Meaning and Modernity

Eugene Rochberg-Halton

Meaning and Modernity
Social Theory in the Pragmatic Attitude

The University of Chicago Press · *Chicago & London*

EUGENE ROCHBERG-HALTON is assistant professor in the
Department of Sociology at the University of
Notre Dame. In 1985–86 he was a Humboldt
Scholar at the University of Tübingen. He is co-
author of *The Meaning of Things: Domestic
Symbols and the Self.*

THE UNIVERSITY OF CHICAGO PRESS, CHICAGO 60637
THE UNIVERSITY OF CHICAGO PRESS, LTD., LONDON
© 1986 by The University of Chicago
All rights reserved. Published 1986
Printed in the United States of America

95 94 93 92 91 90 89 88 87 86   5 4 3 2 1

LIBRARY OF CONGRESS CATALOGING-IN-PUBLICATION DATA

Rochberg-Halton, Eugene.
  Meaning and modernity.

  Bibliography: p.
  Includes index.
  1. Sociology. 2. Pragmatism. I. Title.
HM26.R57 1986   301   86-7060
ISBN 0-226-72330-5
ISBN 0-226-72331-3 (pbk.)

For
JACOB

The thoughts of those divine deep waters, who could fathom them? How could mankind, beclouded, comprehend the ways of gods?

Babylonian wisdom literature

Contents

Preface

At the time of this writing there are ongoing collected-works projects for all four of the major American pragmatists: Charles Sanders Peirce, William James, John Dewey, and George Herbert Mead. What seemed a short time ago to be a completed, and for many, an obsolete movement of thought, has reemerged with contemporary significance for a variety of scholars in America and abroad. Pragmatism, in addressing itself to the question of meaning, in attempting to state rigorously the conditions of meaning within a broadened scientific framework that includes many of the central issues of the arts and humanities as well, speaks to the contemporary hunger for significance in a world where rationalized technique has all too often severed both subject and object from their living context and larger purport.

As the Century of Final Solutions draws to an end, the attempts to reach a terminal state of affairs in both the positivistic and rationalistic ideologies of the sciences, social sciences, humanities, arts, and politics, either under the banner of scientific objectivity or a humanistic or even irrational subjectivity, have revealed themselves as anything but final. Pragmatism had been doomed to the dustbin of history for its insistence on the continuity of thought with action, of biological with cultural life, of emotional with cognitive functioning, of self with environment; for its insistence on the continuity of interpretation itself. Yet it is these very ideas that have begun to bring pragmatism back into the focus of contemporary concern, now that the guiding reductionisms of modern thought have lost their grip.

In 1917 John Dewey, G. H. Mead, and others published *Creative Intelligence: Essays in the Pragmatic Attitude*, a volume that illustrated the broad span of interests stimulated by, but not limited to, pragmatism. Similarly, the present work does not seek to lay out a linear history of the pragmatic movement. Instead, it represents an attempt both to recover and create ideas of contemporary significance, ranging, as in that earlier volume, across disciplinary boundaries and topics, from foundational questions to ongoing researches. Perhaps there is also a resonance with the title (though not the theory) of Kant's *Anthropology in Pragmatic Perspective*, since this book addresses problems of an anthropological nature, in both the German and Anglo-American meanings of this term.

Although drawing heavily from the pragmatists, this book is by no means limited to their work. I am activating dormant concepts of pragmatism, but I am also working out ideas not reducible to those of the four classic pragmatists (yet nevertheless within "the pragmatic attitude" as I conceive it). At the very least this study shows that Mead can no longer be regarded as the central representative of pragmatism in social theory, that he swam within a much broader "stream of consciousness." Meadians should take note that the fiction of Mead as chief source and repository of pragmatic thought is no longer viable: the "Meadian" is no longer the mode! I have sought to show what a social theory in the pragmatic attitude might look like, by engaging in lively dialogue with other social theories of contemporary significance and by undertaking varied researches in Part 4. Throughout the work, though it is not always in the foreground, is a sustained critique of modern culture.

By "modern culture," or "modernity," I mean that total configuration of mind which grew out of the West, which manifests itself in specific and varied traditions in science, industrialized society, in the social organization of institutions, families, and individuals, in philosophy, art, and politics. I mean the term in the broadest possible sense as a cultural template of liberation from traditional ways of thinking, believing, and acting—and later from tradition itself. Modernity introduced valuable new ideas into the repertoire of humankind, yet it is rooted, in my opinion, in underlying dichotomous abstractions such as social versus individual, traditional versus novel, fact versus value, conventional versus original, that, taken to their logical conclusions, lead to self-annulling modes of thought and practice. Much of modern thought bases itself on a false synthesis of a false dichotomy, and I have criticized this tendency toward rigid dichotomizing as it shows itself in philosophical, sociological, psychological, and more general cultural manifestations. I have attempted, especially in the final chapter, to frame modernity as *cultural nominalism*.

This work is an attempt to reconstruct concepts from philosophical pragmatism for contemporary social theory; more than that, it is an attempt to develop a broadened way of thinking, drawing especially from what I take to be the essentials of a pragmatism not yet well-understood. It is a pragmatism most completely and clearly expressed in the writings of C. S. Peirce; a pragmatism antithetical to our so-called "pragmatic" age, with its valuing of expediency as ultimate means and an increasingly abstracted technique as ultimate goal; a pragmatism that reconnects thought with feeling and will, with things and world.

One of the great hindrances to understanding Peirce in contemporary thought is that Peircean terms, to a great extent through the work of Charles Morris, are now associated with a positivistic context that is radically opposed to Peirce's philosophy. Morris's appropriation of Peirce is not merely random but represents and is a classic example of *logical modernism* at work, denying its own foundations while realizing a stark and scientistic foundationalism. Similarly, Morris's term "pragmatics" is based on a positivistic behaviorism antithetical to philosophical pragmatism and has contributed, as I hope to show, to further misunderstandings of what pragmatism means. In many ways Morris is a key player both in the diminution of theories of meaning and in the foundationalist scientism central to twentieth-century modernism. He is, for these reasons, central to this book, albeit in a negative way.

Peirce's pragmatism (later termed pragmaticism) formed the first portion of his broadened logic, or semiotic. I have tried to "translate" many of these seldom-explored ideas into social theory, ranging freely to incorporate whatever concepts I could into *the pragmatic attitude*, the more general outlook or framework or architectonic. In the early chapters, for example, I explore the fundamental significance of inquiry, qualitative immediacy, and semiosis to pragmatism, and the implications of these concepts for broadened theories of inquiry, critical social inquiry, self, semiotics, and culture.

In chapter 1, I attempt to trace out a number of implications for social theory of the concept of inquiry in philosophical pragmatism. Unlike most philosophies of science, pragmatism claimed that the origin of inquiry, the initial framing of hypotheses, is a reasonable process rather than simply irrational intuition. From the pragmatic conception of inquiry also derives a view of social inquiry as a critical science, a process of critical valuation. Finally, the foundations of social life and politics are based on a view of community that is, in turn, based on a semiotic model of a critical community of inquirers. The pragmatic image of man the inquirer is both antipositivistic and anticonceptualistic in claiming that living, existentially and cosmically rooted inquiry animates the human condition. Pragmatism does not reduce the human condition to a restless search for something that is never quite attainable, but, as shown in chapter 2, includes presentness, qualitative immediacy, feeling (in its philosophical sense), celebration and suffering, the myriad uniquenesses that make up the world as aspects of an irreducible mode involved in all social being.

Peirce's realism of signs, though heavily based in John Duns Scotus's scholastic realism, seems to me neither reducible to that realism nor to modern nominalistic "realism" (of either the conventionalistic or positivistic varieties), but to form the basis of a new mind and cultural order only now beginning to reveal their possibilities. Although Dewey may have thought that "the chief characteristic trait of the pragmatic notion of reality is precisely that no theory of Reality in general, *überhaupt*, is possible or needed" (Dewey 1917, 55), he, Mead, and James failed to understand the broad implications of Peircean semiotic realism. Similarly, much as I admire Richard Rorty's attempt to frame philosophy as a conversation or social dialogue, this "conversation," like Kuhn's philosophy of scientific revolutions, is rootless in two senses: In the sense that it neither allows a brute otherness in the world (one that does not change because of what we say to it but that may shape us to itself) nor taps the deeper sources of intelligence beyond conceptual reason. In chapter 1, I claim that the special genius of pragmatism is the way it provides a broadened framework of reason as a process of living, existentially rooted inquiry that includes our deepest biosocial sentiments. Dialogue, or "conversation," is a central concept of pragmatism, but the conversation is one ultimately rooted within a generalized conception of nature: a conception in which nature itself is a biocosmic, emergent dialogue. As the chapters in Part II, on semiotic, show, we live perpetually in a dialogue of signs, a dialogue much broader than situationalist, structuralist, positivist, or relativist theories of meaning can allow. In chapter 6, I have tried to develop an approach to culture influenced by, but not limited to, a Peircean pragmatism (and especially Peirce's "critical common-sensism"), a theory of culture that might begin to recover meaning from the bleak and shrivelled rationalistic landscape of so much contemporary culture theory.

Later chapters move out to explore the questions of materialism, meaning, metropolis as memory, money, and modernism from a broadened pragmatic attitude, by no means limited to the actual influence of pragmatism per se, but inclusive of concepts such as the cultural significance of remembrance, critical animism, and the erosion of qualitative immediacy by abstractionism in modern culture (as discussed in particular in relation to Marx, Simmel, and Veblen in chapter 9), concepts that resonate with themes developed earlier in the book. I am not concerned with the history of pragmatism in this book but with the possibilities (as will become clear in the final chapter) of the pragmatic attitude as a mode of thought, capable of animating new directions for social theory, of coming to terms with present conditions and their conceivable consequences, and of creating new premises for a broadened understanding of the human web of meaning.

Acknowledgments

I am grateful to a number of people whose enthusiasm, encouragement, and criticism have been essential to the completion of this work: Brigitte Berger of Wellesley College; Benjamin Wright, John MacAloon, Milton Singer, Paul Wheatley of the University of Chicago; Edith Turner and the late Victor Turner of the University of Virginia; Richard J. Bernstein of Haverford College; Michael Schudson of the University of California at San Diego; Thomas Buckley of the University of Massachusetts at Boston Harbor; Benjamin Lee of the Center for Psychosocial Studies in Chicago; Barry Schwartz of the University of Georgia; Joan Kron of the *Wall Street Journal*; J. David Lewis, formerly of the University of Notre Dame, and my colleagues Fabio DaSilva, Andrew J. Weigert, and Thomas J. Schlereth; Stephen Turner of the University of South Florida; and especially George and Gene Rochberg, whose warm encouragement, criticism, editing, and vision of a renewed cultural order were most helpful. I also want to thank my other Notre Dame colleagues in the sociology department and the philosophy of social sciences seminar; Justin Stagl of the University of Bonn; Takeshi Ishiguro of Nansan University, Japan; and Friedrich J. Tenbruck of the University of Tübingen.

I first came to terms with Peirce in Chicago at a Hyde Park seminar organized by Kevin McMurtrey, a philosopher of the old school who lives philosophy, though he does not earn his income from it. In grueling line-by-line readings of Peirce, we quickly whittled the seminar down to just the two of us, and decided to write "The Foundations of Modern Semiotic: Charles Peirce and Charles Morris" (chapter 4) as the outcome of some of our explorations of Peirce's semiotic. McMurtrey's knowledge of Peirce and pragmatism is second to none, and his criticisms of my other chapters have been most perspicacious and helpful.

Earlier versions of some chapters appeared in the following places: "Inquiry and the Pragmatic Attitude," in *Pragmatik*, vol. 2, *Der Aufstieg pragmatischen Denkens im 19. und 20. Jahrhundert*, edited by H. Stachowiak (Hamburg: Felix Meiner Verlag, 1986); "Qualitative Immediacy and the Communicative Act," in *Qualitative Sociology* 5, no. 3 (1982): 162–81; "Situation, Structure, and the Context of Meaning," in *The Sociological Quarterly* 23, no. 4 (1982): 455–76; "The Foundations of Modern Semiotic: Charles Peirce and Charles Morris," in *The American Journal of Semiotics* 2, no. 1–2 (1983): 129–56; "The Fetishism of Signs," in *Semiotics 1984*, edited by John Deely (Lanham, Md.: University Press of America, 1985): 409–18; "Object Relations, Role Models, and Cultivation of the Self," in *Environment and Behavior* 16, no. 3 (1984): 335–68. "The City as Living Memory" was also an invited paper for a workshop on "The Meanings of the City" sponsored by the National Academy of the Arts and Sciences, at Wingspread, Wisconsin, October 1984. Special thanks to Anthony Kerrigan, for permission to quote from his translation of "Borges and I."

The Institute for Scholarship in the Liberal Arts of the University of Notre Dame provided a generous subvention for the photographic reproductions used in this book. Though written mostly at the University of Notre Dame, this book was completed at the University of Tübingen, where I spent 1985–86 as an Alexander von Humboldt Research Fellow. The generosity of the Alexander von Humboldt Foundation and the Sociology Seminar of the University of Tübingen are deeply appreciated. I must also thank the Notre Dame steno pool, and especially Nila Gerhold, who typed the manuscript.

I am particularly indebted to my wife, Chessie, who endured more discussions of modernity than an Assyriologist should have to.

I *Pragmatic Roots*

1 Inquiry and the Pragmatic Attitude

PRAGMATIC ROOTS

An outstanding mark of our time is the generalized tendency to abstractionism. Whether in number-crunching mainstream American social science or word-chewing social theory; whether in so-called "conceptual art" or its supposed (and equally ephemeral) opposite "performance art"; whether in the political ideologies of the East or the West, there is a shared domination by the abstract *concept*. More than a century ago Marx could speak of the fetishism of commodities, but could he have foreseen the extent to which the fetishism of the abstract would reduce so many varieties of theoretical and practical life to empty labels and slogans?

Ours is the "pragmatic" age, our legacy the world from which architects have stripped away ornament and facade in the interest of the concept of the "functional," from which philosophers have supposedly stripped away metaphysics in the interest of the concept of the "positive," and in which the obvious failure of functional buildings that do not function for their inhabitants and the extreme metaphysical system of the logical positivists, which holds the ultimate ground for rationality to be the mystical pointing to "things," appear, in the end, to be unpragmatic in the extreme.[1]

Understanding philosophical pragmatism is made all the more difficult

---

1. Charles Peirce, even calling himself a "prope-positivist" (broader than positivist) at one point, sought to refine metaphysics methodically, unlike the modern positivists who tried to erase metaphysics (by using, paradoxically enough, metaphysical erasers). Logical positivists sought to find foundations in "primitive terms." In some ways they succeeded: their foundations are some of the most primitive ever devised. They achieved the diabolical end, which is to seek in one extreme, and to create an unintended answer from the opposite extreme. They sought to do away with metaphysics, and created the most extreme metaphysics ever devised; they sought objectivity, and created a system ultimately based on the subjective experience of a single person; they sought to create for the philosophy of science a foundationalist final solution that was also being sought in diverse and often opposing ways in twentieth-century arts and politics, yet created a feeble and fragmentary philosophy that was obsolete before it was even fully developed.

because of the tyranny of the abstract: it becomes too easy to lump pragmatism with the vulgar uses the word has assumed, so that one simply takes "pragmatic" to mean pure utility or expediency. Not only has the word "pragmatic" taken on a meaning of practical expedience in everyday usage, but the widespread popularity of positivist-cum-pragmatist Charles Morris's term "pragmatics" has further misrepresented pragmatism. By claiming a division of semiotic concerned with the relations of signs to their users (pragmatics), in which "users" and their behaviors are not signs, and in severing "uses" of signs from a normative context of self-corrective inquiry, Morris not only introduced serious distortion into the science of semiotic but contributed new distortions to already existing misconceptions of the nature of pragmatism.

In exploring what the major American pragmatists, Charles Peirce, William James, John Dewey, and George Herbert Mead, meant by the term, it becomes apparent that they were all more or less involved in carving out a view antithetical to heartless expediency and mindless abstractionism. To appreciate pragmatism is to appreciate man's mercurial essence, the transformative power of human nature itself. The root metaphor of pragmatism is not "systematized knowledge," an airtight epistemology, conceptually or empirically based, but *living inquiry*.[2]

Toward the end of his life, disturbed by distortions of the pragmatic maxim in William James and others, Peirce distinguished his own variety as "pragmaticism," a term "ugly enough to be safe from kidnappers." It did not prevent later "Peirce snatchers," such as Charles Morris and the semiotic movement he spawned, from further abusing Peirce's intentions by creating a field seemingly devoted to abstraction for its own sake, a morass of positivistic terminology and conceptualistic obfuscation diametrically opposed to Peirce's first division of semiotic—the method of clarity, that is, pragmaticism. Peirce explicitly stated that "*pragmatism* is not a *Weltanschauung* but it is a method of reflexion having for its purpose to render ideas clear" (CP 5.13n1). Furthermore, pragmatism is "that method of reflexion which is guided by constantly holding in view its purpose and the purpose of the ideas it analyzes, whether these ends be of the nature and uses of action or thought" (CP 5.13n1). To discuss the pragmatic attitude, then, is to go beyond the bounds of Peirce's pragmaticism, which is my intention. I want to describe the generalized "stream of thought" shared by the four major pragmatists, by concentrating on what seems to me to be its most refined expressions in the work of Peirce and Dewey. Peirce's pragmatic world,

2. Peirce considered the view of science as *epistēmē* as fundamentally misguided. As he remarked, "it is plainly important that our notion of science should be a notion of science as it lives and not a mere abstract definition. Let us remember that science is a pursuit of living men, and that its most marked characteristic is that when it is genuine, it is in an incessant state of metabolism and growth. . . . The life of science is the desire to learn" (CP 1.232, 235; references to the Collected Papers of Charles Sanders Peirce [CP] will follow the standard procedure of listing volume and paragraph number, i.e., volume 1, paragraphs 232 and 235, in this reference).

although rigorously expressed in his architectonically constructed pragmaticism, permeates his view of a wide range of philosophical and nonphilosophical issues (CP 5.14; Rosenthal 1983, 20), and it is these wider implications to which I seek to draw attention.

Pragmatism has usually been viewed as closely related to British empiricism, but in order to understand its roots one must also see its many relationships to the German philosophical tradition. Peirce was strongly influenced by Kant early in his career, to the point of claiming that after studying it for two hours a day for more than three years he had almost memorized the *Critic of the Pure Reason* (CP 1.4).[3] It was through examining the foundations of Kant's categories that Peirce came to revise them and later arrived at his own irreducible categories of Firstness, Secondness, and Thirdness (these categories are explained near the beginning of chapter 2; see CP 1.560f.). Peirce went so far as to state that he was led to the pragmatic maxim by reflexion upon Kant's *Critic of the Pure Reason* (CP 5.3), though he believed that Kant was a "somewhat confused pragmatist" (CP 5.525) and that the pragmatic maxim ruled out any notion of a *Ding-an-Sich*. Hegel figured prominently for the four major pragmatists, mostly in a negative way for Peirce and James, positively for the early Dewey and Mead (see Bernstein 1971, 1977; Apel 1980, 1981; Joas 1985a, 1985b). Despite his contempt for Hegel's logic, Peirce saw some analogies in Hegel's *Phenomenologie des Geistes* to his own categories of Firstness, Secondness, and Thirdness. William James devoted a good deal of one of his last major projects, *A Pluralistic Universe,* to refuting Absolute Idealism.

Against what he saw as a "block universe" in the idealist school, James argued for a pluralistic and open-ended universe that would allow for the multiplicities as well as the qualitative uniqueness of experience. In his later work, James struggled against the earlier dualism of his *Principles of Psychology* (1890) toward a more integrated approach that would not simply reduce to a closed system or to meaningless abstractions, but could partially capture the richness, novelty, and open-endedness of experience. He constantly attacked "vicious intellectualism" (a term from *A Pluralistic Universe),* and his targets quite frequently were Hegelians. Against the abstracting tendencies of Intellectualism James sought a more concrete, particularizing philosophy, not in the spirit of reductionism but in a more existentialist spirit, as Barrett (1958, 16–17)

---

3. I follow here Peirce's preference for "Critik" over "Kritik" (in *Critik der reinen Vernunft*), because of the different technical meanings of the two terms. Critik (or critic) is a specific branch of logic, Kritik is "critique, a critical essay," not necessarily a technical term of logic. In tracing the philosophical history of the term "critic," Peirce notes: "This word, used by Plato (who divides all knowledge into *epitactic* and *critic*), was adopted into Latin by the Ramists, and into English by Hobbes and Locke. From the last it was taken into German by Kant, who always writes it Critik, the initial *c* being possibly a reminiscence of its English origin. At present it is written Kritik in German. Kant is emphatic in the expression of the wish that the word may not be confounded with critique, a critical essay (German *Kritik*)" (CP 2.205).

and others have suggested, or in a phenomenological spirit, as Schutz (1962) and others have suggested. Ironically, this vital vision is not only the greatest strength of James's philosophy but also its greatest weakness. James, easily the most fluid stylist of the pragmatists, never could transform his pluralistic pragmatism into a philosophically rigorous form that would do full justice to the inexhaustibility of meaning in determinate action. By comparison, Peirce's difficult style radiates the lucidity of one who chooses his words with the entire history of their etymology and logical purport at his command.

Dewey and Mead, by contrast with James, were swept up in the widespread interest in Hegel that took place in the United States in the late nineteenth century (Dewey through his teacher G. S. Morris at Johns Hopkins University, Mead through Josiah Royce, G. H. Palmer, and others at Harvard University); though both turned away by the end of the century from what they saw as an overly rationalistic spirit in Hegel (although retaining Hegel's emphasis on process and change), toward Darwinian naturalism rooted in a social pragmatism.

The foundations of pragmatism are based in a radical criticism of Cartesian foundationalism, and of the Cartesian-influenced framework of modern philosophy. Beginning with Peirce's powerful criticism of the "spirit of Cartesianism" in the late 1860s, through Dewey's discussions of inquiry in the 1930s and 1940s, the pragmatists consistently sought to undercut both the "dichotomy" of subject and object and the spectator theory of knowledge to which it gave rise, through a view of knowledge as self-correcting triadic mediation. The pragmatists criticized both the rationalist and empiricist traditions, in which knowledge was ultimately disconnected from experience. In the rationalist view, knowledge is based on an innate "faculty," which brings order to experiential chaos. In the empiricist view, knowledge is based on the direct impressions of perception. In both views the knower is essentially passive, the recipient of rational intuitions or immediate sensory intuitions, and the knower's capacities for inference-making are ultimately of a secondary nature in relation to the intuitive foundations of objectivity. Against this "foundational" basis of intuitive knowledge the pragmatists proposed a view that situated knowledge within possible experience as a practice: the practice of inference-making or inquiry.

The Social Basis of Inquiry

In criticizing the "spirit of Cartesianism," Peirce claimed that the Cartesian account of science is inadequate because of its inherent subjectivism. Descartes attempted to replace traditional authority, which provided the basis for scholastic science, with reason, and his method consisted in doubting everything until he arrived at an indubitable principle that could then provide the rational basis for science. He found this principle in the famous

"Cogito, ergo sum," in which one could ground reason through an immediate indubitable intuition that is both clear and distinct.

Descartes' pivotal role in the development not only of modern philosophy but of modern culture as a whole, was to transform the basis of truth from the scholastic emphasis on the testimonies of the community of authorities, themselves ultimately dependent on divine revelation, to the consciousness of the individual thinker, and in this transformation modern individualism was born. The objective world of community became the questioned, and the individual became the unquestioned foundation of knowledge claims, whether rational or empirical. Against this view Peirce argued that the indubitable origin of reason does not provide the basis of scientific rationality; rather, the continuing self-corrective process of science provides its own rational justification. All knowledge, in Peirce's system, is general and of the nature of a triadic sign. To claim there can be indubitable knowledge is to "block the road of inquiry," because inquiry is the living attempt to render doubt into belief, a process in which we as fallible individuals cannot claim *definite belief,* only *probable opinion.* Scientific rationality thus consists in the essential dubitability of any given question, and the ability to revise our opinions until no further revisions are necessary. Though we can, and continually do, hit upon truths in inquiry, our knowledge of these truths always remains probable, because it is always open to the criticisms of any future investigators. Indubitability consists in the final agreement that would be reached by the community of inquirers and that would not be contradicted by further inquiry. Truth then is the ultimate goal of science, rather than the indubitable foundation of inquiry, and is to be realized in the community of inquirers, rather than by the solitary consciousness. Indeed, the Cartesian attempt to replace authority with reason proves in the end to be most unreasonable, because all knowledge ultimately rests on an individual intuition itself inexplicable, irrational, and indubitable.

Peirce's broadened view of science, with its emphasis on the testimonies of an unlimited community of inquirers, represents a renovated version of scholastic realism and a radical critique of the nominalism that characterizes so much of modern thought. Against Descartes' "clear and distinct" idea, in itself inexplicable, stands Peirce's pragmatic maxim for making ideas clear, with its emphasis on the explicability of meaning in future conceivable consequences; that is, "the rational purport of a word or other expression, lies exclusively in its conceivable bearing upon the conduct of life" (CP 5.412). The word "conceivable" is important in this context and distinguishes Peirce's more general and realistic pragmaticism from James's more particularistic and nominalistic pragmatism, with its emphasis on the actual conduct produced as opposed to Peirce's broader inclusion of generalized tendencies toward conduct, whether actualized or not.

All thought is a form of internal conduct, and all conduct is general triadic mediation in Peirce's pragmaticism. From the perspective of inquiry one can see Peirce's emphasis on *conceivable* consequences as a restatement of his idea that all knowledge is probable and subject to criticism and possible correction. In the same way, the meaning of a certain concept, such as a political theory, is not exhausted by actual determinate acts, because further investigation may show these acts to be limited or misguided realizations of the theory or may lead to the revision of the theory itself, and the results of this inquiry would form a further pragmatic consequence of the original concept. In Peirce's words:

> The importance of the matter for pragmatism is obvious. For if the meaning of a symbol consists in *how* it might cause us to act, it is plain that this "how" cannot refer to the description of mechanical motions that it might cause, but must intend to refer to a description of the action as having this or that *aim*. In order to understand pragmatism, therefore, well enough to subject it to intelligent criticism, it is incumbent upon us to inquire what an ultimate aim, capable of being pursued in an indefinitely prolonged course of action, can be. (CP 5.135)

All knowledge, literally each and every sign, in being open to further determination through future interpretation, is intrinsically social and continuous with the unlimited community of inquirers. The pragmatic method is one that finds clarity within "inquiry," broadly defined, and through the consensus of an unlimited community of inquirers capable of continuous inquiry in the indefinite future. In this sense a clear idea is of the nature of a hypothesis, capable of explaining phenomena, intrinsically dubitable, and thereby the ground of the possibility of inquiry. Similarly, a true idea is not the underlying foundation of inquiry but is the pragmatic result and achievement of inquiry.

PRAGMATISM, SCIENTIFIC METHOD, AND THE LOGIC OF DISCOVERY

In his *Logik der Forschung* (strangely translated as *The Logic of Discovery*) Karl Popper expresses the common idea shared by rationalists and positivists alike, that inquiry begins with an irrational intuition, a creative insight that is not an inference made from observed facts, and whose consequences somehow provide the guiding idea of an inquiry, despite the fact that the idea itself is utterly illogical:

> The initial stage, the act of conceiving or inventing a theory, seems to me neither to call for logical analysis nor to be suscepti-ble of it . . . my view of the matter, for what it is worth, is that there is no such thing as a logical method of having new ideas, or a logical reconstruction of this process. My view may be ex-

pressed by saying that every discovery contains "an irrational element," or "a creative intuition," in Bergson's sense. . . . (Popper
1968, 31–32)

Despite its wide acceptance from diverse sources, this idea that the initiation
of inquiry is outside of the inquiry itself is strongly rejected by the pragmatists. In fact, as founded by Peirce, pragmatism is based on the logic of
"abduction," or hypothesis formation (CP 5.196), and so is founded precisely on the very logic denied by Popper and those who share his view of science
as a logic machine rather than as living inquiry. Hypothesis formation,
though not always a purely conscious process, is a reasonable process according to Peirce and Dewey, a genuine mode of inference-making. The pragmatic
view of inquiry incorporates the beginnings and ends of inquiries within the
self-corrective process of inquiry, not as irrational antecedents or consequences of it. Though Popper can state that his criterion for empirical science
is based on an agreement or convention, something in turn based on a shared
sense of purpose that is "ultimately a matter of decision, going beyond
rational argument" (Popper 1968,37), the pragmatists argued that the ends
of inquiry are the ultimate concern of any rational inquiry, and in the long run
are thoroughly determined by the nature of inquiry itself.

Peirce claimed that, instead of a primitive concept or intuition that
serves as a hypothesis but does not meet the fundamental requirement of a
hypothesis to *explain* the known facts, "The elements of every concept enter
into logical thought at the gate of perception and make their exit at the gate of
purposive action; and whatever cannot show its passports at both those two
gates is to be arrested as unauthorized by reason" (CP 5.212). This statement,
with its emphasis on "the gate of perception" and "purposive action," might
seem quite compatible with the various forms of empiricism and logical
positivism, yet when one comprehends Peirce's broadened view it becomes
apparent that he proposed a quite different course. Where positivists con-
strued immediate perception as the foundation of knowledge, the means by
which metaphysics and other varieties of "speculation," including hypothesis
formation as well, could be evicted from the house of science, Peirce used
perception to justify the logic of abduction.

Peirce's perspicuous perspective on perception was that from one
point of view, there are brute, compulsive *percepts* of the mode of being of
Secondness, and simultaneously, from another point of view, all perception
involves *perceptual judgments* (see Bernstein 1964). Knowledge derives not
from discrete, lawless percepts, as empiricists and positivists argued, nor
solely from inner faculties or from a progressive reason that does not recognize the "Outward Clash" of Secondness in its own terms, as rationalists
claimed, but from a truly compulsive Otherness that is yet also general.

Peirce argued that there is no hard and fast barrier between perception and rational knowledge; rather, "perception is interpretative" (CP

5.184). His argument amounts to a criticism of both empiricism and rationalism as having a limited view of reason, as not realizing that perceptual
judgments are themselves infused with elements of generality, though not
subject to self-control. Abductive judgment shades into perceptual judgment,
and the difference between the two is that perceptual judgments are not
subject to self-control. In other words, says Peirce, "our first premises, the
perceptual judgments, are to be regarded as an extreme case of abductive
inferences, from which they differ in being absolutely beyond criticism" (CP
5.181).

As "our first premises," perceptual judgments are uncontrollable
inferences resulting from the interaction of the percept with the totality of
feelings, reactions, and thoughts that have informed and tempered our inference-making perceptual abilities, embodied, over the course of evolutionary
and personal time, in our very being. The sum of it all, says Peirce, is that:

> our logically controlled thoughts compose a small part of the
> mind, the mere blossom of a vast complexus, which we may call
> the instinctive mind, in which this man will not say that he has
> *faith,* because that implies the conceivability of distrust, but upon
> which he builds as the very fact to which it is the whole business
> of his logic to be true.
>   That he will have no difficulty with Thirdness is clear enough,
> because he will hold that the conformity of action to general in-
> tentions is as much given in perception as is the element of ac-
> tion itself, which cannot really be mentally torn away from such
> general purposiveness. (CP 5.212)

"Instinctive mind" was for Peirce mature mind, whereas rational mind was
immature mind. Peirce's break with the tendencies of modern rationalism
and empiricism is perhaps nowhere else clearer, for he is claiming that our
great achievement of rational thought rests on a vaster store of intelligence
embodied in our inference-making nature. Instincts are accordingly, in their
proper environment, *true ideas.* Though the human and sociocultural environmental relationship is many times more plastic than that of other
species, Peirce claimed that it is wrong to assume that, unlike the bird's
instinct for flight, and the bee's for geometrically correct construction, we do
not possess a distinctively human instinct. Ours is the instinct for inquiry, the
capacity for conjecturing, for making abductive inferences and then submitting them to those deductive and inductive tests of self-controlled conduct,
whether in art creations, limited practical affairs, or limitless scientific experimentation. In the history of science many of the important discoveries were
reached not after most of the possible hypotheses had been explored but
through seemingly unconscious predelictions for certain hypotheses that
predominated and vastly quickened the progress of science. This suggests,

according to Peirce, the instinctive capacity of the "well-prepared mind" for making informed guesses, for perceiving nature's laws over the long run because we have "a natural bent in accordance with nature's" (CP 6.478).

To those who might say that the "well-prepared mind" is not truly instinctive because learning has occurred within the web of culture, one could reply that "instinctive" means neither the unconditioned nor solely that conditioned by a biological "deep structure," but, simply, that which is conditioned by whatever habits of experience have shaped it, individually or ancestrally. Certain instincts in dogs, for example, such as retrieving or shepherding, are inseparable from the cultural purposes that created them and from the generalized objects that foster them. Biological structuralism, such as sociobiology, and its secret sibling, cultural or "French" structuralism, both share a withered view of experience, ignoring, on the one hand, how the otherness of the environment serves to temper and condition us, and, on the other, how purpose—whether conceived as the utilitarian individualism of sociobiologists or the cultural codes of the structuralists—is a *transaction* in an environment and not only an acritical underlying structure insusceptible to correction and incapable of growth.

In stating that "every conception is a conception of conceivable practical effects," pragmatism, argued Peirce, "makes conception reach far beyond the practical" (CP 5.196), to include anything imaginable—so long as that which is imagined has some possible pragmatic import. Conjectures having even a slightly greater than chance expectation of being true will lead to valid results in the long run, and thus their provisional acceptance is logically justified. For this reason Peirce was logically correct when he paraphrased the poet Tennyson: "Wildest dreams *are* the necessary first steps toward scientific investigation" (Peirce 1958,233).

In Dewey's approach, developed most explicitly in his *Logic: The Theory of Inquiry* (1938), inquiry consists of "the progressive determination of a problem and its solution." Where many others start with the problem as given, in which the task of inquiry is to arrive at an objective solution through methodical means, Dewey developed a more inclusive view in which the institution of the problem itself is the first phase of inquiry. Dewey's discussion of the discovery of the problem as the first premise of inquiry is parallel to Peirce's discussion of abduction, and is based upon Dewey's theory of qualitative immediacy.

Dewey roots the beginning of inquiry in the pervasive quality of a *situation,* meaning by situation a contextual whole or field that includes the object, subject, and pervasive quality of their relation.[4] Dewey attempted to

4. The "definition of the situation," as discussed by sociologist W. I. Thomas (1928), is one of the key elements of contemporary sociological "symbolic interactionism." Thomas's original

undercut the mistaken notion of original dichotomies of subject—object, or "primary" and "secondary" qualities (in the Lockean sense), by looking at the immediate qualitative situation, or what Santayana termed "tertiary qualities," as the inclusive starting point. An unsettled or indeterminate situation immediately experienced is the antecedent condition for inquiry:

> it is of the very nature of the indeterminate situation which evokes inquiry to be *questionable;* or, in terms of actuality instead of potentiality, to be uncertain, unsettled, disturbed. The peculiar quality of what pervades the given materials, constituting them a situation, is not just uncertainty at large; it is a unique doubtfulness which makes that situation to be just and only the situation it is. It is this unique quality that not only evokes the particular inquiry engaged in but that exercises control over its special procedures. Otherwise, one procedure in inquiry would be as likely to occur and to be as effective as any other. (Dewey 1938,105)

It may seem odd that for Dewey the underpinning of scientific inquiry was none other than aesthetic immediacy, that is, the unique quality of a situation considered in itself, yet Dewey proposed the "problematic situation" as a counter to the ultimately subjectivist dichotomy of a determinate object and doubting subject. In this dichotomy inquiry begins because of the mentalistic doubts in the inquirer. By defining the situation in a way that includes the inquirer, and by claiming that doubt is inseparably connected to the unique quality of a given situation ("*We* are doubtful because the situation is inherently doubtful" [Dewey 1938,105–6]), Dewey located doubt as an existential instigator of inquiry. He also viewed inquiry as more than solely cognitive. The doubtful situation is not at first *known* as such but *felt* to be doubtful. As the situational feeling of doubt becomes known as such, the inquirer discerns there is a problem requiring inquiry, and the process of inquiry is begun. At this point the qualitative situation is transformed into the ground for inferring and articulating the problem itself. A qualitative immediacy becomes a mediated sign.

From the qualitative indeterminate situation emerges the problematic situation and first explicit phase of inquiry itself: the institution of the

---

two-sided emphasis on how both subjective *and* objective factors enter into the ways situations come to be defined has been reduced unfortunately to the subjective side alone in most recent discussions. Yet even his full sense of what constitutes a situation can be placed within the much broader view of the qualitative situation developed throughout Dewey's work, as I hope will become clear in the following discussion. Thomas may have been influenced directly by Dewey's conception of the situation developed in *Essays in Experimental Logic* (1916, 70) or in Dewey's earlier "Interpretation of Savage Mind," which Thomas excerpted in his well-known *Source Book for Social Origins* (1909).

problem. Again, in contrast to Popper and others, Dewey holds that the formulation of the problem-hypothesis is an emergent property of inquiry itself. As he said, "Just because a problem well stated is on its way to solution, the determining of a genuine problem is a *progressive* inquiry; the cases in which a problem and its probable solution flash upon an inquirer are cases where much prior ingestion and digestion have occurred" (Dewey 1938,108). Dewey did not accord *suggestion* a logical status, however, as Peirce did for abductive inference. Yet there is a direct parallel to Peirce's theory of the continuum of acritical perceptual judgments and criticizable abductive judgments in Dewey's discussion of a *suggestion* as psychophysical result of an indeterminate situation that becomes an *idea* when critically analyzed in its context and in relation to other ideas. Such analysis transforms acritical suggestion to logical idea or hypothetical proposition because the suggestion takes on a functional role in directing further operations within the inquiry.

The perceptual is not simply composed of direct copies of physical things, as the empirical tradition held, nor are conceptual ideas the sole basis for ordering "facts," as the rationalist tradition held, because, according to Dewey, "In logical fact, perceptual and conceptual materials are instituted in functional correlativity with each other, in such a manner that the former locates and describes the problem while the latter represents a possible method of solution" (Dewey 1938,111). Although acknowledging Kant's insight that apart from each other perceptions are blind and conceptions are empty, Dewey insisted that Kant was mistaken to assume a radical dichotomy between perceptions and conceptions needing a third activity, synthetic understanding, to weld them together. Instead, the activity of inquiry consists of a functionally related continuum of perceptions and conceptions, which can be *analyzed,* or as Peirce would say, *prescinded,* as perception or conception rather than as requiring a *synthesis.* Dewey's criticism was the basic pragmatic criticism that one does not begin with physical things and mental substances needing to be brought together but with a given indeterminate situation in which and by which objects and subjects are constituted. The given situation is a conditioned situation—conditioned by prior experiences or inquiries, by objective determinations, by whatever has shaped it—yet as the starting point for inquiry the conditioned situation is qualitative. Dewey is *not* saying that the qualitative starting point of inquiry is a raw quality dichotomized from reason. In contrast, he is claiming that the qualitative situation is a *funded quality,* the qualitative resultant of previous transactions and inquiries. Yet Dewey, like Peirce, maintained that the qualitative is a genuine mode of being in its own right, as well as one involved in the sign process of cognition. His logic of discovery begins with a felt problem, that, in the process of being brought to reflection, suggests the further course of inquiry and the possible determination of its solution. Though the determinate situation is the goal of Dewey's theory of inquiry, it is regarded as an "end-in-view," not a final end, because it can be criticized and stimulate new inquiries—in effect, it is open to being made indeterminate through the larger context of continuous inquiry.

Social Inquiry as Critical Valuation

Against the widespread view that there is a radical separation between "is" and "ought" stands the pragmatic view that an inquiry is progressively determined by the truth, which operates *during* the inquiry as a correcting and correctible, regulatory norm, a "should be" or "ought." The pragmatists' conception of truth varied from James's "radical empiricism," which held truth to be that which "works" in concrete instances, through Dewey's and perhaps Mead's somewhat broadened ideas of truth as localized to specific situations of inquiry, yet determinative of those situations, to Peirce's insistence that truth is that conclusion which the community of inquirers is destined to reach, because its object is real.

Although Dewey and Mead deny, more or less, Peirce's insistence on the real as the motivation for inquiry and the summum bonum understood as the final goal of inquiry, they do extend to the social realm the implications of Peirce's notion of science as a process of self-correcting inquiry tempered by its objects. The difference rests in part on the different objects of inquiry. Peirce's concept of the realization of truth through an unlimited community of investigators extending into the indefinite future becomes problematic when applied to social practices and institutions whose natures and problems require interpretations in a limited time frame and localized context, and when these practices and institutions themselves may change as a result of the interpretations of social inquiries.

In social inquiry, as Peirce would probably agree, one deals not with the relatively unchanging properties of a diamond but with a self-reflective object. The laws of human affairs may embody some greater laws, but their significance is found within the human context of purposive conduct, not beneath it in a physical or physiological substratum, and not beyond it in a transcendent unknowable or Absolute.

Mead once claimed (1964,324): "There is no such thing as Truth at large. It is always relative to the problematic situation." Using the Deweyan terminology of "the problematic situation," Mead is expressing the idea, shared by him and Dewey, that truth is not a fixed, eternal entity, not a mere abstraction, but that it is an outcome of a specific inquiry. On Peirce's behalf, it can be said that Dewey and Mead's adversion to truth in general presupposes the presence of guiding norms operating in and through specific situations. Only by assuming overarching transsituational norms could Dewey and Mead ignore them. Yet can we not also say that it is truth itself that leads research to itself. Without "Truth at large," that is, living truth, acting through norms of particular investigations, it is difficult to see how there can be any truth in particular situations.

And when we deal with terms such as "conduct" as the realization of truth, the problem becomes, conduct for whom? Truth, it seems to me, cannot be reduced only to the actual, because it is never exhausted by instances of behavior. Truth is a general, because it causes instances to conform to it. And conduct itself is a general, because it is the concrete manifestation of intelligence. But because it is a general, it is capable of continued correction and growth. And when we ask the question, truth for whom? the answer in my opinion is that, if truth is to retain its meaning, the truths of our particular lives and our particular and localized communities must align themselves with that larger living truth which animates, and is discovered through, the unlimited critical community of all future inquiry.

This difference in focus is why Dewey and Mead are apparently at odds with Peirce. Yet if we realize that their overwhelming concern was social philosophy, and the self-reflective constitution of its object, we can see a much greater continuity (though still not complete agreement) with Peirce's semiotic variety of scientific realism. This also explains the reticence of Dewey and Mead on the claim for a possible final truth or summum bonum (Dewey 1917; Mead 1917). Their concentration on the problematic and probable nature not only of social inquiry but of all inquiry, coincides with Peirce's notion that, even when we do, in fact, hit upon the truth, our knowledge that we have done so remains probable and subject to further criticism. Such a notion of the fallible nature of knowledge is essential in any social investigation, where what is significant does not always have the regularity of gravity, where what is significant is the purposive medium of significance itself, in its qualitative, indexical, and interpretative modes.

When Peirce defines pragmatism as "that method of reflexion which is guided by constantly holding in view its purpose and the purpose of the ideas it analyzes, whether these ends be of the nature and uses of action or thought" (CP 5.13n1), he is also claiming that not only is purpose (or norms) an inherent aspect of any method of investigation but that pragmatism treats this fact explicitly and makes it the object of its methodological principle. The investigation of social life is inseparably bound up with the intepretative medium that is social life, with all those valuations—self-conscious, habitual, and instinctive—that constitute social life and that necessarily enter into the norms of its investigation.

Inquiry, considered as a self-corrective process of interpretation, helps to progressively determine what the facts themselves are, as well as the conclusions to be reached. The facts of inquiry to which the pragmatists attempted to draw attention are that:
— All facts are themselves "the products of complex processes of interpreta-
   tion which have historical origins" (Bernstein 1976,230).

— There are no pure facts outside of the *perspective* in which they are observed. Observation is not immediate perception, as the positivists posited, but is an inferential process. The starting point of an empirical inquiry is not an immediate given but a *perceptual judgment,* and the perceptual judgment, though in itself beyond self-control, nevertheless contains an element of generality.

— All facts emerge through inquiry and all hypotheses are confirmed or disconfirmed through being subjected to the continued scrutiny of inquiry. The inquirer necessarily carries values (or "prejudices"), yet the point of inquiry is not to purge these, but to refine them through inquiry to come into agreement with the objective findings of inquiry. The objective conclusion of an inquiry itself acts as a "should be" during inquiry.

The pragmatists tended to reject that nominalization of the modern world in which values became subjective names or beliefs, purely conventional or arbitrary, because this view (either in its positivist or rationalist manifestations) neglected the tempering role of experience in the acquisition of values, thus disconnecting them from living praxis. Values are not simply arbitrarily or subjectively acquired shackles (though this they can well be). In the pragmatic view, values, as an unquestioned, received tradition, are objective to the degree to which experience has been allowed cumulatively to temper them. In other words, the principles of inquiry, in being existentially rooted and not solely products of a rational system of abstraction, extend as well to cultural practices and to biological life itself. This view does not deny the overwhelming influence of unreasonableness and arbitrary codes in the course of history but simply allows that cultures too can exercise self-control and self-correction.

Values, in this view, are valuations, habitualized acts of judgment rather than simply inert nouns. Values can be seen as the general ground for judgment, for inference-making itself, yet the recognition of this position does not necessarily lead to the excision of values from inference-making in order to achieve a more objective position. It leads, instead, to a recognition that values themselves may be subject to method, to a critical scrutiny that might cause them to accord better with the facts. In the pragmatisms of Peirce, James, Dewey, and Mead, the ineradicability of values in all social conduct is seen. The implications of this view for social inquiry were strongly articulated by Dewey.

In Dewey's view humanity has constructed habits of inquiry that in turn have constructed the nature of our being, enabling us to confront a given situation and make intelligent, rational judgments of what is and what ought to be. Our ultimate purpose is to refine our values, not to ignore them; to bring them into agreement with the broader purposes of life, to make them objective. This involves the discovery and refinement of the broader purposes themselves. Hence the essential questions of life's purposes are themselves to be answered within the critical web of inquiry, not apart from it.

If values are ultimately inseparable from the facts, and are continuously *refined* by inquiry, then those values held at the end of inquiry are, in fact, true values. Values have to be tempered by the inquiry. A prejudice is something we cannot dispel by "scientific fiat," precisely because we are unaware of our bias. Instead we revise our opinions and prejudices as they come under scrutiny in inquiry. In providing the motivating web of thought and context for inquiry, values, as unquestioned yet questionable assumptions, contribute to the critical yet balanced stance of the inquirer. Values are valuable for inquiry, providing a ground on which to stand that is *refinable,* not eradicable. For this reason social inquiry can be seen as a continuing process of critical valuation.

THE PRAGMATIC ATTITUDE

Against both the positivist and rationalist abstractionisms of modern thought, against "vicious intellectualism" in its sensationalist and conceptualist manifestations, stands the pragmatists' image of man the inquirer, animated by the quest for the greater understanding and growth of purpose. The irony of this image is that it is precisely the image of *science,* so-called, that currently defines the modern ideology of the abstract. It is the ideology of science that has animated the major revolutions of the twentieth century, radically reshaping all dimensions of the world to what William Blake termed the "single vision."

Consider the impact of those revolutionaries in turn-of-the-century Vienna led by Sigmund Freud, Ludwig Wittgenstein, Arnold Schoenberg, Adolph Loos, and others, and how deeply held was the ideal of a scientific rationality and a linear progress that informed their works. Consider how the effect of each was to sever the acting, historical, and inquiring human being from the ultimate source or goal, whether it be "das Es" or the "id" (Freud), the ethical (early Wittgenstein), or the concept of rational truth that guided the arts of Schoenberg and Loos. One could also argue that the other side of the twentieth-century "split-brain," irrationalism, whether in various primitivisms, existentialism, etc., claims potency primarily as a *reaction against* the dominant image of rational scientific ideology. Yet even the radical subjectivism of this side tends to accept the myth of a primordial subject over against a primordial object. It is the acceptance of one side or the other of this split that joins the two opposites in secret unison.

As is becoming increasingly clear now that the culture of modernism is on the wane, a dogmatically held image of science (for *or* against) has produced and rationalized many devastating and unenlightened consequences: the modern mass exterminations of people; the radical break with a sense of history and tradition in the arts and philosophy (echoes of the Cartesian presuppositionless inquiry, certain of its own foundations because limited to a seemingly clear starting point); the homogenized "international" architecture, music, and abstract art of much of late modernism or of so-called "socialist realism," both of which characteristically lack their own unique character in individual productions; the massive evisceration of the earth in the name of "development" and progress; and the domination of all human life and "continued inquiry" itself by the fetishism of nuclear commodities in the East and West. Why, then, should pragmatism be considered as an alternative to the deadly ideology of modern techno-science, and as a possible contributor to a new cultural epoch?

Pragmatism involves a conception of a critical public, free inquiry and communication, the growth of the imagination, and the embodiment of purposeful habits of conduct as essential not only to the realization of inquiry but to the ultimate goals of life as well. With its claim that all knowledge is inescapably fallible, it radically opposes the fundamentalist tendencies of this age of abstraction toward final solutions.

Perhaps one of the best expressions of the pragmatic attitude as worldview is found in John Dewey's *The Public and Its Problems*. There Dewey criticizes the idea of "natural" inalienable rights that are given prior to politics, claiming instead that inalienable rights are constituted in and through the social process. The philosophy of individualism posited individuals *apart from* the social world they inhabit, and asserted that constraints on the individual (on private property, etc.) should be severed. Yet, Dewey claimed, human rights are constituted by human relationships, and mediating institutions form the living social web of our consciousness. The long-term effect of English liberalism paradoxically produced a society that worked against democracy—a faceless, unthinking *mass* instead of a real public and genuine social individuals. Against laissez-faire minimalism, Dewey's view includes intelligence, or "the observation of consequences *as* consequences, that is, in connection with the acts from which they proceed" (Dewey 1927, 12). Dewey's concept of the public is rooted in a transactional perspective based on the recognition and regulation of indirect consequences of human communicative acts (a conception that could have broadening consequences for Anthony Giddens's recent discussions of indirect consequences in his theory of structuration, or for Jürgen Habermas's theory of communicative action). Stated pragmatically: "We take then our point of departure from the objective fact that some of these consequences are perceived, and that their perception leads to subsequent effort to control action so as to secure some consequences and avoid others" (Dewey 1927, 12).

Freedom, argued Dewey, is a *political* ideal, not something constituted prior to politics. He grounded his argument in a view that human existence is rooted in purposive community, against what could be called the fiction of Machiavelli and Hobbes that to be human is simply to be a living individual apart from purpose, that political life is a science of techniques rather than of purpose (cf. Habermas 1973). Realpolitik is a nominalism. It claims that community is a mere convention and ideal, that the mediating institutions of language and social relations are not real. Only individual particulars and power-forces which move them for preconceived purposes are real. This is what Dewey (1958, 27) called the "fallacy of selective emphasis," in which a consequence of a certain concept is taken as primary, and the original concept that produced it as derivative of it.

Against the absolutist assumptions of individualists concerning what is truly "natural law," or of Hegelians and/or Marxists concerning what truly moves history, or of any universalist and therefore abstractionist theory, Dewey proposed that:

> Just as publics and states vary with conditions of time and place, so do the concrete functions which should be carried on by states. There is no antecedent universal proposition which can be laid down because of which the functions of a state should be limited or should be expanded. Their scope is something to be critically and experimentally determined. (Dewey 1927, 74)

In delimiting the scope of a concept of publics and states as "something to be critically and experimentally determined" within a specific problematic situation of inquiry, Dewey is reiterating for social inquiry Peirce's description of pragmatism as "that method of reflexion which is guided by constantly holding in view its purpose and the purpose of the ideas it analyzes, whether these ends be of the nature and uses of action or thought" (CP 5.13n1).

Dewey's main point in *The Public and Its Problems* is that political theories and practices need to be based on the model of public inquiry, in which the selection of government officials and the carrying out of governmental affairs are accomplished through a self-corrective intelligence capable of confronting hard facts, changing when necessary, and growing through the critical use of information. Democratic institutions are eroded when special interests, sensationalistic media, and anonymity replace reasoned inquiry, resulting sooner or later (and Dewey believed this had already largely occurred in the United States in 1927, when the book was published) in the eclipse of a true public and its replacement by the faceless mass. Against these tendencies Dewey (1927,178) argued that "Only continuous inquiry, continuous in the sense of being connected as well as persistent, can provide the material of enduring opinion about public matters." Democracy is for Dewey nothing less than the community of inquirers, a continual process of criticism, cultivation, and growth. Similarly for George Herbert Mead (1934), democracy consists in the ability "to take the role of the other," through which one cultivates an internalized community or "generalized other," capable of critical self-dialogue (see the excellent discussion of Mead's political biography in Joas 1985a).

Dewey's position may become clearer by critically comparing it with that of Hannah Arendt. Her book *The Human Condition* (1958) stands as one of the most profound criticisms of modern life and of the technical ideology that guides it.

Both Dewey and Arendt incorporate Greek-inspired ideas of community, in which the living qualitites of action and speech (communication in Dewey's terminology) are needed. For both, action involves the possibility of emergence or natality. Both see the need for a community of *individuals,* a plurality of achieved perspectives: individuality as a social achievement. Without this living web of unique, critical perspectives one is merely left with an aggregate (Dewey) or society (Arendt). Both Dewey and Arendt decry "the eclipse of the public," a phrase that is the title of one of Dewey's chapters in *The Public and Its Problems* and which appears in Arendt's *The Human Condition.*[5]

One major difference is that Arendt sees the rise of the mentality of labor (a conception of human activity as rooted in and determined by life processes, and hence exemplifying necessity instead of freedom), as contributing to the modern culture of science and technology, to its universalizing tendencies, and as directly causing the decay of the public. The social sciences further confirm this trend and are actually manifestations of the dominance of technē itself, not of praxis or theoria (and hence should probably not even be considered sciences). For these reasons social-scientific inquiry is actually an instrument of the tendency in modern life for persons *to behave* rather than *to act,* to form part of a faceless aggregate, a statistical ratio, rather than to embody a qualitative uniqueness and genuine perspective within a community. Hence social-scientific inquiry and method are inimical to the public,

5. One wonders what influence Dewey might have had on Arendt. She reviewed his *Problems of Men* in the *Nation* in 1946 with mild Germanic disdain, yet both drew from similar kinds of sources and made similar critiques of modern society, despite their theoretical differences. We read in Arendt: "The rise of society brought about the simultaneous decline of the public as well as the private realm. But the eclipse of a common public world, so crucial to the formation of the lonely mass man and so dangerous in the formation of the worldless mentality of modern ideological mass movements, began with the much more tangible loss of a privately owned share in the world" (1958, 257). One sees the resonances with the following passages from Dewey's chapter "The Eclipse of the Public": "Our concern at this time is to state how it is that the machine age in developing the Great Society has invaded and partially disintegrated the small communities of former times without generating a Great Community. . . . Till the Great Society is converted into a Great Community, the Public will remain in eclipse. Communication alone can create a great community. Our Babel is not one of tongues but of the signs and symbols without which shared experience is impossible" (1927, 126–27, 142). One gets the impression that Arendt's ties to German philosophy might have prejudiced her from finding any resonances in Dewey, despite the fact that he himself was a Hegelian early in his career.

to speech and action. Dewey, by contrast, recognizes the disparity between science conceived as rational system and science as living practice, rooted in qualitative, problematic situations.

Dewey, then, did not conceive of "life" as Arendt did, as dichotomized from critical intelligence and spontaneous action, but instead, with Peirce, saw the rooting of the higher human capacities within a broadened conception of nature as the ground of the possibility of spontaneous action and critical intelligence. The whole import of "problem finding" and "abduction" is that human faculties of knowledge are themselves tempered capacities, and that our conjecturing is not arbitrary but is rooted in our inference-making and hypothesis-generating nature. Hence science itself is not "systematized knowledge" but *living* inquiry. Dewey also acknowledges the historical factor of abstractionism leading to the decline of the public but sees intelligent, critical inquiry as the means for its recovery. He proposes a critical social (or political, in Arendt's terms) science (1927, 3, 178f.).

Arendt decries the deadening effects of science because science not only ignores but systematically excludes what is most distinctive about human action: its capacity to initiate, to transform and bring about new conditions. Social science, in its search for the regular, destroys the quicksilver of human initiative and freedom. Arendt argues for a critical philosophy, against the acritical logic of empirical social inquiry (and it would seem that her argument also applies against the deadly convention-bound structuralisms that cannot recognize living speech and action—see chapter 3). Inquiry, in this sense, is set up by her as something opposed to living human freedom. Its methodological character is the character of the abstract universalizing tendency that destroys the plurality which is constitutive of the public. Arendt's main criticisms of Dewey are perhaps that he takes the poison of "social scientific" inquiry to be the elixir of reconstruction, and that his view of intelligence and reasoned inquiry optimistically glosses over the obdurate character of people and ruling powers. In this way his thinking might be seen as simply another form of scientific utopianism.

Dewey's criticism of Arendt, in return, might be that her view of community is a kind of idealism that takes its own conceptual validity as a given rather than as a hypothesis to be "critically and experimentally determined." The Greek polis does not necessarily define once and for all the nature of community or what aspects of necessity, such as work and labor, are to be permanently segregated from its life of freedom.

In Dewey's pragmatic view, critical inquiry is constitutive of the public, because inquiry, as the open questioning and "progressive determination of problems and their solutions," is the essence of human freedom: freedom to inquire. Free critical inquiry is at the heart of community, and represents the mode of communication that best enables the continuity of political life. Inquiry tempers both the direction and the goals themselves of the community, and helps to insure the continuity of communication that is the medium of community life. Dewey did not advocate an untethered generalizing inquiry, because he realized how abstracting systematization had uprooted the unique perspectives of individuals and of locality itself. Rather, it is a situated and localized citizenry with media of communication inherently possessing the cultivated ability of free and open inquiry that is requisite to the continued life of the community.

It is simply misguided to conceive of a state without or beyond problematic situations, as so much of modern political thinking has done, because problematic situations requiring critical intelligence are the lifeblood of all social life. A utopia is, on the positive side, an ideal that can infuse new vision into a decaying order, that can provide the motivating spirit for struggle against the frequently overwhelming injustices and blind obsistencies of the world. Yet on the negative side, a utopia that claims to have solved, even in theory, the problems of life once and for all is a miserable fiction indeed. And when this kind of utopianism sets itself up as unalterable truth, it merely asserts its own falsity. A utopia in the best sense is a hypothesis to be tested and tempered. Like any hypothesis, it needs to have the possibility of its own correction built into itself. Like any hypothesis, it needs to be lived in the "experimental community." In this sense a utopia or "the good life" acts as a motivating but revisable template for both individual conduct and community life. The critical community, however, is and always remains, a precarious equilibrium.

The root metaphor of the pragmatic temper is inquiry: science, not as fixed body of truth, that is, "systematized knowledge," but as inquisitive and imaginative human nature tempered through its observations and refined through the self-critical community. The pragmatic *imago mundi* is one of immeasurably rich, fluid, and unique qualities and possibilities; of brute, compulsive facts that testify to the great "Outward Clash"; of the continuity of mind with being; of the possibility, despite enduring oppressive conditions, for the redirection and transformation of individuals, institutions, and worldviews through the continued semiosis of inquiry.

Dewey's great hope for a reconstruction of modern life may strike one as overly optimistic, given the all too frequent brutalities of our time. Yet it is clear that some radical transformation of the now spent voices of modern culture is needed, for we have arrived at that dire time Peirce alluded to in 1893:

> Soon a flash and quick peal will shake economists quite out of their complacency, too late. The twentieth century, in its latter half, shall surely see the deluge-tempest burst upon the social order—to clear upon a world as deep in ruin as that greed-philosophy has long plunged it into guilt. (CP 6.292).

The scope of Dewey's social philosophy of inquiry is enlarged when placed in the broader context of Peirce's realist philosophy of "concrete reasonableness" and "critical common-sensism," which holds that our quest "to find out" the mystery of the universe and our place in it touches the deepest wellsprings of our being, and that the:

> development of Reason consists, you will observe, in embodi-ment, that is, in manifestation. The creation of the universe, which did not take place during a certain busy week, in the year 4004 B.C., but is going on today and never will be done, is this very development of Reason. . . . Under this conception, the ideal of conduct will be to execute our little function in the operation of creation by giving a hand toward rendering the world more reasonable, whenever, as the slang is, it is "up to us" to do so. (CP 1.615)

In the broadened pragmatic attitude, generality itself is rooted in nature, not dichotomized from it, and the laws of mind are not simply inner "faculties" but refractions of larger tempering patterns of nature. The as yet unrealized possibilities of the pragmatic attitude for contributing to a new cultural order rooted in a continuum between purpose and nature, commu-nity and cosmos, could begin to take shape, should humanity survive the age of abstraction.

2 Qualitative Immediacy and the Communicative Act

A distinguishing feature of American social thought is the emphasis placed on immediacy in experience. From Peirce's discussions of "Firstness" (roughly, the phenomenological present) and James's conception of "the stream of consciousness," through contemporary symbolic interactionist discussions of the situation, there is a shared attempt to get at the directness and flow of events, to grasp the mercurial essence that is the vital source of meaning. Critics have charged that these attempts in fact miss the importance of meaning as a system of conventional rules, that in concentrating on the uniqueness of a situation the inquiry becomes bogged down in a morass of subjectivity that ignores the influence of objective norms and social structures (Lewis 1976; Gonos 1977; Giddens 1979, 1984). Although these criticisms may be accurate for some recent trends within symbolic interactionism, they ignore or distort the fundamental importance of qualitative immediacy within the pragmatic conception of meaning as interpretative act. Thus the "qualitative tradition" I will examine is literally a tradition concerned with "quality" in its philosophical sense. I will explore what has been termed "qualitative immediacy" or "aesthetic quality" in the context of the pragmatic tradition by tracing its importance to the theories of meaning and communication of C. S. Peirce, John Dewey, and G. H. Mead.

As mentioned previously, the origins of the philosophy of pragmatism are not to be found, as is often thought, in the work of William James but in that of his lifelong colleague and friend, Charles Sanders Peirce. The foundations for pragmatism can be discovered in a series of articles Peirce wrote in the late 1860s criticizing the Cartesian quest for indubitable foundations of thought (CP 5.213–357). When Descartes borrowed the Augustinian expression *(De Civitate Dei*, XI, 26) "I think, therefore I am," as the clear and distinct idea that could provide a foundation for thought, he helped launch a view that saw direct, immediate knowledge as the goal of inquiry.[1] Through

---

1. As Jacques Choron notes, "Having been advised by his friend, the mathematician Father Mersenne, that his *cogito, ergo sum* is not an original discovery since it can be found in Saint

introspection one could peel away the vaguenesses and uncertainties of the world and attain the realm beyond doubt—the cogito or subjective self-consciousness. "Of thine eye I am Eyebeam," said Emerson's Sphinx in the poem *The Sphinx*, and similarly one might argue that the Cartesian quest to attain the pure "I" through introspection (as if the "eye" could see itself), can only end in blindness, as it did for Oedipus. The point of Peirce's early articles is that all thought or knowledge, including self-knowledge, is inferential and general, that is, it is of the nature of a sign, and it takes time to occur. Thus even in a late article (1905), Peirce answers his own question—"What is the bearing of the Present instant upon conduct"—by replying: "Introspection is wholly a matter of inference. One is immediately conscious of his Feelings no doubt: but not that they are feelings of an ego. The self is only inferred. There is no time in the Present for any inference at all, least of all for inference concerning that very instant" (CP 5.462).

Here Peirce is arguing against immediate knowledge through "introspection" or "intuition," terms which technically mean unmediated, direct inner perception. Yet he does acknowledge the pervasive influence of the present when he says, "One is immediately conscious of his Feelings." Peirce distinguishes feeling from emotion, because for him emotion is a kind of inference, interpretation, or "knowledge"—"Thirdness" as I shall explain later. By "feeling" Peirce means quality or "Firstness," "an instance of that sort of element of consciousness which is all that it is positively, in itself, regardless of anything else" (CP 1.306). This definition of feeling comes very close to the kind of study proposed in philosophical phenomenology (Husserl 1973; Merleau-Ponty 1962; Schutz 1970a), and indeed the analysis of qualitative immediacy considered as "phaneron," formed the basis of Peirce's own brand of phenomenology which he developed independently of Husserl and which he originally termed "phaneroscopy" to avoid confusing it with Hegel's phenomenology. The purpose of phaneroscopy is to ascertain the elemental categories present to mind. Peirce's "epoché" is more radical than Husserl's, however, in that it also excludes any notion of "transcendental subjectivity" as pertaining to the phaneron. (See Rosensohn 1974, for a discussion of Peirce's phenomenology.)

Augustine's *The City of God* (XI, 26), Descartes defends himself in a letter to Andreas Colvius (November 14, 1540) by pointing out the difference between them: 'The use I make of it is in order to show that "I" which thinks is an immaterial substance which has nothing corporeal about it' " (Choron 1968, 640). Not only is Descartes' individualism and rationalism characteristic of modernity, but so is his rigid insistence on differentiating himself from other views in the name of originality. Even his contemporary Gassendi saw through his position: "You will say I am mind alone. . . . But let us talk in earnest, and tell me frankly, do you not derive from the very sound you utter in so saying from the society in which you have lived? And, since the sounds you utter are derived from intercourse with other men, are not the meanings of sounds derived from the same source?" (in Mumford 1970, 82).

In his view, qualitative immediacy is an essential element of an experience, yet the *meaning* of any experience does not consist in its immediacy per se but in its relation to past experiences through continual interpretation dependent on the future. Peirce obviously defines the present much more strictly than Mead (1932), who includes duration—a little bit of the past and future—as an element of the present. Perhaps a better term for Mead's present would be "the emergent present," since he attempted to distinguish a social present influenced by Morgan and Alexander's conceptions of evolutionary emergence.

Although quality is logically (though not necessarily temporally) prior to actuality, we never encounter "pure" examples of it *apart from* its embodiment. Instead we can prescind the quality by "bracketing off," as phenomenologists say, the questions of its existence and relation to other things. Yet qualitative immediacy in itself is not primarily a knowledge affair, it is something we experience directly in the present as feeling. Peirce gives some examples which illustrate the *sui generis* nature of qualitative immediacy:

> The poetic mood approaches the state in which the present appears as it is present. The present is just what it is regardless of the absent, regardless of past and future. Imagine, if you please, a consciousness in which there is no comparison, no relation, no recognized multiplicity (since parts would be other than the whole), no change, no imagination of any modification of what is positively there, no reflection—nothing but a simple positive character. Such a consciousness might be just an odour, say a smell of attar; or it might be the hearing of a piercing eternal whistle. In short, any simple and positive quality of feeling would be something which our description fits that it is such as it is quite regardless of anything else. The quality of feeling is the true psychical representative of the first category of the immediate as it is in its immediacy, of the present in its direct positive presentness. (CP 5.44)

Because Peirce's philosphy is fundamentally in opposition to the idea of unmediated knowledge of the present, the last thing he would want to say is that we "know" qualities of immediacy. Instead, qualitative immediacy is something that can be *felt* but not *known* in the present:

> it is plain enough that all that is immediately present to a man is what is in his mind in the present instant. His whole life is in the present. But when he asks what is the content of the present instant, his question always comes too late. . . . Indeed, although a feeling is immediate consciousness, that is, is whatever of consciousness there may be that is immediately present, yet there is no consciousness in it because it is instantaneous. For we have

seen already that feeling is nothing but a quality, and a quality is not conscious: it is a mere possibility. (CP 1.310)

Dewey, as discussed in the previous chapter, similarly stressed that qualities are felt or, in his word, "had," rather than known.

Peirce's view of qualitative immediacy is significant for social theory because it treats possibility as a fundamental dimension of human experience, not reducible to existential embodiment ("upon the fact that some material thing possesses it"), or to a knowing mind. Peirce claimed that potentiality is itself genuine, and that a common mistake of nominalists lies in "holding that the potential, or possible, is nothing but what the actual makes it to be" (CP 1.422). Thus in delineating a mode of being concerned with potentiality, with what "might happen," with living imagination, Peirce tried to account for the importance of immediacy in experience by showing how essential it is not only to novelty, uniqueness, and the creative aspect of human experience, but also to large-scale human institutions, cultures, and the world at large.

Qualitative immediacy has its importance within the interpretative sign process or mediation (that is, "Thirdness") as well. In this regard it should be mentioned that Peirce distinguishes three elemental categories of all phenomena: Firstness, or quality as described here; Secondness, or the actuality of existence—"otherness," struggle, dyadic reaction; and Thirdness, or mediation, generality, representation, interpretation—what is usually thought of as knowledge or thought (see Rochberg-Halton, forthcoming). All inferences are instances of Thirdness. Firstness is involved in Secondness, and both are involved in Thirdness. Peirce tried to show how the signs constituting language and thought are never absolutely "clear and distinct," à la Descartes, but rather that an essential feature of all communication is what he defined as *vagueness,* which is the involvement of qualitative possibility within the communicative sign process:

> A sign is objectively vague, in so far as, leaving its interpretation more or less indeterminate, it reserves for some other possible sign or experience the function of completing the determination. ... No communication of one person to another can be entirely definite, i.e., nonvague. ... wherever degree or any other possibility of continuous variation subsists, absolute precision is impossible. Much else must be vague, because no man's interpretation of words is based on exactly the same experience as any other man's. Even in our most intellectual conceptions the more we strive to be precise, the more unattainable precision seems. It should never be forgotten that our own thinking is carried on as a dialogue, and though mostly in a lesser degree, is subject to almost every imperfection of language. (CP 5.505–6)

Positivism tried to destroy vagueness, and yet, in the way Peirce describes it, vagueness can provide a very useful methodological tool for obtaining *objectivity* in empirical social research. By reserving "for some other possible sign or experience the function of completing the determination," the researcher can design inquiries that impose the burden of defining the scope of the situation or problem on the respondent, rather than on the a priori assumptions of the researcher. In a broader context Peirce's theory of vagueness enables him to root his theory of inquiry (as well as his philosophical anthropology) in a biocultural and instinctual basis that gives a logical explanation for the creative origins of inquiry. We are tempered creatures who refract the laws of nature, and hence have a proclivity for hypothesis-making. But the intrinsic vagueness of our proclivity demands institutions more or less capable of critical inquiry.

A key aspect of Peirce's formulation of pragmatism and semiotic for contemporary social theory is that all meaning consists of a continuous sign process, communicative acts oriented toward ultimate ends. More precisely, each and every sign, in his definition, constitutes a communicative act. Peirce's most well-known definition of a sign is:

> something which stands to somebody for something in some respect or capacity. It addresses somebody, that is, creates in the mind of that person an equivalent sign, or perhaps a more developed sign. That sign which it creates I call the *interpretant* of the first sign. The sign stands for something, its *object*. (CP 2.228)

A sign, then, consists of the triadic representation of some object (in the broader grammatical sense) to an interpreting sign, or interpretant, and thus intrinsically involves communication. Because it also takes time to occur and is framed within a normative community of interpretation, a sign is by this definition a sign-process, a communicative act. And because the interpretant is itself a sign, it also "addresses" another interpretant, in a continuing process of interpretative communication. In Peirce's simplest threefold division of signs, he distinguishes *symbolic signs,* which convey meaning through convention or rule (for example, linguistic symbols); *indexical signs,* which convey information by being physically affected by their objects (for example, weathervanes indicating the direction of the wind by being pushed by it); and *iconic signs,* which convey information by qualitatively embodying the object (for example, a painting "represents" itself in its own qualities). The fact that there are conventions for landscape painting is not the determining factor in the experience of seeing a given landscape from the iconic perspective. What is important are the qualities of the painting itself—or even how conventions of landscape painting might be directly embodied in the qualities of the painting.

Iconic signs, in this threefold division of signs (Peirce actually developed more detailed divisions of signs which need not be discussed here but see Rochberg-Halton, forthcoming), are signs of qualitative immediacy, and as such, signify the qualitative possibility or pervasive quality of the communicative act. Although Peirce wrote very little on aesthetic experience, he seems to have taken a position very similar to Dewey's theory of aesthetic experience (to be discussed in the next section of this chapter):

> it seems to me that while in esthetic enjoyment we attend to the totality of feeling—and especially to the total resultant Quality of Feeling presented in the work of art we are contemplating—yet it is a sort of intellectual sympathy, a sense that here is a Feeling that one can comprehend, a reasonable Feeling. I do not succeed in saying exactly *what* it is, but it is a consciousness belonging to the category of Representation, though representing something in the Category of Quality of Feeling. (CP 5.113)

By "Category of Quality of Feeling" Peirce means that the aesthetic experience essentially involves a sign of Firstness, or iconicity, in his simplest threefold division of signs. Peirce also discussed the communication of qualitative immediacy in his theory of signs as the *tone* of a sign (Peirce 4.537; 8.363), a distinction that has been repressed in contemporary semiotics. It forms the first level of a threefold distinction between *tone, token,* and *type.* The aesthetic element of experience, as Dewey would later elaborate, involves the communication of qualitative signs, whose meaning is the quality conveyed regardless of what conventions may be used to express that quality.

Although an act always possesses its own inherent quality or character, the meaning always addresses a future interpretation. Thus the pragmatic meaning of any act is the possible conceivable effects it might have on future conduct, not just the actual behaviors or mechanical motions produced in the act. Peirce, who was primarily a logician, did not write much on aesthetic experience, but Dewey dealt with it extensively in his later philosophy. So to get a better understanding of qualitative immediacy in aesthetic experience we turn now to Dewey.

QUALITATIVE IMMEDIACY AND AESTHETIC EXPERIENCE IN DEWEY

Qualitative immediacy is one of the most essential—and overlooked— features of John Dewey's theory of experience. Despite the fact that Dewey's theory of communication figured prominently in the well-known Park and Burgess introductory sociology text of 1921, the Dewey that most contemporary sociologists seem to be aware of is the crass "instrumentalist" and "pragmatist" who emphasized meanings and actions as aimed toward utilitarian goals and who had an image of man, as one sociologist has said, as "an unsocialized calculating man of the jungle" (Lewis 1976,357).

But these are simply caricatures of Dewey's thought, as he himself showed in responding to early criticisms:

> No misconception of the instrumental logic has been more persistent than the belief that it makes knowledge merely a means to a practical end, or to the satisfaction of practical needs—practical being taken to signify some quite definite utilities of a material or bread and butter type. . . . But I again affirm that the term "pragmatic" means only the rule of referring all thinking, all reflective considerations, to *consequences* for final meaning and test. Nothing is said about the nature of the consequences: they may be aesthetic, or moral, or political, or religious in quality—anything you please. (Dewey 1916, 330)

We see again how the pragmatists believed philosophical pragmatism to be the opposite of the modern everyday usage of "pragmatic" as expedient. Despite some important differences between Dewey's and Peirce's versions of pragmatism—which diminished as Dewey became increasingly influenced by Peirce in his later life and came to appreciate the subtlety of Peirce's fallibilism—both shared a view of human conduct as oriented toward correctible ends through self-control, rather than as ultimately motivated by origins or mechanistic determinants. And both saw the ultimate end of human action not merely as a utilitarian adaptation or rationalistic knowledge but as the growth and embodiment of intelligence—in Peirce's words, "concrete reasonableness." They attempted to show how the *summum bonum* is not some abstract, unattainable ideal, but a living presence in all human conduct. Despite the differences between Dewey's situationalism and Peirce's semiotic realism, their perspectives complemented each other.

Peirce was primarily a logician and scientist, yet he came to develop a view that saw truth as dependent upon goodness (that is, logic as dependent upon ethics), and goodness in turn dependent upon beauty (that is, ethics as dependent upon aesthetics),—the qualitative or aesthetic ideal of the intrinsically admirable. In contrast to Peirce's image of humankind as scientific inquirer, Dewey's perspective views man as craftsman, capable of building and cultivating the purposes of life. Dewey (1938) also dealt with the logic of inquiry and the moral influence of philosophy (1946a), yet one of his most important contributions is his discussion of the role of qualitative immediacy in situations, and especially the nature of aesthetic experience.

Dewey first elaborated his theory of qualitative immediacy in *Experience and Nature* (1925). He described, for example, how qualities became infused with intelligence or mind in the course of human evolution, and how this does not make man simply an evolved *homo sapiens*, an abstract knower, but also a being capable of *communicating* the felt qualities of existence:

> As life is a character of events in a peculiar condition of orga-
> nization, and "feeling" is a quality of life-forms marked by com-
> plexly mobile and discriminating responses, so "mind" is an
> added property assumed by a feeling creature, when it reaches
> that organized interaction with other living creatures which is
> language, communication. This state of things in which qualita-
> tively different feelings are not just had but are significant of
> objective differences, is mind. Feelings are no longer just felt.
> They have and they make *sense;* record and prophesy. (Dewey
> 1925,258).

Whereas the experience or act of thinking does have its own inherent quality, it differs from experiences that are acknowledged to be aesthetic, such as art, "but only in its materials." This is because the prominent signs in thinking are *symbolic,* while the prominent signs in aesthetic experience are *iconic,* to use Peirce's simple threefold division mentioned earlier. Dewey develops this idea further in his *Art as Experience:*

> The material of fine arts consists of qualities; that of experience
> having intellectual conclusion are signs or symbols having no in-
> trinsic quality of their own, but standing for things that may in
> another experience be qualitatively experienced. The difference is
> enormous. . . . Nevertheless, the experience itself (of thinking)
> has a satisfying emotional quality because it possesses internal in-
> tegration and fulfillment reached through ordered and organized
> movement. This artistic structure may be immediately felt. In so
> far, it is esthetic. . . . no intellectual activity is an integral event
> (is an experience), unless it is rounded out with this quality.
> Without it thinking is inconclusive. (Dewey 1958,38)

Even though intellectual experience is quite different from aesthetic experience, there is still an element of the aesthetic involved in it. The aesthetic element is what constitutes that neglected realm of human thought celebrated by William Blake, the *poetic imagination,* which in his view not only dreamed us into existence but forever remains the living source of cultural life.

In Dewey's perspective, "esthetic" refers specifically to quality rather than being a synonym for "artistic." He does distinguish art as "a process of doing or making" from the aesthetic as the complementary perceiving and enjoying perspective, denoting "the consumer's rather than the producer's standpoint" (Dewey 1958,47). But the aesthetic is not simply the enjoyment of art, as commonly thought. Instead it is what gives unity to *all*

experience: "no experience of whatever sort is a unity unless it has esthetic quality" (Dewey 1958,40). The aesthetic is a partner of the instrumental in the communicative act; it is the consummation or completion of the experience:

> Discourse itself is both instrumental and consummatory. Communication is an exchange which procures something wanted; it involves a claim, appeal, order, direction or request. . . . Communication is also an immediate enhancement of life, enjoyed for its own sake. . . . Language is always a form of action and in its instrumental use is always a means of concerted action for an end, while at the same time it finds in itself all the goods of its possible consequences. For there is no mode of action as fulfilling and as rewarding as is concerted consensus of action. It brings with it the sense of sharing and merging in a whole (Dewey 1925, 183–84).

Aesthetic experience, or the perception (*aisthētikos* = perceptive) of the inherent qualities of the object, act, or situation, does involve prior habits of convention or interpretation—the instrumental—but does not, strictly speaking, depend on these for its meaning. The reason for this is that from the aesthetic perspective, the inherent quality itself, not the experiencer, is the subject of the experience. True, if there is to be an aesthetic experience there must be an experiencer with a potential for realizing the aesthetic quality. But the aesthetic meaning is possessed by the quality of the total transaction, not just by the experiencer. Mead also expressed this idea in an article on "The Nature of Aesthetic Experience" published in 1926, a year after Dewey's *Experience and Nature,* which Mead claimed was an influence on him:

> The beatitude that permeates the common striving of men after an infinite God of their salvation belongs to the cathedral. The delight which follows upon successful adjustment of one's body to the varied . . . elements of a landscape flows over into the landscape itself. . . . In the aesthetic appreciation of the works of great artists, what we are doing is capturing values of enjoyment there, which fill out and interpret our own interests in living and doing. They have permanent value because they are the language of delight into which men can translate the meaning of their own existence (Mead 1938, 454, 457).

Again, the locus of the aesthetic experience is neither exclusively subjective nor objective but is in the "pervasive quality" of the act (Bernstein 1967, 94–96; Rochberg-Halton 1979a, 1979b).

The experiencer "has" or "feels" the qualities of the aesthetic transaction, rather than only indirectly "knowing" them. The difference here is perhaps like that between an individual immediately enjoying a painting, and an art critic reflectively analyzing and comparing the qualities of the painting. The former activity is aesthetic, the latter intellectual or critical. This is the difference between prizing and appraising, between valuing and valuation, between the immediately possessed and the reflectively understood (Dewey 1939). Poetry may make use of conventional linguistic symbols, and even be expressed in conventional linguistic forms, yet it is the unique qualities expressed that give the poem its aesthetic significance.

In *Art as Experience* Dewey also discussed the role of aesthetic quality in the communicative act by returning to the literal meaning of the term *perception*—to feel or take in. There Dewey distinguishes between *recognition,* in which an object's meaning is solely dependent on previous habits of interpretation, and *perception,* in which an object's meaning includes its unique qualities as well as the viewer's culturally conditioned habits of interpretation (Rochberg-Halton 1979a, 1979b; see my chapter 7 in Csikszentmihalyi and Rochberg-Halton 1981). Recognition is "arrested perception," in which all meaning occurs within the bubble of received cultural convention, and where the qualities of the object have no effect on its interpretation. For this reason recognition is *an-aesthetic,* because there is no "feeling" in Dewey's and Peirce's sense of this term. What is important about the perceptive experience is that a person can learn something new, can have *an experience.* Through aesthetic experience we open ourselves to the spontaneities, the serendipities, the qualities of the surrounding world and make them our own.

The lack of attention given to aesthetic quality is another of the effects of the Cartesian world in which we live. Social scientists tend to ignore aesthetic quality, as if it were solely a matter of convention, or else of physiology. As parodied by Alfred North Whitehead, this spectre of the nominalistic "ghost in the machine" would have us believe that:

> The occurrences of nature are in some ways apprehended by minds which are associated with living bodies. But the mind in apprehending also experiences sensations which, properly speaking, are qualities of the mind alone. These sensations are projected by the mind so as to clothe appropriate bodies in external nature. Thus bodies are perceived as with qualities that do not belong to them, qualities which in fact are purely the offspring of the mind. Thus nature gets credit which in truth should be reserved for ourselves: the rose for its scent: the nightingale for his song: and the sun for his radiance. . . . Nature is a dull affair, soundless, scentless, colorless; merely the hurrying of material, endlessly, meaninglessly. (Whitehead, quoted in Bernstein 1967, 89–90)[2]

2. John Locke's discussion of primary and secondary qualities illustrates the perspective Whitehead had in mind: "What I have said concerning colours and smells may be understood

In Dewey's pragmatic view, however, aesthetic quality is neither wholly "within" the person nor the thing, rather it "belongs" as much to the thing as it does to the person, and can only be realized within the transaction.

Aesthetic quality does have important consequences for the cultivation of the self, as both Dewey and Mead argued. And James Mark Baldwin, a colleague of the pragmatists and the source of inspiration for theories of cognitive development now associated with Jean Piaget, proposed a detailed theory of aesthetic development that has been lost in the field of cognitive developmental psychology because of Piaget's abstractionist overemphasis on the cognitive and "logical" (see Parsons 1980). Yet in the perspective outlined here it could be argued that aesthetic quality is the most prominent feature of the infant's world. A feeling of warmth or irritation can be the infant's entire universe at this early stage of development, one not reducible to "sensori-motor" movements. When the self begins to develop, it already has its own aesthetic quality, or what traditionally has been called "character," which in normal development remains open to further cultivation. Aesthetic quality or qualitative immediacy thus may be one of the most important constituents of the self, perhaps original to it, and makes genuinely new developments of the self possible. Turning to the pragmatic tradition, we see that qualitative immediacy is regarded as an essential feature of the self.

Immediacy, Individuality, and the Self

Dewey and Mead, like Peirce, view the communicative act as the locus of social life and as fully social and objective in itself, even when it occurs within a single person. Dewey said, for example, concerning the modern emphasis on individuality and private experience:

> The modern discovery of inner experience . . . implies a new worth and sense of dignity in human individuality, a sense that an individual is not a mere property of nature, set in place according to a scheme independent of him, as an article is put in its place in a cabinet, but that he adds something, that he makes a contribution. . . . But here also distortion entered in. Failure to recognize that this world of inner experience is dependent upon an extension of language which is a social product and operation led to the subjectivistic, solipsistic, and egotistic strain in modern thought (Dewey 1925, 172–73).

---

also of tastes and sounds, and other like sensible qualities; which, whatever reality we by mistake attribute to them, are in truth nothing in the objects themselves, but powers to produce various sensations in us; and depend on those primary qualities, viz.; bulk, figure, texture, and motion of parts. . . . They are, in the bodies we denominate from them, only a power to produce those sensations in us: and what is sweet, blue, or warm in idea, is but the certain bulk, figure, and motion of the insensible parts, in the bodies themselves, which we call so" (vol. 1, bk. II, chap. 8, pars. 14, 15).

Hence even individuality in Dewey's and Mead's views is fully socialized. There is no "real me" severed from the social *persona* or mask. The *persona* is not simply the veil of illusion, obscuring the really real beneath it; it constitutes the very social fabric of the self.

In the pragmatic view the self is not based on some underlying "cardinal conception" as Cartesians might claim, but instead is a living, feeling, personalized, communicative sign-process oriented toward goals through self-control. Similarly the self is not simply an effect of self-presentation, as it is for Goffman, but is possessed of a potentially unique character, though this may be routinized out of existence in faceless mass society, where "face" means all. The individual self is created and grows only by a process of internalizing the surrounding social world through the communicative medium of gestures, artifacts, and language. Intelligent human communication always involves community, which Mead termed "the generalized other," because even our own thought is an internal dialogue with representations of community, for example, language itself. In Peirce's words,

> a person is not absolutely an individual. His thoughts are what he is "saying to himself," that is, saying to that other self that is just coming into life in the flow of time. When one reasons, it is that critical self that one is trying to persuade, and all thought whatsoever is a sign, and is mostly of the nature of language. The second thing to remember is that the man's circle of society (however widely or narrowly this phrase may be understood), is a sort of loosely compacted person, in some respects of higher rank than the person of an individual organism. (CP 5.421)

"The man's circle of society," which acts as a "sort of loosely compacted person," is similar to Mead's concept of the generalized other—that set of attitudes of interpetation which become internalized in the creation of the self through the process of role-taking. It is also possible to interpret Peirce's statement in terms of the dialectic of the "I" and the "me" discussed by Mead, who acquired it, with changes, from William James. When Peirce says that a person's thoughts are what he is "saying to himself" and that it is "that critical self that one is trying to persuade," he is emphasizing the dialogical nature of thought and the fact that the interpreting thought, or interpretant, or "critical self," is a general—which can be directly translated into Mead's terminology as "the generalized other," or "the me." That which is addressing the me is the first element of a sign, the qualitative element, if we remember that in Peirce's triadic definition a sign consists of sign (first), its object (second), and its interpretant (third). This element is the "I." That which is "discussed" is the object of the sign, or object of the "I-me" dialogue. In Peirce's semiotic a sign is also defined as:

> a First which stands in such genuine triadic relation to a Second,
> called its Object, as to be capable of determining a Third,
> called its *Interpretant,* to assume the same triadic relation to its
> Object in which it stands itself to the same Object.
> (CP 2.274)

In other words, that which addresses the interpretant is of the category Firstness, or qualitative immediacy. The sign as a triadic whole is Thirdness, but it *involves* this Firstness. The upshot of the argument, then, is that the "I" is the element of qualitative immediacy within the communicative act. The many commentators on Mead's "I" tend to miss the essential point he is trying to make—that the emergent present is what introduces novelty, the unpredictable and unexpected, into the self, and that reflection is always an interpretation of what is already past. The present is the "I," the reflective interpretation, the "me."[3]

It should be added that Mead seems to reverse William James's formulation of the "I" and "me" in some ways, that seem to me to overcome the inherent dualism in James. James expresses the distinction in "The Consciousness of Self," in his masterwork, *The Principles of Psychology:*

> We may sum up by saying that personality implies the incessant presence of two elements, an objective person, known by a passing subjective Thought and recognized as continuing in time. *Hereafter let us use the words ME and I for the empirical person and the judging Thought. . . . If the passing thought be the directly verifiable existent which no school has hitherto doubted it to be, then that thought itself is the thinker,* and psychology need not look beyond. (James [1890] 1950, 371, 401).

James suggests here that the "I" is the direct knower in the stream of consciousness rather than the interpreting "me" or reflective mediation, thus falling prey, it seems to me, to a variant of Cartesian dualism. Dewey

---

3. One reading of Jorge Luis Borges's short story, "Borges and I," reveals it as a literary realization of the I-and-me dialogue of the self. Borges himself claims that William James made a strong impression on him (interview, The University of Chicago, April 1, 1980). Even if James is not one of the sources for the piece, Borges's dialogue of pronouns does illustrate the I-and-me distinction, as in the following excerpts from "Borges and I":

> Things happen to him, the other one, to Borges. . . . It would be an exaggeration to say that our relationship is a hostile one; I live, I go on living, so that Borges may contrive his literature; and that literature justifies me. . . . In any case, I am destined to perish, definitively, and only some instant of me may live on in him. . . . I shall subsist in Borges, not in myself (assuming I am someone), and yet I recognize myself less in his books than in many another, or than in the intricate flourishes played on a guitar. . . . I don't know which one of the two of us is writing this page. (Borges 1967, 200–201)

criticized this tendency to dualism in James, in an article called "The Vanishing Subject in the Psychology of James" (Dewey 1946a, 396–409).

There may seem to be some similarity between James's "judging Thought" and Mead's use of the "I" as response. J. David Lewis has claimed that Mead speaks of the "I" as response, but Lewis seems to think of the response as the immediate action produced, or even the physiological functioning of the unconscious moment—in other words, *quantitative immediacy* rather than *qualitative immediacy* as described here. Lewis (1979, 278–81) does offer an interpretation of the "I" as "imagery," which has some similarities to the interpretation given here, but in seeing imagery or inherent quality as reducible to the "neurological conditions" that determine the behavioristic response of the "I," he ignores qualitative immediacy, a common concern of the four major pragmatists, in favor of a positivistic behaviorism quite at odds, it seems to me, with the theoretical foundations of pragmatism. In contrast, I suggest that Mead's use of "response" is similar to Dewey's discussion of the consummatory phase of the act described earlier—that is, the aesthetic—which Mead himself discusses elsewhere (1938, 23–25).

The importance of the "I" in Mead's view of the self is in many respects similar to Firstness—feeling or quality—in Peirce and aesthetic experience in Dewey. It is the element through which emergence, novelty, originality, uniqueness, creative impulse, and free expression enter into the self-process and endow it with vitality and growth. Of course if taken out of its context in the cultivation process, taken as an end in itself, it can lead to empty sensationalism or blind narcissism—equally self-destructive consequences. In Mead's words (1934, 178) the "I" is something "that is never entirely calculable." It is always somewhat different from what is expected by the "me," the conventional and habitual (Mead 1934, 209), and is in this sense novel. What separates the pragmatists' emphasis on habit as the basis for the organization of meaning from crass behaviorism is their insistence that qualitative immediacy enters into habit; in other words, that human habit lives and involves real possibility. Mead says in various passages,

> That movement into the future is the step, so to speak, of the ego, of the "I." It is something that is not given in the "me." . . . The "I" gives the sense of freedom, of initiative. . . . However carefully we plan the future it always is different from that which we can previse, and this something that we are continually bringing in and adding to is what we identify with the self that comes into the level of our experience only in the completion of the act. . . . Now it is this living act which never gets directly into reflective experience. It is only after the act has taken place that we can catch it in our memory and place it in terms of that which we have done. It is the "I" which we may be said to be

continually trying to realize, and to realize through the actual conduct itself. (Mead 1934, 177, 203).

Many interpreters have taken this placing of the "I" outside of the conventional to mean that it is some kind of *unmediated* knowledge, transcendental ego, or direct perception. Anthony Giddens, for example, claims that, "the 'I' appears in Mead's writings as the given core of agency, and its origins hence always remain obscure. To relate the 'I' to agency, it is necessary to follow the detour suggested by structuralists in respect of the decentring of the subject, without reaching conclusions which treat the subject simply as a sign within a signification structure" (Giddens 1984, 43). Although Giddens's interpretation itself remains a bit obscure, he apparently conceives of Mead's "I" as mistakenly foundational and privatized, while yet wanting to keep it outside of sign mediation. It seems clear, however, from Mead's remarks quoted previously that the "I" is the *immediate* rather than the *unmediated*. More precisely it is the *immediate* phase of *mediation*, rather than something outside of or prior to the mediation process. The "I" cannot be separated from the dialogical sign-process that constitutes the self, rather it is that process of mediation or interpretation considered in its immediacy. It is not simply reducible to mediation since it does carry its own potential as qualitative immediacy. But just as important, *it has no separate existence of its own.* For this separate "I," the "private I" if you will, is the fiction of modern individualism.

Mead himself (1934, 209) discussed how modern art often seemed to be a demand for the unconventional and unmediated (or, one might add, even the destruction of all mediation) in a quest for pure novelty, the pure "I." He did not live long enough to see the Cartesian blindness produced by certain late modernists—empty canvasses, silent music, and very blank verse—the culminating stages of the culture of nominalism, in which the quest to grasp the pure "I" amounted to the plucking out of creative vision rather than to its realization. The modernist emphasis on the pure originality, novelty, and uniqueness of the "private I" is as one-sided, from the pragmatic perspective, as that of many preliterate peoples whose self is determined almost exclusively by the "me," and for whom individuality means to be an "enemy of society" (Turner 1975, 27). But even there, the "I" may be personified by a single individual such as the king or village headman, who is relatively freer from everyday constraints and norms to express choice, initiative, caprice, and novelty. Or the "I" may be embodied in the role of the medicine man or shaman, whose liminal position makes him the embodiment of the exploratory "I," the diviner of things to come (Turner 1967, chap. 6).

Thus the importance of qualitative immediacy in the pragmatists' conceptions of the self is that it acknowledges the uniqueness and creative potentiality of the person, and at the same time includes these qualities as social constituents of the self, rather than as asocial attributes of individualism, unconditioned by the communicative act. The meaning of uniqueness, individuality, and originality always resides in and for the discourse of the common good, the cultivation of the community both within and outside the individual person, the living and the not yet born.

IS THERE ROOM FOR QUALITY WITHIN CONTEMPORARY SOCIAL THEORY?

By now it is generally acknowledged that a turn toward more "qualitative" or "interpretive" approaches is being taken within the social sciences (Geertz 1973, 1980; Bernstein 1976, 1983; Smith 1978). The limitations of purely quantitative approaches that to a great extent have dominated midcentury sociology and psychology have become increasingly apparent (except perhaps to those ensconced within the mentality of the mainstream), and many sociologists have attempted to reach out for conceptual frameworks that can adequately deal with the human communication of meaning. But too often these frameworks are only "conceptual" or "cognitive" and, as such, are merely a continuation of the modern dominance of epistemology over ontology, "knowing" over "having" or "feeling." There does not seem to be much room for qualitative immediacy, as discussed here, to be considered an essential element of communication and social life.

Perhaps phenomenology attempts to concentrate on this qualitative element of experience, but, at least as proposed by Husserl, it conceives of qualities as Cartesian "objects of knowledge." Symbolic interactionism, the self-claimed child of pragmatism, with its emphasis on the uniqueness of the communicative act, would seem to illustrate the approaches described here, but, as defined by its definer, Herbert Blumer, it does not seem to allow for inherent and immediate qualities as constituents of all experience and as elements of the communicative act: "An object—that is to say, anything that an individual indicates to himself—is different from a stimulus; instead of having an intrinsic character which acts on the individual and which can be identified apart from the individual, its character is conferred on it by the individual" (Blumer 1967, 141; 1969, 4ff.).

The problem with symbolic interactionism is given in its title: it is a view of meaning and experience as *symbolic*, which does not include the *iconic* or qualitative signs as contributing in their own right to the communicative process. The inclusion of qualitative immediacy could at least clarify symbolic interactionist discussions of why a "situation" should be considered unique, by showing that uniqueness is qualitative rather than subjective.

Piaget's "cognitive developmental" psychology is an excellent example of an influential conceptualistic and rationalistic theory that has no room for qualitative immediacy. But the paradox is that Piaget's theory, as mentioned earlier, is founded on that of James Mark Baldwin, a colleague of the pragmatists, who developed a theory of "esthetic development" within his general "genetic epistemology" (Parsons 1980). An aesthetically based theory would provide a wholly different view of human development.

The inclusion of qualitative immediacy as a genuine modality of being, and of communicative sign-being, could contribute to a much needed broadening of the sociology of art, which is often limited these days to conceptualist and conventionalist views (e.g., Wolff 1981; Becker 1982; Bürger 1984). Art institutions do involve ideologies, reputations, power politics, and markets, whose study is a legitimate enterprise for sociology, but to limit the social significance of art to these externals is to retreat into formalism, a formalism that denies the human capacity to transmute felt experience through communicative forms whose substance can convey feeling itself. Art is the inner life of humanity made public. Yet to a great extent contemporary sociology of art, in denying qualitative immediacy, not only retains a limited conception of the extent of our social being, but also denies our mercurial essence.

I have incorporated the concept of qualitative immediacy in my own empirical research on the meaning of materialism, as will become apparent in some of the later chapters of this book. In describing how valued things acquire meaning I found it important to distinguish different modes of meaning or modes of transaction with things. The dominant conceptualist and structuralist views of culture as a "system of symbols and meanings," mediated solely by conventional norms, did not seem to account for the variety of levels often described by my respondents, nor for the importance of the intrinsic quality of the thing as an element of the communicative act (however seldom realized in mass-dominated American culture). Dewey's description of aesthetic experience and Peirce's "iconicity" seemed to provide a broader perspective for interpretation than the purely "conventional" accounts.

We so often think of pragmatism as the voice of American practicality, yet it should be clear by now that the very ground of pragmatism is qualitative immediacy, a concept that undercuts both the positivistic "atoms" and the solitary "cogito" of modern social thought. Presently, however, the concept of qualitative immediacy remains for the most part an unexplored possibility. In modernity, as Simmel noted, all qualities become reduced to quantities. Unfortunately, the same tendency is true for theories of the qualitative. It is now time for those turning to "qualitative" approaches to consider qualitative immediacy, the long dormant vital source of the pragmatic tradition, as a welcome addition to our understanding of the nature of human *being*.

II *Semiotic*

3 Situation, Structure, and The Context of Meaning

THE SIGNIFICANCE OF MEANING

For years neglected as a central sociological concern, the question of meaning has reemerged with a vengeance and now is demanding some kind of answer from those who would further social theory. Two of the approaches at the forefront of contemporary interest, symbolic interactionism and structuralism, share an interest in the role of signs and symbols in social life yet take radically different standpoints concerning the nature of signs and the locus of meaning. Both claim that meaning forms the very basis of society, not instincts or genetics, materialist economics, or asocial psychological laws; and that the foundation of meaning is the sign or symbol. These approaches by and large reject the idea that social science is a search for empirical, causal "facts," and in quite different ways they argue that "values" are what we are really after—that "significance" binds society together. One persistent problem in these and other interpretative approaches is the locus of meaning: whether it is to be found in existential and unique "situations" or in a deep-rooted system or code, i.e., a "structure." By comparing and contrasting some foundational concepts underlying these traditions, such as the nature of the sign in Peirce and Saussure and Durkheim and Mead, and then exploring recent developments in symbolic interactionism, structuralism, and related work, I hope to evaluate critically their strengths and weaknesses in the context of an emerging semiotic sociology.

The term "symbolic interactionism" was formulated in the late 1930s by Herbert Blumer (1969, 1) to reflect the milieu of social theory developed primarily at the University of Chicago in the early part of the century. Blumer himself cites the pragmatists William James, John Dewey, and George Herbert Mead, Chicago sociologists W. I. Thomas, Robert E. Park, Florian Znaniecki, Robert Redfield, and Louis Wirth, and also Charles Horton Cooley and James Mark Baldwin, as among those who significantly contributed to the foundations of symbolic interactionism. The common theme uniting these theorists is an emphasis on the situational context of meaning—a view of meaning as a communicative process located in interpretative acts, whose study demands close attention to the uniqueness and variability of situations as well as to the way situations reflect habitual attitudes of mind. W. I. Thomas, influenced by his friend and colleague Mead, as well as by Dewey and James, developed an explicitly "situational" approach to sociology that stated: "If men define situations as real, they are real in their consequences. The total situation will always contain more and less subjective factors, and the behavior reaction can be studied only in connection with the whole context, i.e., the situation as it exists in verifiable, objective terms, and as it has seemed to exist in terms of the interested persons" (Thomas and Thomas 1970, 154–55). Thomas's two-sided concept of *situation* as the configuration of conditioning factors that are selectively defined by the person and that shape behavior (Thomas 1966, 154–67) reveals a concern somewhat similar to Weber's concept of *action* as subjectively intended meaning oriented to a conditioning "outer world" of objects and processes of nature and as meaning determined through objectively rational means (Weber 1981; Levine 1981, 10). Yet contemporary symbolic interactionists (and even their critics) have virtually ignored the objective component of the situation that contributes to "the whole context, i.e., the situation as it exists in verifiable, objective terms," in favor of meaning as it is subjectively defined in the situation. The contemporary symbolic interactionist sees interaction itself as the medium of the symbolic process and for this reason has been criticized as both atheoretical and unsystematic, as illustrated by Lewis Coser's extremely negative comments:

> Blumer and his co-thinker wish, in fact, to teach a lesson of humility to the sociological theorist, who is seen as incapable of constructing enduring, objective, theoretical structures, but who must, in their view, be attentive to the subjective interpretations, the definitions of the situations, and the emergent meanings that arise in human interaction and be content with that. Needless to say, though functionalists have availed themselves of many particular insights provided by Mead and his successors in the elucidation of social-psychological processes, they have rejected, as a kind of scientific Luddism, the extreme idiographic and antitheoretical bias inherent in symbolic interactionism. They, as well as other critics, have asserted that this orientation prevents the understanding of social structures and their constraining characteristics or of patterns of human organization such as class hierarchies or power constellations. (Coser 1976, 156–57)

"French" structuralism has developed largely out of the ideas generated by Ferdinand de Saussure, Emile Durkheim and his circle, and more recently, Claude Lévi-Strauss. In Lévi-Strauss's definition of the term "social structure" one sees how structuralism stands in opposition to symbolic interactionism: "The term 'social structure' has nothing to do with empirical reality but with models which are built up after it. . . . It will be enough to state at this time that social relations consist of the raw materials out of which the models making up the social structure are built, while social structure can, by no means, be reduced to the ensemble of social relations to be described in a given society" (1967, 271).

Lévi-Strauss views the goal of social science as the achievement of an understanding of the invariant laws of thought, the "deep structure" that provides the ordering of meaning and therefore of society itself (e.g., 1966, 263–64). His heavy reliance on Saussure's concepts of the sign and of meaning as based on binary opposition, as well as his attempts to seek a scientistic universal logic as the ultimate basis of society, has drawn negative criticism from Clifford Geertz similar to that of Coser's concerning symbolic interactionism, but for precisely the opposite reasons:

> It is all terribly ingenious. If a model of society which is "eternal and universal" can be built up out of the debris of dead and dying societies—a model which reflects neither time, nor place, nor circumstance but (this from *Totemism*) "a direct expression of the structure of the mind (and behind the mind, probably of the brain)"—then this may be the way to build it.
>
> For what Lévi-Strauss has made for himself is an infernal culture machine. It annuls history, reduces sentiment to a shadow of the intellect, and replaces the particular mind of particular savages in particular jungles with the Savage Mind immanent in us all. (Geertz 1973, 355)

Neither the extremes of a structuralist "infernal culture machine" nor a symbolic interactionist "scientific Luddism" can provide the comprehensive theory of meaning that seems to be the goal of the ongoing restructuring of social theory (Bernstein, 1976; 1983; Geertz 1980). Yet these two traditions cannot be reduced solely to the work of Lévi-Strauss and Blumer, and by exploring the concept of *sign* and the locus of meaning in the underlying foundations of the symbolic interactionist and structuralist traditions, I will trace the parallel threads of situation and structure that define each tradition. My purpose, however, is to critically investigate these sign theories of meaning as possible contributors to a broadened contemporary social theory.

PEIRCE AND SAUSSURE ON THE SIGN: SEMIOSIS VERSUS STRUCTURE

Let us begin the discussion of symbolic interactionism and structuralism by examining their foundations in the definitions of the sign given by semiotic and semiology. The sources of symbolic interactionism can be traced, through Chicago sociology, to pragmatism, whereas the origins of structuralism are often attributed to Ferdinand de Saussure (1857–1913). For many contemporary symbolic interactionists, pragmatism simply means the work of Mead, who emphasized the role of gestural signs and significant symbols located in communicative acts. Yet social scientists and those interested in semiotic have become increasingly aware of the contemporary relevance of C. S. Peirce (1839–1914), who not only founded pragmatism but also founded modern sign theory, which he termed *semiotic*. Peirce's interest in signs was little appreciated in his lifetime, and one of the ironies of modern sign theory is that the bulk of both Peirce's semiotic and Saussure's semiology was published posthumously (and in Saussure's case, was based on lecture notes). If we explore the Peircean and Saussurean definitions of sign and meaning, the contrasts between situationalists and structuralists should become more apparent, though Peirce was not, in the end, a situationalist.

Saussure viewed the sign as consisting of the two-sided *signified* and *signifier* ("I call the combination of a concept and sound-image a *sign*" [1966, 67]. In this perspective, meaning occurs through binary opposition within a system: "Instead of pre-existing ideas then, we find in all the foregoing examples *values* emanating from the system. When they are said to correspond to concepts, it is understood that the concepts are purely differential and defined not by their positive content but negatively by their relations with the other terms of the system. Their most precise characteristic is in being what the others are not" (1966, 117). The very basis of meaning in the Saussurean model is *difference* (see Barthes 1977), for "In language, as in any semiological system, whatever distinguishes one sign from the others constitutes it. Difference makes character just as it makes value and the unit" (Saussure 1966, 121). *Vive la différence!* says the Saussurean.

Peirce defined the sign as a triadic process rather than as a dyadic structure and viewed meaning as essentially *relation* rather than *difference:* "A sign . . . is something which stands to somebody for something in some respect or capacity. It addresses somebody, that is, creates in the mind of that person an equivalent sign, or perhaps a more developed sign. That sign which it creates I call the *interpretant* of the first sign. The sign stands for something, its *object*. It stands for that object, not in all respects but in reference to a sort of idea, which I have sometimes called the *ground* of the representamen" (CP 2.228). Peirce argued that a sign only has meaning in the context of a continuing process of interpretation. Because each sign is part of a continuous temporal process of interpretation, his theory is intrinsically processual and thus incompatible with Saussure's dyadic and intrinsically static theory (see Singer 1977). The arrow of time, the *diachronic*, is ultimately separable from the underlying system or synchronic dimension in the Saussurean view. One clear difference between the two theories is that the continuity of the temporal interpretative process assures freedom in the pragmatic tradition (e.g., Mead's "emergent present") but for Saussure

(1966, 78) "cancels freedom" in the sense of limiting the rational arbitrariness of language and the sign.

Saussure's emphasis on the arbitrariness of the sign and the context of cultural conventions as the sole basis for a sign's "reference" can be seen as an argument against the nominalistic assertion that only individuals or particulars are real and that signs ultimately refer to these particulars. Only differences within the language system constitute meaning, Saussure (1966) assures us, and "we shall find nothing simple in it regardless of our approach; everywhere and always there is the same complex equilibrium of terms that mutually condition each other. Putting it another way, *language is a form and not a substance*. This truth could not be overstressed, for all the mistakes in our terminology, all our incorrect ways of naming things that pertain to language, stem from the involuntary supposition that the linguistic phenomenon must have substance" (122). Language is like a single sheet of paper with an inseparable obverse and reverse, thought and sound, signified and signifier, whose combination produces a form and not a substance. This "linguistic fact" explains the arbitrariness of the sign: "Not only are the two domains that are linked by the linguistic fact shapeless and confused, but the choice of a given slice of sound to name a given idea is completely arbitrary. If this were not true, the notion of value would be compromised, for it would include an externally imposed element. But actually values remain entirely relative, and that is why the bond between the sound and the idea is radically arbitrary" (113). The arbitrary nature of the sign, Saussure continues, "explains in turn why the social fact alone can create a linguistic system. The community is necessary if values that owe their existence solely to usage and general acceptance are to be set up; by himself the individual is incapable of fixing a single value" (113). Saussure argued for one of the basic tenets of semiology, structuralism, and poststructuralism: that the system or structure and not the individual person or instance constitutes meaning. Not even the linking of a certain sound with a certain concept determines value, because this isolates the term from its system: In fact we begin with the interdependent whole and through analysis, rather than through the synthesis of individual elements, obtain the elements of the sign (113). Hence meaning resides wholly within *langue* (the general language system), not *parole* (the actual speech act). In the Saussaurean view any given instance of communication has significance by virtue of its underlying structure, not by virtue of the uniqueness of the situation.

Though Saussure's approach seems to argue against one strain of nominalism (the tendency that led to British empiricism and resulted in "naive realism" and Carnap's logical positivism [see Carnap 1967]), it can be argued that Saussure retains a basically nominalistic theory of meaning, one that claims to reside on the nominal side of mind rather than on the physicalistic side of "body," and which retains the nominalistic tendency to dichotomize thought and things, system and instance, social and individual, fact and value. Saussure held a variation of the Kantian view that we know the world only through the categories of thought and not as it is apart from mind. In a way Peirce agreed with Kant's idea that our knowledge of the world is constrained by the laws of mind, yet he differed in allowing that the laws of mind are objective products and refractions of the general laws of nature. It should be remembered that for nominalism only particular instances are real, and signs are arbitrary names for these instances. Where scholastic realists such as John Duns Scotus held that some signs (or generals) are real, nominalists such as William of Ockham (famous for his scientific "razor") denied the reality of signs, arguing that although all thought is in signs, these signs are mere arbitrary conventions for real individual instances. In this way nominalism, the philosophical basis for modern Western thought and culture, drove a wedge between thought and things. Saussure, from this perspective, is thoroughly nominalist in agreeing that values are entirely relative and radically arbitrary, "mere names," having no "substance," and that all meaning resides in the conceptual system of language and not at all in any given instance of speech or action. In contrast, Peirce's pragmaticism, which forms one domain within his wider theory of signs, is based on a thoroughgoing criticism of nominalism and its dichotomizing tendencies. In comparing these two theories one finds a modern version of the old realism—nominalism debate.

To return to Peirce's definition of the sign, each sign consists of three elements: the *ground*, its *object*, and its *interpretant*. The middle element of the Peircean sign, the object, is not included in the Saussurean conceptual-psychological definition of the sign. The ground, or inherent quality of the sign, would come closest to Saussure's signifier, the formal phonetic and graphic structure of the sign, and the interpretant would most nearly resemble Saussure's signified, i.e., the meaning conveyed by the structure. Yet each of the elements of Peirce's triad is quite different from the elements in Saussure's scheme. The ground of a sign is the inherent quality of the sign, which represents through its own qualitative possibility rather than through opposition. The interpretant is not limited to arbitrary concepts in the Peircean scheme but may include nonconceptual emotions or physical action. Interpretants are not solely examples of arbitrary conventions but have as their aim the growth of Reasonableness through the future interpretants they will determine. Reasonableness, in Peirce's view, is real rather than arbitrary or nominal.

Peirce distinguished many kinds of signs on the basis of his categories of "Firstness," "Secondness," and "Thirdness," and perhaps the most well known is his trichotomy of *iconic, indexical,* and *symbolic* signs. Peirce's term "symbol" most closely approximates Saussure's arbitrary sign (Saussure uses the "symbol" in approximately the opposite sense of Peirce, however, as an example of a less arbitrary or "motivated" sign). A symbol, in Peirce's view, is given its meaning by its interpretation as a law, general rule, or convention. A symbol is what Peirce referred to. as a *type*, a general regularity that will determine specific instances, called *tokens* (CP 4.537). This distinction appears to resemble that of Saussure between *langue* and *parole*, except that in Peirce's view the instance is itself a general or a sign communicating information. An orchestral score, for example, is a *type* capable of determining many different kinds of performances, all of which are *tokens* of the score. Strictly speaking, Saussure would not view the performance as meaningful in itself but only as an instance of the score, where the meaning resides. Peirce's inclusion of the token (or indexical sign) as a genuine mode of sign is an attempt to give account to existential meaning. Peirce also developed a third mode of sign functioning, which he termed the *tone* of a sign, which deals with the inherent quality of the sign as significative, apart from convention and logically prior to "opposition." Thus the tone of the performance of the symphony is its qualitative uniqueness considered in itself, apart from other performances. The tone of a sign is its inherent quality and unique character, and this is the level of aesthetic experience in Peirce's semiotic. Peirce accounts for a mode of signification not dealt with in structuralist approaches, namely, how the immediate qualities of experience also can act as mediating signs which impart information. In the same way, Dewey's theory of the situation is based on the concept of "a pervasive and internally integrating quality" (1960, 180). Tokens point to their types, they are indexes or actualizations of the general type, but the tone of a sign is the unique, inherent character of that sign. There may be a type of painting called "still life," there may be many tokens or instances of this type, but its unique realization is to be found in the tone or quality of those tokens.

As with Saussure, individuality has no meaning qua individuality in Peirce's scheme, for all meaning is general and all generals are signs in Peirce's view. But Peirce considers more phenomena as signs than does Saussure. Thus just as the communication of a type is a general, so also is the communication of an individual token (or *index*) a general, and so also is the communication of tone or qualitative immediacy a general. For all communication is semiosis, the sign-process, in which a representation of some object is communicated to some interpretant. Although unique character or quality of feeling does occur in the immediate present, it can also act mediately as a communicative sign, which Peirce termed the *icon*. What Peirce tried to distinguish in discussions of the icon, or of the tone of a sign, was a qualitative mode of communication not reducible to conventions. Still lifes make use of conventions, yet their aesthetic significance depends on the unique qualities conveyed, not on the conventions. Peirce's inclusion of the qualitative within mediation illustrates why it is not only our ability to *know* (as Saussure would argue) that differentiates us from other animals but also our ability to *communicate feeling*. Great works of art give testimony to (and even help create) the deepest expressions of human sentiment and do so through the qualities directly conveyed.

We find then in the Peircean scheme a thoroughgoing attempt to undercut the dichotomizing tendencies of modern nominalism and a comprehensive theory of signs that accounts for how not only thought but also volition and feeling are involved in meaning. Peirce rejected the idea that meaning could be found only in an "underworld" of deep structure and, quite to the contrary, saw the ultimate outcome of all semiosis as the growth and embodiment of what he termed *concrete reasonableness*, inherently of the nature of a community. His comments on the sign illustrate his views that instances are also general, and that the ultimate basis of meaning is not to be found in arbitrary conventions per se but in the correctible process of interpretation that will "live down all opposition" and which in his view can grow into a true convention:

> It is of the nature of a sign to be an individual replica and to be in that replica a living general. By virtue of this, the interpretant is animated by the original replica, or by the sign it contains, with the power of representing the true character of the object. That the object has at all a character can only consist in a representation that it has so—a representation having power to live down all opposition. In these two steps, of determination and of correction, the interpretant aims at the object more than at the original replica and may be truer and fuller than the latter. The very entelechy of being lies in being representable. . . . A symbol is an embryonic reality endowed with power of growth into the very truth, the very entelechy of reality. This appears mystical and mysterious simply because we insist on remaining blind to what is plain, that there can be no reality which has not the life of a symbol. (Peirce 1976, 4:262)

In this way the Peircean view of signs leads to a very much different view of tradition and social conventions than that given by Saussure and consistently followed by structuralists and poststructuralists, who stress arbitrariness. Though Peirce admits arbitrariness in the shaping of cultural traditions and social conventions, he further admits the role of experience, the brute factuality of the world in time, as also shaping and informing traditions. In the Peircean view traditions are not arbitrary deep structures with no purpose or inherent quality of their own nor can they be reduced, as some symbolic interactionists might argue, to the whims of individuals in specific situations. Traditions are the source of the common sense, *general habits* forged through the experiences of generations, and in practical life, far superior as the relatively unquestioned basis for orientation than the mere arbitrariness of reason. Peirce developed a view he termed "critical common-sensism," which was an attempted synthesis of the insights of the Scottish "common-sensists" and the critical philosophy of Kant and his heirs, and which allowed that traditions themselves are subject to correction and growth through criticism. What further distinguishes Peirce's "critical common-sensism" from structuralism is that *sentiment* may provide a valid form of sign-inference in the affairs of practical life; in other words, sentiment is intelligent.

DURKHEIM AND MEAD: THE STRUCTURE OF COLLECTIVE REPRESENTATIONS AND THE PROCESS OF THE GENERALIZED OTHER

The next "moment" in our discussion of the foundations of symbolic interactionism and structuralism is the relationship between the social theories of representation proposed by Emile Durkheim (1858–1917) and by George Herbert Mead (1863–1931). Whereas Saussure and Peirce discuss the sign in its linguistic and logical contexts, Durkheim and Mead discuss the sign in its social web. Durkheim's concept of "collective representations" is frequently compared to Mead's concept of "the generalized other" (Hinkle 1960,277–79; Parsons 1960,144; Lewis and Smith 1980; Habermas 1981; cf. Stone and Farberman 1970). The two concepts do share a number of similarities, such as the emphasis on the generality and communicability of representations or signs, the view of the self as formed in social interaction through the internalization of representations, and especially the idea that "collective representations" and "the generalized other" act as the signs through which society represents itself to itself, thus reproducing itself. Durkheim and Mead also share an emphasis on the objectivity of signs that forms a critique of their intellectual progeny. Durkheim has been criticized by Lévi-Strauss and other structuralists for undervaluing the role of arbitrariness in social conventions, yet he would not have accepted the all-out assault on the "empirical" by recent structuralists and poststructuralists (e.g., Manning 1978; many of the chapters in Rossi 1982; Rossi, 1983). Durkheim's concept of collective representations and general philosophy was, after all, an attempt to reconcile positivism with idealism (e.g., Durkheim 1965,32). Though Durkheim argued that the arbitrary social conventions of a culture are not reducible solely to empirical conditions or individuals, he allowed that institutions are tempered by experience (1965,14). Similarly, a collective representation "presents guarantees of objectivity by the fact that it is collective: for it is not without sufficient reason that it has been able to generalize and maintain itself with persistence. If it were out of accord with the nature of things, it would never have been able to acquire an extended and prolonged empire over intellects. . . . a collective representation is necessarily submitted to a control that is repeated indefinitely; the men who accept it verify it by their own experience" (1965,486).

Durkheim did not seem to account for the fact that institutions and collective representations, like individuals, are subject to error, and that it may take centuries or more to correct false beliefs, but his point is that the accumulated experience of a people does place some limitations on the arbitrary character of conventions, so that conventions in effect have a "reality" as social facts. Similarly, Mead did not share the reservations concerning objectivity expressed in recent symbolic interactionism, because his philosophy in general was an attempt to develop an objective theory of meaning—to see nature itself as general, and as giving rise to mind. In the pragmatic tradition conventions, though largely arbitrary in character, are cultural habits determined not by their arbitrariness but by the goals they represent. Despite numerous points of agreement, Durkheim and Mead ultimately diverge for the same reasons as do Saussure and Peirce; the former seeing a-priori structure, the latter goal-directed sign-process, as the basis for meaning.

Durkheim elaborated his theory of collective representations in his last major book, *The Elementary Forms of the Religious Life,* where he sought the foundations of religion, which, in his view, constituted the fundamental institution of human life. His inquiry would seek fundamental *universal* conceptions, a point that reappears in Lévi-Strauss and other structuralists: "At the foundation of all systems of beliefs and of all cults there ought necessarily to be a certain number of fundamental representations or conceptions and of ritual attitudes which, in spite of the diversity of forms which they have taken, have the same objective significance and fulfill the same functions everywhere. These are the permanent elements which constitute that which is permanent and human in religion; they form all the objective contents of the idea which is expressed when one speaks of religion in general" (Durkheim 1965,17).

Because Durkheim believed complex religions—such as those of great civilizations—were formed out of such varieties and hybrids that one could hardly distinguish "the essential from the accessory," he sought the simplest religions through which the "elementary forms" could be discovered. In considering religious belief as reducible to universal fundamental representations he went in the opposite direction from Max Weber, who sought in his studies of Judaism, Christianity, and the religions of China and India the variety and complexity of human social life in its cultural *specificity* (see Giddens 1978,107–8, for a critical commentary on Durkheim's method).

Durkheim (1965,15,16) described his method as similar to that of Descartes, which consisted in founding the inquiry upon a "cardinal conception," a "primitive" concept, except Durkheim based his inquiry on a "concrete reality," discovered through "historical and ethnological observation":

> Every time that we undertake to explain something human, taken
> at a given moment in history . . . it is necessary to commence by
> going back to its most primitive and simple form. . . . It was one
> of Descartes' principles that the first ring has a predominating
> place in the chain of scientific truths. But there is no question of
> placing at the foundations of the science of religions an idea
> elaborated after the Cartesian manner, that is to say, a logical
> concept, a pure possibility, constructed simply by force of
> thought. What we must find is a concrete reality, and historical
> and ethnological observation alone can reveal that to us. But
> even if this cardinal conception is obtained by a different process
> than that of Descartes, it remains true that it is destined to have
> a considerable influence on the whole series of propositions
> which the science establishes.

Even though observation, as opposed to introspection, is needed to
discover an elementary form, it remains true for Durkheim that the
elementary provides the a-priori foundation of meaning, the underlying
structure upon which all later developments appear as "secondary," mere
"accretions" and "luxuriant vegetation" (1965,17). And as with Saussure, it
is the form and not the substance that constitutes the representation. Durkheim stated that symbols not only represent social life ("clarifying the sentiment society has of itself") but also create social life and shape its sentiments.
Yet the action of the symbol is caused by its social form, not by its substance,
in other words, by the ideal "superstructure" considered as separate from its
material embodiment.

Durkheim (1965,260) viewed the objects of experience ultimately as
mere manifestations of the idea, and the idea alone as the locus of reality.
Although we live in a physical world and need to embody symbols in material
forms, the importance of the symbol lies not in a particular physical object
but in the intangibility of the "superstructure," or what contemporary structuralists term the "deep structure":

> Thus there is one division of nature where the formula of ideal-
> ism is applicable almost to the letter: this is the social kingdom.
> Here more than anywhere else, the idea is the reality. Even in
> this case, of course, idealism is not true without modification.
> We can never escape the duality of our nature and free ourselves
> completely from physical necessities: in order to express our own
> ideas to ourselves, it is necessary, as has been shown above, that
> we fix them upon material things which symbolize them. But
> here the part of matter is reduced to a minimum. The object
> serving as support for the idea is not much in comparison with
> the ideal superstructure, beneath which it disappears, and also, it
> counts for nothing in the superstructure . . . for the ideas thus

objectified are well founded, not in the nature of the material things upon which they settle themselves, but in the nature of society.

Durkheim illustrated his argument for the idealism of things with examples of objects that may be endowed with sacredness for arbitrary reasons or that may be subdivided, with each part possessing the full sacred character of the whole. For instance, relics of a saint or fragments of a flag may be regarded as being just as sacred as the whole objects from which they derive, because their significance consists in being embodiments of the ideal superstructure, not in having inherent properties. We see here the same nominalistic point made by Saussure, that the conventional system, not particular instances, is the locus for meaning. When the "object serving as support for the idea . . . counts for nothing in the superstructure," when it "disappears" as Durkheim says, then we are left with an environment which is a mere facade.

Although Durkheim's discussion of the arbitrary selection and "sacredness" of objects—the representative power of society itself—is a valuable insight, it also highlights the limitations of a purely conventional account of meaning. From this perspective, the vast array of ritual artifacts and practices of the cultures of the world are not meaningful in their own right but only insofar as they carry out various cultural beliefs that ultimately have the sole purpose of representing the ideal superstructure of society. Similarly, Durkheim viewed human nature as essentially dualistic, consisting of individual body and social soul, and he saw the task of collective representations as bringing the asocial aspects of individual consciousness into communion with social consciousness (1965,262–63). In his 1913–14 lectures on pragmatism, which concentrated primarily on James, less so on Peirce, Dewey, and F. C. S. Schiller, and do not mention Mead, Durkheim goes so far as to say:

> This pressure that truth is seen as exercising on minds is itself a symbol that must be interpreted, even if we refuse to make of truth something absolute and extra-human.
>
> Pragmatism, which levels everything, deprives itself of the means of making this interpretation by failing to recognize the *duality* that exists between the mentality which results from individual experiences and that which results from collective experiences. Sociology, however, reminds us that what is *social* always possesses a higher dignity than what is individual. (Durkheim 1983,68)

Durkheim maintained a Kantian-based position by claiming that otherwise asocial individuals are "synthesized" into the social through mediating collective representations; he did not see, as the pragmatists did, that the individual human being is already a social sign "analyzed"—or in Peirce's terminology, "prescinded"—from the ongoing process of mediation. Human individuality is a consequence of, not a condition prior to, collective representations.

Peirce, Dewey, and Mead, although sharing Durkheim's insight that sociality is fundamental to representation, argued that the individuality of a person (and even the biological body) is a social outcome and not a given, and that every sign (or sign act) has its own quality which is involved in the sign's significance to a greater or lesser degree, and which constitutes a genuinely different mode of signification from that of purely conventional accounts. Instead of seeing the "ideal superstructure" as something apart from its physical manifestations and individual members, they all stressed, as we see in Mead's concept of "the generalized other," that a collective representation, as well as an individual person, is a *social dialogue of signs*.

Like Peirce and Dewey, Mead argued that there is more to significance than purely conventional meaning. Mead's "conversation of gestures" (derived from Wundt), although retaining the idea that signification is a communicative dialogue, holds that the generality of gestural communication is found in the gestures themselves, i.e., in their instances or what Peirce termed their "indexicality," and that this level of signs is not limited to human intelligence. Mead's concept of "the generalized other" derives from his attempt to develop a broad theory of sociality that could include reflective intelligence as an emergent property of nature. The generalized other differs from Durkheim's collective representations because the mere existence of collective representations as structures does not make them social; rather "collective representations" arise in and through communication—through a process of role-taking (Duncan 1962,92). Whereas Durkheim found the ideal level of the representation, apart from its manifestation, to be the true locus of sociality, the pragmatists attempted to undercut the modern dichotomies of thought and action, individual and social, by viewing mind as a social, communicative act. Mead, as a pragmatist, defined structure itself as a communicative social process of role-taking:

> In social conduct the individual takes the attitude of another in a co-operative process. If there are a number of persons engaged in the process, he must in some sense take the attitude of all of them. He accomplishes this in getting the attitude which each assumes in relation to the common end which each has. He finds an identical element in the attitude of each, which expresses itself in the different responses of the individuals. It is his ability to go from one of these attitudes to another in so far as each calls out the other that constitutes the structure of the system which imports the group into his experience. (Mead 1938,612–13)

The individual is an element in that communicative process which consists in the determination of a common end through internalizing the perspectives of the others who make up the group. This communicative process, which Mead said "constitutes the structure of the system," is in fact his concept of "the generalized other." Structure is not a timeless, passive entity in this view, but an *ability,* capable of real growth and decay. And structure is not dichotomized from its manifestations but includes its "instances" and embodiments, as Mead said in a criticism of Alfred North Whitehead: "For him [Whitehead] these relations constitute the individual but do not appear as other things in its experience; the world constitutes the thing but does not appear in the thing. In our experience the thing is there as much as we are here—our experience is in the thing as much as it is in us. Organization is being in a number of things at the same time. We attain this through participating in organized reactions of groups—the common content makes it possible to take the different attitudes and keep their relations. The organization is that of the act" (1938,613).

Pragmatism frequently has been caricatured as a philosophy of individualism, and one can see how structuralists might object to Mead's emphasis on society as a process of individuals internalizing attitudes, but Mead's generalized other is not reducible to determinate individuals per se. For the generalized other is that sign-dialogue that constitutes reflective thought, consisting in the *dialogue between* social self and social environment and internally between the interpretative spontaneity of the "I" and the organized and internalized others comprising the "me." Thought itself is an internal dialogue for Mead, as it is in James's theory of self that Mead inherited, and in Peirce's semiotic. Thus Mead could say in the previous quotation, "our experience is in the thing as much as it is in us," for it is in the communicative act as a whole (including its consequences), and not solely in an individual or social subject, that meaning is located. This is further illustrated in Mead's comments on the objective significance of situations as communicative acts:

> But signification is not confined to the particular situation within which an indication is given. It acquires universal meaning. Even if the two are the only ones involved, the form in which it is given is individual—it would have the same meaning to any other who might find himself in the same position. How does this generalization arise? From the behavioristic standpoint it must take place through the individual generalizing himself in his attitude of the other. . . . Mind, which is a process within which this analysis and its indications take place, lies in a field of conduct between a specific individual and the environment, in which the individual is able, through the generalized attitude he

assumes, to make use of symbolic gestures, i.e., terms, which are significant to all including himself. (Mead 1964,245,247)

Unlike Durkheim, Mead argued that not only other persons but also physical objects could act as true elements of the generalized other, and that the cult, instead of being reducible to an underlying elementary form or structure, acts as the means for a dialogue between a social group and its environment:

> Any thing—any object or set of objects, whether animate or in-
> animate, human or animal, or merely physical—toward which he
> acts, or to which he responds, socially, is an element in what for
> him is the generalized other. . . . Thus, for example, the cult, in
> its primitive form, is merely the social embodiment of the rela-
> tion between the given social group or community and its physi-
> cal environment—an organized social means, adopted by the in-
> dividual members of that group or community, of entering into
> social relations with that environment, or (in a sense) of
> carrying on conversations with it; and in this way that environ-
> ment becomes part of the total generalized other for each of the
> individual members of the given social group or community.
> (Mead 1934,154n)

The generalized other of a child, said Mead, is variable and "answers to the changing play of impulse," yet even this level of the generalized other is universal in form. Whereas Durkheim argued that the varieties of religious life *mask* the underlying universal, Mead argued that varied experience and differences *refine* the universal: "Education and varied experience refine out of it [the generalized other] what is provincial, and leave 'what is true for all men at all times' " (1964,245). The generalized other asserts increasingly universal standards as it grows, standards that impart objectivity to the given situation, and whose realization it is the task of the situation to achieve. This is not the colorless, bland, unmediated objectivity proclaimed by positivism and denounced by many structuralists and symbolic interactionists, but an objectivity whose elements (the individuals and their indications) form per-spectives within it and give it the character of a mediated unity.

TOWARD THE STRUCTURED SITUATION?

There has emerged out of the structuralist tradition what has been termed "poststructuralism," a pastiche of scholars whose work stems from the assumptions of French structuralism and Saussure's semiology, but who have attempted to link this style of thought with other significant intellectual movements, such as Marxism (Althusser 1979; Godelier, 1970, 1982) or, as in the case of Jacques Lacan, with Freudianism. At their best, these hybrid developments offer fresh new perspectives, but all too frequently they either merely restate the basic structuralist premiss that the foundation of social life resides in an "underworld" of deep structure, or shift their emphasis to the other side of the split: the radical flux and semiological "fission" outside the margins of structure.

The question of structure versus situation as the locus of meaning is particularly apparent in the work of "structural Marxists," such as Maurice Godelier or Jean Baudrillard. One would think that Marx's lifelong concern with developing the concept of *praxis* (Bernstein 1971,13; contrast Althusser, 1979) would link him with the pragmatists, who similarly sought to view meaning as a form of intelligible conduct, i.e., praxis, rather than with structuralists, who deny continuity between meaning and experience. Yet what structuralists find relevant in Marx is his emphasis on what is before our eyes being the veil of maya, an illusion obscuring the real working of the "invisible" deep structure: "For Marx, as for Lévi-Strauss, a structure is *not* a reality that is *directly* visible, and so directly observable, but a *level of reality* that exists *beyond* the visible relations between men, and the functioning of which constitutes the underlying logic of the system, the subadjacent order by which the apparent order is to be explained" (Godelier 1982,262–63).

Marx's idea that the product of labor is the objectification of the laborer, and that specific historical conditions may distort that relationship of objectification, producing alienation and the fetishizing of commodities, is denied by Godelier, who says instead that the fetishizing of commodities is "the effect *in* and *for* consciousnesses of the disguising of social relations *in* and *behind* their appearances" (1982,268). In other words it is the "true, underlying logic of the system" that is essential, not the objectifying process of praxis. Indeed Godelier says that the aim of science is theoretical knowledge of the deep structure (1982,267) and in so doing merely replaces the dichotomies of empty idealism and blind materialism Marx himself was trying to overcome, as is clear in the following: "Their resolution is therefore by no means merely a problem of knowledge, but a *real* problem of life, which *philosophy* could not solve precisely because it conceived this problem as *merely* a theoretical one" (Marx 1972,75).

Jean Baudrillard's program in his *For a Critique of the Political Economy of the Sign* (1981) is to press beyond Marx, by showing how the critique of the commodity form in Marx needs to be reconceived in a more pervasive critique of the sign, because in his view all objects are fundamentally the outcome of a "generalized code of signs": "one forgets that what we are dealing with first is signs: a generalized code of signs, a totally arbitrary code of differences, *and that it is on this basis, and not at all on account of their use values or their innate 'virtues,' that objects exercise their fascination*" (91). Baudrillard puts the concept of code to work in his provocative studies of consumption, the signature of paintings, the "potlatch" quality of art auctions, and the system of interior design. Although tending to agree with Marx's criticism that the exchange of goods constitutes a general sign system of values rather than utilitarian facts, Baudrillard claims that Marx should have pressed his criticisms further, and that, if he had, he would have seen, as a kind of born-again semiologist, that even use-values and needs derive from the generalized sign code rather than provide the material basis of it. System, and not nature, therefore, constitutes the sole source of meaning. Yet although Marx may be criticized for being influenced by the very utilitarianism he was arguing against, it is not as clear as Baudrillard would have it that Marx saw nature only in its modern mechanical sense. In many ways Marx's theory of meaning is broader than Baudrillard's and that of other structural Marxists precisely because he included nature, in Aristotle's sense of the perfection of being, within the realm of meaning.

In this sense Marx is an *environmental philosopher,* who criticized materialism and conceptualism for disconnecting the person from the "human sensuous activity, practice," that constitutes his or her relation to the environment; and for not realizing that humans shape and even create their environments, as well as reacting to them. Praxis, as Marx uses the concept, is not mere behavior dichotomized from thought, but the synthesis of the two. Marx uses the term in Aristotle's sense, as intelligible action aimed toward the good life in the community, and hence intrinsically moral. The environment, from this perspective, is a moral and aesthetic *practice.* And to an extent perhaps underestimated by many contemporary Marxists, Marx also relied heavily on Aristotle's conception of nature as having an inherent end or goal ("for what each thing is when fully developed, we call its nature, whether we are speaking of a man, a horse, or a family" [*Politics,* bk. 1, 1252]), so that humans are by nature political animals, whose conception of the end enters into the end or goal of life itself, i.e., the good life in the community. The spirit of mechanical law destroyed this conception of nature by the seventeenth century, and the modern utilitarian view that replaced it is the one Baudrillard continually rails against as self-contradictory.

Yet, in seeing nature as purely mechanical and asocial, hence inadequate to account for the systematic essence of meaning as code, Baudrillard (and other structuralists, such as Marshall Sahlins [1976a, 1976b]), merely sits on one side of a dichotomy created by the very utilitarian worldview he criticizes and is thereby linked with his sociobiological and functionalist opposites.

The fundamental idea of these varieties of structuralism is that meaning derives from an underlying system or structure. Surely this is a useful insight, yet the tendency to sunder meaning from experience need not be a necessary consequence. In the structural Marxism of Godelier and Baudrillard (see also Althusser 1979; Gimenez 1982) meaning does not include praxis. Structural Marxism therefore appears not to be a furthering of Marx's thought but what might be termed *the fetishism of structure,* in which

Marx's "human sensuous activity, praxis" evaporates into meaninglessness. Like Marx's critique of religion and money as forms of reification, structure is the sole currency of meaning and is surgically removed from the flesh and blood of life and treated as a totally independent existence.

Even in Baudrillard's critique of the political economy of the environment uprooted conceptions of signs dominate. Here the role of design is seen as an inevitable extension of the political economy into the environment, signified by the functionalism of the Bauhaus, in which everything becomes the object of a calculus of function and signification: "The whole environment becomes a signifier, objectified as an element of signification. Functionalized and liberated from all traditional implications (religious, magical, symbolic), it becomes the object of a rational calculus of signification" (186–87).

What concerns Baudrillard is a theme also discussed in earlier chapters—the transformation (or reduction) of the symbol, which in his particular usage means ambivalence, the irrational (in short, Freud), into the rationalized code of the sign: "This aesthetic order is a cold order. Functional perfection exercises a cold seduction, the functional satisfaction of a demonstration and an algebra. It has nothing to do with pleasure, with beauty (or horror), whose nature is conversely to rescue us from the demands of rationality and to plunge us once more into an absolute childhood (not into an ideal transparency, but into the illegible ambivalence of desire)" (188–89).

Not even surrealism is a protection from political economy; because it still makes reference to function through strange juxtapositions, it is not fully symbolic in Baudrillard's sense of ambivalence and desire, and not fully liberated into the floating realm of pure signifiers. One can surely sympathize with Baudrillard's criticism of the dominance of rationalistic design ideologies, but it is certainly an exaggeration to say that *all* codes or systems of design in our time must necessarily be tied to the functionalist logic of political economy. It also seems to be the mark of the very rationalism he is trying to criticize, to say that the symbolic is set apart, as in Freud, into the realm of the nonrational (or, as he says in the last essay in the collection, it is divorced as ambivalence) from the totally unambivalent systematized code of the sign.

Baudrillard preaches revolution in all dimensions of the economic, communications, media, physical, and design environments; a revolution that would have us float freely from necessity, needs, "motivated" meaning, and ultimately praxis itself, in the world of arbitrary signs. One desires only that Baudrillard would squarely confront the otherness of the environment and allow it to get its words in; perhaps then he could begin to liberate himself from the structuralist straightjacket he has constructed in which everything is a dichotomy, with the "other" as the private and particular and himself as the general of the general.

Pierre Bourdieu has attempted to develop a less constricted position by turning to the concept of *habitus* as that which mediates "the system of objective regularities" and "the system of directly observable conducts" (1968, 1977). Though retaining the basic structuralist premiss that all knowledge is conceptual and systematic, and that even "experience is a system" (1968,683), Bourdieu criticizes both the purely situational approach as a false "realism of the element" and the purely structural approach as a "false realism of the structure": "Without falling back into a naive subjectivism or 'personalism,' one must remember that, ultimately, objective relations do not exist and do not really realize themselves except in and through the *system of dispositions* of the agents, produced by the internalization of objective conditions" (1968,705). Bourdieu's concern with meaning as habit, with the realization of structures through agents, themselves produced by "the internalization of objective conditions," marks an implicit turning to precisely the central issues considered by the classic American pragmatists.

A similar broadening turn has been taken by Anthony Giddens, who has attracted wide interest in his attempts to develop a theory of *structuration* that can do justice to structure as well as individual agency. Giddens has drawn from French structuralism, yet has criticized it as being too inflexible in denying individual agency. In Giddens's view, structures at some point involve agents, who enact intentions and whose actions involve unintended consequences. He also draws from Wittgenstein-influenced language analysis in his discussions of agency and intentionality in action. His mediation of structure and agency in "structuration" attempts to retain what he considers the valid insights of each tradition, while rejecting their limitations. The structuralist tradition is best able to deal with the large-scale organization of meaning (which becomes actualized in social systems, as opposed to structure, which remains only virtual) but excludes subjectivity, whereas those schools of "agency" such as language analysis or symbolic interactionism may treat intentionality and subjectivity but do not encompass the larger totality.

But what is the essence of structuralism? As described thus far, it is a closed logic system based on a conception of an inorganic static code outside of or underneath experience. And though Giddens seeks to borrow the best from structuralism and put it into his own frame, he retains the transcendental claim of nontemporality as well as the static ateleological view inherent to it: "According to the theory of structuration, an understanding of social systems as situated in time-space can be effected by regarding structure as non-temporal and non-spatial, as *a virtual order of differences* produced and reproduced in social interaction as its medium and outcome. *Unser Leben geht hin mit Verwandlung*, Rilke says: Our life passes in transformation. This is what I seek to grasp in the theory of structuration" (Giddens 1979,3). Though agreeing that transformation is key, I do not think it possible to achieve genuine transformation in a timeless, spaceless netherworld of "differences" disconnected, even theoretically, from living, embodied human purpose. In later chapters it will become clearer that I view transformation as a human possibility rooted in the deepest sources of our biocosmic nature, a view that Giddens would strongly oppose. Giddens also assumes the radically antinaturalistic posture of structuralism, suggesting, for example, as "a fundamental theorem: in all forms of society, human beings exist in contradictory relation to nature" (1979, 161) because of a seemingly incorporeal and immaterial "human nature." Giddens accepts the mechanical view of nature, as do structuralists, and in so doing he reifies nature negatively, as functionalists do positively. Giddens's etherialization of structure resonates with, and may be in part borrowed from, Umberto Eco's distinction between signification and communication (See Giddens 1979, 82, 98). Yet in holding an abstract realm of signification independent of any possible communicative acts, Giddens may be retaining the worst fallacy of structuralism: that there can be an autonomous significatory realm clearly and distinctly separated from lived experience. Is it simply a collective *res cogitans*? Where did it come from? And where does it go?

On the other side, what Giddens is drawing from language analysis problematically overstresses both the individual in making choices, and intentionality, in being the sole source of teleology, as overly separate in definition, from the larger picture. What Giddens is pursuing may be necessary for contemporary social theory at one level, but it does not go deep enough; he fails to realize that the whole problem may reside in defining general structure and individual agency as radically different and in having then to find a linking concept to mediate them: structuration. In fact, as discussed previously, one starts out with mediation from which structure or agency can be prescinded. Much as I admire Giddens's project, it seems to me that he does not fully realize to what extent he is buying into the modernist Cartesian pathology of autonomous objectivism or autonomous subjectivism.

In his book *Vertical Classification: A Study in Structuralism and the Sociology of Knowledge* (1981), Barry Schwartz uses the core structuralist concept of binary opposition to its best advantage by examining systems of vertical classification. Yet Schwartz also criticizes structuralism for ignoring the specificity and context of meaning: "The problem with all structuralist approaches to the semiotics of knowledge is this: in reducing knowledge to an understanding of relationships rather than things, they fail to explain why certain media are used to encode specific kinds of information. Defining the relation between the signifier and signified as 'arbitrary,' structuralists close off rather than stimulate inquiry. They ignore the role of the medium in human conception" (124). Schwartz's inclusion of empirical methods within his larger study also shows that a more flexible structuralist framework is possible.

Another structuralist study that has concerned itself with the actualization of codes is S. N. Eisenstadt's (1982) "Symbolic Structures and Social Dynamics." There Eisenstadt takes a basically structuralist orientation toward social organization, stating: "This analysis has indicated that, as in other spheres of symbolic patterning of human experience, it is the 'schemata' of the respective sphere and not the 'objective' contents of the objects of such experience that provides the decisive principles of cognitive and evaluative organization of human behavior, of the hidden structure or contexts of such behavior" (172). Yet he also says that the schemata are not purely cognitive, "prelogical," or logical but are "closely combined with the more existential dimension of human life and social organization" (172). Eisenstadt argues that the "instanciation" (embodiment or institutionalization) of social codes introduces elements of openness, choice, and uncertainty. Though *code* remains key, he argues from within a structuralist position that *situation* and concrete interaction give structure variability and color and must be included within the analysis of any level of human activity. In dealing with the central problem of the relation of hidden structure to the actual workings of institutions, Eisenstadt implicitly turns to the vocabulary of symbolic interactionism, stressing the situational character of interpretation and the importance of the reconstruction of meaning: "The various symbols of collective and personal identity which are constructed in the process of institutionalization of such models and patterns of codes—even if they are taken out of the reservoir of traditional symbols—are rarely simply given. They are continuously being reconstituted and reconstructed" (165). Eisenstadt clearly sees the limitations of a model that must stop short of action and the significance of specific situations, a model that does not allow for the reconstruction of meaning (a key term in Dewey's philosophy, and in Eisenstadt's usage strikingly similar to the symbolic interactionist concept of "negotiated order" [Strauss et al. 1963; Glaser and Strauss 1965]). Yet one might argue that by taking his insights further he might see that a more fundamental correction to the idea of deep structure realized in variable and reconstructed surface "institutionalizations" is needed.

One should not assume, however, that all structuralism needs to do to correct its limitations is to incorporate the insights of symbolic interactionism. Critics of symbolic interactionism have argued that it places too much weight on subjectivist, transitory phenomena at the expense of enduring patterns of meaning (Meltzer, Petras, and Reynolds 1977), and that it ignores social structure (Coser 1976; Lewis 1976; Stryker 1980). In a frequently cited article George Gonos (1977) attempts to show that Erving Goffman should be considered a structuralist rather than a symbolic interactionist because of his concern with "frame." Gonos attacks symbolic interactionism as an approach dedicated to the exotic and trivial (857–58), as individualistic (864), as unable to deal with the continuity of structures (859–60), and as ultimately subjectivist. Gonos claims to use methodological hyperbole (a strange method for an article concerned with the objectivity of meaning in symbolic interactionist and structuralist approaches), and the argument suffers from excessive caricature and an inability to see that Mead, regardless of the directions his followers later took, attempted to develop an objective theory of meaning. Yet it does underscore some of the problems in the symbolic interactionist view of the objectivity of the situation; for example, in "A Theory of the Definition of the Situation" (1967), Stebbins defines the meaning of a situation as consisting in its definition, which is a process of reflection. Any changes in meanings or goals are found in the definition and "not rooted in the experience or information per se" (162). The consequence of Stebbins's definition is a return to precisely the kind of mentalism the pragmatists sought to avoid, a separation of the self from the medium of signs in which it exists (cf. 157; Perinbanayagam 1974, 523–24) and a reversal of the pragmatic view of thought as a form of internal conduct to one of a person projecting subjective meanings onto conduct. Others have criticized the symbolic interactionist tendency to overemphasize the subjective choice of the person in a given situation at the expense of the objective preconditions and consequences of actions taken, but, according to Maines (1977), those symbolic interactionists using the concepts of "negotiated order" and "structural process," such as Strauss and Glaser, avoid this tendency. Perinbanayagam (1985) is one symbolic interactionist who has attempted to overcome subjectivist tendencies by linking symbolic interactionism with structuralism.

A major controversy in symbolic interactionism emerged in the last decade concerning the objectivity of meaning. Much criticism has been directed at Herbert Blumer by the then "Illinois school" of sociologists for his alleged subjectivizing of Mead's theory of meaning (Huber 1973a, 1973b; Lewis 1976, 1977; Lewis and Smith 1980; McPhail and Rexroat 1979, 1980; for countercriticism see Blumer 1973, 1977, 1980, 1983; Johnson and Shifflet 1981). Both Blumer and his critics share an almost mythic attachment to Mead as the central representative of pragmatism, and one hopes that the current questioning of roots will at least open up the relatively untapped ideas of Peirce and Dewey for contemporary social thought. If one looks at Blumer's formulations of symbolic interactionism, however, there does seem to be room for criticism of his interpretation of Mead. Blumer attacks reductionism in social theory, arguing that societies and human beings cannot be explained alone by "social factors" (which would include structuralism) or by "psychological factors"; rather, human societies are "composed of individuals who have selves" (1969, 83), and "group action takes the form of a fitting together of individual lines of action" (1969, 82). Blumer's language is excessively individualistic, making it sound as if one can be an individual apart from a self, as if society is a mere aggregate of individual choices rather than itself a kind of larger self that can determine "individual lines of action" (the point made so well by structuralists). One could argue that in Mead's view society is the generalized other, a self in its own right, and that the individual self is a microcosm of society, the internalized generalized other. Blumer constantly discusses the role of choice and conscious interpretation in conduct, and perhaps this can be seen as a turning away from the pragmatists' central concept of *habit*. Nevertheless, he reveals an understanding of the way habitual conventions or "structure" enter into the situation:

> Usually, most of the situations encountered by people in a given society are defined or "structured" by them in the same way. Through previous interaction they develop and acquire common understandings or definitions of how to act in this or that situation. . . . Social organization enters into action only to the extent to which it shapes situations in which people act, and to the extent to which it supplies fixed sets of symbols which people use in interpreting their situations. (1969,86,88)

These recent criticisms of Blumer have centered on his conception of objectivity and his alleged misinterpretations of Mead. Joan Huber (1973a, 1973b) charged that Blumer and the pragmatists were not capable of scientific objectivity because they do not rely on a-priori theorizing. In his reply Blumer noted that "the likelihood of introducing unwitting bias is much less when the problem is developed through a close, flexible and reflective examination of the empirical world than when the problem is formed by using a model not derived through such intimate, empirical examination" (1973,798). In other words Blumer, like the pragmatists, stressed that scientific inquiry is a self-corrective process, and that objectivity is assured by observation and correction rather than by an a-priori foundational approach. McPhail and Rexroat (1979, 1980) attack Blumer for his emphasis on "sensitizing concepts" as marking the beginning stage of inquiry, but in so doing they reveal an ignorance of Peirce's theory of "abduction" or hypothesis formation, Dewey's "problem finding," and the problematic situation in Mead; in other words, they fail to see the discovery of the problem itself as the first stage of the inquiry. Lewis (1976, 1977) has developed the idea that Blumer has fundamentally misinterpreted Mead, and that Blumer's subjectivism is much closer to an alleged nominalistic pragmatism of James and Dewey (whom Lewis sees as biological individualists).

Lewis's ideas concerning the objectivity of meaning in the pragmatic tradition are placed in a larger context in his book on pragmatism and Chicago sociology (Lewis and Smith 1980). Lewis and Smith claim that there are two pragmatisms—a realistic one characterized by Peirce and Mead and a nominalistic one (which Lewis and Smith claim has no value) illustrated by James and Dewey. They argue that Chicago sociology, including the work of Blumer, was under the influence of the nominalistic pragmatism and that Mead exercised little influence during his lifetime. The argument is based on an ahistorical, a-priori "metatheoretical" realism-nominalism distinction that claims an origin in Peirce's discussions of realism and nominalism (though one could argue that Peirce's method of pragmatism is antithetical to Lewis and Smith's method of a-priori metatheory, itself unrevisable by the inquiry). Pragmatism, as originally formulated by Peirce, is clearly a variety of realism, a renovated version of the scholastic realism of John Duns Scotus rather than of the modern nominalistic forms of "naive realism" that claim the basis for reason is to be found in particulars outside of reason. The discovery of the realistic foundations of pragmatism by the sociological community marks an important turn in the search for the origins of symbolic interactionism, yet one in my opinion marred by Lewis and Smith's nominalistic interpretation of realism. Perhaps the clearest example of their positivistic and nominalistic interpretation of Mead (which would reduce the context of situation to an epiphenomenon, "in name only") is found in their remarks that

> Ultimately, the meaning of a significant symbol must be grounded in the nonhuman world of pure resistance. We previously discussed the same point in connection with Peirce's theory of signs. The ultimate meanings of concepts must be located in some nonmental and nonlinguistic reality if we are to escape the infinite regress of verbal definitions of definitions, ad infinitum. . . . . Mental objects must be referred to worlds that are not mental. (Lewis and Smith 1980, 130)

Lewis and Smith do not realize that although Peirce and Mead agree that the physical is *involved* in the symbolic (e.g., "indexicality" or the "conversation of gestures"), the symbolic is not reducible to a nonsymbolic foundation. In contrast to Lewis and Smith's interpretation, Peirce's argument for reality *is* based on an "infinite regress": all hypotheses must be capable of explanation because science does not admit the inexplicable. "Pure resistance" explains nothing qua pure resistance, hence cannot provide an acceptable hypothesis for the foundation of meaning. Moreover, the positivistic idea that meaning is based in individual reaction with an object is ultimately subjective, because it is based on a single person's experience rather than on a normative conception of an unbounded community of inquirers capable of continuous inquiry and eventual agreement in the long run. The Lewis and Smith programatic "metatheoretical" method leads them to serious distortions, pro and con, of pragmatists and Chicago sociologists, and their positivistic interpretations have been criticized in a number of reviews and articles (Blumer 1983; Johnson and Shifflet 1981; Johnson, 1983; Batiuk 1982; Rochberg-Halton 1982, 1983a; Campbell 1982, 1983; Miller, 1982; Mills 1982; Denzin 1984; Kuklick 1984; Joas 1985b). What will be needed to counter both mentalistic subjectivism and positivistic subjectivism in symbolic interactionism is a rediscovery of the pragmatists' idea that the most fully objective is the most fully mediated—that objectivity is the achievement, not the a-priori foundation, of the sign-process of inquiry.

THE CONTEXT OF MEANING

The turn toward "meaning" in recent sociological theory can be seen as both a rejection of reductionism and an attempt to develop a more comprehensive understanding of the nature of society. Structuralists have argued for the general sign system as the source of meaning as opposed to specific enactments of the system; symbolic interactions have claimed that only through specific interpretative situations can we appreciate the essence of meaning. Yet structures completely separate from content any empty; formless interactions are blind. Paradoxically, some recent criticisms from within structuralism have attempted to deal with the situation level as a corrective to what is percented as an inflexible reduction to the general, whereas "objectivist" symbolic interactions have tried to reformulate the "deep structural" foundations of symbolic interactionisms as a corrective to what is perceived as a flaccid reduction to the particular. These developments suggest a growing need for a more comprehensive theory of signs and society.

Structuralism has claimed their action and speech are not of themselves meaningful, and symbolic interactionism has tended to side with the choices of social individuals to define meanings of situations, and in doing so both have underestimated the role of the *critical community of inquirers* as the objective public realm that is the compelling source and sim of signs. In denigrating the concepts of action and public sphere as mere meaningless instances or illusions, structuralism destroys the possibilities of politics and critical inquiry, since both are reduced to a hidden underworld of deep structure, insusceptible to correction and cultivation through the life of the community. For its part symbolic interactionism has frequently highlighted the arbitrariness of the individual in creating meanings at the expense of the real aims of the broader community in which all situations are involved. Though the "native's" perspective in a given situation is a valid perspective in its own right, it is still subordinate to the interpretation of that situation by the "unlimited community."

Although Saussure and Durkheim emphasized the social nature of language and signs, both were limited by the dichotomizing tendencies of nominalism into viewing individual speech and individual cognition as asocial, and these tendencies have continued in later structuralists and poststructuralists. Mead, though stressing, with Peirce and Dewey, the thoroughly social nature of speech and cognition, developed an objective theory of meaning but not an explicit and truly comprehensive theory of signs. It was Peirce, the founder of pragmatism and semiotic, who articulated the broadest theory of signs and meaning, one that accounts both for system (considered as correctible habit) and for the uniqueness of the situation, which is not "subjective" but is involved in the social meaning of the sign (i.e., all signs or "sign situations" possess their own inherent *quality*, as *iconic signs*).

Let me here illustrate Peirce's three modes of sign-being by showing how they can lead to a much different understanding of situated meaning than that given by symbolic interactionism and, by implication, structuralism. The term *symbolic interactionism* itself may be somewhat misleading, since it seems to make human communication sound purely conventional, dependent on the rule-governed norms of interpretation which constitute *symbols*. But clearly Peirce, Dewey, and Mead emphasized iconic and indexical elements as essential features of all communication as well.

An iconic perspective means that the immediate qualities of experience can also act as mediating signs or sources of information, not reducible to convention alone. The usual discussion of iconic signs as signs which impart information about their objects through resemblance misses the main point, which is that it is the quality or Firstness of the object that is being conveyed. Dewey's discussions of aesthetic experience, for example, reveal how qualitative immediacy is an essential element of all communication and is the source of novelty and uniqueness. Symbolic interactionists, by contrast, stress the uniqueness of the situation, as against the conventional elements, by paradoxically appealing to conventional elements, such as the subjective interpretation given by the "actor" and imposed on the situation (Blumer 1969). Yet strictly following the pragmatic tradition of Peirce, Dewey, and Mead, one would have to see uniqueness and novelty as qualitative rather than as subjective. J. David Lewis, taking a social behaviorist position, has argued that Dewey is a nominalistic individualist (Lewis 1976), but in my opinion Lewis misses both the central importance of qualitative immediacy to Dewey and the intrinsically social theory of inquiry proposed by Dewey in his later work (Rochberg-Halton 1983a). In Dewey's discussion of the role of the situation in inquiry, he located *both* knower and known within an objectively determinable, and inherently social, problematic situation.

A second implication is that there is an existential element of situations not reducible to the subjective interpretation of the "actor," or to a deep structure, so that in certain situations the physical conditions will *compel* the interpretation, regardless of what the actor (or structure) would like to think. This is precisely the "obdurate" character of the empirical research situation emphasized by Blumer in his discussions of method, but overlooked or underemphasized in his descriptions of how meaning is ascribed to the situation by the "actor." A person may think himself or herself well, for example, but if a temperature reading taken from an accurate thermometer reveals a very high fever, that person is compelled to reinterpret his or her situation. The sign registered on the thermometer is an indexical sign of the actual situation. The indexical element of the situation is similarly ignored by structuralism, though in the name of objective convention rather than subjective choice. Though there may be a cultural convention regarding thermometers, the actual instance of a given reading communicates meaningful information and is determined by the kinetic interaction of person and thermometer, not solely by cultural convention.

The third point is that all situations have a certain reality, in Peirce's sense, which in no way depends on what the actor thinks or on an arbitrary convention, although it does influence what the actor should think and the ultimate direction of a convention or "structure." The reality of a situation does not depend on what subjective interpretation the person gives to it, but only on the fact that any and all inquirers would agree on what the reality of that situation is, if they carried the inquiry far enough. The strength of symbolic interactionism is perhaps its emphasis on the living process of interpretation which gives novelty, uniqueness, and an individual character to a situation. Uniqueness and individuality are surely of central importance, but only as they contribute to the common discourse, that is, only as they themselves are real. The fact of a subjective interpretation is not what is important from the perspective of the real—and one can see how different this definition of the real is from current usage—but what is really important is that the person can cultivate the interpretations and refine them and integrate them with the ultimate goals of his or her existence as a member of the wider critical community. This is the meaning of *praxis* and pragmatic, from the pragmaticist's perspective. Peirce's semiotic is a critical theory of interpretation quite at odds with positivistic expediency and arbitrary subjective fiat, and involves a view of the interpretations of the individual as ultimately guided by the interpretations of the unlimited community, of "the generalized other" if you will, in which we live and which gives to our lives not only their qualitative uniqueness but also the possibility of enduring significance.

In Peirce's semiotic each and every sign is social, and the sign-process is inherently a critical process of interpretation and self-correction, guided ultimately by an unbounded community of "inquirers." Peirce's semiotic is framed in a logical context, where questions such as the reality of the hardness of untested diamonds are in the foreground, and needs to be "translated" into the context of social theory, where the objects of inquiry— human beings and institutions—are, unlike diamonds, intelligent forms capable of self-induced change, of growth and decay. Though it has not yet been incorporated into social theory, Peirce's semiotic offers a genuinely new alternative to existing theory and provides a radical critique of the guiding ideas of modern culture and social theory as a whole. Perhaps the renewed interest in meaning that characterizes contemporary social theory signifies a readiness to go beyond the dichotomizing tendencies of modern thought.

4 The Foundations of Modern Semiotic: Charles Peirce and Charles Morris

The emerging field of studies known as "semiotics" is presently a welter of intellectual perspectives and tongues. Although the current lack of consensus as to what constitutes semiotics may be a sign of its vitality and broad scope, it is also quite possible that it symbolizes a Tower of Babel, a community of practitioners without a common language and an understanding of a shared premiss. About the only thing a student entering the field can be sure of is that its practitioners share a concern with the role of signs and symbols in whatever happens to be the object of study. Yet beyond this common denominator lie innumerable and often irreconcilable ideas concerning how signs and symbols should be studied, and even what constitutes a sign or symbol. Semiotic, or sign theory, has come to serve for many as an all-inclusive term, subsuming such diverse enterprises as semiology, cybernetics, hermeneutics, and so forth; yet the contemporary use of the term "semiotic" derives from the highly influential theory articulated by Charles Morris, who in turn acquired it from C. S. Peirce, the founder of modern semiotic.

The term "semiotic" was first used in modern times by John Locke, who mentioned it near the end of his masterwork, *An Essay Concerning Human Understanding*. Locke only suggested a division of science in which semiotic would form the third of three sections, and would be identified with logic. It was first used as a term denoting a specific and detailed theory by Peirce, who spent the greater part of his life working out his semiotic, which for him was a normative theory of logic. This theory is at the heart of Peirce's philosophy, and he considered pragmatism, which he founded, to form one area within its domain. For various historical reasons Peirce was not widely known (even less understood) as a philosopher during his lifetime. Despite an enormous output of published articles covering a host of topics—as if a whole community rather than a single man had written them—Peirce never had a book of his philosophical writings accepted for publication during his life-

This chapter was written with Kevin McMurtrey.

time, although he wrote more than one. His *Collected Papers* did not appear until the early 1930s, twenty years after his death. Surely one of the ironies of modern sign theory is that the major work of each of its founders, Charles Peirce and Ferdinand de Saussure, was published posthumously.

One chronic problem in understanding Peirce's semiotic is that his interpreters have largely misunderstood his work, because it goes against the grain of modern thought. Peirce considered himself a student of the medieval schoolmen, especially the scholastic realist Duns Scotus, and he attempted to renovate scholastic realism in accord with a modern scientific framework. As the central tenets of twentiety-century philosophy, and, indeed, the whole culture of modernism itself in the arts and sciences, have been called into question in recent years, the clouds of obscurity surrounding Peirce have begun to dissipate, and he has reemerged as an original thinker of contemporary significance. We are beginning to see how thoroughly contemporary Peirce actually is, how he not only anticipated and contributed to many developments in present philosophy, but how much of his thinking on the nature of science and philosophy "leapt over" the guiding ideas of twentieth-century thought, and only now are beginning to be appreciated.

In tracing the foundations of modern semiotic we hope to show that Peirce's legacy has had an important influence on semiotic but one that has been subject to serious distortion, resulting in widespread misconceptions that have created barriers to understanding his theory of signs. Semiotic, originally based on a criticism of Cartesian nominalism and foundationalism, has been turned completely around into its nominalistic opposite through the work of Charles Morris. Morris undertook to synthesize some of the principal philosophical movements of his time in a new "science of science" based on the study of scientific method as a sign system. The branches of this metascience were to be "syntactics," "semantics," and "pragmatics"; or the study of science as a language, as a knowledge of objects, and as a type of activity. The first two of these branches were drawn from the interests of the logical positivists and the third from the pragmatists.

Morris acknowledged that pragmatism might appear to be incompatible with logical empiricism, but he argued that an adequate understanding of science must take account of "the psychological, methodological, and sociological aspects of scientific practice" (Morris 1938a, 72). However, Morris himself did not successfully reconcile or even fully grasp the profound differences in point of view between logical positivism and pragmaticism, differences that go to the very roots of modern semiotic. The result is that his work has tended to obscure rather than to clarify certain fundamental assumptions of contemporary semiotic. A thorough examination of the foundations of modern semiotic with especially careful attention to the arguments of the pragmatists is now required. By examining Peirce's arguments for semiosis, and comparing his ideas with those of Morris, we can see that the Peircean semiotic is not only based on quite different premises from those commonly associated with it, but that it forms a radical critique of much that now goes by the name of semiotics.

THE FOUNDATIONS OF PEIRCE'S SEMIOTIC

Peirce laid the foundations of his semiotic in a series of articles that appeared in the *Journal of Speculative Philosophy* in 1868. The theme of these articles was the inadequacy of the Cartesian account of science. The alternative that took shape in Peirce's criticism, although not yet named, was semiotic.

Peirce summarized his objections to Cartesianism in these four points (CP 5.265):
1. We have no power of Introspection, but all knowledge of the internal world is derived by hypothetical reasoning from our knowledge of external facts.
2. We have no power of Intuition, but every cognition is determined logically by previous cognitions.
3. We have no power of thinking without signs.
4. We have no conception of the absolutely incognizable.

Let us take the second point first. Descartes began with skepticism, claiming that no science could be secure until its foundations were established beyond all possibility of doubt. He observed that contemporary science was not so founded. To remedy this, he proposed to doubt everything until some principle proved itself to be indubitable and thereby provided the basis for a new, secure, and genuine science.

Peirce's denial that we have the power of intuition is a denial of the Cartesian skepticism. By "intuition" Peirce meant a cognition completely undetermined by any prior cognition or, what amounts to nearly the same thing, a premiss not itself a conclusion, an absolutely first premiss.

Descartes offered his philosophy as an alternative to scholastic logic. The schoolman's picture of science was one of a chain of syllogisms, the first premiss of any one of which was justified as the conclusion of a prior syllogism whose premises were, in turn, themselves justified as the conclusions of still prior syllogisms, and so on. At the very beginning of this chain of syllogisms stood the unconditioned first premisses of all scholastic science: divine revelation and the testimony of authorities. Descartes' innovation consisted in attempting to replace authority with reason. He undertook to found science upon a principle that would rationally justify itself and therefore stand as more than a tenet of faith.

But scholasticism and Cartesianism share the assumption that science is justified by the infallibility of its first premisses. Peirce argued against this assumption. He concluded that science is justified not by its starting point but by the continuing activity of science itself. Truth is not something that has to be established once and for all in order for science to be able to begin. It is rather the guiding ideal of the scientific enterprise.

Peirce's alternative to both scholasticism and Cartesianism is that inquiry always takes place against a background of premises taken on faith. These premises are not infallible, for inquiry eventually might reveal them to be false. Nevertheless, every inquiry is conditioned by certain preconceptions that it does not even occur to us to doubt. In the course of our inquiries we either come to revise our original premises or we do not. If we do revise them, these new opinions function as the premises of our continued investigations until we are forced, in turn, to revise them, and so on. If at some point we achieve opinions that we would never be forced to revise, then we have reached the goal of our inquiry, the truth of the matter. For truth is just that opinion that no course of investigation, no matter how prolonged, would ever lead us to revise. Science, thus, is a process of self-correcting inquiry. It is the capacity of inquiry to correct itself, not the infallibility of fundamental premises, that guarantees the validity of science.

Further, in asserting that science cannot begin without establishing its principles beyond all possibility of doubt, Descartes made a claim that cannot itself be scientifically justified. Modern science recognizes only one justification for admitting a hypothesis: that it helps to explain observed facts. Now by definition intuition is cognition completely undetermined by prior cognition. It is the starting point of reason, the ultimate given. An intuition is itself inexplicable, for it is the ground upon which all explanations are constructed. But this claim in favor of the power of intuition is itself only a hypothesis in the science of logic. Like any hypothesis it is justified only insofar as it helps to explain the observed facts. But it is no explanation of any fact to assert that it is utterly inexplicable. Therefore the supposition that we possess the power for intuition is inadmissible.

The schoolmen understood more clearly than Descartes all that is involved in the notion of unconditioned premises: either the unconditioned can be explained or it cannot. But explanation only consists in putting forward the conditions that justify belief. Therefore the unconditioned cannot be explained. To assert that certain premises are unconditioned is just to assert that they must be taken on faith. Thus faith was the acknowledged foundation stone of scholastic reasoning.

Descartes tried to reform the scholastic logic by introducing the notion of a rationally justified but nevertheless unconditioned premiss, an intuition. Peirce argued that such a thing is impossible. Reasoned justification consists in setting forth the conditions that account for what otherwise would be unaccountable. Therefore the only genuine alternative to scholasticism is that there is no absolutely first premiss.[1] This is Peirce's position. Every explanation is capable of explanation. There is nothing reasonable that is exempt on principle from reasoned inquiry.

Finally, discovering an indubitable is a much more difficult matter in Peirce's eyes than it is in Descartes'. Descartes seemed to suggest that all we need to do in order to grasp the indubitable is clear our minds of prejudice by an act of will, and proceed to accept anything of which we are then clearly and distinctly convinced. Peirce had greater appreciation for the ways in which our experience is conditioned by an immensely complicated web of cultural and historical prejudices. This cultural background is not to be dispelled by fiat. Although prejudice can be overcome, and we are not doomed to the arbitrary opinions of the society or class or group from which we happen to come, we cannot free ourselves from prejudice by abstract good intentions. We must engage in a never-ending criticism of beliefs actually held, and continually attempt to replace our critical assumptions with ever

---

1. Against the assumption shared by Cartesianism and scholasticism, that reasoning must begin somewhere and that therefore there must be some premiss which is absolutely first, Peirce replied with a characteristically subtle argument: First, suppose some thought to be represented by a horizontal line of a certain length. The premiss that determines this line thus can be represented by another line a little shorter than the first, and the premiss of the premiss by a still shorter line, and so forth. On this principle a point having no length will represent an absolutely first premiss. Now suppose an inverted triangle to be dipped in water. At any instant the surface of the water makes a horizontal line across the triangle. This represents a thought. As the triangle is dipped further into the water a longer line is marked by the water. This represents a subsequent thought. The point of the triangle represents an absolutely first premiss. Now to argue that reasoning must begin with such an unconditioned premiss is like claiming that there must be a moment at which the water will mark out a line under which it can mark out no shorter line. But there is no such line. For no matter where you mark the line, you can still make as many lines as you please below it and below one another. And each of these lines will be shorter than the one above it. Let us say that you mark out the line a very small distance, A, from the apex of the triangle. You can still mark out a line $\frac{1}{2}$A and $\frac{1}{4}$A and $\frac{1}{8}$A and so on, and each of these lines will be shorter but still of a finite length. There are an infinite number of rational fractions that could be marked out (compare CP 7.536). Thus, although thought may have a beginning in time (that is, the triangle may be dipped into the water), there is no absolutely first thought in the logical sense.

This subtle distinction is the same one that is the key to the solution of the motion paradoxes from ancient Greek philosophy. If we suppose that in order for us to traverse the stadium we first must traverse half the distance across, then traverse half of the remaining half, then half of the remaining quarter, etc., it is clear that we can never traverse the stadium. But of course we can traverse the stadium. Therefore the initial supposition is absurd. It is absurd in this way: We suppose that Achilles must make an infinite number of finite efforts. In fact Achilles only has to make a single continuous effort. Likewise when we begin to reason we do not need to begin with a distinctly first premiss. We need only to enter into a continuous process of thought—continuous from the beginning. And because there is no distinctly first premiss, the security of our reasoning does not depend on the indubitability of such a premiss.

more justified beliefs. We all start from prejudices we never think of doubting. But experience constantly forces us to revise these beliefs in favor of others. Science is the systematic effort to bring prejudice to trial in the court of experience. A genuinely indubitable opinion is not achieved through facile skepticism. Nor, on the other hand, is any given belief, however sacred, entirely exempt from scrutiny. Truth is the goal to be realized, the ideal end of inquiry.

Peirce's first objection to Cartesianism was to its claim that we have a power of introspection. Descartes had argued that science must be founded upon intuition, upon premisses that justify themselves. But the only perfectly self-justifying premiss that Descartes thought he had discovered was "I think, therefore I am." Thus Descartes concluded that science ultimately must rely upon intuitive individual self-consciousness, that is, upon introspection.

Peirce's objection was based on a number of grounds. In the first place, investigations in what we nowadays call developmental psychology contradict the claim that our awareness of self is a primary datum. On the contrary, the notion of self seems to be developed relatively late, certainly much later than the child's general powers of thought. In the second place, the Cartesian view makes science depend upon a single strand of reasoning. Science should be rather "a cable whose fibers may be ever so slender provided they are sufficiently numerous and intimately connected." (CP 5.265). Although a conclusion cannot be more certain than all of the premisses that support it, it can easily be more certain than any one of those premisses taken individually. However, it is Peirce's final objection that goes to the heart of the matter:

> to make single individuals absolute judges of truth is most
> pernicious. . . . We individually cannot reasonably hope to attain
> the ultimate philosophy which we pursue; we can only seek it,
> therefore, for the *community* of philosophers. (CP 5.265)

Just as an opinion of the moment always must be subject to revision in the course of future inquiry, so any individual opinion must be subject to the criticism of the community—not any particular community, but the community at large, unbounded in time or place.

Once again the question is best understood when viewed against the background of scholasticism. The great debates of the thirteenth century concerned the issue of nominalism and realism. On the one hand, the realists held that "universals," or generals, were real. For instance, "Man," in general, is real. On the other hand, the nominalists held that "Man" is merely a name, a sign, which we use to describe individual existing persons generally. "Man" in general is merely a concept. Only existing individuals are real.

Nowadays, if the whole debate is not dismissed as irrelevant, the tendency is to regard nominalism as the only position that could be held by anyone with any sense. Peirce said that this is because we fail to appreciate the subtlety that realism achieved in the philosophy of a great thinker like Duns Scotus. Sophisticated realists did not hold that universals exist in such a way that one might, for instance, meet "Man in general" walking down the street. They admitted that all generals are signs, or thoughts. What they did hold was that the mere fact that something is a sign does not necessarily mean that it is unreal. "Man" is a real general because, although every man is an individual man, there is nevertheless also a human character present generally in men, but yet not dependent on any one man. Therefore the question of nominalism and realism comes down to this: the nominalist admits that all signs are general, but denies that any general is real. Consequently the nominalist denies that what a sign represents is real. On the other hand the realist admits that all generals are signs, but also holds that *some* generals are real. Consequently, the realist allows that what a sign represents *may* be real. In other words, the object truly represented in a sign *is* real.

Cartesianism is a nominalism. It holds that our conceptions can be brought to the level of science if we make sure that they conform to the character of objects as they exist in the world apart from its relation to mind. The adequacy of our knowledge must finally depend upon the valid apprehension of these objects. For the apprehension to be valid individual inquirers must examine the contents of their consciousness carefully and make sure that there are no vague notions or prejudices affecting their understanding.

Peirce argued that modern science requires a renovated realism (and one quite different from the "naive realism" of modern philosophy). Reality is not something altogether independent of mind; rather, it is simply that belief the truth of which is not dependent on what you or I or any individual in particular thinks it to be. Scientific objectivity as Peirce conceived it is the result not of a successful apprehension of an object otherwise out of consciousness but the product of the continuous scrutiny of preconceptions by the scientific community. Whatever conception the community would agree upon in the long run is the truth, and its object is real. Agreement may take generations to achieve, and no individual or group of individuals can ever be certain of having reached it once and for all. Nevertheless it is the ultimate concern of the community, whatever that may be, and not individual objects as they may be supposed to exist apart from any conceptions of them, that defines objectivity.

Peirce took up the question of the relation of objects to consciousness in his fourth objection to Cartesianism, namely, that the absolutely incognizable is absolutely inconceivable. He remarked:

That upon the Cartesian principles the very realities of things can never be known in the least, most competent persons must long ago have been convinced. (CP 5.310)

Peirce evidently had in mind the whole dialectic of modern philosophy that culminated in Kant's explicit recognition that the thing-in-itself cannot properly be known to science. That dialectic can be said to have begun with modern philosophy's rejection of scholastic realism in favor of nominalism. From this point of view the logic underlying the development of Cartesian philosophy can be summarized in this way:

— Only particulars are real. Universals are mere inventions of the mind.
— Nevertheless it must be admitted that universality is an ineluctable aspect of all scientific thought.
— Therefore science can grasp only its own inventions. It cannot lay hold of the real as it is in itself.

On the other hand, the Cartesian claims that if science is to be possible at all, we must have some power of immediately knowing particulars. Science is knowing things as they really are, and things as they really are, are particulars. Thus the Cartesian comes to insist that we have a conception of what is, properly speaking, incognizable.

Peirce replied that, rather than hold fast to paradox, the Cartesian had better reexamine his premises, especially the nominalistic assumption that only particulars are real. According to Peirce, science can base itself only on the recognition that some universals are real after all. The best argument for scholastic realism is that, if it is not true, science is impossible.

The first precept of the Cartesian method was that science should accept only those concepts that are clear and distinct. But a concept was supposed to be clear if after attending to it without prejudice or haste we still found ourselves unable to doubt it. This was a standard adequate to a philosophy that was mostly concerned to replace traditional authority with the authority of individual consciousness. In contrast, Peirce aimed to replace individual authority with the objectivity of the scientific community. This requires in its turn a revised standard of clarity, which Peirce does indeed propose in a logical principle still widely misunderstood more than a century after it first appeared. It is the doctrine of pragmatism, which asserts that

> if one can define accurately all the conceivable experimental phenomena which the affirmation or denial of a concept could imply, one will have therein a complete definition of the concept and *there is absolutely nothing more in it*. (CP 5.412)

In other words, a clear conception is one that permits us to design an experiment bearing on that conception's truth or falsity.[2] If we knew all of the

2. Despite superficial similarities, this doctrine has little in common with the spirit of logical positivism's "verifiability criterion." Peirce proposed that a meaningful hypothesis can be tested, not that an infallible perception can be "verified."

experiments that ever could be relevant to a given concept, our conception would be absolutely clear.

Now by this standard we can have no conception whatsoever of the absolutely incognizable. Such a conception is unclear, because it is completely untestable. Thus, in contrast to Descartes, Peirce concluded that:

> Over against any cognition there is an unknown but knowable reality; but over against all possible *cognition*, there is only the self-contradictory. In short, cognizability (in its widest sense) and *being* are not merely metaphysically the same, but are synonymous terms. (CP 5.257)

To sum up, Peirce asserted that Cartesianism mistakenly tried to base science upon the principles of intuition, introspection, and our ability somehow to know what is admittedly incognizable. Peirce's alternative makes reasoned knowledge depend instead upon such features as continuity of inquiry, publicity, and the testability of hypotheses.

The third of Peirce's objections to Cartesianism is the one that opens the door of semiotic: "All thought is of the nature of a sign." From Descartes' own point of view the great problem was how the substances *res cogitans* and *res extensa*, soul and body, could have anything to do with each other. Peirce suggested that this problem is the logical consequence of Cartesian assumptions about the nature of science. Descartes first assumed immediate self-consciousness. We are supposed to know ourselves not through hypothetical reasoning from known facts but by virtue of a special faculty. In the second place Descartes supposed that the object as it really is, is completely unrelated to mind. Thus, it could only be known by means of an "intuition," a cognition completely undetermined by any prior cognition. The inevitable conclusion from these premises is that we have no grounds for supposing that self-consciousness is in any way related to objects at all. We appear to be locked into our own consciousness. The Kantian philosophy simply acknowledged that science could never know things-in-themselves and proceeded to try to salvage the objective validity of science by other means.

Peirce's position is more radical. In broad outline he argued that science does not consist in bringing together substances supposed to be immediate. Science is rather a continuous process from which certain elements may be prescinded but which nevertheless always manifests a mediated unity. Thus the Cartesian question becomes not one of how to synthesize the immediate but one of how to analyze the mediate. Only when the underlying assumptions of Cartesianism are reformed can we understand how science can know the real world.

The key to the solution of the Cartesian question is Peirce's understanding of mediation. There is mediation when a first is related to a second by means of a medium, or third. An unbounded complex of mediums is a continuum. Science, by which Peirce, of course, meant not merely laboratories and test tubes but reason in the broader classical sense as well, is a great continuum in which each inquirer, and indeed in which each idea, stands to others through the medium of continued inquiry.

Another way of saying this is that all thought is of the nature of a sign, for by definition a sign is the medium through which one thing is represented to something else, which sign itself may be represented then to other things by means of further signs and so on. Inquiry is this continuing process of sign interpreting sign. From this point of view Peirce's criticism is that the Cartesian philosophy, instead of recognizing that the sign-process itself is fundamental, makes inquiry depend upon elements which by their very nature cannot themselves be the object of inquiry, "in short [upon] something resulting from mediation itself not susceptible of mediation" (CP 5.265). In contrast, Peirce insists that all thought is an aspect of semiosis.

In Peirce's semiotic the unmediated substances of Cartesianism are transformed into "presciss" elements of the mediating sign-process. Instead of a self of which we are conscious through a special power of introspection, a sign is said to have a *ground*. Like the Cartesian ego, the *ground* is immediate consciousness, abstracted from all relation. Unlike the Cartesian ego, however, the *ground* is not an object of immediate cognition. It is, rather, the element of immediate consciousness *in* the cognition of the object, "the thought itself, or at least what the thought is thought to be in the subsequent thought" (CP 5.286).

Similarly the *object* is like the Cartesian object, the other-than-self, but we do not know the *object* through immediate relation, but only through its representation in other thoughts.

> Let us suppose, for example, that Toussaint is thought of, and first thought of as a *negro*, but not distinctly as a man. If this distinctness is afterwards added, it is through the thought that a *negro* is a *man*; that is to say, the subsequent thought, *man*, refers to the outward thing by being predicated of that previous thought, *negro*, which has been had of that thing. If we afterwards think of Toussaint as a general, then we think that this negro, this man, was a general. And so in every case the subsequent thought denotes what was thought in the previous thought. (CP 5.285)

Finally, the relation of *ground* and *object* is not immediately posited but is rather represented to mind through a mediating representation, or *interpretant*. Indeed, "mind," as it is used here, is to be understood as nothing but semiosis, the continuing interpretation of interpretations.

Therefore, all thought and science are in signs, and all signs are inferences. In the words of Max Fisch:

> Every thought continues another and is continued by still another. There are no uninferred premises and no inference-

terminating conclusions. Inferring is the sole act of cognitive mind. No cognition is adequately or accurately described as a two-term or dyadic relation between a knowing mind and an object known, whether that be an intuited first principle or a sense-datum, a "first impression of sense" (CP 5.291). . . . The sign theory of cognition thus entails rejection not only of Cartesian rationalism but also of British empiricism. (1978, 36)

Signs, not intuition, are the very foundation of Peirce's semiotic. When we turn to Charles Morris, who perhaps more than any other person was responsible for the actual spread of semiotic, a quite different view emerges.

FOUNDATIONS OF THE THEORY OF CHARLES MORRIS

I feel very strongly, just as you do, that philosophy is entering upon one of the most important synthetic periods in its history. The entire condition of our civilization makes it almost inevitable that philosophy will assume a more commanding position in both the practical and theoretical aspects of life,—provided that philosophers are able to sense the nature of their task and develop a point of view large enough to meet the new demands. Past philosophy is dead; the new child is only now being born.   (Morris 1927)

Charles Morris first came to appreciate the importance of the philosophical issue of signs while a student of George Herbert Mead at the University of Chicago. From Mead he learned to view meaning in terms of experimental consequences. But Morris also was influenced by the logical positivists, and especially by one of the leaders of the Vienna Circle, Rudolph Carnap. The logical positivists argued that the meaning of language must depend upon the existence of one or another sort of basic statement, the truth or falseness of which ultimately could be verified. Morris saw logical positivism not only as a continuation of the pragmatic movement but also as a way of saying clearly what the pragmatists had only said vaguely (Morris 1938a, 67).[3]

3. Morris's *The Pragmatic Movement in American Philosophy* (1970), extends the ideas that pragmatism and semiotic are behavioristic theories and that Peirce was unnecessarily vague and ambiguous in his definitions of "sign" and "pragmatism." Morris says: "Peirce himself had no single clear-cut comprehensive formulation of the nature of 'meaning.' There is, to be sure, a 'hard-core' doctrine which is quite definite. But, as we shall see, this is surrounded by supplementations and qualifications which arise out of Peirce's own dissatisfactions with his 'hard-core' formulation. . . . The issues here are very complex, and no rounded-out behaviorally-oriented semiotic was developed by the pragmatists. To this extent the pragmatic view of the relation of meaning and action, and hence the nature of pragmatism itself, remained nebulous. An analysis of some of Peirce's statements will illustrate the situation" (Morris 1970, 7–18). Morris then goes onto quote Peirce's definition of sign as standing to somebody for something in some respect or capacity, and creating in the mind of that person an equivalent or more developed sign. He notes: "the term 'sign' is not completely clarified since the interpretant of a

Morris's semiotic was an attempt to synthesize these two influences. In our view it failed because Morris was not fully aware of the profound differences between pragmatism and logical positivism (see, for example, Morris 1964, 33; 1970, 148). Specifically Morris most fundamentally failed to grasp the full import of the fact that the Vienna Circle had tried to found science upon "certain fundamental concepts" and "elementary experiences" and then to erect a "constructional system" (see Carnap 1967), whereas Peirce had sharply criticized the Cartesian assumption that science must be based on indubitable foundations. In contrast to the logical positivists, as well as to Descartes, Peirce's "foundation" was continuing inquiry, the self-corrective process of interpretation. The validity of scientific inquiry in its turn is determined by reality itself, understood not as some primary sense datum but as the belief that the community of inquirers is destined to reach in the long run. There is no infallible foundation of science because experience may show what we think infallible to be wrong. The logical positivists' search for the ultimate sense datum, for example, only showed us how fallible our conception of the ultimate is. The result of Morris's attempted synthesis was a philosophy that combined the basic assumptions of logical positivism with a deceptive admixture of pragmatistic vocabulary.

Morris, imbued with the logical positivist's desire to purify language, saw semiotic as the means of facilitating immediate knowledge:

> it has become clear to many persons today that man—including scientific man—must free himself from the web of words which he has spun and that language—including scientific language—is greatly in need of purification, simplification, and systematization. The theory of signs is a useful instrument for such a debabelization [sic]. (Morris 1938b, 3)

Presumably Morris himself was to lay the foundations for the new purity in his pivotal *Foundations of the Theory of Signs*, the first complete monograph in the *International Encyclopedia of Unified Science*. This work not only influenced many linguists and philosophers but laid the groundwork for much of contemporary semiotic (we are not including here the the developments of semiology). However, the contemporary reader familiar with Peirce cannot help but be struck by Morris's considerable unacknowledged debt to

---

sign is itself said to be a sign; there is no reference to action or behavior. In general, there is no hint of pragmatism, or the 'pragmatic maxim,' in this particular formulation" (Morris 1970, 19).

Clearly Morris does not realize that all conduct, "action or behavior," *is* of the nature of a sign, that it is semiosis, or *sign-action*. Nor does he realize that a "hint" of pragmatism *can* be drawn out of the "problem" that the interpretant is itself a sign, if we see that the pragmatic maxim's emphasis on future *conceivable* consequences of a concept is an emphasis on the continuity of signs.

Peirce and Morris's even greater failure to grasp what Peirce fundamentally tried to achieve.

Morris borrows many of Peirce's key technical terms in this monograph, and makes use of some concepts derived from Peirce; but the only explicit mention of Peirce's influence appears when Morris misuses Peirce's "sinsign-legisign" distinction. Morris owned the first six volumes of Peirce's *Collected Papers,* published in the early 1930s, and had elsewhere written on Peirce and pragmatism (1938c). He was also a colleague of Charles Hartshorne at the University of Chicago, one of the editors of the papers. But Morris does not state why he chooses to use the term *semiotic* for the science of signs, or *semiosis* for the sign-process. It could be that he was influenced by John Locke, who, as mentioned, introduced the word near the end of *An Essay Concerning Human Understanding;* but Morris also could have used Ferdinand de Saussure's term, *semiology.* A monograph on the foundations of semiotic might well have drawn attention to the founders of semiotic (not to mention the foundational terms), but it appears that only twenty-five years after the encyclopedia monograph, in his 1964 book, *Signification and Significance,* Morris finally mentioned Peirce as the one responsible for the modern usage of *semiotic.* The earlier monograph gives the impression that Morris himself was the founder.

Like Peirce but unlike many others, Morris analyzed semiosis triadically (although his definition also introduced an obscure fourth "factor"):

> This process, in a tradition which goes back to the Greeks, has commonly been regarded as involving three (or four) factors: that which acts as a sign, that which the sign refers to, and that effect on some interpreter in virtue of which the thing in question is a sign to that interpreter. These three components in semiosis may be called, respectively, the *sign vehicle,* the *designatum,* and the *interpretant;* the *interpreter* may be included as a fourth factor. These terms make explicit the factors left undesignated in the common statement that a sign refers to something for someone. (Morris 1938b,3)

The last statement, "a sign refers to something for someone," which Morris implied was the vague language of the older tradition, was actually a paraphrase of one of Peirce's definitions of a sign: "something which stands to someone for something in some respect or capacity" (CP 2.228). Morris suggested that this triadic definition of signs was common, but it was not. Signs usually were defined dyadically as something which stands for something else. Likewise, the term "interpretant" is Peirce's. In the place of Peirce's first two elements of a sign, the ground and its object, stand Morris's terms *sign vehicle* and *designatum.* Morris defined the *sign vehicle* as "that which acts as a sign," whereas "that which the sign refers to," whether actual or not, is the *designatum.* Those designata that actually exist Morris termed *denotata.* The denotatum seems to correspond to what Peirce called the *dynamical object,* and the designatum to the *immediate object,* except that Peirce argued that the sign object is an element prescinded from the sign-process and therefore cannot be known immediately but only as it is represented to be in further signs.

Concerning the sign vehicle, Morris said:

> In any specific case of semiosis the sign vehicle is, of course, a definite particular, a sinsign; its "universality," its being a legisign, consists only in the fact, statable in the metalanguage, that it is one member of a class of objects capable of performing the same sign function. (Morris 1938b,50)

Here is one of the basic differences between Morris's and Peirce's theories of signs. For Peirce, the "ground" element of the "ground-object-interpretant" relation is the immediate quality of self-consciousness *in the sign.* The object (or designatum-denotatum) is the relative other in the sign, and would correspond roughly, in Morris's usage, to sinsign. But Peirce's qualisign-sinsign-legisign distinction belongs in a systematic science of semiotic in which a sign is related to its own ground or inherent quality through quality (qualisign), existence (sinsign), or law (legisign). Another way of saying this is that it is *quality* that makes a sign a qualisign, sinsign, or legisign; in the latter two cases it is a quality of existence and a quality of law that constitute, respectively, a sinsign and legisign (see Fig. 1). But in Morris's positivistic view there is no room for quality, positive possibility, or vagueness; in short, for that which is essential in Peirce's semiotic. For Morris there are only universals and particulars, and "universals" belong only to the metalanguage (Morris 1938b,51). Thus Morris's position is directly opposed to that of Peirce, and indeed to those of Mead and Dewey as well. The point of the pragmatists is that generality is real, that it is *in* nature and *in* experience, and that even "thing language," as opposed to metalanguage, must make use of "universals," because the object of a sign is not given apart from semiosis but only in and through semiosis. For the pragmatists there are, strictly speaking, no "things" in Morris's sense at all, that is, no designata that are not signs, for we have no power of intuition. In other words Morris failed to understand that pragmatism is a renovated scholastic realism. He remained a nominalist.

Morris's emphasis on the distinction between universal and particular (or legisign and sinsign, type and token) is similar to Ferdinand de Saussure's distinction between *langue,* the language system, which is universal, and *parole,* the utterance, which is particular and which derives its meaning from *langue* (Saussure 1966). And both of these accounts completely oppose Peirce's discussions of legisigns and sinsigns, types and tokens; for in Peirce's view all signs are general. Even individual, actual "speech acts," although concrete, carry a universal significance. For instance, when a

FIGURE 1   Peirce's Triadic Theory of Signs

	Ground (First)	Object (Second)	Interpretant (Third)
Quality (Firstness)	Qualisign	Icon	Rheme
Actuality (Secondness)	Sinsign	Index	Dicent
Law (Thirdness)	Legisign	Symbol	Argument

particular cross symbolizes Christianity, the cross's inherent qualities (its iconic element) and its physical characteristics (its indexical element), are both involved in, and emerge through, the symbol and thus are aspects of the sign's general significance. Similarly an indexical sign, such as a thermometer, which signifies only by virtue of an immediate factual relation to its object, nevertheless conveys a meaning that is general, the temperature.

The theories of Morris and Saussure also completely ignore that dimension of Peirce's semiotic dealing with the communication of qualitative possibility. Peirce's discussions (see CP 2;4.537) of *qualisign* and *tone* (in the tone-token-type division) as well as of *iconic* and *rhematic* signs, revealed an aspect of "firstness" or qualitative immediacy in semiosis that nominalistic theories, such as those of Morris and Saussure, cannot include.

Morris also borrowed, without acknowledgment, Peirce's trichotomy of *icon, index,* and *symbol.* Perhaps he believed that no acknowledgment was necessary, that terms should take precedence over the person who introduced them. But even if this were so, the fact that Morris radically changed the meaning of Peirce's carefully considered terminology (CP 2.219f.; Ketner 1981), as well as the fact that Morris's monograph was, after all, supposed to deal with foundations, should have led to some discussion of the original significance of the terms. Morris "introduced" the trichotomy of signs in his discussion of semantics, perhaps because he thought this distinction had to do with the relation of a sign to its object:

> In general, an indexical sign designates what it directs attention to. An indexical sign does not characterize what it denotes . . . and need not be similar to what it denotes. A characterizing sign characterizes that which it can denote. Such a sign may do this by exhibiting in itself the properties an object must have to be denoted by it, and in this case the characterizing sign is an *icon;* if this is not so, the characterizing sign may be called a *symbol.* . . . A "concept" may be regarded as a semantical rule determining the use of characterizing signs. (Morris 1938b,24)

Morris's use of "indexical sign" retained Peirce's emphasis on denotation through immediate factual relation of sign and object, in which the object compels the interpretation, but once again Morris's use of the term throughout the text betrayed his nominalistic assumptions that denotation lies outside the sign-process and that meaning depends upon intuition rather than upon semiosis. This is in sharp contrast to Peirce's view that, although denotation is an aspect of all signification, sign and object are not immediately given entities but abstract elements of a sign continuum. Also in sharp contrast to Peirce, Morris continually defines key concepts by means of one another, a strange practice for someone who purports to be freeing man from the "web of words" he has spun. For instance, it is not clear how "designates" is to be distinguished from "characterizes," for on the one hand " 'Designates' is a semantical term, since it is characterizing sign designating a relation between a sign and an object" (Morris 1938b,22,23); but on the other hand, in the passage just cited, a "characterizing sign characterizes that which it can denote."[4]

4. Some examples from Morris's 1946 glossary of semiotic terms in *Signs, Language, and Behavior* may illustrate what we are criticizing as a fundamental lack of clarity:

Ambiguous sign	A sign-vehicle that is not unambiguous.
Behavior	This term is presupposed by semiotic and not defined within it. Roughly speaking, behavior consists of the sequences of responses (actions of muscles and glands) by which an organism seeks goal-objects that satisfy its needs. Behavior is therefore "purposive" and is to be distinguished from response as such and from the even wider class of reaction. Behavior is *individual* or *social*, and when social may be *co-operative, competitive,* or *symbiotic.*
Denote	A sign that has a denotatum or denotata is said to denote its denotatum or denotata. All signs signify, but not all signs denote.
General sign	A sign that is not singular. There are various degrees of generality depending upon the interrelationship of significata.
Interpersonal sign	A sign is interpersonal to the degree that it has the same signification to a number of interpreters; otherwise *personal.*
Language sign	*See* Lansign.
Lansign	A sign that is a member of a lansign-system. In this book "language sign" is often used in place of "lansign"; strictly speaking, only the latter term is defined.
Personal sign	A sign is personal to the degree that it is not interpersonal.
Plurisituational sign	A sign that is not unisituational.
Precise sign	Signs, not vague, are precise.
Reliable sign	A sign is reliable to the degree that members of the sign-family to which it belongs denote; otherwise unreliable.
Singular sign	A sign whose signification permits only one denotatum; otherwise it is general.
T-ascriptor	As ascriptor that denotes. "T" is used to suggest "true" though the latter term is not here defined. Similarly, an *F-ascriptor* is one

Morris's definition of icon also seemed to represent Peirce's notion that an icon signifies its object by virtue of a common quality. Yet Morris's nominalism did not allow for qualitative possibility, which is the mode of relation of an icon to its object in Peirce's scheme (CP 2.276f.). Morris's substitution of "properties" ("exhibiting in itself the properties an object must have to be denoted by it") made an icon signify through imputed character (in Morris's term, "values") rather than through shared quality (Morris 1946b,81; 1964,70f.), and thus missed the point of Peirce's theory of icons. In a later elaboration of his monograph on the foundations of signs, *Signs, Language, and Behavior,* Morris stated:

> A portrait of a person is to a considerable extent iconic, but is not completely so since the painted canvas does not have the texture of the skin, or the capacities for speech and motion, which the person portrayed has. The motion picture is more iconic, but again not completely so. (Morris 1946b,23)

Morris fails to appreciate Peirce's crucial transformation of Descartes' concept of immediate self-consciousness into qualitative immediacy, a prescinded but real aspect of semiosis freed from Cartesian subjectivism. Consequently Morris distorts the icon, making it into a conventional sign of a peculiar nature rather than a properly qualitative sign. The notion of a "pure" icon becomes the notion of an exact physical duplicate, a clone. An object of visual art, which in Peirce's view would communicate by virtue of inherent quality, must, in Morris's view, reproduce itself in the viewer quite literally. A "pure" iconic representation, therefore, would not be representative at all. Iconicity becomes mere duplicity.

Peirce also remarked that a portrait may be regarded as an icon, saying that an icon

> is a Sign whose significant virtue is due simply to its Quality. . . . We say that the portrait of a person we have not seen is *convincing.* So far as, on the ground merely of what I see in it, I

---

	that does not denote. Ascriptors in any mode of signifying may be T-ascriptors or F-ascriptors.
Unambiguous sign	A sign-vehicle is unambiguous when it has only one significatum, that is, belongs to only one sign-family; otherwise it is ambiguous.
Unisituational sign	A sign that signifies a given significatum in only one situation; hence, it is a sign-vehicle that belongs to no sign-family. Most signs are plurisituational.
Unreliable sign	A sign that is not reliable.
Vague sign	A sign is vague to a given interpreter to the degree that its significatum does not permit the determination of whether something is or is not a denotatum; otherwise it is precise. (Morris 1946b, 345–56)

am led to form an idea of the person it represents, it is an Icon. (CP 2.92)

And Peirce, like Morris, also recognized that a portrait may not be a *pure* icon. However, his reasons for saying so are completely different from those that Morris gave. Peirce observed that we are influenced by knowing that the portrait is an effect, through the artist, of the original's appearance, and so may be interpreted as an indexical sign, and not only as an icon. Also, we may be influenced by knowing that portraits "have but the slightest resemblance to their originals, except in certain conventional respects, and after a conventional scale of values, etc." (CP 2.92), and so may be interpreted as symbols rather than as icons. The "pure" icon is thus by no means merely a sign having an absolutely determinate resemblance to its object. Instead it is a sign that signifies through internal quality rather than actual relation or conventional representation:

> A possibility alone is an Icon purely by virtue of its quality; and its object can only be a Firstness. But a sign may be *iconic,* that is, may represent its object mainly by its similarity, no matter what its mode of being. If a substantive be wanted, an iconic representamen may be termed a *hypoicon.* Any material image, as a painting, is largely conventional in its mode of representation; but in itself, without legend or label it may be called a *hypoicon.* (CP 2.276)

Morris's previously cited definition of symbol is that it is a characterizing sign that does not exhibit in itself the properties of the object it denotes, that is, is not iconic. Morris seemed to be emphasizing, as Peirce did, that a symbol is related to its object through convention. In his 1946 glossary Morris defined a symbol as "A sign that is produced by its interpreter and that acts as a substitute for some other sign with which it is synonymous; all signs not symbols are signals" (Morris 1946b,355). Again Morris's nominalism caused him to reinterpret Peirce's term and use it for a purpose quite different from the one Peirce intended. Instead of seeing a symbol as a sign "produced by its interpreter," Peirce proposed that a symbol is a rule that produces its interpretant: "A Symbol is a Representamen whose Representative character consists precisely in its being a rule that will determine its Interpretant" (CP 2.292).

For Morris the semantical rule for a symbol rests on a foundation of primitive terms that ultimately refers to definite "things" indicated by indexical signs (Morris 1938b,24, 25). In other words, Morris thought that the possibility of meaning depended upon intuition. Peirce viewed a genuine symbol as a law, or "regularity of the indefinite future" (CP 2.293), whose meaning would consist in the practical consequences that an unlimited community of inquirers would conceive it to have in the long run, rather than in a single interpreter's pointing at a "thing." For this reason a symbol is neither determinate (because it is a type, not a token) nor completely arbitrary (because it is a convention that will cause future events to conform to it [see CP 2.292]). Morris's misunderstanding of the symbol brings us back to the problem of the interpretation of the sign.

One of the biggest controversies surrounding Morris's semiotic is his use of Peirce's term "interpretant" and of Morris's own innovation, "interpreter." Morris defined the interpretant as "that effect on some interpreter in virtue of which the thing in question is a sign to that interpreter." His definition is unclear about whether "that effect" is itself a sign, as it is in Peirce's scheme, or whether it is something outside of signs, such as behavior. Although Peirce viewed conduct, or "behavior" as a kind of sign, that is, as general, Morris's discussions elsewhere in the text (for example, concerning "behavioristics") suggest that he viewed behavior as something outside the sign continuum. In his view the interpreter is the organism or person who interprets the sign. Whereas the "takings-account-of" are interpretants, "the agents of the process are interpreters" (Morris 1938b,4). The notion that instead of the term "interpretant" Peirce could have been more clear by using "interpreter" is a misunderstanding rooted in nominalism. For Peirce the sign a man uses is the man himself (CP 5.314); thus, the fact that there is such a thing as an interpreter depends upon there being such a thing as an interpretant, not the other way around. Or as Peirce expressed it elsewhere, we should say not that the thought is in us, but that we are in thought.

As mentioned earlier, Morris's definition of the elements of a sign was ambiguous on the "interpretant-interpreter" relationship. He says that the common view of semiosis is that it involves three factors, but he equivocates by adding "or four" in parentheses. He also says that "These three components" may be called the sign vehicle, the designatum, and the interpretant, but after the semi-colon he hedges—"the *interpreter* may be added as a fourth factor" (Morris 1938b,3). This ambiguity suggests that Morris set out from Peirce's tripartite conception of signs, but, failing to understand that for Peirce man himself is a kind of sign, introduced a fourth term, the "interpreter," which to him seemed clearer and more concrete than "interpretant." This hypothesis finds some confirmation in the fact that Morris disregards his own definition and substitutes his fourth component, the interpreter, for the third component, the interpretant, which drops out of the account completely: "In terms of the three correlates (sign vehicle, designatum, interpreter) of the triadic relation of semiosis, a number of other dyadic relations may be abstracted for study" (Morris 1938b,6). This sleight of hand brings him back to a triadic conception of sign, but one in which the interpretant has disappeared. Upon this magic rests the foundations of what Morris dubbed "pragmatics." Again, Morris's nominalism, his emphasis on a behavioral interpreter already given outside of the sign-process, rather than on an interpretant within it, his tendency to regard things as real and thoughts as mere concepts, diminished the scope of Peirce's semiotic.

SYNTACTICS, SEMANTICS, AND PRAGMATICS

Perhaps the most influential contribution of Charles Morris to contemporary semiotic is another threefold division of the science of signs, that of *syntactics, semantics,* and *pragmatics.* This division, also utilized by Morris's colleague Rudolph Carnap, has been accepted by many semioticians, linguists, and philosophers. Morris claimed to have based this division on "dyadic relations" abstracted from the "three correlates (sign vehicle, designatum, interpreter) of the triadic relation of semiosis" (Morris 1938b,6). Thus syntactics is defined as "the formal relations of signs to one another" (p.6), semantics as "the relations of signs to their designata and so to the objects which they may or do denote" (p. 21), and pragmatics as "the relation of signs to their interpreters" (p. 30). One wonders why Morris gives "dyadic relations" such prominence, since just two pages before advancing these definitions he had explained that all semiosis is triadic and mediate. This division of signs thus based on dyads seems to suggest that the division must itself be grouped outside of semiosis. But the basic argument Morris seems to be making by his division of semiotic is that the three divisions should correspond to the relations of a sign to its three elements: sign vehicle, designatum, and interpreter. Now this division also appears to be based on an unacknowledged debt to Peirce. By comparing Morris's divisions with Peirce's division of semiotic into *pure grammar, critical logic,* and *pure rhetoric,* one can see both the basis of Morris's divisions and the radical departures from that basis his theory makes.

In a manuscript written in 1897 Peirce proposed the following breakdown of semiotic and gave these reasons for making it.

> In consequence of every representamen being thus connected with three things, the ground, the object, and the interpretant, the science of semiotic has three branches. The first is called by Duns Scotus *grammatica speculativa.* We may term it *pure grammar.* It has for its task to ascertain what must be true of the representamen used by every scientific intelligence in order that they may embody any *meaning.* The second is logic proper. It is the science of what is quasi-necessarily true of the representamina of any scientific intelligence in order that they may hold good of any *object,* that is, may be true. Or say, logic proper is the formal science of the conditons of the truth of representations. The third, in imitation of Kant's fashion of preserving old associations of words in finding nomenclature for new conceptions, I call *pure rhetoric.* Its task is to ascertain the laws by which in every scientific intelligence one sign gives birth to another, and especially one thought brings forth another. (CP 2.229)

On the surface, it appears that pure grammar must correspond to Morris's syntactics, critical logic to Morris's semantics, and pure rhetoric to Morris's pragmatics. But a closer examination reveals that at every level Morris's nominalism creates a systematic inversion of Peirce's divisions.

Pure grammar, as that branch of semiotic that seeks to state the conditions under which a sign may have meaning, culminates in pragmatism, as the doctrine that attempts to explain how our ideas may be made clear. Because pragmatism is in the first branch of Peirce's semiotic, it would appear to be closer to Morris's syntactics than to his pragmatics. But the content of even these two sciences is radically different. In treating the "formal relations of signs to one another" Morris seems to be suggesting something akin to certain aspects of linguistics, which in Peirce's view is a "psychognostical" science (CP 7.385) rather than a branch of general semiotic. For Morris,

> Syntactics is, then, the consideration of signs and sign combinations in so far as they are subject to syntactical rules. It is not interested in the individual properties of the sign vehicle or in any of their relations except syntactical ones, i.e., relations determined by syntactical rules. (Morris 1938b,14)

Critical logic, or Peirce's science of what must be the nature of signs if they are to represent their objects truly, seems to correspond to Morris's semantics. But again, on closer inspection, it can be seen that there are crucial differences between the Peircean conditions for truth and Morris's logical positivistic truth criteria. In Morris's semantics the object designated by the sign is not part of the sign process but a "thing," which, in imitation of Carnap, may be represented in a "thing sentence": "let us use the term *'thing sentence'* to designate any sentence whose designatum does not include signs" (1938b,15). Truth is based on intuition rather than semiosis. Paradoxically, the insistence that science must be founded upon unquestionable objective knowledge, direct apprehension of "things," led Morris and the logical positivists to the same subjectivism for which Peirce had criticized Cartesianism (compare Dewey 1946b,88f.).

The third branch of Peirce's semiotic is "the doctrine of the general conditions of the reference of Symbols and other Signs to the Interpretants which they aim to determine" (CP 2.93). Pure rhetoric is no mere "rhetorical device" in Peirce's scheme—not persuasion for the sake of persuasion, but persuasion as determined by the real. It is concerned with inductive validity, that is, with what makes a conclusion valid. Peirce's own conclusion is an argument for reality as being that which an unlimited community of inquirers would eventually agree upon. The meaning of these inquirers or "interpreters" is general and is found in the conclusion they aim for, not in the particular instances of behavior they exhibit.

Pure rhetoric is not in the least concerned with who is doing the interpreting, but only with the validity of the interpreting signs (interpretants). One can see how Morris, who substituted "interpreter" for Peirce's "interpretant" in an attempt to be more objective, could also "correct" Peirce's idea of the references of signs to their interpretants, doing this with a division of semiotic (pragmatics) concerned with "the relations of signs to their users" or, as he later reformulated it, with "the origins, uses, and effects of signs within the behavior in which they occur" (Morris 1946b,219). One also can see why this move ultimately is subjectivistic, even solipsistic, because it has reference to particular individuals rather than to a normative conception of an unbounded community of inquirers. Morris says, for example:

> To the degree that what is expected is found as expected the sign is confirmed. . . . In general, from the point of view of behavior, signs are "true" in so far as they correctly determine the expectations of their users, and so release more fully the behavior which is implicitly aroused in the expectation or interpretation. (Morris 1938b,33)

Morris's unusual statement describes well the ignorant person, who, free from the irritation of doubt and fallibility, seeks only the expected and, in "finding" it, learns nothing new. Morris reserves the issue of the actual objective truth of signs for the semantic level, while trying to account for the perspective of the sign "user" at the level of pragmatics. One can sympathize with the attempt to deal with the level of the "agent," but in defining the user as an individual organism instead of a fully socialized being existing in an objective web of goal-oriented signs, he moves far afield from pragmatism.

Dewey criticized Morris for his interpretation of pragmatism and interpretants in 1946, saying:

> The misrepresentation in question consists in converting *Interpretant,* as used by Peirce, into a personal user or interpreter. To Peirce, "interpreter," if he used the word, would mean, *that which interprets,* thereby giving meaning to a linguistic sign. I do not believe that it is possible to exaggerate the scorn with which Peirce would treat the notion that *what* interprets a given linguistic sign can be left to the whim or caprice of those who happen to use it. But it does not follow from this fact that Peirce holds that the interpretant, that which interprets a linguistic sign, is an "object" in the sense of an existential "thing." (Dewey 1946,87)

Peirce did use the word "interpreter" on occasion, as a "sop to Cerberus," an attempt to phrase his theory in a way his nominalistic audience could understand.[5] But it is clear that the interpreter is an interpreting *sign*—as

5. In a letter to Lady Welby dated 23 December 1908, Peirce remarked, "It is clearly indispensable to start with an accurate and broad analysis of the nature of a Sign. I define a Sign

Dewey said, "that which interprets" (compare Morris's replies [1946a; 1971]).

Morris's use of the term "pragmatics" has little to do, in fact, with what Peirce meant by pragmatism. Peirce's pragmatism would be in the first branch of semiotic, not the third. But more generally Morris does great violence to pragmatism by virtually defining "pragmatics" as expediency, viz., the relation of signs to their users, "within the behavior in which they occur," regardless of the norms of continuing inquiry. For Peirce, the "final interpretant" is not particular instances of behavior but the embodiment of general, self-correcting habits, the fruition of semiosis, the growth of "concrete reasonableness":

> The deliberately formed, self-analyzing habit—self-analyzing because formed by the aid of analysis of the exercises that nourished it—is the living definition, the veritable and final logical interpretant. (CP 5.491)

Despite some important differences between the pragmatisms of Peirce, James, Dewey, and Mead, the major American pragmatists were united in their opposition to the subjectivism that had been the heritage of the Cartesian philosophy. But in attempting to synthesize pragmatism and the nominalistic theories of logical positivism, Morris reintroduced the old Cartesian subjectivism in "pragmatics."

In reply to Dewey's article Morris said:

> Professor Dewey's discussion . . . of the relation of my monograph, *Foundations of the Theory of Signs,* to Peirce's semiotic may have given to some of your readers the impression that my analysis claimed to be a presentation of Peirce's views. This was not the case. The result may be that the central problem which bothered Dewey (the problem of the relation of a behaviorally oriented semiotic to the work of such "formal logicians" as Carnap) will be missed by his focusing of attention on the historical problem of how far my views do or do not agree with those of Peirce. (Morris 1946a,196)

Morris the modernist, who proclaimed past philosophy dead, pretended that his theory was original by denying Peirce's influence and relegating it to a mere "historical" question. He says that the question of Peirce's influence is of little importance in itself, and that he need acknowledge neither the original meanings of the Peircean framework he used nor his own reasons

---

as anything which is so determined by something else, called its Object, and so determines an effect upon a person, which effect I call its Interpretant, that the latter is thereby mediately determined by the former. My insertion of 'upon a person' is a sop to Cerberus, because I despair of making my own broader conception understood" (1977, 80–81).

for changing that framework while retaining much of its terminology. These are "merely historical" issues. Philosophy had to begin anew by building not upon the efforts of the past but upon an indubitable foundation of objective knowledge. The myth of intuition, that there can be a first sign or foundation not determined by previous signs, seems to have had Morris in its grasp, forcing him to deny his own foundations while purporting to explain them.

Language, too, had to be purified by rigorously excising whatever could not certify its legitimate birth from immediately verifiable facts. Of the analogous Cartesian undertaking to accept only those beliefs grounded in rationally indubitable premises Peirce commented:

> We must begin with all the prejudices which we actually have.
> . . . These prejudices are not to be dispelled by a maxim, for they are things which it does not occur to us *can* be questioned.
> Hence this initial skepticism will be a mere self-deception, and not real doubt; and no one who follows the Cartesian method will ever be satisfied until he has formally recovered all those beliefs which in form he has given up. (CP 5.265)

In Morris's case the pretense of complete renunciation of the past led to the suppression of all explicit acknowledgment not only of Peirce's influence but of Morris's honest attempt to make pragmatism more rigorous as well. Paradoxically, the result was not a work of model clarity, free of all assumptions, but rather a monograph filled with hidden premises, internal inconsistencies, obfuscation, and technical jargon that changed in meaning from one page to another. Morris attempted to lay the foundations for a brave new science of signs that would free man from the web of words, but the result of his Cartesian foundationalism has been the erection of the New Tower of Babel, which is contemporary semiotics.

To a great extent "semiotics" owes its current foundations to the magic of positivism, which, in positing that the true objects of knowledge lie outside knowledge and signs, that the firm foundation for all cognition and reason is incognizable and irrational, created one of the most extreme metaphysics ever devised, a perspective that in our view ultimately would destroy the science of signs. If we are to regain a consistent, enduring theory of signs, whether it is based on the work of Peirce, Morris, Saussure, Wittgenstein, or others, we need to develop a deep understanding of the traditions of semiotic, so that the theory and its various terms can become real instruments for inquiry rather than opaque means of mystification.

5   The Fetishism of Signs

LAGADO BRAVADO

Semiotics has been hailed as a revolutionary breakthrough in the various disciplines, a breakthrough beyond disciplinary thought, indeed, the revolutionary breakthrough of our time. It challenges accepted modes of thought across the sciences, humanities, and practicing arts. Yet, like money (and before that, religion), semiotics can also be seen as the new equivalent to Marx's "fetishism of commodities," one fitted to an Age of Abstractionism.

I would like to claim that contemporary semiotics, on the whole, represents a cultural distortion; that it tells us much more about the advanced culture of Abstractionism, or uprooted rationality, than about the nature and purpose of signs.

One of the key problems in contemporary semiotics is the question of how meaning is organized. Whether it be called structure, code, or some kind of system ("system of signification," "system of symbols and meanings," and so forth), the organization of meaning appears as a rather remote and inflexible system frequently not susceptible to criticism and correction, or, for that matter, to self-destructive consequences. This theoretical tendency seems to me to be itself a mirror of our culture of nominalism, in which label and technique have replaced living interpretation rooted in concrete sign-practices. If one is merely an avatar of a code or system, with no critical capacities of one's own, then surely the world is arbitrary and no one can be held accountable: Blame it on the system.

The tendency to espouse semiotics as a technical panacea that will melt down all obdurate facts, disciplinary boundaries, biosocial imperatives, or human individuality into a sea of semiosis obscures the fact that semiotics is, in the end, a means for interpretation and not a religion. Hence, despite the attention devoted to it, the concept of sign remains acritical. And the frequently opaque language of semioticians, whether the high-tech jargon of positivism or the fancy footwork of postrationalist rationalism, more often acts as a means of mystification than as a means of clarification and fuller understanding.

In Gulliver's travels to Lagado, he meets with scholars who could be described by today's standards as positivists, or, with a slight twist, as postmodernist semioticians. Realizing the unnecessary hegemony of words, words, words, they propose a project to abolish words completely on the principle that, "since words are only names for *things,* it would be more convenient for all men to carry about them such things as were necessary to express the particular business they are to discourse on."

Think "sign" for "thing," and continue:

> many of the most learned and wise adhere to the new scheme of expressing themselves by things, which hath only this inconvenience attending it, that if a man's business be very great, and of various kinds, he must be obliged in proportion to carry a greater bundle of things upon his back, unless he can afford one or two strong servants to attend him. I have often beheld two of those sages almost sinking under the weight of their packs, like peddlers among us; who, when they meet in the streets, would lay down their loads, open their sacks, and hold conversation for an hour together; then put up their implements, help each other to resume their burdens, and take their leave. But for short conversations a man may carry implements in his pockets and under his arms, enough to supply him, and in his house he cannot be at a loss. Therefore the room where company meet who practice this art, is full of all things ready at hand, requisite to furnish matter for this kind of artificial discourse.

If we think of this kind of artificial discourse as a kind of X ray of the contemporary semiotician, we might imagine what otherwise looks like an average person as festooned with the elaborate terminology of semiotics: Saussurean, Morrisean, Peircean, Freudian, and other varieties of signs, bulging out of and overflowing every pocket, ready to be conspicuously displayed (and even consumed), weighing down and possessing their possessor by their sheer bulkiness so that communication becomes merely a wearisome and purposeless exhibition of semiotic goods, albeit freed from the strictures of rational discourse.

Despite these tendencies, I must acknowledge what seems to me the broad possibilities of semiotics for contributing to "post postmodern" culture. But in order for this to occur a radical transformation must take place: the fetishism of signs that now constitutes semiotics must give way to an animism of signs.

Just as humankind has frequently been misled into seeing "the definite social relations between men" assume the reified and fantastic forms of religious or, more recently, economic myths that deny human relationship in its own terms, so too does contemporary semiotics, with some exceptions, appear to be the latest incarnation of modern alienated rationalism. I would like to suggest, for example, that in rigidly separating language (as meaning-system) from speech (as mere instance), the semiological tradition appropriates meaning from living human action and speech, denying what for the Greeks was the essence of human nature itself, the capability to engage in living communicative dialogue, to cultivate and criticize purposive community. Meaning, as the medium of human social life, not only is robbed of its critical dimension as human instrument but vanishes from the concrete world itself to that nether region of "the deep structure." Symbolic signs may be constituted by conventional "codes," but codes themselves operate within a broader sign-web of purpose. Structuralism, as well as the positivist variety of semiotics launched by Charles Morris, simply does not address this larger question: What are codes *for?* Yet, it seems to me, this should be the ultimate aim of the semiotic perspective. The fetishism of signs that now dominates semiotics is in many ways simply an updated version of Adorno's 1938 characterization of "The Fetish-Character in Music and the Regression of Listening": "The new fetish is the flawlessly functioning, metallically brilliant apparatus as such, in which all the cogwheels mesh so perfectly that not the slightest hole remains open for the meaning of the whole" (in Arato and Gebhardt 1982,284).

Semiologists, including poststructuralists, like to make the claim that semiology is a critical form of discourse, capable of lifting the veil of illusion that hides from our faces the workings of codes. Perhaps this is the positive contribution of the semiological tradition. But is the notion of conventions or codes so original to this tradition? Marx, Veblen, and a number of other social theorists would clearly say not. And must codes be so rigidly dichotomized from action, from sentiment, from nature? Marx and Veblen would say no, but all the binary thought-world of structuralism would shout, en masse, *Oui!* Should we take them at their word that speech is meaningless and that their shout signifies nothing?

Let me briefly discuss two recent works in semiotic social theory that illustrate the tendency toward sign fetishism, or the unquestioned attachment to signs or sign-systems as panaceas. Both derive from the structuralist tradition, one embracing a totalized sign-system, the other a seemingly opposite call for revolutionary semiotic anarchy.

In *From the Sociology of Symbols to the Sociology of Signs: Toward a Dialectical Sociology* (1983), Ino Rossi seeks a "constructive dialogue between sociologists of traditional orientation and French structuralists," and so attempts to bring together in one volume the full range of "traditional" sociological theories with various structuralist approaches, such as those of Saussure, Lévi-Strauss, Piaget, Chomsky, Barthes, Lacan, and others. In Rossi's book everything not structuralist is labeled "traditional" (in the excessively binary manner that characterizes structuralist thought) and then is examined from a consistent structuralist point of view.

As can be seen in his title, Rossi is after a reconstruction of traditional sociology, and the reconstruction is to be brought about by fitting the flawed traditional models into the all-encompassing logical net of "relational structuralism." Where "traditional" sociology expressed concerns for meaning and action manifested in *symbols,* which in Saussurean semiology indicate some "rudiment of a natural bond between signifier and signified," the Rossi revision will reveal that true meaning is to be found in the *sign,* considered as inescapably bound up with "a system of relational differences and oppositions" (p. 135), and in no way determined by empirical reality. "Empiricism," as Rossi tells us, "is the most frequent villain I shall refer to throughout this book" (p. 5). And villain it is, since Rossi constantly claims empiricism, acknowledged or unacknowledged, as source of the flaws of traditional sociology. All roads, it seems, lead sociological theory inevitably to "relational structuralism," which is characterized as antiempiricist, antihumanist, and antihistorical.

The book begins with a discussion of Marx, who is criticized as being insufficiently structuralist and dialectical. One might say on Marx's behalf that if he were as devoutly antiempirical as Rossi, he would never have devoted years to *Capital,* he would never have broken with Hegel (who himself attempted to *include* the empirical within his theory). Marx might have, instead, limited himself to expressing the German ideology (or perhaps nowadays, the "French") instead of criticizing it through tempered observation.

One might say that it is the structuralists themselves who remain tied to the crudest conception of the empirical as a chaotic, formless manifold. Had they a broader conception of the nature of signs and generality, they might have seen that there is some order *in* the empirical and that there is also an essential otherness to it that tempers our cultural codes regardless of conventions. This broader conception might have forestalled the demise of structuralism as a vital theoretical framework.

In his brief conclusion, Rossi himself sees the insufficiency of structuralism that others working out of or "post" this tradition have also criticized. Objective structure alone is not enough, for, "both the objective and subjective focuses ought to be indispensable components of a holistic and dialectic approach because they refer to two facets of the organization and functioning of symbolic systems" (pp. 309–10). He has come full circle to "the larger issue of the relationship between society and individual" (p. 313), an issue which, interestingly enough, animated the classical theorists far more than recent structuralists. And what is "the locus of the dialectic relationship between structure and subjectivity"? Praxis! Rossi, rejecting Sartrean subjectivity and Althusserian objectivity, says that his view of praxis "represents a radical departure from the Marxist notion of dialectic in its objective and subjective version" (p. 317). We come full circle back to Marx, but to an intellectualized, semiologized, rationalized Marx.

The problem with Rossi's dialectical solution is that in the end we are still left with another "one size fits all" approach. Haven't we seen the blinding limitations of the Grand Theory as final solution? Of the domination by System over living human purpose? Rossi attempts to extend a broad, systematic framework, but ultimately his analysis presents us with a fetishism of abstract signs, one that takes the diversity of social theory and reduces it to the limitations of structuralist dogma.

The Time of the Sign (1982), by Dean MacCannell and Juliet Flower MacCannell, belongs very much to the current "post" phase of culture, such as postmodern architecture or poststructuralism (Jacques Derrida's influence looms large throughout the book), and the authors explicitly call it a "post-disciplinary" work with a "postrational" perspective. Like many contemporary works in semiotics, it seems to aim at a level of discourse just over the horizon of comprehension, frequently making pronouncements without arguments or evidence, as if obfuscation were a sign of profundity and clarity a sign of an outdated "rationalism" (Roland Barthes, in his critique of *la clarté*, practically said as much).

The Time of the Sign is an ironic title in a sense, because the book is based primarily on a Saussurean concept of the sign that does not include time as an inherent constituent of the sign. One of the criticisms of structuralism is that it overemphasizes static, underlying codes and does not provide an adequate theory for social change. The MacCannells attempt to deal with this problem by turning to the "revolutionary" origin of signs that allows, in the manner of a semiologized Rousseau (and after the fashion of Derrida), an uncovering of the "original semiotic mechanism by which the value system arises," namely, the sign as "value-free and arbitrary" (p. 34). Nevertheless, the problem remains that change is set over against system as discontinuous revolution, and no room is left for the continuity of a changing and growing system in time. Our binary choice is either to be slaves to a dead, unchanging structure or to slough off history and turn to a revolutionary poststructuralist chaos: the original arbitrary sign. In the same vein, throughout the book the authors criticize the various disciplines as ossified and needing to be reborn as postdisciplinary semiotics.

One can readily sympathize with their criticism of the pigeonholing tendencies of contemporary sociology, yet their posthaste postmortem might be premature. A recognition that individuals, institutions, and societies can be characterized as sign-complexes does not necessarily mean the end of sociology but perhaps only a broadening of it. In itself there is nothing wrong with the call to dissolve rigid disciplinary boundaries, but when, for example, one reads a chapter "On the Nature of the Literary Sign," in which literature plays no part (so typical in contemporary "postliterary" criticism), the suspicion arises that such a "postdisciplinary semiotics" would be merely a new form of theoretical imperialism, not to mention a triumph of Lagadoism: the replacement of unique discourses by a one-dimensional technology of signs.

In their concluding chapter, "A Community without Definite Limits," the authors argue against a unified semiotics by using Peirce's concept of an *unlimited community* as the basis of scientific objectivity, thinking it justifies their belief that a "semiotics of unity" is not possible and that a semiotics of *difference* is necessary. They state: "Assumptions of unity at the level of the individual or the community are based on a desire to return to a state of nature. . . . Within nature there is no deviation and ambiguity. . . . The image of man that emerges from the semiotics of unity is, to our mind, one of the least attractive we have ever devised for ourselves, exactly that of a political animal" (pp. 149,151). To confuse Aristotle's concept of man as a *political animal,* capable of the critical pursuit of the common good in and through community, with a notion of an unreflective, undeviating robot is absurd. The authors apparently do not realize how essential unity (or agreement) is to community; what is required is not their dichotomous idea of unity as homogeneous, acritical, and merely disciplinary thought, that is opposed to free, arbitrary semiological fission, but unity as a common object of a plurality of social individuals. Peirce's semiotic, which is based ultimately on *relation* rather than Saussurean *difference,* and on a conception of an eventual agreement, given sufficient inquiry, by an unlimited community (in many ways a logical expression of Aristotle's idea of community), simply works against their forced dichotomy. Their idea that "within nature there is no deviation and ambiguity," is, along with its profound ignorance of the variety and diversity and transformative nature of living organic nature, further indication of the modern topsy-turvy view that nature is a mechanical system.

The Time of the Sign remains merely a sign of our time: our so-called postmodern time at the end of the modern culture of nominalism, when even the echoes of those vital revolutionary forces of this cenury have played themselves out in formalistic abstraction. What is now urgently needed is not so much a deconstruction of meaning (that, after all, was the implied and sometimes explicit aim of modern culture) as a reconstruction of meaning at all levels—a reunification of the human spirit with the abstract mechanisms of its creation. We see in such a work further evidence of the dominance of vicious intellectualism in contemporary semiotics and social theory—an intellectualism that represses the significance and remembrance of experience, the "empirical," the purposive, and nature itself, as all of these are involved in the play of signs.

The binary tendencies characteristic of semiological structuralism, far from providing a framework for a critique of modern culture, exemplify the discrete either/or mentality so characteristic of the twentieth century and embody the fetishism of the abstract that is symptomatic of the last phase of modern culture: our time.

The semiological tradition does not monopolize the fetishism of signs, however. All one need do is read a selection of Charles Morris's *Foundations of the Theory of Signs,* almost at random, to find there a mind so possessed by mythic scientism that it is incapable of clear and logical expression of ideas and terms—something we would assume should be at the essence of scientific discourse.

AVATARS OF ABSTRACTIONISM

Semioticians (e.g., Sebeok 1978) frequently cite Charles Morris's *Foundations of the Theory of Signs* (1938b) as the most influential work, apart from those of Saussure and the semiological tradition, for the development of the field of semiotics. Morris, drawing from logical positivism and pragmatism, introduced the distinction of "syntax, semantics, and pragmatics" as the division of semiotic, and this threefold division, taken up by the philosopher Rudolph Carnap and others, has since influenced whole generations of philosophers and social scientists. As the previous chapter showed, Morris's triadic division of semiotic is based upon an unacknowledged debt to Peirce, one that not only fails to credit Peirce but which radically and systematically distorts Peirce's carefully conceived semiotic into an antisemiotic positivism, even as it retains Peircean terminology. "Pragmatics," for example, refers to the relation between signs and their users (Morris 1938b,29–30). Involved in this idea is Morris's distortion of Peirce's term "interpretant." Morris identifies "interpretant" with a phenomenal "interpreter" or "user," instead of presenting it as Peirce intended, as itself a sign in the continuing sign process. Hence Peirce's pragmatic theory of signs is reduced to the nominalistic behaviorism he spent his life arguing against (see Dewey 1946b; also Apel's [1980] critique of Morris).

In Morris we see the myth of pseudosemiotic scientism systematically dominating his thought, so that "interpreters" and their dispositions to respond to a sign, that is, "interpretants" (Morris's appropriation of Peirce's term), exist on a purely technical level of "response-sequences of some behavior-family" (Morris 1946b,17), whereby what will complete a sign-interpretation is that which will meet the exigencies of a particular organism's needs or of a behavioral setting. Interpretation is thus reduced to an acritical expediency that remains opaque both to its own fallibility and to its inability to generate new meaning. In this sense Morris (as well as in his own quite different way, Claude Lévi-Strauss) is merely an avatar of the modern myth of scientism, espousing a view that not only erases the purposive and critical individual and community but that ultimately undermines the possibility of science itself.

Another currently popular and widely read semiotician, but in my opinion an equally misguided one, is Umberto Eco. We see in his work a combination of the Cartesian dualisms of semiology with the positivistic scientism of Morris. For example, one of the main distinctions Eco sets up in his *A Theory of Semiotics* is that between "systems of signification" and "processes of communication," in a kind of an echo of Saussure's *langue* and *parole* distinction.

> A signification system is an autonomous semiotic construct that has an abstract mode of existence independent of any possible communicative act it makes possible. On the contrary (except for stimulation processes) *every act of communication to or between human beings*—or any other intelligent biological or mechanical apparatus—*presupposes a significant system as its necessary condition.*
> It is possible, if not perhaps particularly desireable, to establish a semiotics of signification independently of a semiotics of communication: but it is impossible to establish a semiotics of communication without a semiotics of signification. (Eco 1976,9)

A "signification system," contrary to Eco, cannot exist independently of possible communicative acts. Such a system would have to exist in the void, since apart from "any possible communicative act" we could never know of it. If Eco means that the general is not reducible to the particular, that is one thing, but what he says is that signification has no necessary content or embodiment and that communication is not in itself general. In fact, Eco's structuralist formulation is approximately the opposite of what Peirce meant by pragmatism. The Peircean interpretant makes the sign process mediate and processual, and communication occurs *within the sign process itself;* such communication is general and not simply an instance.
Eco later says:

> It is incorrect to say that every act of inference is a "semiosic" act—even though Peirce did so—and it is probably too rash a statement to assert that every semiosic process implies an act of inference, but it can be maintained that *there exist acts of inference which must be recognized as semiosic acts.* (Eco 1976,17)

An example Eco might give of something noninferential is a direct perception, such as the perceived stimulus of a table here in the present. Eco, contrary to Peirce, does *not* regard perceived stimuli as inferential and as signs (Eco 1976,19). For Eco, a thing may be regarded as a sign, "if and only if there exists a convention which allows it to stand for something else" and semiotics is limited to, and synonymous with, a concept of culture (Eco 1976,28) or, more precisely, cultural convention. In Peirce's broader semiotic there can be natural signs (such as a symptom) as well as conventional signs, and even the most basic perceptions are inferential and all inferences are signs. In Peirce's broader view perception is, quite simply, interpretative. The most basic perceptions involve "perceptual judgments," which, although inferential, are acritical and not subject to self-control (see Bernstein 1964). A perception is a sign addressed to an interpretation, the interpretant gives meaning to the sign (e.g., this bundle of perceptions is a table), and because this process occurs *in time* we can never "know" the absolute present noninferentially (our knowledge always comes "too late"). Peirce's semiotic, though available to Eco as a cultural resource, is simply whittled down, as it had been in Charles Morris, to a much narrower view of semiosis. The semiotics of Saussure, Morris, and Eco preserve a positivist substratum to which signs do not penetrate, the fictional substratum of nominalism. In so doing they exclude too much of what should be considered sign phenomena, resulting in a divorce of living human purpose from reality. Reality is cold and impenetrable, and human meaning is arbitrary, unfeeling, and unpurposive. Consider Eco's statement:

> Semiotics suggests a sort of molecular landscape in which what we are accustomed to recognize as everyday forms turn out to be the result of transitory chemical aggregations and so-called "things" are only the surface appearance assumed by an underlying network of more elementary units. Or rather, semiotics gives us a sort of photochemical explanation of semiosis, revealing that where we thought we saw images there were only strategically arranged aggregations of black and white points, alternations of presence and absence, the insignificant basic features of a raster, sometimes differentiated in shape, position and chromatic intensity. Semiotics, like musical theory, states that where we recognize familiar melodies there is only a sophisticated intertwining of intervals and notes, and where we perceive notes there are only a bunch of formants [sic]. (Eco 1976, 49–50)

Here feeling means nothing and purpose is only an illusion based on, festooned with, and dominated by an underlying discrete technology of signs. Semiotics only serves to puncture reality, not to critically further it.

Claiming to base himself "on a highly reliable philosophical and semiotical tradition," Eco says elsewhere that, "semiotically speaking—there is not a substantial difference between peanuts and peanut butter, on the one hand, and the words/peanuts/ and /peanut butter/ on the other. Semiotics is concerned with everything that can be *taken* as a sign" (1976, 7). To be more accurate, Eco should have said there is not a substantial difference between his "theory of semiotics" and peanut butter. For when he says that "semiotics is in principle the discipline studying everything which can be used in order to lie" (1976, 7), and that "the possibility of lying is the *proprium* of semiosis"

(1976, 59) and the basis for an intensional semantics; when he bases truth in existential instances that are irrational, as if the facts of an inquiry can be conceived outside of inquiry or semiosis, he shows us that, like peanut butter, his semiotics is rather hard to swallow.

Eco claims in his recent *Semiotics and the Philosophy of Language* (1984) that semiotics can be "scientifically" predictive, capable of achieving a comprehensive social engineering (1984, 5, 6). These remarks, like many others that pervade his work, display a limited view of science in general and the human sciences in particular, veritably a shrunken view of science when one compares it to that given by Peirce's semiotic. His work signifies, from the unnecessary slash marks, numbering systems, diagrams, and so forth, to the semiocybernetic robot talk that predominates, a domination by the abstract mechanism he purports to explain, with no sense of living, purposive human activity that transcends both the arbitrary and the merely technical. Though his fiction may come out smelling like a rose, Eco's theoretical work thus far is simply too metallic to encompass living human purpose and too narrow to provide the comprehensive theory of meaning social theory is currently attempting to formulate.

FROM FETISHISM TO ANIMISM

One of the problems with the varieties of structuralism, whether French, Freudian, or Marxist, is that they do not allow things to be what they are; instead they must always stand for something else. Yet an object's own qualities and physicality can also convey and signify something about that object beyond cultural convention: sometimes a cigar is, after all, a cigar; sometimes a painting by one's child is a unique token of love, a remembrance of a certain experience not repeatable. The fact that an object is part of a general code or cultural convention does not prevent it from also having its own inherent quality or aesthetic meaning, in the broad sense of this term, as an iconic sign.

A much broader view of signs is needed in contemporary semiotics and social theory, one that can admit that nature itself is general, a "sensuous code" if you will, that includes "necessary" or indexical signs, ranging from genetic signaling material to death itself, as well as the more conventional signs characterizing much of human social life, such as the personal and social meanings of life and death. Instead of the shared views of sociobiologists and their conceptualist opposites in the structuralist tradition that human sentiment and instinct serve only greedy self-interest and mechanical law, a broadened view of signs would recognize that human sentiment and even instinct motivate the highest human activities as well, and that the goal of rationality is not to assimilate all the world into itself, but to give itself, over time, to sentiment: to transform itself from the most immature of our capacities of mind to maturity by gradually becoming instinct, a paradoxical instinct that is also critical. I realize that these words must sound strange to those who accept the modernist dichotomy between nature and culture, but far stranger to me is the idea that nature is unintelligent!

A transformation is needed from our Age of Abstractionism, with its fetishism of signs, to an animism of signs in which the imagination and the signs it gives birth to will not only reconnect us with our biocultural heritage but also animate us to cultivate living purpose, not merely inert code. A healthy culture is not one in which instinct and reason are irreconcilably opposed, as the nature-versus-culture dichotomists hold, but one in which natural inclinations could find expression in and act upon the process of discursive reason. Culture is far more than the signification of rational codes and communication of "information." And semiotics is far more than the conspicuous display of the unintelligible in the name of the obscure. Semiotics must become the living attempt to render meaning clear, to make its language as supple a one as we can fashion and its ultimate object that mysterious, encompassing sign-web that is not only greater than human rationality but that animates the very nature of things. To give ourselves to the task of enlarging the scope of living human purpose through critical interpretation of signs need not be mere fetishism but the beginning of a new cultural attitude in which the *cultivation* of signs *animates* us toward a greater reasonableness.

III   *A Pragmatic Theory of Culture*

6   Culture Considered as Cultivation

> Reason, if it were perfect, would lead men to use the proper means of preserving their own lives and continuing their kind. But the Author of our being hath not thought fit to leave this task to reason alone, otherwise the race would long ago have been extinct.
>
> Thomas Reid, "Bees and Men:
> Instincts and the Limitations of Reason"

> If the Sun and Moon should doubt
>   They'd immediately go out.
>
> William Blake

To say that culture *lives* is anathema to most contemporary social theory. The concept of culture is viewed in most quarters today as an abstract system: a system of symbols and meanings, a system of beliefs, a meaning-system, a "pattern-maintenance" system of value-orientations, a deep structure of codes, and so forth. By most accounts culture in its essence is a meaning-system that arbitrarily or conventionally provides the values and beliefs that orient a society.

The turn toward culture as sign-system marked some the of most significant developments in anthropology since the 1960s (Singer 1968), and indeed the social sciences in general, whether in social theory, cognitive psychology, structuralism and its various offshoots, or the catchall field of semiotics, have by and large discussed meaning as a conceptual system of one sort or another. In most of these approaches, with some notable exceptions, such as those of Clifford Geertz or Victor Turner, culture is the name for the organization of meaning and is an autonomous sphere radically opposed to nature. To even suggest that culture "lives" would mean to some, such as Marshall Sahlins (1976a,b), Anthony Giddens (1979, 1982, 1984), Jürgen Habermas (1984), Claude Lévi-Strauss (1966, 1967), and Umberto Eco (1976, 1979, 1984), a basic confusion of the culture category with the nature category, a kind of naive naturalism that would put one in the camp of sociobiologists, those latest avatars of capitalistic social Darwinism.

When I say that culture lives, I do intend to suggest a continuity of culture with nature. But, as will become clearer, I reject the one-dimensional mechanical view of nature paradoxically shared by sociobiologists and conceptualists. It is strange, to say the least, that evolutionary mechanists should so ignore what is characteristic of evolution, namely *growth*, as a constituent feature of the principle of evolution itself. Sociobiology and conceptualism share an unnecessarily narrow, mechanical view of nature, and both ignore the tempering role of experience. Both also trivialize the social medium through which the biological body and cultural codes are forged, seeing it as merely additive instead of formative. Both make the "fallacy of misplaced concreteness" in denying the fundamental interaction of social practices (as ritual life) and the development of the biological conditions for human being. Human being is the bodying forth of living social relation.

I plan further to claim that signs live, that we live in signs, and that the essence of culture, like that of nature, is the living growth and embodiment of signs: semiosis. Though it resides on a continuum of self-control with nature, culture is that greater capacity for self-controlled conduct, both on the broader institutional as well as personal levels. Culture, to be sure, involves critical capacities that are minimal or largely nonexistent in the rest of nature, yet this does not necessarily signal a categorical distinction, but can also be read as a sign that evolution is itself subject to evolution; that just as the laws of evolution are the results of evolution rather than of a-priori mechanical commandments, so too can the laws of evolution grow to include purposive, critical human conduct as constitutive.

We live *in* a cultural medium, not simply it in us, a cultural medium continuous with the whole range of tempering experiences that have shaped our species-nature and personal temperaments, a cultural medium that lives but that surely can become stagnant or pathological, that can wither away and die. In a living culture we do possess a personal perspective, but it is culture that animates us transpersonally; we live to further the growth of reasonableness, to express and embody in living acts and artifacts a humanized, cosmically rooted intelligence. Culture in this sense is something much more than it is in the limited conceptual views of modern rationalisms, and in fact forms a critique of their narrowly prescribed limits of reason. In the view proposed here, reason is capable of real and living growth, and nature is capable of critical intelligence. It is in this sense that I will consider culture as *cultivation*.

THE TRANSFORMATION OF CULTURE

Both etymologically and historically, the word "culture" originally meant an active, educative process of cultivation, inseparable from the larger goals of the community, the *polis*. In this view culture was the completion of nature, and the word itself derived from a sense of cultivating or tilling the land. But with the turn to a nominalistic worldview in the West, a new perspective emerged by the seventeenth century that came to see culture as unnatural, as dichotomized from nature. As Raymond Williams has noted:

> Before this period, [culture] had meant, primarily, the "tending of natural growth," and then, by analogy, a process of human training. But this latter use, which had usually been a culture *of* something, was changed, in the nineteenth century, to *culture* as such, a thing in itself (Williams 1958, xvi)

Although Williams is primarily concerned with the turning of the concept of culture in the nineteenth century into the idea of an "acquisition," so that one could become "cultured" by being educated at the right schools, knowing the right books, and so on—in other words by an artificially conceived "cultivation"—his statement holds true for the broader temporal span as well. Culture, in becoming denatured, became divested in common usage of its quality as a human practice in favor of a status label or thing.

Nature, which from Aristotle through the medieval schoolmen meant the inherent potentiality, perfectible end, or "final cause" of a thing or being, came to signify only "first causes," the governing mechanical laws that later were seen to determine evolution. Descartes, who believed the body to be a kind of mechanical apparatus, claimed: "The great science of mechanics is nothing other than the order that God has imprinted upon the face of his work, which we commonly call *Nature*" (in Morris 1971, 143). In the emerging modern view nature came to signify those supreme embodiments of modern rationality, namely, individuality and self-interest, whereas culture was the secondary realm of the social contract and community. And community became defined increasingly as *social aggregate*, paradoxically the principal trait we share with other forms of nature such as ants and bees.

Thomas Hobbes articulated the sociopolitical implications of the emerging worldview in his *Leviathan*. There we see a reversal of the Christian "garden of paradise" and Greek conceptions of nature: humanity in its natural state "is a condition of Warre of every one against every one," and culture serves as a limitation of liberty through obligation to the social contract. According to Hobbes, culture and representation are, as they later would be in a different scientistic guise in Freud's psychology, literally a compromise, an artifice superimposed on the real. Hobbes tells us:

> The final Cause, End, or Designe of men, (who naturally love Liberty, and Dominion over others,) in the introduction of that restraint upon themselves, (in which we see them live in Com-mon-wealths,) is the foresight of their own preservation, and of a more contented life thereby; that is to say, of getting themselves out from that miserable condition of Warre, which is necessarily

consequent (as hath been shewn) to the naturall Passions of men. . . . " (Hobbes 1651, 223)

From Aristotle's dictum that, although all animals live, man is a *political animal* determined by nature to live well, that is, to live the good life in the community, we see a complete reversal in Hobbes. Community is not so much the purposive cultivation of purpose itself as it is the mechanism of restraining the "natural" impulses to anarchy. There is no purpose in nature save the mechanical law of self-interest, itself not subject to criticism or correction but only to repression or sublimation. Liberty becomes not the aim and achievement of community but private licence. The domain of privacy itself, held since the Greeks to be the means toward the fuller life of the public, is inverted to become the end of the public life, in the sense that the common or public serves only to harness the primordial private individual. Jürgen Habermas has noted the profound implications of the new view of the human condition effected by Hobbes's transformation:

> In its role as the science of the state of nature, a modern physics of human nature replaces the classical ethics of Natural Law. . . . In place of the *animal sociale* in the Christian-Aristotelian sense of a *zoon politikon* he sets an *animal politicum* in the sense of Machiavelli, in order then to show quite readily that precisely the assumption of these rights, especially the right of all to everything, as soon as it is applied to a pack of "free" and "equal" wolves, will have as consequence a state in which they mutually tear and devour each other. This subtle playing with venerable attributes reveals the radical rethinking of classical Natural Law, so that it becomes the actual absence of all right and justice for the natural environment, which lacks positive regulation and rational compacts. The conditions under which a community of saints was supposed to live, appear, in a diabolical inversion, as the conditions under which human beasts live in a continual life-and-death struggle. (Habermas 1973, 64–65)

"Diabolical inversion" is an apt term. Indeed the term "diabolic" derives from the Greek word *diaballein* meaning "to throw apart" or to separate, and is the opposite of "symbolic" (*symballein*) which means literally "to throw together." The new vision of society was to be based on a fragmenting, individualized worldview that separated thought from things, self from community, culture from nature. The new order of nominalism that first gained acceptance in the revolt of the nominalists and humanists against scholastic realists and gradually came to dominate the emerging cultural epoch proclaimed a world rent into two separate spheres, the rational and physical, both of which rested on a foundation of irrational intuition, a wellspring of unreason.

This depersonalization of consciousness and world in modern culture can be characterized as a process of nominalization, in which relationships formerly treated as basic were transformed into epiphenomena of "things." Classical materialism acted as a cultural belief system and extended itself beyond the realm of physics to political economy, evolutionary biology, and positivism, and produced a worldview that by and large saw human purpose as convention superimposed upon the underlying realities of physical things and mechanical laws. It is as if, and perhaps this is not as metaphoric as it sounds at first, a transformation from verbs to nouns took place, from acting in the world to merely naming and labeling that world. In the classical Lockean sense one's relationship to the world came to consist of the "secondary qualities" or conventions of the mind that stood for the "primary qualities" of which objects consisted, such as mass, figure, texture, and so forth. The living act that joined person and world in a unique and direct qualitative relationship became merely an epiphenomenon of an underlying rational intuition or perceptual impression, depending on what side of the split one took as valid.

One of the consequences of this emerging position is that culture becomes an additive, "in name only," an arbitrary system severed from the "real" substratum of mechanical law, leading either to a denigration of culture or to an overemphasis on arbitrary and conventional elements. Culture becomes a question of arbitrary taste, authority, and legitimation rather than the pursuit and expression of the real goals of community life. Most contemporary theories of culture tend to share this dichotomous view in which community is guided solely by arbitrary conventions rather than by real (and thereby general) laws or ultimate goals, and hence is a social construct apart from nature. The tendency in these views, such as structuralisms of whatever sort, is to see culture as a static system of symbols and as located in the "underworld" of deep structure, rather than in the community of tempered beliefs and critical communication. The new culture of nominalism, which replaced scholastic realism in the European centers of learning, gave birth to a completely new conception of individual and society in the West; one that not only has dominated social thought but that also has become embodied in the guiding principles of modern art and everyday culture, in the very "flesh and blood of the average modern mind" (Peirce). It is this nominalized view of culture now dominating cultural practices as well as theories of culture that I seek to revise.

THE CULTIVATION OF MEANING

The wild pear tree, as Georg Simmel remarked, bears woody, sour fruit. But through human cultivation pear trees can be brought to bear edible pears. What existed as a potentiality in the tree is cultivated to an actuality through human, purposive intervention. The meaning of the pear tree itself grows into something much more than it was in its uncultivated state. Meaning, in other words, is not simply a fixed and static realm "untouched by human hands," but has its existence in and through a process of cultivation, a process involving the development, refinement, or resultant expression of some object or habit of life due to care, inquiry, suffering, or celebration, and whose goal is the greater embodiment of living reasonableness. Meaning is not merely abstract system; nor is it arbitrary whim or inclination. Meaning is transaction, triadic semiosis that not only includes subject and object as constituent but also the modes of transaction between them. For this reason culture is the cultivation of meaning, a triadic sign-process that includes (1) the inherent quality or qualitative possibility of that which is cultivated, (2) the existential otherness or *obsistency* (CP 2.89) involved in the transaction, and (3) the real generalization toward which the process is aimed, that is, the outcome of cultivation.[1]

How meaning consists in living cultivation can be seen in greater relief by considering three exemplary theorists who cut against the grain of contemporary conceptualism: Georg Simmel, Clifford Geertz, and Victor Turner. Simmel's insights into the larger question of cultivation and modernity remain among the most penetrating to date, and so serve as a good illustration of why culture should be viewed as cultivation.

One of the key distinctions in Simmel's social philosophy is that between *objective culture* and *subjective culture*. Simmel's view of culture emphasizes the interaction of the unique subject with the object that becomes product of the interaction, and how subject and object reciprocally cultivate each other. He stressed that, from the perspective of subjective culture, there are inherent qualities that must be realized, that enter into the cultivation process as part of its aim:

> Cultivation implies that some being existed before the appearance of cultivation in an uncultivated, that is, "natural" state, and it further implies that the ensuing transformation of this subject is somehow latent in its *natural structural potential*, even though it could not be realized by itself, but only through culture. For cultivation brings its object to a fulfillment determined by the essential and fundamental tendencies of the object's nature. . . . The *should* and *can* of man's full development are inseparably bound to the *being* of man's soul. Only the human soul contains the developmental potentialities whose goals are determined purely in the teleology of its own nature (Simmel 1971, 228–29)

1. See my Chapter 7 in *The Meaning of Things* (Csikszentmihalyi and Rochberg-Halton 1981) for a discussion of the three modes of meaning transactions, using the framework (but with a different terminology) of Peirce's three modes of being as they apply to the three modes of sign-action.

Subjective culture, or cultivation considered from the perspective of the self, is that development of meaning "which follows the inherent proclivities of the being and as such may be called its culture" (Simmel 1971, 229). Simmel was supremely aware of the crisis of modern culture, in which the unique character or disposition of an individual is subjected to enormous pressures by the general quantification and rationalization of life. Though modern culture made possible new developments of individuality, life in the modern metropolis especially, with its emphasis on the money economy, intellectuality, and the blasé attitude, tended to create individuals whose selves consisted mainly in a veneer of idiosyncrasy and studied cosmopolitanism and that served to repress the development of the inherent uniqueness of the individual.

Simmel was not trying to claim that the self is absolutely determined in advance, only that there is a unique configuration of determining factors in every individual that give the individual unique potentials. He did not believe that cultivation was simply the unfolding of inner stages of development, in which the objects of experience do not make a qualitative difference in development (as someone like Piaget might hold); instead, he made a strong claim for the *otherness* of interaction as constitutive:

> For culture exists only if man draws into his development *something that is external to him.* Cultivation is certainly a state of the soul, but one that is reached only by means of the use of purposively created *objects*. This externality and objectivity is not to be understood only in a spatial sense. The forms of comportment, the refinement of taste expressed in judgments, the education of moral tact which make an individual a delightful member of society—they are all cultural formations in which the perfection of the individual is routed through real and ideal spheres outside of the self. The perfection does not remain a purely immanent process, but is consummated in a unique adjustment and teleological interweaving of subject and object. (Simmel 1971, 230)

Culture is finally a process of reciprocal interaction between the forms of subjective culture and objective culture. There can be no subjective culture without objective culture, though objective culture is partially independent from subjective culture in that its "'cultivated,' that is, cultivating" objects are more general and are available for cultural purposes reaching beyond its immediate subject. Yet the overarching goal of culture remains subjective cultivation in Simmel's perspective.

Simmel manages to encompass both interaction and larger structure, both subjectivity and objectivity, in a more compelling way than many of the recent attempts in social theory to develop a comprehensive meaning theory. Although acknowledging his deeply insightful analysis of the nature of cultivation, I cannot accept his rigid Kantian separation of nature from teleological culture, of form from content, and his idea that subjective culture is the final goal of cultivation. The overarching goal of cultivation is the continued growth and concretization of purpose itself, a process that surely involves subjects and objects, but subjects and objects who ultimately serve, not rationality, but reasonableness, broadly understood as living interpretant and not abstract formal system. As will become clearer later in this chapter, we are bearers of *humanized, cosmically rooted intelligence.*

Clifford Geertz has been a consistent and compelling critic of both functionalist and formalist reductionism, and his work offers rich insights into the ways in which cultures act as webs of meaning that must be explored in their own right and in their own specificity. In his provocative chapters on "The Impact of Culture on the Concept of Man" and "The Growth of Culture and the Evolution of Mind" in his *The Interpretation of Cultures* (1973; also see his discussion in 1983b), Geertz cut through the "stratigraphic" view that there was an underlying, fully formed biological man in a "state of nature" who one day discovered the social contract that is culture.

The apparent fact that the final stages of the biological evolution of man occurred after the initial stages of the growth of culture implies that "basic," "pure," or "unconditioned," human nature, in the sense of the innate constitution of man, is so functionally incomplete as to be unworkable. Tools, hunting, family organization, and, later, art, religion, and "science" molded man somatically; and they are, therefore, necessary not merely to his survival but to his existential realization. . . . The human nervous system relies, inescapably, on the accessibility of public symbolic structures to build up its own autonomous, ongoing pattern of activity. (Geertz 1973, 82–83)

Geertz's interactive approach to biology and culture enables him to let culture saturate being to a deeper level than many contemporary conceptualistic theories would allow. Culture is not merely additive to our nature but formative of it, and not only for our reflective nature but for our somatic nature as well.

Culture is essentially a public discourse of symbols in Geertz's perspective and "denotes an historically transmitted pattern of meanings embodied in symbols, a system of inherited conceptions expressed in symbolic forms by means of which men communicate, perpetuate, and develop their knowledge about and attitudes toward life" (Geertz 1973, 89). In his ". . . as a Cultural System" series, Geertz has explored in turn the subtleties of religion, ideology, common sense, and art considered as cultural systems. He has argued persuasively against contentless universalism and blind relativism, by showing, for example, how art needs to be seen in its social contexts in different cultures, neither as purely formal nor purely functional but as embedded in particular experiences and customs. Similarly in his "Common

Sense as a Cultural System" (1983a) he explores how common sense, expressed, for example, in attitudes toward hermaphroditism, reveal it to be not as universal as one might believe.

Common sense, viewed interpretatively, is not an unmediated presentation of reality "neat," but a mediated system, situationally rooted, as Dewey might say, within specific cultural contexts:

> If common sense is as much an interpretation of the immediacies of experience, a gloss on them, as are myth, painting, epistemology, or whatever, then it is, like them, historically constructed and, like them, subjected to historically defined standards of judgment. It can be questioned, disputed, affirmed, developed, formalized, contemplated, even taught, and it can vary dramatically from one people to the next. It is, in short, a cultural system, though not usually a very tightly integrated one, and it rests on the same basis that any other such system rests; the conviction of those whose possession it is of its value and validity. Here, as elsewhere, things are what you make of them. (Geertz 1983a, 76)

Though Geertz concludes by saying, "Here, as elsewhere, things are what you make of them," one might equally turn this around to say that things have helped temper you to be what you are, and that there might be some commonalities of the tempering experience so ingrained in that web of meaning which is the human temperament as to be indubitable, while still fallible. This view of common sense, which I shall argue for in the next section, is more than cultural construction (though it involves it), yet fully interpretative, and not to be confused with the more rationalized forms of "common sense" in twentieth-century philosophy to which Geertz refers.

If we compare Geertz's "cultural system" approach to religion with Peirce's emphasis on "living belief," we see how, despite very close affinities between Geertz and the pragmatists, his theory ultimately retains a conceptualist tendency that narrows the scope of cultural signification and belief, and, paradoxically, of the public nature of culture.

In one of Geertz's best-known essays, "Religion as a Cultural System," he describes the two-sided nature of religious belief as providing *models of* the wider world, and *models for* conduct. Borrowing the organization of his essay from Kenneth Burke's dictum that "A definition should have just enough clauses, and no more. However, each clause should be like a chapter head, under which appropriate observations might be assembled, as though derived from it" (Burke 1966, 3), Geertz defines religion as: "(1) a system of symbols which acts to (2) establish powerful, pervasive, and long-lasting moods and motivations in men by (3) formulating conceptions of a general order of existence and (4) clothing these conceptions with such an aura of factuality that (5) the moods and motivations seem uniquely realistic"

(Geertz 1973, 90). Religion is a symbol system, like culture in general, whose task is to generate a social construction of reality. Geertz sees the essence of religion as based on the prior acceptance of authority:

> It seems to me that it is best to begin any approach to this issue with frank recognition that religious belief involves not a Baconian induction from everyday experience—for then we should all be agnostics—but rather a prior acceptance of authority which transforms that experience. . . . It is, again, the imbuing of a certain specific complex of symbols—of the metaphysic they formulate and the style of life they recommend—with a persuasive authority which, from an analytic point of view, is the essence of religious action. (Geertz 1973, 109, 112)

The religious experience is here reduced to a cultural system of beliefs, a system of symbols, and the validity of these beliefs is dependent on authority: religion is a sort of ideology. Despite a rooted interpretative analysis that overcomes many of the problems of Parsonian "grand theory," Geertz's use of Parsons' "systems" model of human action retains a limiting view of cultural belief as "pattern-maintenance" or legitimation. If one grants that religions tend to assume the form of a legitimizing mirror of society, both in Durkheim's positive sense of collective representations or Marx's negative sense of a deadening social opiate, this does not exhaust the dynamics of religious or even cultural beliefs, and more significantly fails to penetrate the animating impulse to belief in general and the vital consequences certain beliefs might provide.

Geertz's emphasis on a-priori acceptance of authority is similar to Durkheim's emphasis on "elementary forms" or Cartesian "Cardinal Conceptions" (Durkheim 1965, 16) as the foundation for religious belief. Geertz, like Durkheim, stresses a-priori origins or foundations, rather than ultimate goals, as the essence of the religious life. In both cases everyday experience and the ongoing cultivation of community life toward ultimate goals are secondary phenomena reducible to the underlying principle of religious authority. The a-priori acceptance of religious authority is what "tranforms" an experience into a religious experience, and make religious "moods and motivations seem uniquely realistic" (Geertz 1973, 90). But what is the validity of religious authority?

In Peirce's view, belief in authority is not the essence of religion, or of social life in general, because the validity of authority is itself dependent on reality (see Peirce's article, "The Fixation of Belief" [CP 5.358–387]). Where Geertz himself begins with a prior acceptance of the authority of authority, Peirce begins by accepting the religious experience itself:

> And what is religion? In each individual it is a sort of sentiment, or obscure perception, a deep recognition of a something

> in the circumambient All. . . . when a man has that experience
> with which religion sets out, he has as good reason—putting
> aside metaphysical subtleties—to believe in the living personality
> of God as he has to believe in his own. Indeed, *belief* is a word
> inappropriate to such direct perception. (CP 6.429, 436)

The validity of the religious experience in this view is itself dependent on
reality and community, and should be an experience of true being:

> But religion cannot reside in its totality in a single individual.
> Like every species of reality, it is essentially a social, public
> affair. It is the idea of a whole church, welding all its members
> together in one organic, systemic perception of the Glory of the
> Highest—an idea having a growth from generation to generation
> and claiming a supremacy in the determination of all conduct,
> private and public . . . . The *raison d'être* of a church is to confer
> upon men a life broader than their narrow personalities, a life
> rooted in the very truth of being. To do that it must be based
> upon and refer to a definite and public experience. (CP 6.429,
> 451)

In the long run religion, like social life in general, is not based on
authority but on reality, to which all forms of authority are subject. And the
reality of religious life is not made up of fixed, a-priori concepts, but is living
belief open to change:

> Yet it is absurd to say that religion is a mere belief. You might as
> well call society a belief, or politics a belief, or civilization a be-
> lief. Religion is a life, and can be identified with a belief only
> provided that belief be a living belief—a thing to be lived rather
> than said or thought. (CP 6.439)

Substitute "cultural system" for "belief" in this quotation, such as society as
a cultural system, common sense as a cultural system, art as a cultural system,
and you can see Clifford Geertz as a cultural system, a conceptually based
theory quite at odds, despite other deep-seated similarities, with Peirce's view
of living culture, existentially and cosmically rooted. Cultures considered as
cultivation must include "cultural system," broadly conceived, but must
include as well those broader animating purposes and possibilities whose
task it is for cultural systems to realize.

Perhaps the most eloquent spokesman for culture as a living and
vividly human process has been Victor Turner. Throughout his work Turner
conveys that mercurial essence that is the living source of human individuals
and human cultures, that appears in sacred rites and mundane events, and
that gives to our otherwise inhumane ways the possibility of renewal. Turner
perceptively documents the human form of culture again and again in his
ethnographies while revealing that our humanity itself reaches to deeper and

transcendent realities whose significance we may partially grasp but never capture.

Turner's "social dramas" approach grew largely out of his fieldwork with the Ndembu people of northwestern Zambia. In describing how he came to shift emphasis from the structuralist-functionalist approach of his early work to one emphasizing the play of symbols in ritual life, Turner remarked:

> I found that I could not analyze ritual symbols without study-
> ing them in a time series in relation to other "events," for sym-
> bols are essentially involved in social process. I came to see per-
> formances of ritual as distinct phases in the social processes
> whereby groups became adjusted to internal changes and adapted
> to their external environment. From this standpoint the ritual
> symbol becomes a factor in social action, a positive force in an
> activity field. The symbol becomes associated with human in-
> terests, purposes, ends, and means, whether these are explicitly
> formulated or have to be inferred from the observed behavior.
> The structure and properties of a symbol become those of a
> dynamic entity, at least within its appropriate context of action.
> (Turner 1967, 20)

The symbol here has its meaning in context, not the deadly abstract and static context of the structuralist conception of code, but the living, ongoing social milieu. Turner's ethnographies illustrate in the concrete Peirce's conception of the symbol as a living, growing entity: "For every symbol is a living thing, in a very strict sense that is no mere figure of speech. The body of the symbol changes slowly, but its meaning inevitably grows, incorporates new elements and throws off old ones . . . a symbol, once in being, spreads among the peoples. In use and in experience, its meaning grows" (CP 2.222, 302).

Ndembu culture is far closer to Peirce's view of the symbol than the conceptualist approaches which now dominate cultural anthropology and semiotics. In calling his study of the ritual life of the Ndembu *The Forest of Symbols* (1967), for example, Turner draws attention to the ways trees, as living things, symbolize the deepest values of the Ndembu in a concrete and yet elevated way. The native term for symbol itself derives from the cuts made on trees in the forest that act as signposts for male hunters ("The symbol is the smallest unit of specific structure in Ndembu ritual. The vernacular term for it is *chinjikijilu*, from *ku-jikijila*, "to blaze a trail," by cutting marks on a tree with one's ax or by breaking and bending branches to serve as guides back from the unknown bush to known paths. A symbol, then, is a blaze or landmark, something that connects the unknown with the known" [1967, 48]). The matrilineal basis of the society is multivocally signified through the Mudyi or white-milk sap tree, as becomes most evident in girls' puberty initiation rites. There a young girl and a Mudyi sapling, symbolizing her entrance to the matriliny, are placed in the center of a ring of dancing women, who themselves personify the matriliny, as, for example, when they clash with the males, symbolizing the matrilineal-virilocal conflict that motivates many of the tensions in Ndembu life. Turner's informants led him to a view of society as rooted in living symbolic processes.

Turner also recognizes, with Peirce and the other pragmatists, that human culture and mind is more than simply cognitive:

> Long before I had read a word of Wilhelm Dilthey's I had shared his notion that "structures of experience" are fundamental units in the study of human action. Such structures are irrefrangibly threefold, being at once cognitive, conative, and affective. Each of these terms is itself, of course, a shorthand for a range of processes and capacities . . . persons will desire and feel as well as think, and their desires and feelings impregnate their thoughts and influence their intentions. . . . It became clear to me that an "anthropology of experience" would have to take into account the psychological properties of individuals as well as the culture which, as Sapir insists, is *"never given"* to each individual, but, rather, "gropingly discovered," and, I would add, some parts of it quite late in life. We never cease to learn our *own* culture, let alone other cultures, and our own culture is always changing. (Turner 1982, 63, 64)

Though they embody conventions and are the media for their transmission, symbols do so within lived experience, not apart from it. Experience is what endows the symbol with vitality and through which it, with us, grows. Symbols are means of empathic, volitional, and critical adaptations, both individually and collectively. In *The Forest of Symbols* Turner links a Durkheimian treatment of the social and structural aspects of symbols with a Freudian approach to the psychological dimension of inner needs and the rooting of expressive symbolism in bodily experience, to arrive at his own unique formulation that can do justice to symbolized social experience.

Turner's most influential contribution to cultural theory has been his discussions for the role of *liminality* in cultural life, the creative matrix that so frequently appears in the margins or gaps of routinized existence (such as play, ritual, or festival), and which is a phase in a view of social life considered as *social dramas*.[2] Turner draws his ideas on liminality from van Gennep's discussion of rites of passage as consisting of three phases of *separation*, *liminality*, and *reaggregation*, in which (1) the norms and statuses of the

---

2. For an excellent example of the "social dramas" and culture-as-performance approaches to culture see MacAloon (1984). Culture considered as cultural performance is developed at length by Singer (1972).

relevant group no longer apply, (2) those undergoing the rite enter a "betwixt and between" phase, neither living nor dead, as in the case of the Ndembu puberty initiation rite, and then (3) a phase of reentry into the wider society, now transformed or "reborn" through the initiation. Rites of passage, especially the dynamics of liminality, provide the model on which Turner's much broader "social dramas" approach to culture in general is based, and apply both to the transformation of individuals (as "initiates") and to larger groups, institutions, or cultures:

> The social drama, then, I regard as the experiential matrix from which the many genres of cultural performance, beginning with redressive ritual and juridical procedures, and eventually including oral and literary narrative, have been generated. Breach, crisis, and reintegrative or divisive outcomes provide the content of such later genres, redressive procedures their form. As society complexifies, as the division of labor produces more and more specialized and professionalized modalities of sociocultural action, so do the modes of assigning meaning to social dramas multiply—but the drama remains to the last simple and ineradicable, a fact of everyone's social experience, and a significant node in the developmental cycle of all groups that aspire to continuance. The social drama remains humankind's thorny problem, its undying worm, its Achilles' heel—one can only use clichés for such an obvious and familiar pattern of sequentiality. At the same time it is our native way of manifesting ourselves to ourselves and, of declaring where power and meaning lie and how they are distributed. (Turner 1982, 78)

The social drama that is culture is a dialectical process between structure and antistructure or liminality, between hierarchy and community, between the indicative mood that is everyday life and the subjunctive mood of cultural possibility, expressed in those liminal spheres where artistic imagination, moral action, and reflective commentary are given free play to develop and infuse their insights into the lived cultural heritage.

Turner's emphasis on the dialectic of drama as the moving force of a culture might be criticized for the same reasons as the Hegelian dialectic with which it resonates: it leans too heavily on the dialectical principles themselves as providing long-term solutions through inherent generation and resolution of oppositions and perhaps does not give enough credit to the great "Outward Clash" that may temper a culture even apart from its conventions, turning it to a different direction. In the Hegelian dialectic truth will sooner or later come around, but truth is more than the outcome of rational argument, it is the outcome also of extrarational tempering, and so becomes the aim of *inquiry*, broadly considered. Though Turner did not explicitly connect rites of passage with Hegelian dialectic, he was aware of this problem, and sought to account for it, perhaps, by attempting to include the hard facts of life within social drama, and, especially in his last works, by exploring the long-range tempering manifest in the human brain itself and its relation to culture.

Turner's most persuasive claim for liminality is not simply that it brings creative anarchy or stirs things up by turning them upside down, but that the fantastic forms that liminality often assumes make possible an honesty and clarity that can burn away the obscuring and distorting cultural residues, or what Blake termed "the mind forg'd manacles":

> any society that hopes to be imperishable must carve out for it-self a piece of space and a period of time in which it can look honestly at itself. This honesty is not that of the scientist, who exchanges the honesty of his ego for the objectivity of his gaze. It is, rather, akin to the supreme honesty of the creative artist who, in his presentations on the stage, in the book, on canvas, in mar-ble, in music, or in towers and houses, reserves to himself the privilege of seeing straight what all cultures build crooked. All generalizations are in some way skewed, and artists with candid vision "labor well the minute particulars," as Blake knew. This may be a metalanguage, but all this means is that the "meta" part of it is not at an abstract remove from what goes on in the world of "getting and spending," but rather sees it more clearly, whether more passionately or dispassionately is beside my pres-ent point. Whether anthropology can ignore this incandescent objectivity and still lay claim to being "*the* study of man" I gravely doubt. (Turner 1984, 40)

Our own modern culture, in denigrating the "subjunctive mood,"wherein lies the liminal phase, in favor of a scientistic and rationalizing "culture of the indicative mood," has worshiped a false and hollow idol of objectivity, at once cold, blind to sentiment, and ultimately solipsistic. As Peirce would remind us, reality is itself of the nature of a general, a conditional, a "would-be," and is not reducible to positive instances.

In the recovery of meaning that is how underway in social theory, Victor Turner stands as an impassioned voice for that "incandescent objec-tivity" that should form the heart both of cultural life and of reflective social theory. Just as Simmel reminds us of the need for the uniqueness of the individual in interaction with objective culture, and Geertz of culture as externalized mind which completes us, Turner directs our gaze toward the incandescent human form through which the mystery of creation enters the human web of meaning.

Instinct, Common Sense, and Critical Reason

> If man had not the gift, which every other animal has, of a mind adapted to his requirements, he not only could not have acquired any knowledge, but he could not have maintained his existence for a single

generation. But he is provided with certain instincts, that is, with certain natural beliefs that are true. They relate in part to forces, in part to the action of minds. The manner in which he comes to have this knowledge seems to me tolerably clear. Certain uniformities, that is to say certain general ideas of action, prevail throughout the universe, and the reasoning mind is (it)self a product of this universe. These same laws are thus, by logical necessity, incorporated in his own being.

(CP 5.603)

It seems at first somewhat of a contradiction that Charles Peirce, founder of modern semiotic, original contributor to the development of symbolic logic and innovations in mathematics, and one of the greatest of logicians, should have adopted the view that reason rests on instinct. Surely the person who so devastatingly criticized Cartesianism and its descendants for grounding reason on unreasonable intuition (in the sense of direct, unmediated knowledge) could see that similar problems seemingly arise when one says reason is based on something as irrational as instinct. Peirce was, in fact, quite aware of this problem, and to understand why he could make such strong claims for instinct, it is important to realize that *instinct is reasonable* in Peirce's critical reconstruction of nature. As he says in the previous quotation, instincts are "certain natural beliefs that are true." Peirce is expressing a view quite at odds with the modern nominalistic consciousness of Hobbes, Freud, et al., who hold that truth is a compromise designed to provide order for an underlying "natural" reality that, if given full expression, would ultimately lead to anarchy and death. Peirce held that both truth *and* reality must be that which lead to the fruitful development of relation and law, indeed that are synonymous with an evolutionary love rather than Hobbesian hate.

Peirce formulated a view of evolution quite at odds with the ascendant Darwinian version of his time. Characteristically, Peirce's understanding of evolution was more encompassing and reconciled seemingly opposed views, and in so doing would seem to have anticipated some of the most recent developments in contemporary evolutionary theory. Darwin's theory of evolution made a deep impression on Peirce, and though he regarded it highly he saw it as far too limited an explanation. Peirce proposed in the late nineteenth century a composite of three views that corresponded to his categories of Firstness, Secondness, and Thirdness. Darwin's emphasis on chance variation formed an evolution by Firstness, Clarence King's theory of cataclysmal evolution formed an evolution by Secondness, and Lamarck's theory of acquired characteristics formed an evolution by Thirdness, one accounting especially for human habit and culture. It is important to realize that Thirdness, or the tendency toward habit-taking, considered not simply as behavior but as generalization itself, is "a congenital tendency of the universe" and not simply a product of subjective mind. This view involves the ascription of generality to nature itself.

One of the major implications of Peirce's view was the rejection both of Darwin's idea of imperceptible variations at birth and of Lamarck's imperceptible variations through experience in favor of an account that only very recently has reemerged with new explanatory power in evolutionary theory: evolution by abrupt revolutions (see Eldredge and Gould's discussion of "punctuated equilibria" [1972]; also Gould [1977, 1983]; Eldredge and Tattersall [1982]). Let me quote at length Peirce's late nineteenth-century critique, which today seems so straightforward:

> if we can trust to the lessons of the history of the human mind, of the history of habits of life, development does not take place chiefly by imperceptible changes but by revolutions. For some cause or other trade which had been taking one route suddenly begins to take another. In consequence merchants bring new goods; and new goods make new habits. Or some invention like that of writing, or printing, or gunpowder, or the mariner's compass or the steam engine, in a comparatively short time changes men profoundly. It seems strange that we who have seen such tremendous revolutions in all the habits of men during this century should put our faith in the influence of imperceptible variations to an extent that no other age ever did. Is it because we have so little of Asiatic immovability before our eyes that we do not realize now what the conservatism of old habit really is?
>
> That habit alone can produce development I do not believe. It is catastrophe, accident, reaction which brings habit into an active condition and creates a habit of changing habits. (Peirce 1976, 142)

Peirce viewed instinct not simply as the expression of mechanical law but as a form of intelligence expressing a purposive adaptation of organism to its specific environment ("They relate in part to forces, in part to the action of minds"). He diverged not only from the empiricist view that the environment shapes us blindly according to the forces it exerts on us, but also from the Kantian view that mind only knows the world through its own faculties and therefore that its laws are autonomous. Peirce proposed a genuinely third view that accepts the basically anthropomorphic nature of the human faculties of thought, while holding that these faculties are themselves tempered by those general ideas of action that "prevail throughout the universe" and hence are transilluminations of the general order of nature rather than an autonomous realm apart from it. "Unless man have a natural bent in accordance with nature's," as Peirce said elsewhere, "he has no chance of understanding nature at all." The relative rapidity of the scientific understanding of nature in relation to the possible span of time it would take if all the possible hypotheses were to be explored randomly, was taken by Peirce as a suggestive proof of an innate tendency to make good guesses. The ability to make good guesses in the formation and choice of hypotheses was discussed in Chapter 1 as Peirce's logic of abduction. Because pragmaticism is based on the logic of abduction, it therefore "implies faith in common sense and in instinct, though only as they issue forth from the cupel-furnace of measured criticism" (CP 6.480).[3]

Peirce's views on instinct, common sense, and critical reason are expressed most clearly in his doctrine of "Critical Common-Sensism," one of his characteristically unique attempts to undercut seemingly antithetical modes of thought, in this case Scottish common-sense philosophy and Kantian critical philosophy. Peirce proposed a doctrine that could reconcile the common-sensists' claim that there are indubitable natural beliefs with the Kantian claim that all knowledge must be critically based.

Peirce's critical common-sensism admits that there are original, that is, indubitable (because uncriticized) beliefs of a general and recurrent kind, as well as indubitable acritical inferences (where, although we know that one belief has been determined by another given belief, we are not conscious that it proceeds on any general principle). Although accepting the Scottish common-sensist view, such as that of Thomas Reid, that there are original beliefs of the nature of instinct (broadly considered), critical common-sensism modifies it to include the fact that these beliefs are themselves slightly modified "under varying circumstances and in distant ages" (CP 5.498) through evolution rather than given for all time. This position holds that instinct must be *developed*, like every feature of creation (and in human terms, one could add, must be cultivated). Along with not recognizing how instincts may be modifiable in time, the common-sensists also failed to see that although instinct may be indubitably true in its proper environment, it does not remain so in the vastly extended environment of human endeavor. In other words the common-sensists failed to see "the limitations of indubitability and the consequent limitations of the jurisdiction of original belief" (CP 5.445).

The most distinctive character of the critical common-sensist, Peirce claimed, "in contrast to the old Scotch philosopher, lies in his insistence that the acritically indubitable is invariably vague" (CP 5.446). In discussing a *vague sign* as the antithetical analogue to a *general sign*, Peirce stated, "A sign is objectively *vague*, in so far as, leaving its interpretation more or less indeterminate, it reserves for some other possible sign or experience the function of completing the determination" (CP 5.505). The open-endedness of human experience, or what Max Scheler in the late 1920s called "world-

---

3. Indeed Peirce, a practitioner and innovator in many sciences, believed science in general to be based on the instincts for nutrition and reproduction, and as leading to interests in physical forces and the communication of minds respectively (CP 1.118; 6.418; 6.500).

openness" (*Weltoffenheit*), is not equivalent to the complete absence of instinct, but rather acritical indubitable instinctual truth is essentially vague in its operation; that is, it acts upon us *suggestively* rather than as a "wired-in" determination we cannot avoid. Unlike the ant or bee, we can avoid our instincts and perhaps, over time, even modify them through collective self-control. This use of self-control in modifying instinct would itself be an example of the intervention of human purposive action in the growth of evolution. Finally, the critical common-sensist possesses a high esteem for doubt, for the critical capacity, while at the same time recognizing that what one cannot doubt, one cannot argue about. Critical common-sensism, in its high esteem for the critical is "but a modification of Kantism." It is a modification that goes to the heart of Kant's philosophy, however, because "The Kantist has only to abjure from the bottom of his heart that the proposition that a thing-in-itself can, however indirectly, be conceived; and then correct the details of Kant's doctrine accordingly, and he will find himself to have become a Critical Common-Sensist" (CP 5.452). Such, briefly stated, are the principal characteristics of Peirce's critical common-sensism.[4]

Insofar as general patterns of nature are incorporated into our being, they are refracted as innate capacities or habits and also act as the acritical ground for those beliefs that make up the common sense. For example, how could one deny the place of instinct in the learning processes of early child-hood, such as sucking? And, though still in dispute, the easy facility of the

---

4. Along with the denial of "infallible introspective power into the secrets of his own heart, to know just what he believes and what he doubts," Peirce listed as other clauses of critical common-sensism that:

> there are indubitable beliefs which vary a little and but a little under varying circumstances and in distant ages; that they partake of the nature of instincts, this word being taken in a broad sense; that they concern matters within the purview of primitive man; that they are very vague indeed (such as, that fire burns) without being perfectly so; that while it may be disastrous to science for those who pursue it to think they doubt what they really believe, and still more so really to doubt what they ought to believe, yet, on the whole, neither of these is so unfavorable to science as for men of science to believe what they ought to doubt, nor even for them to think they believe what they really doubt; that a philosopher ought not to regard an important proposition as indubitable without a systematic and arduous endeavor to attain to a doubt of it, remembering that genuine doubt cannot be created by a mere effort of will, but must be compassed through experience; that while it is possible that propositions that really are indubitable, for the time being, should nevertheless be false, yet in so far as we do not doubt a proposition we cannot but regard it as perfectly true and perfectly certain; that while holding certain propositions to be each individually perfectly certain, we may and ought to think it likely that some one of them, if not more, is false.

> This is the doctrine of Critical Common-sensism, and the present pertinency of it is that a pragmaticist, to be consistent, is obliged to embrace it. (CP 5.498)

young child for acquiring language has suggested to many an innate capacity in humans to acquire language in general. The possible instinctive capacity for language in humans is inseparable from the specific linguistic cultural context in which it develops in children. The purely culturist explanation, based on a notion of arbitrary cultural codes, simply does not explain the amazing facility and ease with which language is initially acquired. But what is even more difficult for the modern consciousness to accept is the possibility that higher forms of human activity may be based on, though not reducible to, a foundation of instinct. Human culture is more than the communication of rational codes and social configurations: it involves the deepest roots of our being as well.

Where the Hobbesian/Freudian view would hold that the greatest human achievements are the most remote from instinct, and sociobiologists might hold that these achievements are merely sublimations reducible to an underlying rationalistic calculus of genetic individualism, Peirce's view implies that these achievements are frequently suggested by instinct itself, by our instinct for abduction that leads us, usually quite unself-consciously or even unconsciously, to generate wholly new ideas, feelings, hypotheses, and modes of conduct that then become scrutinized and refined by critical reflection. That vast reservoir of transhuman experience incorporated in our very physical composition is a form of deeply constituted intelligence, what might be called sensuous generality, that can generate inferences transcending the more limited realm (in a certain sense) of reflective thought. This is not to deny that the human instincts were largely developed to deal with environments vastly different from those of literate civilizations and especially of modern humanity. The insistencies of life and locality fed and tempered human instinct in the direction of greater manual dexterity and sensuous vocal utterance, toward more complex ways to touch the world and feel and communicate its significance. Yet left undirected and uncultivated, these deeper impulses could provide no guide to modern experience—they weren't meant to—and perhaps have suffered from the "modern experience" in ways deeply injurious to them. We so often think of modernity as infinitely more complex than the societies of early man, and yet, as Lewis Mumford has so eloquently shown in his two-volume, *The Myth of the Machine* (1967, 1970), modernity can also be viewed as the domination by the *Megamachine*, a system that progressively devours the diversities of human life, assimilating them into its own single standard in the name of rationality and science.

The modern tendency to regard rational cognition as the final arbiter of practical experience is pernicious in denying intelligence or reasonableness to sentiment. It makes only rational "knowing" to be our great achievement in evolution and our distinction from other creatures, when it could be argued that the human ability to *communicate feeling*, as exemplified in great works of art, especially signifies what it means to be human. Along with the idea that instinctually rooted abduction is essential to the logic of science and to the sphere of rational cognition itself, Peirce claimed that especially in those practical "topics of vital importance" sentiment should be prominent as an intelligent guide for conduct:

> Reason, anyway, is a faculty of secondary rank. Cognition is but the superficial film of the soul, while sentiment penetrates its substance. . . . reasoning has no monopoly of the process of generalization—Sentiment also generalizes itself; but the continuum which it forms instead of being like that of reason merely cognitive, superficial, or subjective . . . penetrates through the whole being of the soul, and is objective or to use a better word existant, and more than that is exsistant." (Peirce 1976, 4:xxi)

If there are instincts that produce the indubitable beliefs of common sense, then a culture that attempted to rationalize these out of existence would simply be denying the undeniable; and, as in cases of psychological denial, these beliefs would sooner or later appear precisely in the place where they were most denied, although probably in a distorted or extreme fashion. If, for example, there is an instinctive tendency for belief in God, however "God" be defined, then one can imagine a culture systematically denying that belief, say through an ideology of science, only to have the belief reappear in an inverted or disguised fashion. Perhaps the fascination in the twentieth century with achieving the ultimate transcendence of history and tradition in the arts, sciences, and politics is a good illustration; this fascination left as its paradoxical legacy only formularized dogmas of science and revolutionary art and politics. Or one could point to the appearance of the "numinous" in flying-saucer sightings or science fiction, where the Ultimate Power frequently appears in the guise of an alien traveler or through a primitive force released by scientific experimentation, symbolizing how we have deified science as the "religion" of modernity.

One might argue that the examples just mentioned only illustrate the strength of cultural tradition, and need not imply the existence of instinctive beliefs. If "God" is simply the representation of society to itself, then the dissolution of this representation may call forth something to fill the void, some newer representation of the ultimate purposes of a society, such as money or science, that can then do the significatory task of representing Significance itself. This seems true enough, as does the criticism that money and scientific ideology in the end cannot fill the void because they themselves are representations of an alienated form of culture. Yet this problem itself suggests to me that whatever is to act as a truly overarching representation of the larger totality must itself be in accord with the most general patterns of lived experience and purpose; that the same distorted culture which holds up the rational symbols of money and an ideology of science to represent the ultimate is likely to hold an abstracted view of meaning as well; that the inability to shake off the need for larger meaning, for a sense of an ultimate purpose which, although not yet completely comprehensible, nevertheless draws us on to further inquiry and celebration of its mystery, may be a sign that belief runs deeper than abstract cultural convention.

In this sense I am suggesting that we are saturated with tradition to a degree that goes beyond criticism to indubitable, yet fallible, belief. One reads this more profound sense of the depth of thought and feeling, as compared to modern hubristic rationality, in Babylonian wisdom literature:

> What seems good to one's self, is a crime before the god,
> What to one's heart seems bad, is good before one's god.
> Who may comprehend the minds of gods in heaven's depth
> The thoughts of (those) divine deep waters, who could fathom
>   them?
> How could mankind, beclouded, comprehend the ways
>   of gods? (In Jacobsen 1963, 483)

It is this question, "How could mankind, beclouded, comprehend the ways of gods?" that penetrates to the deepest layers of our being, just as it is the smug and overly self-assured answers given by religious, scientific, and political ideologies that repress this essential mystery and diminish our perceptive capacities. The Babylonian view cannot be dismissed merely as reification, or as acritical "mythic thought" (as a rationalist such as Jürgen Habermas might claim); it is rather a deeply felt sense that purpose extends beyond self-conscious cognition and even beyond cognition. One sees that "the moral law within," to use Kant's phrase, is not separate from "the starry sky above," but extends beyond a self-conscious sense of duty to include the humbleness that results from seeing "heaven's depth" as one's own. Perhaps when this century of destruction, of righteous rationality ready to ruin anything or anyone who stands in the way of its "inevitable" logic, has worked itself to its inevitable conclusion—self-destruction—perhaps then the Babylonian question, "How could mankind, beclouded, comprehend the ways of gods?" will ring with a contemporary significance for a world in ruins.

This same sense of a larger purpose animating human purpose, anthropomorphic yet not anthropocentric, is perhaps what informs William Blake's comment that:

> Man can have no idea of any thing greater than Man, as a cup cannot contain more than its capaciousness. But God is a man, not because he is so perceiv'd by man, but because he is the creator of man. (Blake 1788, 556)

Instinctive belief may be that tempered transhuman achievement of the millennia, prejudice in the literal sense, a potential resource for action need-ing cultivation to bring it to bear on the novel situations it meets. This "it," as opposed to Freud's "it" or "id," is a *general* ground for action, not simply the expression of blind, mechanical, solipsistic force.

Instincts and the common-sense beliefs they generate do need to be tempered by critical intelligence. And critical intelligence continually "out-runs" instinct and common sense, which for the higher human activities are only at the most suggestive of felt inclinations. The freedom from rigid determination by instinct is for this reason both our greatest asset and greatest liability. But by the same token a healthy culture is not one in which instinct and reason are irreconcilably opposed, as the nature-versus-culture dichotomists hold, but one in which natural tendencies could find greater expression and refinement through the forces and play of imagination acting upon the process of discursive reason as well as through rational thought and conduct.

The peculiar human ability that distinguishes us from other species is our capacity for relatively highly developed self-controlled conduct, for not only well-tempered but also generalized sentiment and that subspecies of self-controlled conduct which is self-controlled thought (or what is usually discussed as our capacity for symbolic signification). When Peirce described cognition as 'but the superficial film of the soul" (Peirce 1976, 4:xxi), he meant to counter the hubris of modern rationality that denigrates all other modes of being other than rationalistic cognition, and to reconstruct a balance of the different forms of semiosis in the conduct of life.

And what does Peirce's critical common-sensism hold as the goal of evolutionary reasonableness? It is decidedly not the rationalization of the life-world, as Jürgen Habermas's theory of communicative action (1984) might suggest, but what must strike the modern consciousness as perhaps one of the strangest of Peirce's notions, namely, the instinctualization of reason itself.

Peirce held the view that rational mind is immature mind and instinc-tual mind is mature mind, mature in the sense that it has attained harmony with experience. The maturity of instinctual mind is due to its being nearly perfectly mediated with its environment, resulting in instinctual ideas acting as true ideas, as true guides for conduct. The immaturity of rational mind, by contrast, is due to its essentially unfinished form, to its tendency throughout history, as experience has sadly shown so frequently, to overstep its bounds through uprooted abstraction and hubris. As George Rochberg has said:

> Consciousness is not definable by the rational capacity alone,
> which is only one aspect of the total ensemble whose ultimate
> mystery is memory. . . . The danger to which I have already
> alluded, of believing only in the power of reason, is that reason

> has a propensity to order that leads away from the concrete to
> the abstract and can only be brought to heel by the imagination,
> which ensures the balance and presence of living concreteness.
> (Rochberg 1984a, 202)

"Rational madness," which Rochberg contrasts with Plato's discussion of "divine madness," consists in rationality severing itself from its imaginative, instinctive, and contextualized moorings and pursuing its own abstractions as ends in themselves, paradoxically resulting in the triumph of the irrational.

Rational mind, as anthropologists have shown, is largely made possible by the prolonged immaturity of the human, both temporally in the number of years it takes to mature, and also in the relative weakness of instinct in the direct regulation of conduct. It is this plasticity of instinct that causes humans to *need* culture, to need those living patterns of meaning, as our means of completing nature and becoming fully human. Despite Peirce's admiration for instinct, he yet said:

> The instincts of the lower animals answer to their purposes much
> more unerringly than a discursive understanding could do. But
> for man discourse of reason is requisite, because men are so in-
> tensively individualistic and original that the instincts, which are
> racial ideas, become smothered in them. A deliberate logical
> faculty, therefore, has in man to take their place; and the sole
> function of this logical deliberation is to grind off the arbitrary
> and the individualistic character of thought. Hence, wherever the
> arbitrary and the individualistic is particularly prejudicial, there
> logical deliberation, or discourse of reason, must be allowed as
> much play as possible. (CP 1.178)

Peirce's reason, dedicated to "grind(ing) off the arbitrary and the indi-vidualistic character of thought," is clearly opposed to the genetic individual-ism of sociobiologists, but it is also opposed to the structuralists and other conceptualists who claim that reason is arbitrary cultural code or convention.

To claim that the goal of rational mind is to become "instinct with experience" seems to suggest that there could be an indubitable belief that is yet critical. The human capacity for inquiry, for instinctively rooted abduc-tive inference-making, as well as for critical deductive and inductive infer-ence-making, when viewed as the free communication of ideas, is perhaps one of the most frail of human achievements. Yet Peirce believed that through the continued process of cultivation the truths that guide rational inquiry can come to be rooted in our innermost being:

> And just as reasoning springs from experience, so the develope-
> ment of sentiment arises from the soul's Inward and Outward
> Experiences. Not only is it of the same nature as the develope-
> ment of cognition; but it chiefly takes place through the in-

strumentality of cognition. The soul's deeper parts can only be reached through its surface. In this way the eternal forms, that mathematics and philosophy and the other sciences make us acquainted with, will by slow percolation gradually reach the very core of one's being; and will come to influence our lives and this they will do, not because they involve truths of merely vital importance, but because they are ideal and eternal verities. (CP 1.648)

This process of "slow percolation" in which sentiment is generalized and reason is instinctualized is a task of the generations but one that has become especially crucial in our own time, as the abstractionist consequences of nominalism reach their deadly conclusion. Though our century has been a century of revolutions, their result has not been to bring about a greater emancipation throughout the world but only to plunge humanity into a world crisis of unhinged and destructive reason. The extent to which this crisis is habitualized as the modern consciousness is so great as to suggest that only through some radical transformation, through one of those truly revolutionary, and not simply ideological, acts that mark evolutionary transmutation, can humanity survive and flourish.

Peirce's view suggests nothing less than that the human destiny is to give rise to a new kind of creature for whom critical inquiry is natural, a creature whose innermost sentiment is to complete his or her personality "by melting it into the neighboring parts of the universal cosmos." This new creature is not simply a form of transcendental vegetation, incapable of real and sustained thought because lost in a pipe dream of beatific feeling, but a perceptive incarnation of a new balance. Peirce said at the end of the nineteenth century that the "supreme commandment of the Buddisto-christian religion" (a term that the provincial caryatids who tend to hold power in all organized religions would even today, and perhaps for all time, find incomprehensible) is:

to generalize, to complete the whole system even until continuity results and the distinct individuals weld together. Thus it is, that while reasoning and the science of reasoning strenuously proclaim the subordination of reasoning to sentiment, the very supreme commandment of sentiment is that man should generalize, or what the logic of relatives shows to be the same thing, should become welded into the universal continuum, which is what true reasoning consists in. But this does not reinstate reasoning, for this generalization should come about, not merely in man's cognitions, which are but the superficial film of his being, but objectively in the deepest emotional springs of his life. In fulfilling this command, man prepares himself for transmutation into a new form of life, the joyful Nirvana in which the discontinuities of his will shall have all but disappeared." (CP 1.673)

WHERE IS THE SELF?

One idea that causes no problems for many traditional peoples, but which we moderns have a great deal of trouble with, is how we can be in two places at once, how we usually are in *more* than two places at once. I intend to answer the question "Where is the self?" by exploring how the self is essentially both a sign-complex and a transaction between subject and object occurring in an environment; how it is impossible to have a subject or object without the transaction between them; and how the living self depends for its continued existence on a process of cultivation, one that can and should transcend the life of the organism.

One of the consequences of modern epistemological positions is the tendency to split the self from the environment. Western thought in the past few centuries, as mentioned earlier in connection with the culture concept, developed the strange perspective that mind is somehow identified with brain alone, locked inside the head apart from the actuality of the world. The focus of order, in this view, is to be found in the organizing principles of physiology, whether they be of natural or cultural origin, rather than in the purposive life of the community. It is usually assumed in Western culture that the self is located within the physiological organism, either within the central nervous system (Freud 1900,637f.; Piaget 1929,33) or in the actual physical be-haviors of the organism (Skinner 1953,29f.; Bandura 1969). Too often the self is taken either as a vanishing mathematical point of pure mind, apart from the material world, or as a system of interacting particles or behaviors, somehow "objective" and having nothing to do with mind or consciousness. But this is a relatively recent idea, traceable to the influence of René Des-cartes, who located the self within the *cogito,* the unity of the subjective self-consciousness. Descartes' assumptions have greatly influenced what we now take for granted about the self, and have contributed to what Herman Melville over a century ago called the "Isolato" view that is characteristic of the modern world. On the one hand the self, person, individual, personality, or whatever term is used, is seen as something apart from matter and the physical environment, echoing Descartes' radical separation of mind and body. Most modern epistemological positions support this conceptualistic view. In the social sciences, this is the view of the various cognitive and structuralist approaches of psychology and anthropology. In these views consciousness is "mentalistic" and occurs inside the head or brain of the thinker. This Cartesian view is illustrated as clearly and distinctly as possible by Piaget himself:

> Let us imagine a being, knowing nothing of the distinction be-tween mind and body. Such a being would be aware of his de-sires and feelings but his notions of self would undoubtedly be much less clear than ours. Compared with us he would experi-

ence much less sensation of the thinking self within him, the feeling of a being independent of the external world. The knowledge that we are thinking of things severs us in fact from the actual things (Piaget 1929 [1975],37).

Piaget's "imaginary" being described in this quotation is in some ways actually an approximation of the being of the self proposed here. Though knowing of some distinction between body and mind, specifically that body is both vehicle of mind and embodied mind, our being knows himself or herself to be within thought, not the reverse, and to be continuous with the external world rather than independent of it. Our being knows further that "the knowledge that we are thinking of things" in fact and in general connects us with those things. Our being knows that while the self is not simply a "thing," the Piagetian rigid separation from things would end up making it simply a mental "thing," and therefore this being agrees with Peirce's analogies between man and word:

> A man denotes whatever is the object of his attention at the moment; he connotes whatever he knows or feels of this object, and is the incarnation of this form or intelligible species; his interpretant is the future memory of this cognition, his future self, or another person he addresses, or a sentence he writes, or a child he gets. . . . There is a miserable and barbarian notion according to which a man cannot be in two places at once; as though he were a *thing!* A word may be in several places at once, Six Six, because its essence is spiritual; and I believe that a man is no whit inferior to a word in this respect. (CP 7.591)

The other side of the Cartesian separation of mind and body is perhaps best represented by behaviorism. In this perspective the self is an existent "thing," consisting of the repertoire of behaviors of an organism. Those such as Watson, Skinner, or Homans usually claim that thought and consciousness are either nonexistent or merely subjective and not capable of being measured. At best, the values, goals, and morals that might shape a person are seen as "subjective" and therefore not relevant to scientific study or to a scientific definition of the self. Underlying this view is again the Cartesian idea that scientific ideas should be at bottom "clear and distinct," and that the only clear and distinct statements that can be made about humans are those based on actual behaviors.

But where is the self? Is my self locked up in this physical structure of flesh and blood? Is it somewhere in my brain or central nervous system? If that is where my consciousness exists, then perhaps there may my self be.

Yet it is clear that the self is distinguishable from the physical organism proper. A person may lose a leg and yet the self can remain intact. A number of years ago some doctors wanted to examine Einstein's brain after he died to see what made him such an extraordinary thinker. Their conclusion was that his brain "looked pretty much like everyone else's"; it provided no clue as to how Einstein came to discover that E = mc². If you were to examine the body of Picasso and place all of his works next to the body, which would tell more about the self of Picasso? Which would actually be the truer manifestation of his self? Certainly an analysis of his works would reveal far more about the self of this great artist, and yet they are inanimate objects spatially removed from the man.

How do we know the self? It would seem that the self can be known only through the signs it gives off in communication. When a friend speaks to us, we are conversing with his or her "self" through linguistic signs. That person projects intelligently ordered sound waves into the environment which are perceived and interpeted by us. We may be speaking directly with the person, or his or her utterance may be transformed into electronic signals and back again to sound over a telephone, but in either case the communication is mediated by an environment that can transmit or temporarily store physical expressions of intelligence, signs of a self.

A self exists only in and through communication. When we think we are in a sense talking to our *selves,* our thought itself is a kind of internal dialogue. Freud, Piaget, and G. H. Mead, despite all the differences in their theories, do agree that the self develops only when other personalities become internalized and live within us as representations. This is the meaning of the Oedipus complex for Freud; it is nothing less than the creation of mediation and representation, which forms the basis for culture. Role modeling and the development of an ego-ideal is also stressed by Piaget and Mead. Role modeling enables the development of the bio-logical structures to unfold for Piaget, while in Mead's view it makes the internationalization of the norms, expectations, and goals of the community possible, and hence gives rise to the generalized other that forms the basis of the self.

But while Freud and Piaget limit the self or personality to internal cognitive processes that work themselves out on the world, Mead stresses the fact that the self arises in the course of social experience *as a transaction with the environment:*

> Our contention is that mind can never find expression, and could never have come into existence at all, except in terms of a social environment. . . . If mind is socially constituted, then the field or locus of any given individual mind must extend as far as the social activity or apparatus of social relations which constitutes it extends; and hence that field cannot be bounded by the skin of the individual organism to which it belongs. (Mead 1972, 242, 243n)

Mead's statement is strikingly similar to Georg Simmel's observation that "A person does not end with limits of his physical body or with the area to which his physical activity is immediately confined but embraces, rather, the totality of meaningful effects which emanates from him temporally and spatially" (Simmel 1971,335).

Mead, like the other pragmatists, viewed meaning not as an affair purely of the head but rather as a process of interpretation that included the object of that interpretation (cf. Peirce, CP 7.591; James 1890, 291; Dewey 1934,104). Becoming a self means becoming an object (in the broader grammatical sense) to oneself, becoming the object of one's own interpretation. If all thought is in signs, and is of the nature of an internal dialogue, then even self-knowledge is inferential and mediated by signs. Even the feeling I have of myself also acts as a qualitative sign, an inference indicating my self as its object. Photographs or other things that we identify with, or that form some part of our life-worlds, can act as signs of the self, and in so doing become parts of the self. It is important to realize, then, that the self is of the nature of a sign or complex of signs. To be a self means to be a living, embodied, objectified form of intelligence.

Thus it may not seem so far-fetched to say that things can be actual manifestations of the self. The process of becoming an "object" to oneself, which Mead, Baldwin, and others have emphasized as essential to the development of the self, occurs through a communicative medium, usually through linguistic thought-signs. But clearly gestural and tangible signs are also essential to this process, and are perhaps the only medium available to the infant before the development of language. With the appearance of language, the develoment of self-consciousness clearly shifts to linguistic symbols, but are we to suppose the gestural and artifactual levels disappear? Recent studies in kinesics and "body language" have demonstrated the importance of the gestural level even in linguistic conversations. Likewise, artifacts can serve as a medium for socialization and self-expression, and hence transactions with one's cherished possessions, either actually or symbolically, can be seen as sign expressions of the self. The person, as a complex of living, feeling, sign-habits, extends into and derives from the spatiotemporal environment through signs. The self can thus be seen as a habitual predisposition to act in accordance with certain aims while critically cultivating the aims themselves, that is, as a living, embodied rule for conduct. From a semiotic perspective, the meaning of the self does not consist in the mechanical motions it might cause—or physical behavioral patterns per se—but rather in the aims that are cultivated and realized in the physical actions, expressions, relations, and tangible signs of the self.

The absolutely individual self and falsity are one and the same, which is to say that the self arises through cultivation out of a social milieu and is intrinsically social. The psychological disorder known as "multiple personality syndrome" illustrates, though in pathological disassociation, how the self is by nature a composite, a plurality of identities, a family and a community, rather than a primordially isolated subject. Similarly, different dimensions of self can be viewed as forming different perspectives within the social medium. I will distinguish three levels of the self—the *personal, social,* and *cosmic*—and show in each case how the self extends beyond an individual existential "thing." The notion of multiple levels of self is certainly not new. William James distinguished three levels of self in his *Principles of Psychology* (the material self, the social self, and the spiritual self) that may seem similar to those drawn here. These levels constitute the "empirical me" in the dialectic of the I and the me: "Hereafter let us use the words ME and I for the empirical person and the judging thought" (James 1950 [1890],371). This is the dialectic of the self usually associated with Charles Horton Cooley and George Herbert Mead, who both acquired it from James. Similarly Cooley distinguished self-consciousness, social consciousness, and public consciousness (1909,12). But my levels are actually more influenced by the broader divisions of consciousness made by Peirce (CP 7.572–78). There he distinguishes between the *carnal, social,* and *spiritual* consciousnesses.

The first and most immediate level is the *personal self,* the awareness of our body, our own thoughts, moods and emotions, perceptions, gestural expressions, and the character of our physical being. This is what is usually called the self in most social science literature, but in my perspective it forms only one level of the self—and at that a still incomplete self. Again, even the personal self is not an absolutely immediate consciousness, perfectly "clear and distinct," but is also mediated by signs. Early socialization in infancy largely consists in building up a sense of one's own body, learning to make use of one's own limbs for movement or for grasping objects. What is being learned are rules for action, or sensuous ideas that are literally embodied in the habitual patterns of physical movement. One learns to take possession of one's own body. Out of this process develops a "body image," a "cognitive map "of oneself as a being with physical extension in space and relatively differentiated from the surroundings. The development of a sense of one's place marks the beginning of the self.

Again, this personal consciousness is not an immediate, clear, and distinct given but is inferential and mediated by signs (or rather, *is* sign mediation). A clear example of this is when a person loses a limb but still has feeling "in the limb." If you hit the area where a missing leg would be, for example, and the amputee doesn't know the leg is missing but sees you swipe at the leg, the person will experience as much pain as the force of the hit would have caused. This serves to illustrate that even consciousness of our most personal and immediate "possession," our own body, still occurs through the medium of signs.

The argument that the self can be in two or more places at the level of the personal self amounts to the following. The object of a sign is a part of that sign, is an essential element of the meaning of that sign. When the self interacts with some object, that object, or what it represents, becomes the object of that sign, the self. It is more correct to say, then, that the self is a transaction between interpreting organism and object, and in this sense is in two places. One could add that the self as transaction also includes the resultant interpretation or conceivable consequences of the transaction, and hence can be in many places. Let me illustrate this with a concrete example from my research on the meaning of household possessions. An adolescent girl talked about her cat, which, though technically not an object, is certainly a kind of possession:

> Whenever I have a problem, sometimes I go up to him and I hold him real tight and he gives me a little meow. He feels so good, he's so fluffy, and when I hold him I love to talk to him. I love cats. He's real special. . . . If I didn't have my cat, then I wouldn't have something to hold when I had a problem and I like to be alone, but then I'd really be alone. If I didn't have him then I'd be empty. There'd be a spot in me that was empty.

Obviously there is metaphoric intent in this statement, but it is also quite literally true. When this girl says that without the cat, "There'd be a spot in me that was empty" she is also literally correct, if we interpret the "me" in Mead's sense as the embodiment of the generalized other. Through a "conversation of gestures" as well as the "significant symbol" of the cat itself, the girl carries on a dialogue with her self. The animate cat as well as inanimate possessions are physical things which are animate signs of the self as well as "instruments," in Aristotle's sense (see his *Politics* bk.1,chap. 4f.), for its continued cultivation. The cat has its own inherent character as a sign. It serves to concentrate the attention of this girl and channel her emotions, and enables her to realize intentions—the goal of enjoyment or of resolution of some problem. To phrase this according to Peirce's definition of signs mentioned earlier, the cat is something which stands to this girl as a reflection of the self and its goals and problems. It creates in the mind of this girl (and "mind" is meant here as including the entire transaction) an accomplishment or emotional resolution, in Peirce's words, "a more developed sign" (see Rochberg-Halton 1985a).

When we imbue an object with qualities of our self, we literally impress our being into that object, whether it is the words we write on a page, or the chair that we fashion, or the photograph someone takes of us. These objects become objectified forms of consciousness no less than the words we speak into someone's ear, and all form a portion of the *social self*. Through these objects a part of our self comes to be embodied in the consciousness of others and can continue to exist long after our own personal consciousness has ceased. Our own personal consciousness forms only a portion of the larger social consciousness of the self. In this view, general ideas, such as a cultural tradition or a social institution, have a kind of life, and we live in them as much as they live in us. Indeed, as Peirce once wrote, just as we might say, "That bicycle is in motion" but would not say, "Motion is in that bicycle," it is more proper to say that we live in ideas than it is to say that they live in us. This means that not all consciousness is limited to single brains, but that the social consciousness, say, of a corporation, involves a *community* of brains, the body social, and that it occurs in multiple places.

The idea, and I use the term "idea" in its broadest sense, of the great Gothic cathedrals is another example. When these buildings were constructed the spirit that animated the builders could be realized only through a community of minds who thought and labored whole lifetimes to bring about the realization of the medieval mind in concrete actuality. These monuments are still living representations of the social selves who built them. Though the individuals who built them died long ago, their purpose remains alive today and speaks to us through these structures.

As Marx pointed out so clearly, human traditions and institutions easily lend themselves to reification, assuming a life of their own that can dominate us for destructive purposes. An institution that would crush the human spirit or anesthetize it is an abstract idol, a devouring Moloch. Institutions should serve human purposes, but institutional human purpose also serves a broader development of reasonableness in the Peircean realist view proposed here. Hence, though Marx was on the right track in his discussions of alienation, his statement that "The more man puts into God, the less he retains in himself" is incorrect. Substitute "the purpose of life" for "God" in this sentence and the fallacy becomes apparent. If "God" is synonymous with the purpose of life, then one gives his or her own life this purpose by cultivating and hence serving it. One might say that Marx should not have confused the real ultimate purpose with existent God-images of the times, just as one would not confuse fully humanized praxis with alienated and distorted versions of praxis.

Yet another level of self should be distinguished, the level of the *cosmic self.* I do not mean "cosmic" in any mystical sense of something transcending all human understanding in a realm beyond signs, conception, physicality, etc. Rather it is that dimension of the self whose ultimate goal or end is the larger harmony of things in general. Another way of putting it might be to say that it is the portion of the self involved in the creation, discovery, and embodiment of the laws of the universe, the cosmos, although this sounds a bit grandiose for modern man. But it is not only scientists who further the laws of the universe, for these laws—which include creation and death, love and hate, good and evil, truth and ignorance, the great moving principles of humanity—pervade all human endeavor. In this view the cosmic self is a dimension of human existence repressed by the mechanical principles underlying the modern mentality: the behaviorism of a Skinner, the "sensori-motoric" of a Piaget, the "id" or "it" of a Freud. These underlying mechanical principles deny that the "It" may include purpose as emergent possibility. This cosmic self, with its relentless and passionate questions, "What and why is It?" "Why am I here?" is the essence of both religion and science. It is the manifestation of the inquisitive nature of mankind. We are so used to thinking of religion and science as providing authority or final answers that we forget both are, in essence, manifestations of humanity's need *to question the universe* and discover its meaning. The cosmic self is that portion of the self which merges in sympathy with one's neighbors to express or inquire into the glory of creation. It praises the personification of creation, the creator, through acts which express the full potential of that ultimate purpose toward which they are aimed. When this occurs the cosmic self can be said to become creation, creating. Creaturing might be another term to express this, since the creation is "bodied" and personified, say, as a work of art, a work of imaginative projection concretized with a fully realized personality. The "highest business and duty" of the cosmic self is to recognize, "a generalized conception of duty which completes your personality by melting it into the neighboring parts of the universal cosmos" (CP 1.674). The "highest business and duty" of the modern self, by contrast, has been an isolating and privatized self-interest under the banner of rationalization. Needless to say, the dimension of the cosmic self, so essential to the origin and development of humanity, and to our destiny if Peirce is correct, is in a state of advanced atrophy in that hubris of individualism (including the collectivist antithesis wherein the state becomes a ruthless and dominating individual) which is modern culture.

In defining the cosmic self this way, I am proposing a radically different approach to meaning than those theories which have been most important in modern social science and epistemology. I am claiming that the cosmic self, in seeking to answer "What and why is It?" and "Why am I here?" can become part of the larger totality of meaning; that is, I am ascribing purpose or meaning to "It." "It" is the total cosmic configuration of which we are all partial elements, but interconnecting and interrelating elements. This is the "foundation" of Peirce's theory of reality and of the philosophy of scholastic realism he adapted to his own purposes. It means that reality itself is a "general" or sign, rather than a thing outside of signs.

The cosmic self has for its object the cosmos, the intelligible universe, and the more one cultivates this self the more one becomes a manifestation of the laws of the universe, the more one is *in* the universe. Where is the cosmic self? The answer may seem strange, but it is *in* the universe, and becomes increasingly so the more it develops. The cosmic self increasingly becomes a *microcosmos,* through giving embodiment to the laws of the universe in particular ways, and for this reason can be said to be our immortal self.

If there are rights of possession for these three levels of self, they are that we possess our personal self, we are copossessors of the social self, and we are possessed by the cosmic self. It "possesses" us by inspiring the broadest possibilities for the development and cultivation of the self, by introducing us to the wider patterns of order in the intelligible world which become personified through us.

The modern world seems not to believe in the possibility of a cosmos; it sees instead two worlds: one a steam engine whose destination lies at the end of a fixed track, and the other the "rational" world of mankind, which imposes its own order, as it wills, onto the world of nature. The result is that the self, that living, embodied, personalized and objectified form of intelligence, has a split existence, either apart from its body and environment or apart from its mind and soul. It becomes possible to reconcile the split by showing how purpose and meaning "extend into" or, rather, involve, the environment as a process of cultivation between subject and object, a process that implies a renewed version of animism, a critical animism of signs that links us with the generalized objects of experience, with the broader transhuman patterns of meaning, and with those humanized creations that are the task of culture to create.

The Further Reaches of Semiosis: Seeds for a New Cultural Order

Peirce's proposal for a new balance of critical reason and sentiment implies nothing less than "a transmutation into a new form of life" involving a radically new conception of culture and self, one in which our immature and deadly playing with symbolic signs in the name of abstractionism (in its conceptualistic and even positivistic guises) is matured into a much broader horizon of semiosis, one recognizing that our own sign-nature resonates with, and is embedded in, the larger sign-nature of nature itself. One need not go all the way with Peirce, however, to see that the abstractionist tendencies of modern culture, which are also reflected in most contemporary theories of culture, involve many self-defeating and even destructive consequences.

The tyranny of the rational is a diabolical one that grows more irrational as it pervades all dimensions of life. But reason does not, as Weber seems to have thought, necessarily lead to the iron cage of a completely rationalized existence. Only a distorted version of reason, rooted in nominalism and its tendency to divide what is continuous into discrete parts and then to call the part the whole, could found the rational on an irrational basis, so that the more the rational grows, the less rational are its consequences. Only a nominalistically rooted reason would see the obliteration of tradition and unreflective action as necessary to an ultimate goal of totalized rationality.

If we turn to human sensuous activity or practice in the ways it is usually practiced we note at every level, from the most simple to the most abstract, that the unself-conscious act precede the self-conscious reflection. Yet rationalistic theory, such as that of Jürgen Habermas (1981, 1984), tends to concentrate only on the latter, reflective aspect as "communicative" and, in doing this, destroys the rightful place of unquestioned assumptions as the ground of action.

The tendency to make explicit the unexamined, when carried to an extreme, can become quite self-conscious in the everyday sense, creating a paralysis of conduct. Yet one of the most essential features of a thriving culture is precisely the opposite tendency: the unself-conscious expression of new forms of activity. Vital cultures are frequently characterized by the unself-conscious immersion of their members in a larger motivating attitude, one that charges the culture with an animating energy that only gradually becomes reflected upon. How to tap that transilluminative energy, while simultaneously renewing critical intelligence, is perhaps the central problem of our time.

Culture is more than abstract rational code or arbitrary conventions; it is a living sign-process of cultivation involving not only multiple modes of being but multiple modes of sign-being. Cultivation in the first mode involves the inherent quality (or what was discussed in Chapter 2 as qualitative immediacy) of sign-practices. This includes the unique character not only of cultural products but of those other sign-complexes that are individual selves, institutions, or even a whole people. The prominent mode of communication at this level is the qualitative communication of feeling or sentiment, which, though general, is noncognitive. The reality of imagination as generative source of cultural life is a central fact of this domain. The repression of this domain is a central fact of our time.

Cultivation in the second mode is existence, that genuine otherness which tempers us to come into accord with our surroundings and challenges us to better them. The willingness to live on in the face of seemingly insuperable obstacles is culture in the second mode. The prominent mode of communication at this level is volitional or energetic: in a living culture it is the energy that can move mountains.

Cultivation in the third mode is the generalization, and generation, of real law through those symbol-practices by which it is conveyed. Just as all humans are living symbols, all real symbols are living beings, animated by, and in turn animating, individual and collective human existence. This is the sense in which Samuel Taylor Coleridge could say: "For if words are not THINGS, they are LIVING POWERS, by which the things of most importance to mankind are actuated, combined and humanized" (Coleridge 1960, 1:128). The prominent mode of communication at the third level is the cultivation of symbols, the reciprocal giving of life through intelligible conduct to symbolic forms and the giving to human life of the larger meanings that the symbols in turn convey.

Through the cultivation of symbols we make intelligible the larger patterns of reasonableness, whether in rational, moral, or aesthetic forms. It is the task of cultivation to humanize these forms, not to give them over to those inhuman tendencies in ourselves and our institutions that seek unbalanced domination; and also to realize that to be fully human is to be cosmically rooted: we serve a mysterious unfolding of reasonableness that is, in the long run, larger than the human race.

It is in this growth of reasonableness in all its fullness that the human essence is rooted, but it is in the uncontrolled spread of rationality that modernity is rooted; a rationality that denies the validity of other forms of intelligence that are its own sources, in the name of "reason alone." The modern culture of nominalism has undercut instinct, common sense, and the reasonableness of sentiment to such an extent as to virtually insure, as the epigraphs by Reid and Blake at the beginning of this chapter suggest, our imminent extinction at the hands of unhinged reason. Our great hope to avoid this fate lies not so much in a piecemeal change as in a radical transformation comparable in scope to that of the "axial age" proposed by Karl Jaspers. In short, as Lewis Mumford said in 1956, "the moment for another great historic transformation has come" (1956,138). Evolution in general and human evolution in particular are marked not simply by slow cumulative growth but also by those incandescent transformations that mark a radical redirection. Let us hope that that mercurial essence of which we arrogantly proud moderns seem so ignorant might yet assert itself purposively for a new epoch.

IV *Meaning, Materialism, Metropolis,*
and Modernism

7   Object Relations, Role Models, and Cultivation

And some certain significance lurks in all things, else all things are little worth, and the round world itself but an empty cipher, except to sell by the cartload, as they do hills about Boston, to fill up some morass in the Milky Way.

Herman Melville, *Moby Dick*

Two of the most significant developments in the social sciences in the past decade and a half are the emergence of environmental studies, broadly defined, and the turn toward "symbolic" studies, or semiotics, again broadly defined. Perhaps in reaction to what C. Wright Mills termed the "abstracted empiricism" of mainstream post–World War II social and psychological research, environmental and symbolic studies have provided new contexts in which to analyze social life, and multidisciplinary perspectives to counter those fragmenting tendencies that always threaten to reduce living inquiry to dead world-play.

One criticism that might be directed against each of these trends, at least until recently, is the tendency to ignore or deny what the other assumes: environmentalists, even those in the field of "cognitive mapping," often tend not to fully appreciate the claim of the "symbolists" that all human behavior, perception, consciousness, and environments form a web of signs, whereas symbolists often tend not to fully appreciate how signs are rooted in *some* environment, not a mentalistic netherworld. What is needed is an approach that can reconcile what amounts to, roughly, the old materialist-idealist dichotomy. Such an approach, it seems to me, can be culled from the insights of the philosophical pragmatists and early "Chicago" sociologists (such as Charles Horton Cooley, who in fact taught at the University of Michigan).

I will consider two very different approaches to meaning, classic psychoanalytic "object relations" theory and pragmatic sociology.[1] Both

1. I am using the term "pragmatic sociology" instead of "symbolic interactionism." Much recent work in symbolic interactionism exaggerates a subjectivist approach to the "definition" of

emphasize the mediating role of representations in the socialization process, yet the relationship between the external environment and the constitution of these representations is quite different in the two approaches. The inherent subjectivism of the Freudian tradition is criticized through an examination of the role of personal possessions in the objectification of self; that is, we will see how material objects serve as important signs of the process of *cultivation*, and how they *literally* act as role models to reveal goals and values, and serve as means to realize those aims. I hope to show how Freudian object-relations theory undervalues the external environment ultimately through a misconceived understanding of the reflex arc concept, and how the pragmatic understanding of the reflex arc and the internalization of role models provides a corrective that includes external things as real signs of the self. Finally, I will explore the implications of pragmatic sign theory for the field of cognitive mapping.

One would think a theory calling itself "object relations" would be primarily concerned with objects, and it seems strange upon reflection that the psychoanalytic theory of object relations refers to people and not objects. Those who use this term habitually never think twice about it, assuming as a matter of course that "object relations" means the representation of *persons*, the development of an inner system of representations that mediates between the raw impulses of the unconscious and the outer world. In the area of socialization the "object" refers to some socializing figure, loved one, or role model, usually a parent. A "role model" commonly means a person who acts as an influence on one's future conduct. But if we reflect on *this* term, it becomes obvious that a role model is not necessarily an actual person. The word "role" is taken from the theater, as is the word "person" (which in Greek originally meant the mask worn by an actor), and derives from a physical object, the "roll" or paper on which an actor's part was written, which was a script for conduct. Most people would agree that some of the most influential role models are not actually living persons but fictional *characters*, such as Oedipus, Hamlet, Superman, Wonder Woman, and even R2D2 of *Star Wars*, the sublimated version of Toto, Dorothy's "transitional object"—the only "object" who accompanied her in her adolescent separation fantasy to Oz. These fictional characters *personify* the role, endowing it with the quality of personhood. Similarly, other social roles, such as fireman or teacher, may be personified by specific individuals, real or fictional, and act as a general "script for conduct" not reducible solely to those individuals. Just as fictional characters constitute some of the most essential role models, it can also be argued that physical objects, such as possessions, also act as essential models for certain roles in the socialization process. A toy rocket, a

---

situations, and this subjectivism seems to me to diverge radically from the more integrated perspectives of the earlier "school" (Rochberg-Halton 1983a).

dollhouse, or a video game can indicate to a child certain values of the culture, which can be personified and internalized through fantasy and play activities.

What is necessary for someone or something to act as a role model is that it must *represent* something to someone. A role model is *representative* of the values of a culture; to put it in semiotic terms: a role model is a *representation* or sign. The terms "sign" and "symbol" are weasel words these days. Not only are there a plethora of theories of symbolism, but these theories tend to use the terms "sign" and "symbol" differently, producing what must seem to the uninitiated to be a veritable Babel of signs. I follow here, as in previous chapters, Peirce's use of sign as the most general term, and symbol as one kind of sign, that which is related to its object by convention (CP, vol. 2). By *sign* I mean simply *that which represents something to someone*. Signs are representations, and what they represent may be any-thing—qualities, physicality, or other signs. In one sense signs are vehicles for our emotions and thoughts, but they are even more than that, they are the very medium of emotion and thought. In saying that signs represent some-thing *to someone*, I want to emphasize that the sign is a kind of *dialogue*. Each and every sign is not only an interpretation of what has happened, but also represents itself to further interpretation. A sign, then, represents something to someone, and in so doing acts as a communicative dialogue within an objective web of meaning.

Indeed "representativeness" is the primary meaning of the term "role model" for George Herbert Mead: it is a representation or sign of the social norms or "attitudes" of the community that become internalized as the *generalized other*. A hero or parent can symbolize through their actions how one should behave or should not behave. An inanimate book also can impart similar information through the signs it conveys. This is precisely what Mead implied when he said that inanimate objects could serve as elements of the generalized other: "It is possible for inanimate objects, no less than for other human organisms, to form parts of the generalized and organized—the completely socialized—other for any given human individual. . . . *Any-thing—any object or set of objects, whether animate or inanimate, human or animal, or merely physical*—toward which he acts, or to which he responds, socially, is an element in what for him is the generalized other; by taking the attitudes of which toward himself he becomes conscious of himself as an object or individual and thus develops a self or personality" (Mead 1934, 154n; emphasis added).

In Mead's view the self originates through assuming the role of "the other," first specific others and gradually the generalized other of the group or community. Mead's original sense of roles and role models as elements of the *generalized* other, and hence personified symbols of community life, has become narrowed, so that now social scientists tend to emphasize the be-havioral patterns of an actual person as constituting a "role model," consequently ignoring the fact that Mead includes "any object" or "set of objects" as having this power as well. Yet just as there are "personified" role models, there can be "objectified" role models. The importance of a role model in Mead's perspective lies in its *representativeness as a sign*, and an inanimate doll can symbolize the role of mother or father to a child just as an animate person can; a musical instrument can symbolize the role of musician just as, in other contexts, a musician can. In other words, objects can *objectify* the self. In telling us who we are, what we do, and who and what we might become, things can act as signs of the self and as role models for its continued cultivation.

This representative ability of role models brings us back to object relations, or the mental representation of others. The term *object relations* is itself an abbreviation for something like "relations with the objects of representations." It essentially refers to an internal process, to an internal representation that in Freud's view was the object of "cathexis," i.e., the object onto which psychic energy or "libido" was discharged. Freud's approach is summarized in a recent article on object relations by analyst Jacob Arlow:

> It was in connection with Freud's revolutionary approach to the subject of sex and love that he developed the concept of the object. Discussing the nature of the energy of the erotic drive, the libido, Freud (1905) distinguished between the zone of origin of the libido, the aim of the libidinal instinct, and the object of the instinct. It is upon the object that the libido is discharged and this process of discharge is experienced as pleasure. He said that the object is the *mental* representation of something which is the source of intense libidinal gratification, something highly cathected with libido. The mental representation grows out of a mnemic image . . . . it should be emphasized, we are dealing with technical terms, the concept of a *mental* representation. According to libido theory, it is not the external thing which is vested with energy; it is the mental representation of the thing or person so cathected. (Arlow 1980, 112–13)

Clearly the emphasis is on an internal idea rather than an external thing. The concept of object relations highlights the need of individuals to develop interpretative schemes in order to function in the first place; more especially, it shows how interactions with others are based on inner mental representations quite often at odds with the real attributes of the other and ultimately rooted in the underlying biologically based needs of the psyche. The external other is essential to the development of the self in this view, but is a secondary development, an accretion on the underlying intrapsychic foundations. Ultimately the external world only amounts to the raw perceptual impressions of the individual's sensory field, and for this reason psychoanalysis places a theoretical wall between the self and the surrounding world of people and things, which appear ultimately in Freud's metapsychology merely as discrete "arrows" of perceptual input (Freud 1900, 576–80; see Basch's [1976] powerful criticism of Freud's metapsychology and theory of perception).

Freud wrote many sensitive case studies of patients, historical figures, and himself, yet these seem to me, in the end, to do an injustice to the real social world in which experience occurs, by ultimately grounding meaning in an underlying private world of the unconscious. In Freud's view the actual existing environment itself is a faceless stimulus field; the real stuff goes on in what could be called the "cognitive functioning of the genitals," that is, in the libidinally determined mental representations of objects. Consciousness never actually *touches* the world surrounding it, but only projects its vital fluid of libido, as it were, onto that world.

The Freudian view of representation, elaborated in Freud's metapsychological Chapter 7 of *The Interpretation of Dreams*, is based on the reflex arc concept of the nineteenth century, the traditional stimulus-response account of human behavior. In part B of Chapter 7 on regression, Freud says: "All our psychical activity starts from stimuli (whether internal or external) and ends in innervations. Accordingly, we shall ascribe a sensory and a motor end to the apparatus. At the sensory end there lies a system which receives perceptions; at the motor end there lies another, which opens the gateway to motor activity. Psychical processes advance in general from the perceptual end to the motor end. Reflex processes remain in the model of every psychical function" (Freud [1900] 1962, 575–76).

The reflex arc concept is based on three distinct elements: (1) sensory stimulus or input, (2) central idea or activity, ranging from memory images to mental representations, and (3) motor discharge, or in more contemporary terms, response. Four years before Freud published *The Interpretation of Dreams*, John Dewey criticized the reflex arc concept in his landmark article of 1896, "The Reflex Arc Concept in Psychology," as a fundamentally untenable account of psychic behavior:

> The result is that the reflex arc idea leaves us with a disjointed psychology, whether viewed from the standpoint of development in the individual or in the race, or from that of the analysis of the mature consciousness. As to the former, in its failure to see that the arc of which it talks is virtually a circuit, a continual reconstitution, it breaks continuity and leaves us nothing but a series of jerks, the origin of each jerk to be sought outside the process of experience itself, in either an external pressure of "environment," or else in an unaccountable spontaneous variation from within the "soul" or the "organism." (Dewey 1896, 42).

Freud makes use of the latter explanation, variation from within the organism, through the concept of psychic energy as libido, a sort of *élan vital*, a force that gives meaning and purpose to the act but is itself outside of meaning and purpose and the specific context of the act itself.

The problem with the nineteenth-century concept of the reflex arc is that it conceives of each of the three stages as independent units only externally related to the others (Bernstein 1967, 15–19) and essentially unaffected by the specific context, that is, the "environment," in which they occur. Dewey's criticism is that the concept grossly distorts the reality of purposive behavior in seeing the stimulus as a decontextualized, raw starting point, in seeing the central idea as disembodied psychic entity, and in seeing the motor discharge as purely mechanical activity. The concept thus retains "a mixed materialistic-spiritualistic assumption" (Dewey 1896, 47) that falsely dichotomizes experience. Against this conception Dewey argued that the three independent units should be reconceived as functional phases within specific environing situations. A response in one context can serve as a stimulus in another, and all stimuli are contextualized within the act. Dewey proposed that the reflex arc concept should be reconceived as organic coordination, in which the purposive concrete act is the starting point. One of the implications of Dewey's argument, which grew into his mature formulations of pragmatism, is that "psychic behavior," that which forms the self, is an organized coordination that includes the external object, representation, and resultant conduct as interdependent phases, thus linking self and world.

Freud stressed a mechanistic energy-based definition of psychic energy, in which the mentalistic "psychic" component is reducible ultimately to mechanistic determinants. These a-priori determinants provide the Cartesian foundation for the apparatus of the self, a self ultimately divided internally, and also clearly and distinctly separated from the actual object.

Where Descartes saw human bodies as machines animated by soul or rational capacities, Freud saw the sexually based libido as the animating principle. Freud, like his Vienna contemporaries, overturned traditional values and made the low the high and the means the end, just as Arnold Schoenberg raised dissonance to an end in music and Adolph Loos stripped away ornamentation in architecture so that function became the single valid definition of a good house or office building.

As Schorske (1980) has so vividly shown, the decadent culture of Vienna at the turn of the century retreated from the public sphere that had been its central focus since the building of the Ringstrasse in the 1860s, to a more subjective world symbolized by the garden of an inner courtyard. In the chapter titled "Politics and Patricide in *The Interpretation of Dreams*," Schorske analyses Freud's own dreams using politics, instead of sex, as the ground for interpretation. He shows how Freud, too, confronted with rising anti-Semitism in the 1890s that hurt his career, developed a theory of psychology that reduced the social realm of public life to an epiphenomenon of the subjective psyche. A curious point of urban intellectual history is that Dewey, who at the same time was using the nineteenth-century reflex arc as a basis (albeit a negative one) for a new functional psychology, went in the opposite direction from Freud, in large part from his interaction in Chicago with Jane Addams and Hull House, and Dewey's own "lab school": from neo-Hegelian idealism to a view that saw the self as fundamentally immersed in the environment of social life and only derivately individual. Like Peirce and Mead, Dewey developed a view that saw the individual as an achievement of the social process rather than a precondition to it.

Rephrasing the reflex arc discussion in a broader context, we have the basic Cartesian problem of how to bring together an independent mental subject and a physical object. Against the Cartesian assumption of a mental subject and an external object needing to be brought together or mediated, the pragmatists began with the process of sign-mediation, from which could be *prescinded* a subject or object. In this view even the impulses of instinctual life are purposive products of social life, rather than Hobbesian asocial and even antisocial needs. The self is a living, feeling, sign-complex continuous with its environment of signs.

From the Deweyan view it is more accurate to give the psychic component of "psychic energy" its full due and to see it arising in the context of the environmentally situated interpretative act—which Dewey called "organic coordination" and much later in his philosophy "transactions" (Dewey and Bentley, 1949),[2] what Peirce termed the "sign" (CP 1931–35, vol. 2; Singer 1980; Part II of this book), what Mead characterized as "the act" (1938), and what I have designated as "cultivation." By cultivation, I mean the web of meaning that is medium for the self and that is not merely a noun, "culture," not merely a static, conventional "system of symbols," but is an active process of interpretation reciprocally requiring care and inquiry and endowing one in return with the broader perspective of community life. Because the self-controlled intelligence that constitutes mind, or the psyche, only arises as a result of cultivation, it is incorrect to posit an a-priori energy element apart from its context in mind. Indeed culture, considered as cultivation, is itself "psychic energy," because it provides the "moods and motivations" (Geertz 1973, 94f.), the ultimate goals, to inspire an individual or

---

2. By "transaction" Dewey meant that the elements of any act of intelligence are not determined as independent entities but only gain their status as elements in and through the act itself. In the words of Richard Bernstein:

> From a transactional perspective, an "element" is a functional unit that gains its specific character from the role that it plays in the transaction. From this perspective, it is the transaction that is primary. A transaction does not occur with an aggregate or combination of elements that have an independent existence. On the contrary, what counts as an "element" is dependent on its function within a transaction. (Bernstein 1967, 83)

group to a given course of action. The mistake of the Freudian and many "cognitive" approaches, not to mention bioreductionistic schools, is to conceive of mind only as individual and inside the person, for in many ways it is we who live *in mind* and not the reverse. The meaning of the self is to be found in its contributions to the community of discourse, both externalized and internalized, and not in its alleged foundations through what Paul Ricoeur has referred to as Freud's "archaeology of the subject" (Ricoeur 1978, 169–83).

Charles Horton Cooley also addressed the role of "object relations" from his own perspective at approximately the same time as Freud, in 1902 (Cooley 1964, 187f.), but saw the representation as ultimately a social dialogue rather than as an individual image. In the views of Cooley, James Mark Baldwin, Dewey, Mead, and others in the American social psychological tradition, the essence of the self consists in a communicative relationship with its object, a relationship that includes the real social object as well as its representation in mind. The self grows through a progressive internalization of the empathic, gestural, and verbal dialogues it carries on with its surroundings, and for this reason the foundation of the self is seen as a social self-dialogue, rather than an asocial reactor core of libido. In Cooley's words:

> The imaginary dialogue passes beyond the thinking aloud of little children into something more elaborate, reticent, and sophisticated; but it never ceases. Grown people, like children, are usually unconscious of these dialogues; as we get older we cease, for the most part, to carry them on out loud. . . . But, speaking broadly, it is true of adults as it is of children, that the mind lives in perpetual conversation. (Cooley 1964, 89)

One consequence of the Freudian approach is to see the meaning of a possession, like that of a dream, not in its *manifest* content but only in its underlying *latent* content (1900, 311). Although there have been some recent developments in psychoanalytic theory, such as the greater emphasis on the transference relationship in therapy (when the patient projects strong emotions onto the therapist [see Basch 1980 for a lucid discussion]), which seem to be correctives to the intrinsic subjectivism of the Freudian legacy, an adequate view of mind would still demand that more be said on behalf of the physical object and concrete world.

One of the limitations in the various psychoanalytic perspectives is that there is no room for aesthetic experience, that is, the experience of the inherent qualities of things. Whatever characteristics things do possess are always "translatable" into the previous experiences of the experiencer and an underlying sexual component, ultimately, some form of the "pleasure principle." For all of its Viennese emphasis on fantasy life, psychoanalysis remains a variant of English utilitarianism, not recognizing fantasy in its own right but only as a servant of Jeremy Benthams's ultimate masters, pleasure and pain: "Nature has placed mankind under the governance of two sovereign masters, *pain* and *pleasure*. It is for them alone to point out what we ought to do, as well as to determine what we shall do" (Bentham 1948, 1).

It must be stressed that artifacts in a certain sense do have a "purpose" of their own. Objects have a definite character or inherent quality that will have an influence on the possessor and that is realized through the transaction of person and thing. And as Marx (1978, 71, 150) pointed out, we do in fact invest external things with psychic energy through our labor. The product of our labor is the external representation of that labor, whether it be our professional work, a shelf that we make at home, or a plant that we tend. Through our transactions with these things we cultivate the self, and these things are representations of the self, just as the words one utters or the thoughts and emotions one has are representations of the self. Transactions with cherished possessions are communicative dialogues with ourselves. As Charles Horton Cooley or George Herbert Mead might say, we engage in "conversations" through these signs, communicating with internalized representations of community life, the "generalized other," embodied in the objects of the home environment. In this sense the home is a sign-practice, a craft to be cultivated. It forms an important part of both the individual and family self, as well as representing the wider culture. Just how external things carry a world of meaning not reducible to the dynamics of the individual psyche will become even clearer if we examine the role of possessions in everyday life.

SELF POSSESSIONS

The limitations of a mentalistic theory of representation and socialization, such as psychoanalytic object-relations theory, structuralism, or even recent tendencies in "cognitive mapping," as I will argue later, became very apparent in my empirical study of household possessions (for an extended discussion see Rochberg-Halton 1979a and the enlarged and published version of my dissertation, Csikszentmihalyi and Rochberg-Halton 1981). The views of everyday life as a fragile surface crust just waiting for *parapraxis* (i.e., a "Freudian slip") to allow preconscious materials to intrude (see Freud 1953, 6), or as meaningless "surface level," dominated by the codes and conventions of the "deep structure" (Barthes 1977; Baudrillard 1981), were simply inadequate to explain what I observed. In interviewing families about their most special belongings, I soon could see that meaning also resides *in* experience not only underneath it, and that "codes" are tempered by their specific embodiments. On the one hand, many possessions legitimized by cultural codes, such as high-status appliances, "lowbrow" or "highbrow" furniture, etc., although possibly present in a household, simply were not highly regarded in a respondent's hierarchy of values; on the other hand, seemingly idiosyncratic objects, or common objects that held idiosyncratic meanings, could assume profound significance because of their relation to personal experiences of the respondent.[3] The purpose of interviewing whole families was to map out a comprehensive view of the cultural environments people create in their homes at different stages of the life cycle, both to give order to their lives and to express what they consider significant in their lives. What was discovered was that different family members often inhabit vastly different symbolic environments even while living in the same household.

The interviewing was conducted in 1977 and was based on a socioeconomically stratified sample of 82 three-generation families, comprising 315 respondents, in Evanston and north Chicago. To the extent possible, both parents, one child, and one grandparent were interviewed, usually in the home of the respondents. Along with questions concerning admired persons, community symbols, and important life-events, a number of questions regarding possessions were asked, including what things in the home were "special" and why, what it would mean not to have the possession, when and how the object was acquired, and where it was located. The word "special" in the question represented an intentional use of *methodological vagueness*. In leaving the precise meaning of "special" to be determined by the respondent, one could then code the respondent's own valuations of the object as data without predetermining them; for example, the object was special because it was a memento, it was expensive or functional, it was a gift, etc.

Although an inventory of living-room objects was also made, following Laumann and House (1970) and earlier studies (Chapin 1935; Goffman 1949; Junker 1954; and Davis 1955), it is important to realize that the primary data were based on what the respondent *selected* from the household environment as most special. The inventory approaches tend to illustrate how social-class structure is reflected in the kinds, styles, and arrangements of living-room objects, and although this information is useful, it certainly does not exhaust the range of meanings present in the symbolic ecology of the household. One of the interesting findings of my study, in fact, was how few class differences appeared. Despite a sample stratified into upper-middle and low-middle classes, and households whose contents reflected different economic buying powers and status codes, there were very few class differences in the kinds of things selected as "special." It appears that when the question of *having* is shifted to that of *meaning*, many class differences collapse, so

3. Erving Goffman, whose master's thesis (1949) involved an analysis of living-room objects, remarked in conversation in his kitchen in 1979 that the things that meant the most to him in his own home were the unique and irreplaceable objects he had found over the years in flea markets, antique stores, and junk shops. Many of Goffman's numerous examples in his works share this same quality of uniqueness, and perhaps it is not entirely off the mark to suggest that both his possessions and examples embodied his concern for meticulous observation of everyday life.

that, for example, "upper" and "lower" can both mention things such as inexpensive photos, or an old couch, that provide tangible signs of one's life-experiences or those of one's family.

Perhaps the central finding was the shift over the life-span from an emphasis on objects of *kinetic interaction* in youth to an increasing emphasis on objects of *contemplative memory* (see table 7.1). The most dramatic difference between generations is that children tend to be attached to things that involve kinetic interaction, such as stereos, musical instruments, pets, sports equipment, vehicles, refrigerators, and stuffed animals. All of these objects usually require some physical manipulation to release their meaning. Grandparents, by contrast, single out things that do not necessarily have to be touched to release a wealth of associations, thus allowing for contemplation: photographs, books, painting, sculpture, plateware, silverware, etc. Stereos and photos best reflect the kinetic interaction versus contemplative memory distinction that characterizes age-related differences. Almost half (46 percent) of all children named a stereo as one of their most special objects, compared to 18 percent of parents and only 6 percent of grandparents (chi square 40.62, p.<0001). Table 7.1 shows how this pattern is reversed for photographs, where 37 percent of grandparents mentioned at least one photo, compared to 22 percent of parents and 10 percent of children (p.<0002). Most children who mentioned a stereo cherish it as a means of

TABLE 7.1   Special Objects Mentioned at Least Once by Respondents of Three Different Generations

Children (N = 79)	% Mentioned	Parents (N = 150)	% Mentioned	Grandparents (N = 86)	% Mentioned
1. Stereos	45.6	1. Furniture	38.1	1. Photos	
2. TV	36.7	2. Visual art	36.7	2. Furniture	
3. Furniture	32.9	3. Sculpture	26.7	3. Books	
4. Musical inst.	31.6	4. Books	24.0	4. TV	
5. Beds	29.1	5. Musical inst.	22.7	5. Visual art	
6. Pets	24.1	6. Photos	22.0	6. Plates	
7. Miscellaneous	20.3	7. Plants	19.3		
8. Sports equipment	17.7	8. Stereos	18.0		
9. Collectibles	17.7	9. Appliances	17.3		
10. Books	15.2	10. Miscellaneous	16.7		
11. Vehicles	12.7	11. Plates	14.7		
12. Radios	11.4	12. Collectibles	12.0		
13. Refrigerators	11.4	13. TV	11.3		
14. Stuffed animals	11.4	14. Glass	11.3		
15. Clothes	10.1	15. Jewelry	11.3		
16. Photos	10.1				

hearing their records and creating moods (usually with rock-and-roll music—"rock and roll" suggesting "kinetic," even "frenetic"). Photos, by contrast, are often described as "irreplaceable" by older respondents. The qualities of the photos themselves include moods of remembrance of particular occasions for older people. Stereos and photos are thus objects well suited to induce sentimental moods, and perhaps they are so highly regarded by children and grandparents respectively because they can induce moods in ways that are felt to be appropriate to meet the inner needs of children for lively activity and of the aged for reminiscence.

The inherent qualities of photographs and stereos also reflect the different senses of time and significance between youth and the aged. A photo is a completed object; it can take on new meanings only in reflection, as the possessor compares those present in the photo with a current situation. But a stereo system can take on new meanings with each new record played, since its function is to serve as a medium for music. The stereo thus acts as a vehicle through which adolescents can "try on" a continuous series of identities, easily discarding last month's favored musical role models for new ones that, for a very brief time perhaps, express the "ultimate." Although the form of pop music may represent a narrowly prescribed and banal commercial marketing code, it still remains important to realize how the stereo record and tape system has possibilities in its object-character that lends itself to the meaning needs of youth. Thus not only were there inner needs of youth for action, and of the aged for reminiscence, but these needs could best be cultivated through objects which inherently possessed the appropriate means for meaning.

Not only the *kinds* of objects mentioned share this distinction between action and contemplation-orientations, but also the *meanings* associated with special things. The youngest generation emphasized the ongoing experience that the object provides, its context in some kind of activity, or the enjoyment or release it makes possible. The meanings of these things also tend to be much more egocentric, whereas with age in adulthood, memories evoked by belongings become the dominant meaning, and significant other people become increasingly associated with one's possessions, suggesting widening boundaries of self.

Household artifacts do not exist atomistically, except perhaps in a museum display; rather they form part of a gestalt for the people who live with them, a gestalt that both communicates a sense of "home" and differentiates the types of activities that might be more appropriate for one part of the home than for another. Hence the meanings of the things one values are not limited to the individual object itself but also include the spatial context in which the object is placed, forming a domain of personal territoriality. In other words the background context or gestalt of the thing also communicates something, and the results show how different rooms in the household reveal different conceptions of self.

Approximately half the special objects of children of ages eight to fourteen are located in their own bedrooms. The importance of the bedroom then continuously declines into adulthood, to a point where an average of 11 percent of the respondent's special objects are found there, and then becomes more important in old age, when about 24 percent of the special possessions of respondents over seventy years old are again located in the bedroom (see table 7.2).

The bedroom was generally valued by respondents of all ages as a space providing autonomy. For children it is a private area that gives a greater feeling of control over activities and objects than other rooms and thus is a place where autonomy itself can be cultivated through "dialogues" with the self, mediated by cherished possessions. Because children place a higher value on action-objects that hold predominantly egocentric meanings, it is more important that they be physically surrounded in the same room where they sleep and spend time in play and recreation with those things most closely associated with their developing identity.

The importance of a private sphere for developing adolescents was even more striking in the responses to the question, "Where in your home do you feel most 'at home'?" Whereas only a little more than 10 percent of parents and grandparents name the bedroom, over one-half (p.<001) of all the children feel most at home in their own bedrooms, and the importance of

TABLE 7.2   Percentages of Special Objects Found in the Most Frequently Used Rooms for Different Age Groups

Ages	Number of objects	Living Room		Respondent's Bedroom		Dining Room		Entire House		Study		Kitchen	
		N	%	N	%	N	%	N	%	N	%	N	%
8–14	168	20	12	80	48	1	1	9	5	14	8	8	4
15–21	185	31	17	70	38	9	5	8	4	5	3	16	9
22–28	92	33	36	14	15	15	16	5	5	—	—	5	5
29–35	185	63	34	31	17	17	9	21	11	18	10	7	4
36–42	220	74	34	26	12	18	8	22	10	21	10	14	6
43–49	208	87	42	24	12	20	10	10	5	19	9	15	7
50–56	198	83	42	22	11	25	13	12	6	12	6	12	6
57–63	113	35	31	9	8	20	18	9	8	9	8	8	7
64–70	95	39	41	10	11	14	15	9	10	5	5	2	2
71–77	83	35	42	19	23	15	18	5	6	2	2	5	6
78–96	83	35	42	21	25	3	4	1	1	5	6	8	10

autonomy and privacy were usually cited as the reasons for selecting this room. As one girl said:

> In my room. It has all the needs I want in there, except for food, and I go to the kitchen for that. All the needs, and if I'm scared of something, I go to my room and sit on the bed.

The autonomy provided by the bedroom appears to be a less prominent aspect of the patterns of meanings that adults cultivate. Instead, the social atmosphere of the living room becomes the most appropriate context for structuring and expressing what they consider most significant. The bedroom again increases in importance for the very old, presumably again because of the autonomy it provides, either as a private sphere where older people living in their children's home can keep personal belongings or also possibly because the person spends more time resting in the room.

It is frequently forgotten how central the bedroom was (before, for example, the intervention of the hospital) in the most culturally marked and signified life activities: the birth of an infant, the consummation of a marriage, death. Much of our dream-life transpires in the privacy of the home's bedroom, that frame of quasi-conscious familiarity in which the most fantastic visions can take place. The changing significance of the bedroom as one ages seems almost to trace the course of the self over the life cycle. In childhood and adolescence privacy is valued because it enables the child to cultivate a sense of autonomy through transactions with an environment charged with personalized meanings. The sense of personal autonomy is internalized with adulthood and thus the self can be signified more broadly throughout the home (not to mention the public sphere) and through more socially oriented patterns of meaning. With old age, however, the self itself becomes increasingly internalized as the social activities of the old person diminish, and thus the bedroom again becomes important as a private sphere in which the autonomy and memories of the old can be cultivated in the immediate environment of objects of contemplation (for some interesting work on the relation of the house to the self, see Kron 1983; Korosec-Serfaty 1984, 1985; Schutz 1970b; and in cross-cultural contexts, Duncan 1982).

Transitions of an Adolescent

The empirical results reported thus far give some indication of how cherished possessions can act as signs and role models in the process of cultivation, but to give a richer view of this process at work, and to contrast it with the psychoanalytic framework, let me turn to an extended profile of one sixteen-year-old girl I will call Dorothy. Dorothy emigrated with her family from the Phillipines when she was ten. Her most special possessions are of the kind indicated by psychoanalyst D. W. Winnicott's (1958) concept of the *transitional object*, yet, as I hope to make clear, she also makes use of her belongings not only to resolve current tensions and problems but to cultivate new developments in her self not reducible to infantile needs.

Winnicott's concept of the transitional object refers to external things not completely distinguished from the individual's own person. Transitional objects are those things, such as a security blanket, that initially come to take the place of the breast before the infant has distinguished a sense of self and other. Winnicott also includes some sublimated versions of transitional objects that are applicable to later stages in the growth of the self but that retain the underlying psychological meaning of breast substitute (Winnicott 1958, 236).

Dorothy comes from a large family and lives with her parents, maternal grandmother, and four other brothers and sisters. Like many other adolescents, Dorothy felt most "at home" in her own room, which she shared with a sister, because "I can be by myself, think, and everything. It's a private place." Most of her valued possessions are in her bedroom, and some of her most special objects are her stuffed animals, especially one in particular. She started acquiring these about a year earlier, when she was fifteen. She said:

> They've been hugged a lot, so it's kind of dirty now. They're cute and soft and lovable. With no stuffed animals I'd have nothing to hug. I'd feel pretty bad about it, especially one of the stuffed animals. [*Why?*] I usually had one of them, and that's the oldest [*pointing*]. It's been cried on and everything. It's been given to me by a special friend. She's very nice, we were born on the same day. This one was given to me and like I told you, it's been cried on and everything. I wouldn't have anything to hold, too.

These stuffed animals are gifts signifying friendship, as well as objects that give her comfort and nurturance when she feels upset; apparently she has a strong need for a make-believe friend and the sense of affection and nurturance she can give to herself through transactions with these personified things. Stuffed animals are obviously emotional objects for children, but pets act similarly for the whole family, adults included, in providing a surrogate "family member" on whom emotions can be lavished to an extent frequently greater than with other family members (Rochberg-Halton, 1985a). Because this was not a clinically oriented study, we do not know the source of Dorothy's troubles, but perhaps the problems of moving to a new country and an alien environment have placed extra stress on this family. One does sense a need in this girl throughout the interview both for more attention and more autonomy.

One of her belongings does approximate a pure example of Winnicott's transitional object, which, as mentioned, is an external thing not yet completely distinguished from the individual's own person. In Dorothy's response to the question "Are there any objects that have been special in your life, but which you no longer possess?," she said: "My security blanket. When I came here, it was in the Phillipines, when I was very young. My Mom wouldn't let me take it." Psychoanalytically one could justifiably interpret the stuffed animals as sublimated versions of her security blanket, which, in turn, if we follow Winnicott (1958, 236) merely stands for the breast. Although one might see some validity to this psychoanalytic interpretation, in the sense that the stuffed animals and security blanket provide warm, soft, emotionally nurturing objects, the explicit reductionism strips away important elements of these objects. These things exist for her in her present environment and fulfill functions as surrogate love-objects when she is sad. In this way they enable her to carry on a dialogue with herself about her feelings, and to work through and resolve her bad feelings through what Mead, drawing from Wundt, termed a "conversation of gestures," in which the qualities of soft-ness and huggableness "respond" to her needs. And this girl is not limited only to these more infantile objects, she has created a "language" of emotional expression for herself with some of her other special possessions, such as her family's piano and her own sketchings as well. She says about these things:

> I love playing the *piano*. Sometimes when you're angry or sad, it lets it out, you know, when you play? Well, I just like to touch it when I play it. (Without it I would be) sad. You won't have any place to throw out your feelings in. It's the same with art. My *sketchings*. Like the piano, you can throw out your feelings through it. And sometimes after you're tired, you just draw something and it just gives you peace of mind. . . . I'm proud of them, especially when I do a good job. [*Without them?*] It's like the piano. You won't have any place to put your feelings in. And then you'd have to keep it to yourself and that's awful. . . . I had them for a long, long time. I started it in the Phillipines when I was 4 years old. Sometimes I just like drawing things that I see, that I feel.

These physical objects and the activities associated with them enable this girl to channel her emotions and to express her feelings through artistic activity. Yet these processes are not simply "internal," because they involve the meeting of this girl's feelings and abilities with the objective "rules" of music and drawing. Dorothy can, as she says, "throw out" her feelings through these activities, yet she must do so *within the medium of expression*. In other words, the expression of her feelings actually involves the objects that form the medium of that expression, and in this sense the piano and sketchings are quite literally parts of her self. Successfully releasing her feelings through the piano involves "taking the role of the other" in the sense of her having to take on the attitude or feeling of the music she is playing—to *feel* what she is trying to play. In this way the piano and the craft of music it represents act as a socializing role model for this girl not only by telling her what she is and what she can do, but also by revealing possibilities for what she can *become*. It enables her to vent her frustrations, resolve bad feelings, as well as carve out new domains for her growing self as a musician.

It becomes even clearer how the piano and the sketchings act as role models when we turn to the people she most admires. Consider the unusual complex of values symbolized by the following admired persons. Along with her older sister, Ernest Hemingway, and rock disc-jockeys, she mentioned Beethoven and Rembrandt, who together personify the ability to put one's feelings into music and paintings:

> [*Beethoven*] He's written real good—I guess you call it songs, no? [*You mean music?*] Yeah, music. He's written real good ones. It seems he puts his feelings in it.
> [*Rembrandt*] The paintings he did, it's real good. [*What makes it good?*] His brush strokes, and the way he puts life in it. It's not like a flat picture. It looks real; it's there. . . .

Object-relations theorists (such as Fairbairn 1954; Kernberg 1976, 1980; Mahler 1979; Arlow 1980; and, though he termed his own work the psychology of the self, Kohut 1971, 1977),[4] who seem devoutly interested in keeping a clear and distinct separation of the object representation and real external object, could learn something from Dorothy. Her understanding of art as the throwing of one's feelings into an object so that, like Rembrandt, one creates a living reality is in many ways more accurate than the utilitarian view that art is merely illusion. Winnicott (1958, 230, 240) may view art, religion, and creative scientific work, with Freud, as sublimated versions of transitional phenomena, the original "illusion" that replaces the mother's breast, but in the long run it is they that are eternal while the person is transitory: *Ars longa, vita brevis.*

All respondents were asked what all of their special objects mean, taken as a whole. This question represented an attempt to get something like the Rorschach test global "W" or "whole" response, that gestalt which reflects one's overall view, and Dorothy's answer to it is quite interesting. She

---

4. I have chosen to concentrate on the classic foundations of object relations theory in Freud rather than on contemporary work. Much contemporary work seems to me to retain the basic Freudian subjectivism, despite its authors' claims to the contrary (but see Jonte-Pace, in press). Kohut in particular is an example of the provincial little world in which psychoanalysts tend to operate: How else is one to account for a theorist who spent a significant portion of his career in Chicago, and yet proclaimed a revolutionary "psychology of the self" as if the Chicago tradition of sociology had never existed, never acknowledging the significance (positively or negatively) of Mead, or, for that matter, of Harry Stack Sullivan or, for that matter, of the entire social psychological tradition.

said: "Life. It's what you look for, it's there when you need them. It's something to hold onto." Now what could be a better description of the primal breast that underlies Winnicott's transitional object? The objects as a whole are "life," "what you look for," "there when you need them," "something to hold onto." And yet, do we not undervalue the tangible world of meaning this girl has created by seeking its ultimate or real meaning in an internal conceptual realm? The world of meaning that we create for ourselves, and that creates our selves, involves the objective surroundings, and the things we value do indeed act as signs of the self that are essential in their own right for its continued cultivation.

THE ENVIRONMENT AS SOCIALIZING SIGN-COMPLEX

In contrasting the psychoanalytic view of representations with that of the pragmatic perspective, I have argued that the self consists of a communicative dialogue of signs rooted in an environmental context and requiring cultivation for its emergence and continued growth. The view proposed here denies the materialism of those environmentalists who consider signs and symbols an addition to a material substratum (including the notion of a perceptual noninferential substratum, e.g., Downs and Stea, 1973, 23–24, and contra, Rochberg-Halton 1979b, app. 1) and denies the conceptualism of those "symbolists" and semiologists who consider the actual environment itself the meaningless "surface stuff" of a separate mental system, whether psychological (as in the case of Freud or, it could be argued, Piaget) or cultural (Barthes 1977; Baudrillard 1981; Eco 1976). In the context of environmental studies it would appear that this view of the relationship between self and environment as a continuous, socializing, inference-making sign-complex is analogous to the concept of "cognitive mapping," yet it seems to me that as currently defined, cognitive mapping suffers from the same dichotomizing tendencies toward materialist or conceptualist reductionism criticized here. Let me briefly review the concept of "cognitive mapping" to further illustrate the view developed here, and to suggest further implications for environmental studies.

The term "cognitive mapping" was first introduced by the experimental psychologist Edward C. Tolman in his 1948 article, "Cognitive Mapping in Rats and Men." There Tolman argued against simple stimulus-response models of how rats learn to run mazes. Over fifty years after Dewey introduced the concept of "organic coordination" as the mediating principle between organism and environment, in his reflex-arc article discussed earlier, Tolman reintroduced to the American psychological community, now dominated by behaviorism, the idea of a mediating and tentative "cognitive map." Tolman's position, influenced by Lewin's "field theory" (itself a descendant of the Chicago functional psychology Dewey had been in-

strumental in creating), was that learning involves something like the organizing gestalt of a mental map:

> We believe that in the course of learning, something like a field
> map of the environment gets established in the rat's brain. . . .
> Secondly, we assert that the central office itself is far more like a
> map control room than it is like an old-fashioned telephone ex-
> change. The stimuli, which are allowed in, are not connected by
> just simple one-to-one switches to the outgoing responses.
> Rather, the incoming impulses are usually worked over and
> elaborated in the central control room into a tentative, cognitive-
> like map of the environment. And it is this tentative map, in-
> dicating routes and paths of environmental relationships, which
> finally determines what responses, if any, the animal will
> finally release. (Tolman [1948] 1973, 31)

Tolman emphasized, as had Dewey, not only that stimuli and responses are contextually related rather than mechanically produced (which is
to say in the language of Peirce's semiotic [CP, vol. 7], that perception and
conduct are inferential sign-processes), but also that "a tentative, cognitive-
like map of the environment" is a purposive rule or model for conduct.
Although expressed in behavioristic terms, Tolman's metaphor of a cognitive
map provided a broader conception of person-environment relations than
allowed by the mainstream of his day (e.g., Hull 1952), but it still tends to
reduce the social world to a by-product of individual experience.

The term "cognitive map" eventually came into general use by
geographers, environmental sociologists, and psychologists to describe the
ways in which people orient themselves to the external environment through
mediating representations.[5] Yet Tolman's original emphasis on the *purpose*
of the representation, how it acts as a communicative rule for behavior,

5. Perhaps the most influential book in the emerging field of cognitive mapping was Lynch's
The Image of the City (1961). In Lynch's model the person's relation to the environment is
mediated by "environmental images," and the person is a much more active agent in a transaction than in Tolman's behavioristic model (Lynch 1961, 6). In using the term "image" Lynch
claimed to be primarily concerned with visual image and not with meaning or expressiveness,
"sensuous delight," stimulus, or choice. His environmental images, built out of an experiential
process, seem to be close to the mediating sign-habits of the pragmatists, but Lynch does not try
to relate his environmental images to the interpretative sign-process, as do pragmatists. Perhaps
his work can be seen as an implicit empirical description of the purposive sign-process and its role
in socialization.

When one compares Lynch's *The Image of the City*, however, to Mumford's *The City in
History*, also published in 1961, one realizes how thin the standards of environmental and urban
research were (and remain), so that Lynch's small-scale monograph could assume such central
significance in the next two decades while Mumford's historically informed wisdom and schol-
arly insights on the purposive nature of the city and its representations could be virtually ignored.

somehow tended to drop out of account in cognitive mapping studies in favor of an account of the structure of the map itself, apart from its purpose. This has resulted, rather paradoxically, in a reification of the metaphor, in which a concept designating a *process* through which space and conduct are organized is itself turned into a *thing*.

When we examine some recent cognitive mapping studies they seem to have missed the purpose of Tolman's concept: to account for purpose itself. Some cognitive mappers, such as Kaplan, have sought to reduce an individual's relation to the environment to physiological mechanisms:

> But at present the idea that people have a map in their heads remains essentially a metaphor. . . . Yet the idea is sufficiently attractive that it is hard to resist the challenge to take the next step, to move from metaphor to mechanism. "Mechanism" is used here in the sense of the machinery that underlies the observed phenomena, in other words, the specification of how it is constructed and how it works. (Kaplan 1976, 33)

A more "sophisticated" machine is proposed by Stea and Blaut, but the mechanistic purpose remains similar:

> The search for a physical analogue to the cognitive map has led us to consider the hologram, a recent product of laser technology, as a model, or, perhaps, a metaphor. . . . Extending this to spatial conceptualization, we might speak of a "psychological hologram," a conceptual three-dimensional projection of the three-dimensional object. It is a representation presumably located structurally or functionally somewhere in the central nervous system. (Stea and Blaut 1973, 56)

More recently Kuipers (1982) has criticized the cognitive mapping metaphor for not being capable of portraying the brain processes that are more complex than a geographical map. Kuipers may be accurately criticizing the tendency toward spatial reification, yet he commits the same fallacy he is attempting to criticize in taking a literal-minded approach toward a metaphor and in interpreting the metaphor as standing for spatial mechanism rather than for the purposive nature of conduct.

In these examples we are left with the spectre of a Cartesian "machine" that "underlies the observed phenomena" in a way analogous to that proposed by Freudian metapsychology, rather than a model that might account for how experience and communication are possible in particular contexts, and that could explain how cognitive maps act as *rules for conduct*. These approaches do not tell us the purpose of the cognitive map, which is precisely what Tolman stressed (Tolman 1961).[6] Thus what is essentially a pragmatic question, in Aristotle's sense of the cultivation of the good or virtuous life through conduct, is reduced to a technical one. The technical question asks how the thing works, the pragmatic one, in the philosophical sense, how conduct can best be oriented to accord with the purposes of community life, purposes themselves subject to cultivation. An application of pragmatic sign-theory, such as Peirce's theory of perception as an inferential process (not as an immediate given, as Stea and Blaut [1973] and many others suggest) or Dewey's and Mead's views of perception and representation as mediated within the purposive, environmentally situated act, provides an integrated theory of cognition, self, and society that cognitive mapping studies lack. This environmental semiotic includes emotion, as well as cognition, as a purposive sign-process. Too often signs have been seen as "merely" aesthetic and hence "subjective" and somewhat extraneous aspects of social life (e.g., Orleans 1973, 115), as if social worlds can exist independently of signs and symbols. Rather, it is by virtue of signs that our social worlds are organized. Signs are not inessential additions to experience, they are the very medium of perception itself.

It is in this sense that we are thoroughly immersed in an environment of socializing signs, internal and external. Even before the infant is born, its parents have begun to project an environment of clothing, toys, and furnishings that will begin the socialization process. The self arises in a milieu that is constantly "addressing" it, telling it who it is through its surroundings, telling it how to become he or she. Transactions with one's cherished possessions, either actually or symbolically, can thus be seen as sign-expressions of the self. The person, as a complex of living, feeling, sign-habits, does not stop with his or her physical organism but quite literally is in continuous transaction with the broader spatiotemporal environment through signs.

6. ". . . all gestalts are for us sign-gestalts—and all relations, in the last analysis, means-end-relations. Types of organization of the environmental field are for us always held together by, threaded upon, means-end-strands. . . . In a word, the fact of purpose, as we conceive it, is an objective fact. It is the fact that behavior is docile relative to objectively determinable ends. Our psychology is a purposivism; but it is an objective, behavioristic purposivism, not a mentalistic one" (Tolman 1961, 779).

8   Remembrance of Things Present

William James, in a letter of 1896 to his brother Henry, described his summer home in Vermont with characteristic Jamesian vividness:

> The little place is the most curious mixture of sadness with delight. The sadness of *things*—things every one of which was done either by our hands or by our planning, old furniture renovated, there is n't an object in the house that is n't associated with past life, old summers, dead people, people who will never come again, etc., and the way it catches you round the heart when you first come and open the house from its long winter sleep is most extraordinary. (James 1926, 2:37)

It has been remarked often enough that our time is one in which people increasingly produce information rather than things, but perhaps the home is the last retreat for *homo faber*, the maker and user of things. The home is in many ways one of the few spheres remaining in the modern techno-piecemeal world where it is possible to have a direct and continuous relationship to objects either produced or cultivated by oneself. Yet the home is also the destination of that plethora of household goods signifying the culture of consumerism, objects whose principal meaning seems to be simply their presence as pecuniary trophies rather than as objects of personal significance and value. The average American home contains an array of artifacts that would convey a fantastic notion of wealth to other times or to people living in most other cultures today. Despite this wealth, it also seems that the larger cultural codes of American consumer culture do not provide material to touch the deeper human needs for meaning. The obvious target for criticism is the materialism which characterizes modern life, a materialism that levels everything to a quantitative standard. Yet things per se are not the problem, for to say that they were would be to accept a variant of the very materialism one is criticizing. The question of materialism, as I hope to show, is ultimately one of meaning, and the home is one of its primary staging grounds.

For the Haida of the American Northwest Coast described by Marcel Mauss in his classic essay *The Gift*, the home is much more than a physical container, it is a living personality:

> The large *abalone* shells, the shields covered with them, the decorated blankets with faces, eyes, and animal and human figures embroidered and woven into them, are all personalities. The houses and decorated beams are themselves beings. Everything speaks—roof, fire, carvings and paintings; for the magical house is built not only by the chief and his people and those of the opposing phratry but also by the gods and ancestors; spirits and young initiates are welcomed and cast out by the house in person. (Mauss 1967, 43)

As Mauss says, "everything speaks" in this traditional household, and examples of the same attitude could be given from many other cultures as well (e.g., Bourdieu 1973, 98–110). Most peoples at most times have lived in a personified world, and have personified their surroundings with animate representations that bring life to the material environment.

Is there a sense in which the animate world of goods described by Mauss is applicable to the exchange and possession of material objects in contemporary life? With possible exceptions for pets, stuffed animals, and plants, we moderns do not commonly regard household possessions as animate personalities. And yet, as I hope to make clear, the domestic environment does speak to us through the signs with which we personalize it. Cherished possessions evoke a whole range of sign-habits or meanings through our transactions with them: they are repositories of personal and collective memories, they embody kinship ties, they are valued as tangible evidence of friendship and family bonds, they are signs of our presence in a paradoxically material yet evanescent world.

Valued belongings are means through which to objectify the self, to create an external extension of personal identity, a tangible presence in one's surroundings. Yet presence alone is not enough when disconnected from its human context of significance. "Things present are judged by things past," as the sixteenth-century English proverb has it (Hazlitt 1907), which is to say that what we *have* gains its meaning through its connection to those experiences and memories that have shaped us into our present condition. "Having" something means to be in a relationship to it, a relationship mediated by all those experiences that have conditioned the possessor and the thing possessed, and that form the medium between person and thing. To have stood in the sun fifty years ago for a photo with one's brothers is to have formed a link physically captured and preserved by the camera, a tangible memory powerful enough to bring one to tears, as happened to an otherwise gruff grandfather during an interview in my research. The photo itself is not simply a "raw" presence and inert thing, it is a conditioned remembrance, whose very survival over the years gives testimony to the need to externalize and hold onto what we consider worth preserving.

Remembrance means the ability to reminisce selectively, to bring to mind a memory that has made a lasting impression. A remembrance can also be an artifact that serves the same purpose—a keepsake or souvenir. The capacity for remembrance is one of the distinguishing features of humanity, for through those songs, objects, practices, and words that helped to recall the memorable events of a people, humanity developed symbolic consciousness. Symbols provided a means through which humanity could free itself from immediate sensation and unconscious habit, and could people the present with the voices of the past, thus radically enlarging the possibilities for self-controlled conduct and the growth of the imagination. The human being became not only a descendant, but an heir, capable of conserving and accumulating the experiences of those who had gone before. With an enlarged spatiotemporal field of tradition a people could also reject past mistakes or take on new directions. The traditions made possible by symbol usage and cultivated through remembrance became the "second nature" of humanity, external artifices, that to a great degree took the place of instinct as the basis for purposeful conduct (see Peirce, CP 1.178). In a culture of forgetting, it would seem that those ignorant of their own history would be doomed to repeat its mistakes. Similarly a culture shackled to the past, incapable of coming to terms with the present because blinded by clouds of habituation, ideology, and exaggerated sentimentality, would risk cutting itself off from the vital sources that energize a culture. Remembrance, though it may degenerate into nostalgia, is much more than mere nostalgia. As Hannah Arendt has said, remembrance and tangibility provide the continuity that is essential for human conduct:

> The whole factual world of human affairs depends for its reality and its continued existence, first, upon the presence of others who have seen and heard and will remember, and, second, on the transformation of the intangible into the tangibility of things. Without remembrance and without the reification which remembrance needs for its own fulfilment and which makes it, indeed, as the Greeks held, the mother of all arts, the living activities of action, speech, and thought would lose their reality at the end of each process and disappear as though they had never been. (Arendt 1958, 95)

Valued possessions are living signs, whose life consists in the transactions between person and thing. As living signs, objects must be cultivated to retain their significance; as cultivated objects, things can grow in significance over time and take on new layers of meaning. One can see the living presence of an inanimate object in the following woman's description of a portrait that has been in the family for five generations:

> This is my great, great grandfather. I've had it since childhood. It's more than just a portrait—it's a person! I'd grab it right away in a fire. [Without it] my life would be lessened. I'd go on living, but it would deplete my secure "lump." It would mean that I wouldn't be able to hand it down to my children. The kids already say, "I'm gonna inherit this and that." . . . It's part of the continuity of who I am, where I came from, where I'm going. People who settled in this country—150 years is *old* in this country! But it's important for a memorable history.

This contemporary Chicago woman almost sounds like one of the traditional peoples portrayed in Mauss's study, in her description of the portrait as being "more than just a portrait—it's a person!" Perhaps animism is not as primitive and obsolete a belief as the modern consciousness has claimed, once we realize that one's relationship to valued surroundings is an *animism of signs*. The portrait is a family icon, a veritable ancestor totem, which lives in the remembrance of the generations who receive and come to cherish it, and in turn transmit it to their descendants. Hence when the mother says, "It's part of the continuity of who I am, where I came from, where I'm going," she is correct not only figuratively, but ontologically as well. The portrait forms an essential element of those habits of conduct in which her self consists: it is a direct physical link with preceding family members, with her individual sense of identity, with what she will become individually, and what her family will become collectively. It is both a socializing sign and sign-expression of her self, just as the other feelings, experiences, memories, and thoughts that shape her self are.

Having the portrait is a family responsibility taken on and cultivated by succeeding generations, and one that illustrates the two senses of what it means "to have." Having is the direct pervasive quality of the person-thing transaction, something, as Aquinas said, that is the "medium between that which has and that which is had." It is in this sense that when one thing makes, and another is made, *making* is the medium, the pervasive quality of the maker-made situation. The having of a thing is also the *habit* of relationship over the course of time, in which the person acquires a general tendency to behave toward or interpret the object in a certain way.

"Things present" not only "are judged by things past" but also have pragmatic import for future conduct. As sign-habits, things socialize and can create new possibilities for development. A piano, for example, might be merely a silent bulk of status-furniture for one family, but in the hands of a young Mozart or Thelonious Monk it can act as a physical means for the growth and transformation of self, and culture as a whole. Even as we cultivate things, they in turn cultivate us, and this capacity for self-controlled intervention in the environment, the capacity for artifice, is not only one of the great achievements of humanity but has also made possible the darker aspects of human greed and domination, culminating in our age of possession.

The term "possession" means both the relationship of ownership and the thing owned. We speak both of "taking possession of property" and of the property itself as a possession. And the two-sided nature of the person-thing relationship is highlighted when we speak of "being possessed." Modern culture, as Simmel repeatedly pointed out, (1971, 234; 1978) is an increasingly one-sided development in which things are cultivated at the expense of the subjective culture of the person, in which things seem to take on a life of their own, to dominate, in the economy of both the public and private spheres, the destinies of the very people for whom they were supposedly created. Our consumer culture is indeed a culture of possession, a culture of a whole people consumed with the passion to possess: to possess people and things, and to possess but briefly, transiently. Yet who, in this culture of totemically named cars needing to be made anew each year, of commercially sterilized popular music with a life expectancy of a few weeks or months, in this culture where one of the few things made to endure for years is frozen food, who is truly possessor and who possessed?

THE ACQUISITION OF SPECIAL POSSESSIONS

> But for the moment it is clear that in Maori custom this bond created by things is in fact a bond between persons, since the thing itself is a person or pertains to a person. . . . The thing given is not inert. It is alive and often personified, and strives to bring to its original clan and homeland some equivalent to take its place.
>
> (Mauss 1967, 10)

One of the major differences between the traditional Maori way of life described by Mauss and modern Westernized society is the dominance of the money economy in modern life, where most exchange occurs through the anonymous and supposedly utilitarian medium of money rather than through tokens of intrinsic worth and significance. Money has come to be the pure symbol of exchange par excellence, the standard of all value, capable of being transformed into any material object it can buy. Hence it could mean something completely different to acquire a valued possession through purchase rather than through nonmonetary exchange, because there is not necessarily an intrinsic connection between seller and purchaser, as does exist between the two parties involved in a gift exchange. One might expect, for example, that cherished possessions acquired through purchase might be more individualistic in meaning than those received as gifts, because their acquisition is determined by the purchaser and implies no continuing symbolic obligations to the previous owner, as a gift frequently does. Here I want to concentrate on one aspect of the meaning of valued possessions in contemporary American life: how the acquisition of possessions also reflects their context of significance.

In my research, as discussed in the previous chapter, family members were asked to describe what objects in the home were "special," why they were special, how the object was acquired, where it was located, etc., and all responses were tape-recorded and transcribed verbatim. One noticeable finding from the perspective of materialism was that most respondents tended *not* to mention the bulk of technological and common consumer items that are usually associated with materialism and that most of these respondents actually owned. The common consumer items such as clothing and appliances tended not to be mentioned, whereas artifacts embodying ties to loved ones and kin, valued experiences and activities, and memories of significant life-events and people were named. It would seem that the central values in people's lives can be expressed by objects that are significant because of their personal meaning, not just because of their exchange value. There seems to be an idea in America that an enormous number of objects must be consumed just to have the basics of a good life, as if the good life consists of props conspicuously displayed. Yet when we reflect on what we consider our most cherished possessions to be, it turns out that the bulk of consumer items is excluded and more or less taken for granted.

Common consumer goods do, however, act as reliable indices of one's socio-economic class, age, gender, and so on, as recent studies by Caplow (1982; 1984) on Christmas gift-giving in Middletown and by Rathje (1974) on garbage patterns in Arizona have shown. Caplow reports that clothing was by far the most common type of Christmas gift, comprising 35 percent of all gifts, and that "The preference for clothing over all other categories is probably accounted for by the automatic individualization of items of clothing. In effect, they describe the receiver by age, sex, appearance, and style" (Caplow 1982, 385). What is interesting is that despite the unquestioned centrality Christmas has assumed in American culture in this century as an emotional symbol of family life, signified by the large-scale purchase and exchange of consumer goods (department stores make about one-third of their annual sales during this "season"; see Schudson 1981, 1984), despite this celebration of love in which the normal constraints of the capitalist "Scrooge" mentality are transcended by millions of consumers purchasing billions of dollars of goods, clothing is simply not a highly memorable special possession, being mentioned by a mere 2.7 percent of parents, 5.8 of grandparents, and 10.1 percent of children.

In contrast to my study of the most highly valued household objects, archeologist William Rathje and his workers, dressed for sanitary reasons in hospital coats and masks, examined the least valued things of the American household: the wretched refuse. This may strike one as an odd object of inquiry, perhaps, yet the study of garbage is a traditional method in archeology that provides a very rich indicator of everything from eating patterns to pottery styles. Sooner or later, it would seem, most things find their way to the garbage.

WHEN SPECIAL OBJECTS WERE ACQUIRED

As one might expect, the older the respondent in my study of American materialism, the longer he or she possessed the objects named as special. Fully 25 percent of the grandparents' belongings mentioned as special were acquired over thirty-five years earlier, whereas almost the same percentage of children's possessions were acquired in the last two years (see table 8.1). The peak period for parents was about ten years previously, possibly suggesting that setting up the household after marriage is the time when most special objects are acquired for adults. This might also explain why grandparents have such a high percentage of possessions acquired over thirty-five years previously. It would appear that the significant events that occur in early adulthood, such as marriage, setting up a household, and birth, "imprint" themselves into one's memory and identity through palpable remembrances. Youth's transient flux of meanings and identities tends to give way to more quasi-permanent paraphernalia of life as one "settles down."

TABLE 8.1   Date of Acquisition of Special Objects for Three Generations

	Percentages of Objects Acquired in a Given Time-Period		
	Children	Parents	Grandparents
1975–1977	39	19	11
1973–1974	20	11	6
1971–1972	13	11	6
1967–1970	14	19	9
1962–1966	6	18	11
1952–1961	6	13	15
1942–1951	0	7	15
1900–1941	0	2	26

Purchased

As table 8.2 reveals, almost half of all special objects are purchased by either the respondent or, in the case of children, by the respondent's parents (further information on these coding categories can be found in Rochberg-Halton 1979b, and Csikszentmihalyi and Rochberg-Halton

TABLE 8.2   How Special Objects Were Acquired

	No. of Objects	Percentages[a]			
		Purchased	Gift	Inherited	Handcrafted
Furniture	187	46	26	16	6
Bed	43	63	12	19	—
Visual art	136	54	28	7	15
Sculpture	108	38	44	3	18
Collectibles	49	71	29	4	4
Musical instruments	77	55	30	10	3
TV	68	72	24	2	—
Stereo	74	62	35	—	1
Radio	24	54	42	—	—
Books	79	70	29	5	3
Photos	93	32	23	12	37
Plants	48	52	65	2	8
Plates	68	31	32	34	—
Silverware	17	35	47	29	—
Glass	36	22	44	33	—
Pets	29	41	48	—	7
Aquarium	11	36	64	—	—
Appliances	56	57	27	4	2
Refrigerator	16	88	6	—	—
Lamps	31	48	26	3	3
Clocks	30	20	40	33	3
Tools	12	83	25	8	—
Sports equipment	33	49	52	—	—
Trophies	21	5	5	—	10
Camera	8	63	13	—	13
Toys	15	47	47	—	7
Stuffed animals	18	6	83	6	6
Clothes	21	71	24	—	5
Jewelry	31	26	48	19	—
Textiles	31	23	23	16	36
Carpets	20	80	5	—	5
Fireplace	15	7	—	—	—
Bath	11	9	—	—	—
Whole room	26	19	4	—	12
Miscellaneous	67	25	22	8	16
All	9	33	—	—	22
Scrapbooks	23	9	13	—	44
Vehicles	20	60	35	—	—
Telephone	9	78	22	—	—
Yard	15	—	—	—	20
Candlesticks	9	11	22	56	—
Totals	1,694	45.7	30	9	8.8

[a]The percentages in this table sometimes total less than 100, because they were acquired in a less frequently mentioned category that was not included in the table; sometimes they total more than 100, because more than one category was mentioned.

1981). Gifts are also an important means of acquiring cherished possessions, as almost 40 percent of all special objects were received by the respondent as a gift (gifts, 30 percent; inherited 9 percent), and together these categories, purchases and gifts, comprise 85 percent of all special objects. The next most important category included special objects that were hand-crafted by the respondent or someone known personally to the respondent (9 percent). The remaining categories of acquisition occur much less frequently, such as objects already in the dwelling when the respondent moved in, found objects, awards, or things acquired by combinations of these categories, such as collections.

Things acquired by purchase range across almost every type of special objective except lawns, which were usually acquired when the respondent moved into his or her dwelling, thereby implying the purchase category. The types of things acquired most frequently by purchase tend to be objects of *kinetic interaction* rather than of *contemplative memory*, and even more specifically, they are things usually used for functional purposes, such as beds, televisions, stereos, carpets, telephones, refrigerators, tools, cameras, clothes, and vehicles. The only frequently mentioned objects without perhaps a clear functional use were collectibles and books.

The emphasis on objects used most frequently for functional purposes also appears in the meanings associated with special objects acquired by purchase (table 8.3). These belongings are more likely to be valued because of their utilitarian function, or because of the experiences they provide, such as release, or ongoing occasions, or enjoyment. Things valued as collections, or because they are embodiments of ideals are also acquired more frequently by purchase, as are artifacts associated with admired persons, self, and spouse. The patterns of meanings associated with objects acquired by purchase suggest they are self- rather than family-oriented, and refer to current experiences rather than past memories.

Gifts

Things acquired most often as gifts include living "objects" such as plants, aquariums, and pets, as well as representations of living things: stuffed animal toys. Plants and pets are usually thought of as the most natural of objects, but these results suggest that they are also important indicators of social relationships (see Rochberg-Halton, 1985a, for a discussion of pets as symbols of the "family metaphor"). Plants are especially good examples of how social networks are embodied in the home. The keeping of large numbers of plants in the home emerged as one of the major trends in interior decoration in the 1970s. But since it was a new trend, it was also a practice that had to be learned, and one of the primary ways that respondents usually

TABLE 8.3   Meanings Associated with Acquisition Categories

| | No. of Objects | Percentages[a] | | | |
		Purchased	Gift	Inherited	Hand-crafted
Memento	321	36	28	16	14
Recollection	285	43	35	9	8
Heirloom	140	5	18	74	2
Souvenir	145	52	26	17	3
"Long Time"	79	44	44	10	6
Intended heirloom	63	35	25	32	5
Ethnic	50	30	32	30	2
Religious	25	32	40	12	—
Collections	60	58	32	5	8
Gift	250	11	80	9	1
Enjoyment	689	55	29	5	8
Ongoing occasions	263	57	25	3	7
Release	99	66	28	3	3
Craft	205	26	24	7	43
Uniqueness	81	33	31	16	20
Physical description	274	46	28	11	13
Style	473	50	29	8	7
Utilitarian	300	61	22	2	4
Embodiment of ideal	112	56	29	5	5
Accomplishment	166	40	17	2	31
Personification	58	35	50	7	7
Self	1,031	54	27	3	9
We	190	48	17	13	6
Spouse	197	52	26	7	11
Children	210	38	36	10	15
Mother	137	19	41	37	4
Father	86	23	38	27	9
Siblings	41	17	27	22	17
Grandparents	65	8	31	65	2
Grandchildren	32	19	44	9	16
Whole family	97	33	23	12	24
In-laws	54	13	37	35	7
Relatives	41	22	44	32	12
Ancestors	27	7	4	85	4
Friends	117	39	52	4	3
Associates	42	36	38	7	14
Admired persons	89	60	20	6	8
Total	6,585				

[a]See footnote to table 8.2.

learned about plant-keeping was through social networks of neighbors and friends. Often a new plant would be acquired as a cutting from a friend's plant, and the friendship was thus symbolized through a bond of living matter.

A plant given to one respondent's husband by a patient became a central symbol of the critical social relationships that are a part of her husband's work as a doctor and a part of the whole family's daily life:

> We have a plant that a patient of my husband gave that prob-ably has significance because she died shortly after. I don't like to be that spiritual but it meant a great deal to him, and to both of us. You know, people do continue, in some very obscure way, but it's there. . . . It isn't that it's such a magnificent plant. It's just its relationship. If something happened to it, it happened to it. I wouldn't be too terribly upset about it. . . . The woman re-ceived a similar plant and my husband liked it so she sent a simi-lar one. My husband is a hematologist and . . . treats people with chemotherapeutic drugs. They have a very intense relationship because the therapy is so critical. You know you really live with these people day and night. Even though I don't know these peo-ple it's part of your household.

This plant symbolizes for this woman both the intense relationship of her husband and his patient who gave the plant, as well as the critical rela-tionships that her husband experiences in general with his patients because of the nature of his work. As a family symbol the plant represents the fact that in a sense the husband "brings home" his work to his family, that the family shares this critical relationship ("You know, you really live with these people day and night"). The plant itself is a beautiful living organism, a gift from someone now dead. Like one of the themes of Saul Bellow's novel *Hum-boldt's Gift,* it reveals to this woman that the dead can continue to live in our memories through symbols, and may have a real presence in our lives.

Decorative objects, such as jewelry, silverware, and glass were also frequently received as gifts. Respondents would often mention, for example, a wedding present such as ring given to them by their spouses. Over half of sports equipment items were received as gifts, and usually by males. These sports-related items are accepted through sociocultural conventions as more appropriate gifts for males, while the decorative items, such as jewelry, silverware, and glass were more frequently the content of gifts to females.

Gifts also often referred to friends, mother, grandchildren and rela-tives, indicating the importance of symbolizing friendship and family ties.

Further evidence of the symbolization of these social networks is seen by examining who the donors of the gifts were. After coding how respondents acquired special objects received as gifts, additional categories were added to determine who the gifts were received from and on what occasions these gifts were received. Although 19 percent of gifts did not have the donor specified, the majority (62 percent) of cherished possessions received as gifts were given by the respondent's family or kin. Special objects were most often received from parents, followed by friends and associates, nonrelatives, children, spouse/lover, and other relatives. Only 4 percent of gifts were given by grandparents, 3 percent by siblings, and 2 percent by grandchildren.

An attempt was also made to determine on what occasions these gifts were exchanged, but most (78 percent) of the responses did not specify the occasion. The remaining responses do indicate, as expected, that the objects cherished as special and acquired as gifts were usually received on occasions associated with the custom of gift giving. As Mauss and others have pointed out, the exchange of gifts is one of the oldest and most effective means of symbolizing friendships and family ties, and my results indicate that this practice remains a valued aspect of contemporary American culture.

Inherited

The 9 percent of special objects that were inherited by respondents are almost entirely decorative objects whose use involves contemplation rather than action, and include candlesticks, plateware, glass, silverware, and textiles. The exceptions to this pattern are beds, furniture, and perhaps jewelry—all items used in kinetic interactions but which are also usually used for decorative purposes. Inherited things that are preserved and handed down in families are also gifts, but they tend to be more highly prized and unique, on the average, than the items acquired under the specific category of gifts. One example of this can be seen in the fact that many of the functional special possessions acquired by purchase are conspicuously absent from the inherited category, which suggests that the objects handed down in families are chosen more for their purely symbolic meaning than for their functional attributes.

The meanings associated with inherited special possessions indicate that these artifacts are important repositories of family continuity. Cherished possessions that are handed down in families are more likely to be valued because they remind respondents of their ancestors, grandparents, mother, father, in-laws, relatives, or siblings. The importance of furthering the family continuity symbolized in these artifacts is expressed in the fact that about one-third of all meanings explicitly signifying intended heirlooms are associated with objects that the respondent received in the same way. Just as the family itself forms a living archive of memories and "lineage" (Weigert and Hastings, 1976), the remembrances selected and handed down through the generations form a tangible presence of persons and things past.

MATERIALISM AS VALUATION

We know of no culture that has not, in some way, made use of material artifacts to express its most central values, and indeed urban life and civilization seem to be dependent upon tangible, material artifacts and structures for their very survival and continuity. Occasionally during an interview respondents would say that the objects they owned were not what was important because they were not materialists; rather, it was the *people* connected with these objects who were important and that these things merely served to remind them of loved ones and friends. One member of the Christian Science religion denied that *any* objects were special, claiming that only the spirit matters; yet, when pressed, he admitted that his Bible indeed was something he greatly valued for its spiritual significance.

Though we nowadays in America call a "materialist" someone who lives for the self-centered pleasure of status prestige derived from material wealth, it remains true that not only is some level of material existence inescapable but that material goods can act as genuine *materials* for the cultivation of their possessors. Hence the question of materialism is not simply one of physical things per se, but of the purposes embedded in and derived from things.

To illustrate how the question of materialism is a question of valuation, let us turn to two brief case studies that illustrate what I have elsewhere distinguished as *instrumental* versus *terminal* materialism (Rochberg-Halton 1979b; Csikszentmihalyi and Rochberg-Halton 1978). The first case illustrates the valuation of goods as essential instruments or means for furthering one's goals in a wider social context, whereas the second portrays the valuation of objects as decontextualized ends in themselves—possession solely for the sake of self-gratification. This distinction was influenced by Dewey's *Theory of Valuation* (1939), and is meant to emphasize that, as all human acts have consequences, the valuation of goods involves the consequences entailed by the person-thing transaction, consequences embedded in a context of goals that may extend beyond the individual to include family and wider institutions. Instrumental materialism includes immediately enjoyed and consumed goods, as "consummations" of immediate experience that also exist in a web of social consequences for the individual and not simply as privatized, decontextualized "pleasures." When a quality of feeling such as "pleasure" is used as the ultimate criterion for valuation, though not itself subject to criticism because it is merely a feeling in and of itself and not a judgment of value, then the materialism involved is terminal. There is no sense of reciprocal interaction in the relation between the object and the end in terminal materialism, because the end is valued as final and not subject to criticism and possible correction and growth.

Those who pursue the terminal end most fervently have a goal of becoming a pure individual, yet they can never satisfactorily attain this goal because they are always dependent upon other people to appreciate their individuality and give them the status they so desperately want. In terminal materialism the objective end remains social, serving the purpose of a competitive comparison with others' goods, though the foundation remains paradoxically to *approach* individualism, to stand alone and to be seen standing there.

The case of F. D. partially illustrates how a person can realize values and ultimate goals in cherished possessions, activities, and heroes, and how in turn these things act as instruments for the expression and development of the self. F. D. is a tool-and-die-maker whose main hobby is to build and fly model airplanes. The place where he feels most at home is the basement, where his tools are located and where, he says, he has the most "control over the entironment." His possessions are special because through them he can realize those acts that best express what is most uniquely individual in his life. His lathe, for example, enables him to build and modify his planes, which he flies in competitions:

> . . . and I got it to learn about my business. But then I found I enjoyed it, because you can fashion things within a thousandth of an inch. It's a very fine instrument. A lot of men would like to own a lathe but they never got the opportunity to do so. . . . I could probably sell it now for three times what I bought it for, about ten years ago. In that sense it doesn't cost you anything, it's an investment. It also ties in nicely with the model airplane hobby—there are certain things I can make or fashion. It's doing something with my hands which I enjoy. [*And what would it mean to you not to have it?*] It's certainly not one of those things that's necessary for survival. But I'm sure it's important to me. I had a dream that the house was on fire. And I don't know if my wife and kids got out, but I was down in the basement, frantically trying to dismember the lathe, and get it out, piece by piece. It's a very special tool, the kind of thing a lot of men would like to have. And I feel very fortunate to have it.

The concern with the lathe to the point of dreaming that in a fire he would retrieve it before his family suggests an almost obsessional relationship, perhaps some problem in the family relationship or an overemphasis on self-activity. Yet central to its meaning is his statement that "there are certain things I can make or fashion." In other words things produced by his actions in the home, mediated by the lathe, confirm his identity and goals, confirm his character as *homo faber*. Elsewhere in the interview, F. D. described a supervisor at work who taught him that "There wasn't anything that was insurmountable, you could always accomplish it, if you put your mind to it." The importance of having a sense of purpose also occurs in his description of the astronaut John Glenn, one of the five people F. D. most admires:

> I don't have too many heroes anymore. . . . He went into space, but a lot of people have done that. He has showed a lot of character, displayed a strong sense of purpose, a man totally dedicated to his profession. He struck me as totally unselfish, taking little credit personally for what he accomplished, giving all or most of the credit to his associates.

Again, when asked what the most important events in his life were, one of F. D.'s most crucial memories involved the time he first soloed as a pilot in the Navy:

> In the Navy I always wanted to be a flight pilot. And the day I soloed was an important event in my life. There's a deep sense of accomplishing something that I wanted to do, where your very life depended on your skill and implementing what you learned. A tremendous sense of satisfaction.

His most cherished possessions, activities, memories, and heroes, then, all refer to the same meaning; they indicate his past achievements and serve as models for what he might accomplish. He has made the flight of John Glenn into outer space somehow *his* flight, and his exploit in the Navy is described in very similar terms. And now his model airplanes link his experience of flight with the experiences he derives from the skillful use of tools. The model airplanes also provide a relaxing activity that is connected (through the lathe) with his work, and (through flying them) with his family, especially his son. Though one sees an overreliance on the technical, as distinct from the pragmatic, there is also a clear sense that this man's possessions have their value as they relate to and help realize his relations to his family, his friends and associates, his imagination, and his deepest values. His favorite objects, though material and in some cases expensive, are not valued primarily for extrinsic reasons like their monetary or prestige value; they are instrumental not only toward realizing his goals but also toward refining those goals through the levels of craftsmanship they make possible. He describes all of his special objects in these terms:

> But it's your familiar surroundings, your anchor to reality, your
> anchor to the world you identify or associate with.

Like the Greek craftsman Daedalus, this man seems to have harnessed his
creative and technical potentials into one activity that is playful yet related to
his occupation, his most outstanding achievements, and his deepest life goals.

The significance of objects is quite different for B. L., a young
professional with three separate "households": one that includes his former
wife and children (who were also interviewed), one his lover and child, the
third where he lives occasionally with another lover. This man has moved up
in the world from a poor ethnic family to a lucrative profession. This is how
B. L. describes the objects that have special significance to him:

> Well, it's unfortunate, I have to admit, I always like to have
> something different, something which appears to be "better"
> than somebody else or something "different" than somebody
> else, so I spent a lot of money on that. And I like pretty things.
> Pretty women, pretty cars, pretty clothes, pretty houses. And
> clean women, clothes, houses, cars. . . . My carport, I built that
> for my BMW. I'm very materialistic. But I'm very benevolent: I
> give. But I have a BMW that I can afford, almost as much as I
> paid for the house. But I believe in getting those things I can. . . .

B. L. seems to have placed all of his values on a monetary standard: women
and cherished possessions are equally goods to be appraised, pecuniary
trophies. He calls himself "materialistic" but claims to be "benevolent" as
well. Yet his benevolence here and in other responses consists in his giving
money and possessions away: generosity is also a purely financial transaction
that distinguishes him in the eyes of others. Possession seems to have become
an end in itself rather than a means to furthering goals, as can also be seen in
this description of what all his objects mean:

> No more than an ego trip. Nothing I would go down fighting
> for. [An ego trip?] It makes me feel good while I'm enjoying
> those things to know that I have them and, equally as important,
> that other people know I have them.

When asked to describe his most personal or private objects B. L.
named his BMW, because it is meant to be seen and admired by others as a
status symbol. Although it may seem peculiar to name as one's most personal
or private object, the one object frequently displayed outside the home in
public, and whose meaning derives from its effect on others, a few other men
mentioned their high-status cars for this response as well.

> My car—probably because of the images it creates, to be very
> frank. Being different than most people. Most people don't have

a BMW. It's more different than having a Mercedes at this time.
. . . It's an ego trip which I admit. I don't think it's so wrong. I
hope a lot of people let me do my thing.

Moving up the social ladder appears to have caused a split in this
man's life, which is embodied in his love relationships, personal objects, and
even in the geographical perception of "home." When asked to describe what
his home meant to him, B. L. responded:

> It's a place where I know I can go at all times. It's a place that's
> my house, that is, mine in the mortgage sense of it. . . . I live
> with a lady there who is different from the lady I live with on
> the South Side. My home up there is a place from which I can
> operate locally. It's a place where I go to sleep, eat, and have
> things done for me. I don't spend a lot of time there, and it's
> somewhat conscious. It's not as warm as I feel it should be.
> However, the fact that I now have a new child by the lady with
> whom I live, makes it somewhat different. At least I can enjoy
> being there for a specific reason, whereas in the past, I have not
> enjoyed going there for the most part. It's not live to me. I don't
> feel live. It's a hell of a bad thing to admit, but it's true. . . . The
> decor is live but the house is not live.

He sometimes lives with a woman who has his child in a north Chicago
suburb, sometimes with a younger woman on the South Side. His North Side
residence, relationships, and objects embody his rise on the social ladder and
the resulting bourgeois respectability, whereas his South Side attachments
connect him with his own ethnic roots and provide him with a "live"
environment that can gratify his desire for pleasure. He admits that his North
Side residence is better than it used to be now that he has a new child there,
because he can, "enjoy being there for a specific reason." He seems, however,
to regard his new child as a kind of good that can provide him with pleasure.
The objective environment seems to exist for the purpose of satisying B. L.'s
needs to stand alone and *to be seen standing there.* He does not seem to feel a
deep responsibility to give *himself* to other people, such as his various
children of different households, but rather to be "benevolent" by giving
money and possessions away. His goals are terminal because the ownership
of distinctive goods and people are what he values most. A consumptive
culture that would legitimize such terminal, self-centered, and rootless values
would surely wither and die very quickly.

The Past Recaptured

A present from one person to another involves more than the temporal present. It involves the past context of relationships and future consequences symbolized by the gift. Similarly, the domestic environment of

cherished possessions is more than a simple, perceptual present. It is personal time embodied, a storehouse of signs of treasured people, events, and achievements that communicate one's personal and cultural identity and that serve as contexts for further cultivation.

In this sense the view I am proposing might be termed *critical animism*. Animism has traditionally referred to the belief that certain animals, plants, or inanimate things such as ritual objects, are actually spirits, and as such should be treated as autonomous personalities. Animism is a view rather antithetical to anyone brought up in the modern Western tradition who believes that thought and things are radically different substances. Now I am not suggesting that we should believe in fairies and leprechauns, but what I am proposing is that objects are not merely inert matter but are living signs whose meanings are realized in the transactions we have with them and that need to be critically cultivated in the context of the consequences they bring about. This critical animism of signs means that all three elements of the transaction—person, thing, and what the thing represents—are intrinsically involved in its meaning. In other words, against the idea that meaning is a disembodied conceptual entity located in a brain, cultural system, or "deep structure," it is more accurate to view meaning as including the sign-objects through which representation occurs.

Let me illustrate this point with a concrete example drawn from one of the interviews, in this case with a thirteen-year-old girl. In describing the things in her home that are most special for her, she named one toy in particular that had special meaning, her stuffed dog. She said:

> My stuffed dog. He has his own special way. When I was little I used to talk to him and he used to talk back to me. We'd carry on a conversation. And everytime I'd look at him, I feel he's saying something to me. And my grandmother was going to throw him out. She said, "He's all beat-up." But I said no, I'm never throwing him out. We have a special communication together. I can't explain it. [Without the stuffed dog] It'd be something missing. I have a lot of other toys, but he's my favorite. If I didn't have him I'd feel uptight. Kind of tight. Sometimes when I have a problem, I just go cry on him.

This inanimate dog is clearly an *animate sign,* an external object, which, by being endowed with qualities of personhood, makes possible a self-dialogue in which this girl can communicate her own feelings to herself through an external means. Just as we develop internal habits for dealing with problems, this dog is a kind of external habit for this girl, a readily available means of coping with problems in a safe way, one in which she has control. This is a cute childish example, but are adult fishing poles, automobiles, stereos, photographs, and popular psychology books so very different? They too can act as surrogate partners in a relationship that can either help one to grow or simply alienate one from other people through a facade of things.

Through transactions with the animate signs of the domestic environment, one is constantly reminded of the links to one's past, links that are in turn fostered by the remembrance one cultivates. A particularly striking example of how simple, inanimate things can be alive with a multitude of complex meanings is given by the following woman's description of her family photos. In an otherwise normal interview, she seemed, when discussing these photos, to tap deeper regions of herself, expressed with compelling eloquence:

> That is the link with the past, the pictures of people that I never knew, and whom my children will certainly never know. I'm the kind of person who looks up relatives. It's a link with the past, the knowledge that these people are a part of our lives. I consider the loss of an irreplaceable photo a terrible, terrible loss. When I took a photo I liked, I always had a zillion copies made—but often forgot to give them to people—but I wanted to make sure somewhere there was another copy, in case anything happened to the original. But the ones my mother has from Europe are just irreplaceable, the people are all dead. All of their belongings were confiscated. There's nothing left.
>
> It's a very emotional issue for Jews who lost family during the Holocaust, and I don't know any Jewish people who didn't lose someone, some members of his family, whether it was someone he knew or didn't know. . . . All of my mother's five brothers and sisters, their husbands and wives, their children, her cousins, all of her childhood friends, everybody was slaughtered. Some died in the concentration camps, starvation and torture. Some were killed, pulled right out of their homes, and murdered, not just by the Nazis. One niece remained, the one whose paintings I have, she lives in Paris. And her contact with her sister—the only other one left of the whole family, dozens and dozens of people—she learned from her sister what happened to the family. They all lived in neighboring towns. . . . Some were sent to concentration camps. Others were just killed on the spot. Butchered by the local townspeople, who were given free rein by the Nazis to kill the Jews.
>
> My mother came to America when she was fifteen, her brother and sister were here. The rest were killed, and their homes were looted. It's very obvious that this has colored our feelings and thinking about a lot of things. There's no denying that what we call the Holocaust has had a profound effect on Jewish people living all over the world. My mother went through a terrible emotional, a terrible few years. She's never stopped crying about her family. But in recent years it affected her mentally—she

would say, "The trucks are coming, they're coming for me!" She had terrible dreams that were so real she would say, "My brothers and sisters, I saw the blood running!" On her it was even worse, because she knew these people, I didn't. But I have the pictures and I see them. It's heartbreaking to know that these little children—one of my mother's brothers was killed when he wouldn't give up his children, when they were taking them away. And they just battered him to death, on the spot. The whole thing was just so horrible. . . . My mother said to us, "Do you know what they're doing, they're making soap out of Jewish people." And my brother and I both said, "Ma, don't get so upset, this is the twentieth century, things like that don't happen now. That was in the middle ages." And it turned out to be true. The whole horrible nightmare. And that was a terrible thing to take. And even now we know of people who perpetrate pain, torture, and suffering on the other people and seem to enjoy it. It's a terrible, frightening thing.

Perhaps more than any other response, this remarkably vivid discussion of family photographs conveys the power of remembrance, and how simple personal belongings can express deep human needs for relationship and continuity in a world of oblivion. The woman who described these photos was born and raised in Chicago, far from the dark horror of Nazi Europe that exterminated her mother's family and forced her mother to move to America at age fifteen. She did not directly experience the Holocaust and yet it is a deeply and painfully felt part of her life, and, as she said elsewhere, of her children's lives, all so vividly symbolized by the photographs of her murdered ancestors and kin. She portrays the personal tragedy of the Holocaust with a searing directness that has been imprinted on her from the photos. The photos are tangible reminders not only of "the whole horrible nightmare," but of the precariousness of moral and material life, reminders of how what may seem so solid may be so easily swept away, reminders of the fact that the most abominable barbarisms can, and so frequently do, take place in this, the enlightened twentieth century. These photographs enable her to keep alive images of family and a sense of family and ethnic tradition. They enlarge her sense of self by connecting her with her murdered kin and the historical events in which they were involved; by acting as touchstones with which to confront the contemporary world; and as treasured keepsakes and reminders to be preserved and passed down to her children. Through her remembrance, mediated by the photos, the living memory of her family acts as an animate socializing sign in the cultural microcosm of the home.

Valued household objects are concrete manifestations of past valuations in the present. They infuse the present with a larger context of kinship ties, friendships, important experiences, and remembrances in a way that expresses who and what went before. Remembrance, like the two kinds of material valuation, is a critical process of cultivation. When remembrance becomes an end unto itself, mere nostalgia, it degenerates into a terminal bubble of the past that both closes one off from the living spontaneity of the present and denies the possibility of a future. Without remembrance, a life is subject to all the transient social fashions of the day, a leaf in the flux of a stream, incapable of calling anything truly its own, without its own conditioned history and ground for self-control.

Remembrance is one of the chief vehicles of sentiment, that vast reservoir of social feelings, emotions, prejudices, and common sense that reaches deep into habitual mind and biological mind, to the sum of all those ancestral, collective, and personal tempering experiences that almost imperceptibly shape our natures. Pure sentimentality alone is not enough as a guide for action, yet when informed by experience and cultivated by critical application, it can provide a much wider ground for development than that of pure rational mind.

We are mysterious creatures who mark our time on earth through tangible remembrances. We transform time itself, as it were, into tangible space through our makings and doings, personalizing our environment while objectifying ourselves. In our own time it might be said that things themselves have got the better of us, dominating our lives with their claim that buying and selling is the ultimate goal of existence. Yet in this economic age of possession, it remains possible, and indeed all the more essential, to reclaim significance from our surroundings. As Jorge Luis Borges has said, "Time is the one essential mystery," and, "Our task is to turn memory into beauty."

9   The City as Living Memory

> I could tell you how many steps make up the streets rising like stair-
> ways, and the degree of the arcades' curves. . . . but I already know this
> would be the same as telling you nothing. The city does not consist of
> this, but of relationships between the measurements of its space and the
> events of its past. . . . As this wave from memories flows in, the city
> soaks it up like a sponge and expands. . . . The city, however, does not
> tell its past, but contains it like the lines of a hand, written in the cor-
> ners of the streets, the gratings of the windows, the banisters of the
> steps, the antennae of the lightning rods, the poles of the flags, every
> segment marked in turn with scratches, indentations, scrolls.
>
> Italo Calvino, *Invisible Cities*

Of the many abilities that set us apart from the rest of nature, surely
remembrance is one of our most distinguishing features. Other animals and
even plants have innate biological clocks or habitualized memories of persons, places, or things, but remembrance, the ability to reminisce selectively,
to call to consciousness the significant biography and geography of one's
mind, is at the core of what makes us human. Through remembrance we
could people the imagination with a symbolic environment extending far
beyond the spatial and temporal limitations of individual existence. What
formerly had to be learned through direct contact could now be preserved
and handed on as cultural legacy. Not only was remembrance our chief
cultural legacy but it was the very means to our becoming human.

But the development of remembrance was not simply an inner
mental event, it required the creation of artifices—language, ritual, and
artifacts. Through these externalized forms of mind, emerging humanity
created the media of enlarged possibilities of communication and intelligent
conduct. These vital forms shaped from the vast reservoir of sentiment and
instinct could transform the narrow boundaries of lived experience into
wider environments of shared experience, environments that included beings
representing an extended temporal domain—gods and ancestors—who

could signify the broader temporal perspective and thereby overcome the tendency in individualized conduct toward forgetting.

As with all distinctively human abilities, remembrance also brought with it the danger of cultural nostalgia, the dulling of an individual's or a whole people's ability to encounter the present perceptively through a broadened framework, in favor of a reduction of all things present to an overly sentimentalized past that distorts rather than informs the present. "Remember the Alamo!" may once have been a brave call to collective action, but when that memory becomes simply an excuse for ethnic separatism, it is reduced to haunting spectre rather than living memory. As Doris Lessing reminds us in her Swiftian account of the problem of memory and modern rationalized consciousness in *The Sentimental Agents*, the more advanced we become in our culture of words, the easier it becomes to slip into exaggerated forms of sentimentality and nostalgia. Living memory, by contrast, is purposive memory that touches the present and infuses its wisdom onto the world of experience.

From the earliest graves come not only key signs of our transformation into humankind and into the settled patterns of life that form the basis of urbanism, but also records of the obvious role of remembrance in that transformation. The dead were the first to attain a permanent and even memorable dwelling place, and, as Lewis Mumford said,

> perhaps the first form of the city is the cemetery, the city of the dead, a place to which people returned to keep a sense of family identity and continuity. As a matter of fact, one might write a whole interpretation of the city in this vein. . . . In time, when the city at last develops, it serves as a kind of tomb, filled with dead institutions as well as dead bodies, so that, even when it is destroyed as often as Troy, the survivors return to the same spot out of piety to the dead. (Mumford 1960, 226)

Just as language contains the "bricolage" or debris of past cultures, the signs developed in prior modes of culture that still serve as essential building blocks for contemporary communicative needs and purposes—such as, for example, the enduring influence of medieval scholastic terminology on English—so too the city is a composite of times, where the eternal meets the circadian. I remember my shock in seeing the neighborhood boys playing darts on the great doors of the Church of the Carmine in Florence where the Renaissance was born. I wondered how many generations of boys had played darts on those doors, how many more generations it would take for time's work to be done, and also how many generations had grown up and then claimed the golden achievements of their city's past as something worthy of preservation. The old woman inside the church who was pumping coins into the box under a cheap, glowing commercial picture of Jesus and the Apostles could not care less that the Old and New Testaments had first assumed humanized and local form in Masaccio's paintings on the walls surrounding her. Legacy, like all other dimensions of human culture, does not automatically act upon its inheritors. It only acts as a conduit of possibilities, just as the city is a container and conduit of possibilities. Both must be actively cultivated to realize their vital potentials.

THE SEMIOTIC VIEW OF THE MODERN CITY

> The city is redundant: it repeats itself so that something will stick in the mind. . . . Memory is redundant: it repeats signs so that the city can begin to exist.
>
> Italo Calvino, *Invisible Cities*

The buildings, places, and institutions of the city are not merely static entities or inert objects, or even simply structural codes, but are signs that live objectively in the transactions people have with them. They signify history, relationships, current practices and goals; communicate a sense of place and participation; and grow, through cultivation, in the minds of those who care for and about them. The metropolitan environment, from this semiotic perspective, is a living sign-practice transcending the present moment and objectively situated in the minds and hearts of its inhabitants as well as forming an external dimension of their minds and hearts. The city is itself a public possession, but one which should also simultaneously possess its inhabitants by endowing them with the energy, communicative forms, and opportunities for participating in the larger drama of urban life. In this sense the city is a larger personality, one that should be our means to an enriched life, but one which can also act as an all-devouring Moloch, swallowing all vitality for its own destructive purposes, as Fritz Lang's 1926 movie *Metropolis* so masterfully and prophetically showed.

The metropolitan environment is a communicative medium of signs, ranging from materiality per se to the memories or "cognitive maps" of its inhabitants; and the significance of this environment of signs resides in the ways it makes an expressive, cohesive, and vital social life possible and practicable. To use the terminology of Charles Peirce's semiotic, metropolis is icon of the expressive feelings it embodies, index of the energies it animates, and symbol of the growth of all the purposeful modes of conduct it makes possible. In Peirce's words "every symbol" (and I should reiterate that a symbol is but one mode of sign in Peirce's semiotic, that which signifies through conventional understanding) "is a living thing, in a very strict sense that is no mere figure of speech. The body of the symbol changes slowly, but its meaning inevitably grows, incorporates new elements and throws off old ones. . . . a symbol, once in being, spreads among the peoples. In use and in experience, its meaning grows" (CP 2.222, 2.302). Peirce's description of a symbol could just as well be that of a city, a "living thing" whose body "changes slowly, but its meaning inevitably grows" as it "incorporates new elements and throws off old ones."

My apologies to those familiar with the high-tech field of semiotics for whom this appropriation of Peirce may sound unfamiliar, or even unsemiotic! But I must stress that to the extent the city is viewed simply as structural code, apart from any vital or purposeful aim, it is alienated—even as semiological structuralism is one avatar of that advanced poison of abstractionism that dominates our cities and entire cultural life, claiming that an inhumane logic is and should be at the heart of cultural "codes" and urban planning, and that sentiment is either superfluous or mere ornamentation. It would be much more correct, and, I might add, semiotically correct, to say that rationality is at present but an ornamentation on the far vaster depths of sentiment that compose the human psyche and soul, an ornamentation, however, that has deluded itself with its power and unhinged itself, progressively downgrading or obliterating anything that does not meet its own now distorted norms.

Symbolic signs may be conventional "codes," but codes themselves operate within a broader sign-web of purpose. As mentioned earlier, structuralism, as well as the positivist variety of semiotics launched by Charles Morris, simply does not address this larger question—What are codes *for?*—yet this is the whole point of the semiotic perspective proposed here. I am adopting the concept of the polis as *purposive community*, a concept shared by Aristotle, Mumford, and Peirce, in which the community is defined as the common object of a plurality of perspectives (politics in the ancient Greek sense, or city as citizenry). The ultimate foundation for the metropolis is the same as that for the sign in Peirce: the unlimited community capable of realizing through the continued life of interpretation the purpose of purpose—the truth or the right conduct of life. The city is not simply an aggregate of goods, services, things, and people who happen all to be lumped together engaging in certain types of behaviors, it is intrinsically purposive: it is in its own constitution a purposive sign. And one of the primary purposes of all cities, and particularly the modern city, is to bring out the best in its citizens.

In its own physical structure a great city symbolizes a much larger society than one's own family or neighborhood, and in so doing can personify the impersonal and thus provide a broader conception of self. And a symbol, like a metropolis, is meant to unite people. The term "symbol" itself literally means to throw together or unify. To be an individual person is to be a living symbol and member of that commonality of meaning which is the wider community. The words common, community, and communication are related around the same root, *munis*, meaning a gift exchanged. Communication itself depends upon the possibility of a common ground, and the common ground is the life of the community: that purposive web of social individuals whose symbols, that is, gestures, language, artifacts, buildings, and practices, constitute a culture. Each and every sign, in representing something to someone, acts as a communicative dialogue within an organic, objective web of meaning.

A metropolis is meant to unite people not only in physical proximity but in the shared symbols of a common, however diverse, culture; symbols that can signify a vital and complete existence. One sees this in a number of ancient cities of the far east, such as Angkor Thom, whose sacred centers— the temples, palaces, or squares—symbolize their position as center of the cosmos (Wheatley 1967, 10f.). Through a symbolism that attempted to elevate the city as microcosm of the sacred macrocosm these cities linked their citizens with representations of the world center, uniting the inhabitants with the larger purposes not only of their community but of the all-surrounding cosmos. As Wheatley has noted in describing Persepolis, that city stood as

> the quintessentially sacred enclave of the Persian culture realm, a *Civitas Dei* designed as an appropriate setting for the hierophanies of Ahura Mazda himself. There is scarcely a foot of wall which does not bear the stamp of this grand essay in the establishment of a parallelism between the worlds. . . . Persepolis constituted a magnificent demonstration of abundance, the contribution of the Persian people to the maintenance of harmony between the heavens and the earth, an unequivocal declaration that they were enacting their assigned roles in the cosmic process. (Wheatley 1967, 33, 34)

This does not mean that there were not serious political conflicts or diverse points of view in traditional cities, but only that there tended to be a shared worldview embodied in the very physical structure of the city itself.

One has only to view the architecture of many ancient cities, such as Angkor Thom or Persepolis, and then compare those cities with a large modern metropolis, such as Chicago or Los Angeles, to see how the modern city seems to signify almost the complete antithesis: instead of unified microcosmos, it emphasizes seemingly unlimited differentiation; instead of sharing in an overarching community, modern urban dwellers seem to be exemplars of externalized individuality and idiosyncrasy—cosmopolitans without a cosmos. In the views of Georg Simmel, Max Weber, and Lewis Mumford, the rise of modern culture and forms of individuality in the West are intrinsically bound up with the evolution of Western urbanism, and in Mumford's case it would be more accurate to call it a process of devolution or, to use his term, "deurbanization."

It would seem that we can no longer characterize the modern city in terms of the unified worldviews of traditional cities and their inhabitants. Or perhaps our task becomes drastically more difficult and indirect. Given the secularization of modern life, there is an almost unbridgeable symbolic gap between the *axis mundi* of the ancient city and what would be its modern equivalent, say, the Sears Tower of Chicago and its meanings to Chicagoans. Although the need to symbolize the city as center of the cosmos may still persist, for example, it is apparent that the modern consciousness has transformed the spiritual world center into the world trade center, the *axis money*. The religious sentiment has given way to the economic sentiment, just as Simmel argued in *The Philosophy of Money* (1900); God, as ultimate purpose, has given way to Money, as ultimate modern purpose. And yet the often conflicting signs of contemporary urban life—the erection of a new steel and glass skyscraper (with a corner lopped off so as to look "postmodern") next to an old church undergoing renovation—often do somehow point toward the complex whole or personality of a city. "Characterization of the city, and of the life lived in it," as Richard Wohl and Anselm Strauss have said, "is indispensable for organizing the inevitably ambiguous mass of impressions and experiences to which every inhabitant is exposed, and which he must collate and assess, not only for peace of mind but to carry on daily affairs" (Strauss 1961, 17).

Without something to remember, something that lives as a sign in memory and can serve to give shape to and organize conduct, the city remains a blur of meaningless signs. For the city, as Emerson observed, "lives by remembering" (in Mumford 1961, 98). How then may we begin to uncover the physical "grammar of signs" that makes a city memorable, and in so doing infuses the present with broader possibilities for meaningful conduct?

TOWARD A GRAMMAR OF METROPOLITAN SIGNS: CHICAGO

A number of ways of uncovering the grammar of metropolitan signs in Chicago are possible. One could, following Strauss, discuss the images that appear most persistently in literary and popular historical sources (Strauss 1961). Another route might be the detailed ethnography of a specific community, as exemplified in Suttles's study of the "Addams area" of the Near West Side of Chicago. Albert Hunter examined the symbolic definitions of local community by interviewing approximately ten people in each of the seventy-five community areas of Chicago and then analyzing a number of geographical and social variables (Hunter 1974). Kevin Lynch interviewed thirty people in Boston, fifteen in Jersey City, and fifteen in Los Angeles, and had them draw maps and discuss the mental images associated with their own city (Lynch 1960). The approach taken here was to interview a sample of Chicagoans and simply ask them what stood out for them as "special" about the city of Chicago. It was hoped that a diverse group of Chicagoans might provide a more representative image of the commonly shared symbols of

Chicago than a group that might be selected solely from literary accounts, and thus serve as a basis for critical interpretation. By examining the representations of the modern metropolis, we can explore how a city comes to be personified, what makes urban living a specific and (for some) desirable way of life, and how the vast complexity of a city like Chicago comes to be organized and used as a rule for conduct. If, following Mumford, Simmel, Mead, and others, mind is a dimension of the community or *polis*, then representations of this broader community can illustrate some of the ways the modern metropolis contributes to the cultivation of its inhabitants and is itself an indicator of modern culture.

The respondents in my 1977 research—mainly residents of Rogers Park (a North Side neighborhood in Chicago) and Evanston, forming a socioeconomically stratified sample of eighty-two three-generation families—were interviewed in their homes concerning not only possessions, but also "things" and places in the broader urban environment. They were asked, following Lynch (1960), what first comes to mind on hearing the word "Chicago," to broadly describe the city, and then to name the places that were most special for them by day and by night, as if they were showing these places to a friend from another city. They were also asked to describe the places in the city that made them feel certain emotions, such as "sad" and "free." Rather than impose a-priori typologies upon those interviewed, I hoped that the grammar of signs would begin to emerge from these open-ended questions. A number of common-sense categories were drawn from responses in order to outline the broad features of Chicago, and although these are meant to represent "native" categories, they should not be regarded as rigidly fixed or exhaustive. Other ways of categorizing the data are possible, but these seemed to work quite well for my purposes.

The main locations described as "special" are landmarks of Chicago, and include museums, Lake Michigan, noted buildings, artworks, and various other well-known public areas. In many ways they match the officially designated tourist attractions, and are overwhelmingly centered in the Loop. These metropolitan symbols, as one might expect, have more stereotyped meanings than the personal possessions of these same respondents described previously. But a stereotype need not be a dead convention; it can serve just as well to impress a living image of the city on the minds of its possessors, and to create a lasting impression. A powerful urban symbol will usually either possess inherent imageability (or iconicity) or have a cultural convention associated with it (such as the association of the North Michigan Avenue water tower with the Great Fire of 1871), but its vitality as symbol will depend on how it reciprocally cultivates and is cultivated by those it addresses.

For most people, the question "What comes to mind when you hear the word *Chicago* and how would you broadly describe Chicago?" elicits descriptions of gangsters and blues, of the Chicago Fire of 1871, and the great Chicago architecture that was born in the aftermath of that fire. Like New York, it is a city of immigrants and, also like New York, one that can be described as a city of vast slums. But there is also the romantic Chicago, a city of stereotypes and images from the past, such as the slaughterhouses, that are no longer actually present in the city. When we think of cities we usually think of prominent stereotypes that are associated with them and that Chambers of Commerce usually tend to promote. These stereotypes can serve as vague markers on which to attach our own personal experiences of a particular city, and in this sense can serve either negatively as mere worn-out clichés or more positively as living symbols of collective identity, of the metropolitan consciousness. Consider, for example, the following description of Chicago given by a grandmother and lifelong resident of the city. The gangster image and Chicago Fire are significant, not in the usual stereotypical way, but because of her own memories of people and experiences connected with these themes:

> My youth, because I lived on the Near North Side and I remember Dion O'Banion and his florist place and I remember the kindness he offered by always giving me one flower a day. I remember Oak Street Beach with its rickshaws. It was a very colorful time because I saw all the gangsters' funerals. That was very impressive because they had walking musicians. It was really a colorful time of my life. Then there was the Michigan Avenue stores, the old McCormick place. I went to the Ogden School. At that time the principal was Mrs. Martha Priggles, who was crippled in the Chicago Fire. She is in the Chicago Society—a replica. I remember the wooden floors in the hallways going up and where she stood at the head of the stairs with a cane tapping and marking time. I had to play a march——I was only eight years old—on the piano. This is the colorful part.
>
> Chicago to me is what my young days offered. [*Could you describe?*]. Now? I am turned off by Chicago. I think the people that have come in are not of the calibre to bring any beauty. They destroy. Sheridan Road at one time was nice—now the houses are defaced. The people now that are coming in destroy the streets, the neighborhood; they are destroying the world. I'd take those professional gangsters against any of the hoodlums walking the street. Because they never touched you. I remember Dion O'Banion. He was the kindest man. It's disgusting today. I'd like to run.

Ah, "Sweet Home Chicago" (as the blues song says), where one can remember "the kindest man," who gave flowers to children, and the principal of one's elementary school, who marked time while you played a march.

Though these sorts of reminiscences are no doubt common for many an older person, it is not everywhere that the subject of such reminiscence could happen to be one of the most notorious gangsters ever to challenge the Capone gang (he lost), and who was given a testimonial by the Democratic Party bosses before the 1924 election, as well as the grandest gangster funeral of all a short time later, with 122 funeral cars and 26 truckloads of flowers. Or a school principal, now enshrined in the Chicago Historical Society, and similarly touched by the spectre of violence that has been part of Chicago since its earliest days: crippled by the Great Fire of 1871. What is remarkable about these reminiscences is how this woman not only interacted with these "archetypes" of Chicago, who have now come to symbolize Chicago's memorialized past, but how these people and experiences have entered into her perceptions of contemporary Chicago as standards for conduct ("I'd take those professional gangsters against any of the hoodlums walking the street"). Or to take it even further, the memories of Chicago *are* Chicago for this woman; what she confronts on a daily basis, what a behaviorally oriented social scientist asking about "attendance and activity patterns" would call "her Chicago," is not Chicago for her, but only a falling away from it. But the memories she carries with her, although she cannot perhaps point to them as actualities today, are signs that invest her environment with meaning, even if it is a meaning rooted in the past and not capable of fully touching the present.

This same theme of Chicago as signifying the remembrance of things past was common for older respondents of my study, just as, when describing their most significant possessions, they stressed the importance of contemplation and reminiscence. One lifelong Chicagoan described the significance of Chicago as follows:

> I've lived here all of my adult life and I like the city of Chicago. I don't like what happened in the past ten or twenty years, where you can't go out in the street at night, and the crime, although this neighborhood here is much better than the other side of the tracks. . . . You see, I've lived in Chicago since I was three. When I was a boy, my brother and I, we used to live at 60th and Dorchester, where the Del Prado Hotel was, across the street. And we roamed this park, we got our names under all these bridges. And the old German building, its gone now; this was after the World's Fair and some of the old buildings were still there. We were out there fishing one day, my brother and I, with a bent pin for a hook and a limb of a tree, and we were catching one fish after another. And an old man sitting next to us, he must have had a hundred dollars' worth of equipment and he wasn't catching any fish. And he began to laugh and laugh and he said, "Boys, look at all this equipment." And he invited us over to the

German building for lunch, which for us, we were six, seven
years old, it was a big treat.

I like Chicago. I don't like the change in the people. Nobody
likes that. And of course at my age, I live in a different world
than you do, or my daughter does.

This last point, "I live in a different world than you do," by a
seventy-nine-year-old man who has spent his entire life in Chicago highlights
the fact that people living in the same physical environment may inhabit quite
diverse symbolic environments. Chicago is largely the memories of his child-
hood, where he fished and marked his territory with his name just as, though
probably in a less benign way, the graffiti terrorist youth of today continue to
do.

Building/Architecture

Despite a long record of destruction of its architectural heritage,
architecture remains an outstanding objective feature of the city of Chicago.
Widely regarded as the birthplace of modern architecture, Chicago has still
standing many of the works of Louis Sullivan, Frank Lloyd Wright, and
others: embodied testimony to the revolutionary ideas these architects introduced as Chicago rebuilt itself after the Great Fire of 1871 and expanded into
a great trade center in the early part of this century. Yet the Chicago
architectural tradition seems not to be all that significant for Chicagoans; it is
probably fair to say that, like Chicago sociology and philosophy and, more
recently, Chicago blues and jazz, Chicago architecture generates far more
interest elsewhere, especially abroad, than in the city itself. The historical and
aesthetic value of the city's architecture was, however, important for some
respondents, such as one woman who described the beauty of the Auditorium
Theater (designed by Dankmar Adler and Louis Sullivan in 1889) in the
context of the current "modern" trend of buildings:

> The Auditorium Theater is an exquisite work of art. A beautiful
> structure which was beautiful when it was built and is still
> beautiful. Although the lines of buildings being built now are
> straight and plain, I don't believe it will ever lose its appeal. I
> can't imagine not using this building and don't feel that the city
> will lose it to the changes that are occurring.

Others would mention a building because of the activities that it
once housed or now houses, e.g., hospitals and universities, rather than for its
architecture. One man singled out one of the more notorious Chicago dens of
iniquity, the North Michigan Hotel, because it served as Al Capone's headquarters, although he also recognized its architectural merit:

> We've never had visitors who didn't enjoy Chicago. . . . They al-
> ways want to know about Al Capone. On the way to China-

town, I show them the Michigan Hotel, which Al Capone used as headquarters, and which, by the way, is a beautiful piece of architecture.

The most important architectural feature of Carl Sandburg's "city of the broad shoulders," however, were the tall buildings, such as the Sears Tower, the John Hancock Center, and the Standard Oil Building. Though architecturally perhaps not as beautiful or significant as other Chicago buildings, these modern monoliths represented the raw *power* of Chicago, as well as its uniqueness as the center of the world's tallest buildings:

> The Hancock Building. Especially the restaurant and lounge. It affords a view of the shore and skyline of the city, which is quite beautiful. It's as high as you can go without going into an airplane. . . . With the naked eye you can see the lake, the ferries, the city sprawled out before you, the city's traffic. It's all quite fascinating.

> The Sears Tower. It's so big and there's only one of its kind.

> The Sears Tower. We can go up to the observation deck and see the lights of the city. There's a beautiful view, and it makes you feel important in this large city.

Tall buildings symbolized both the relative insignificance of the urban dweller who looks up at them and, at the other extreme, the feeling of omnipotence when looking down at the city from the observation decks or restaurants.

What does not at all emerge at the personal level of interviews and yet is intrinsic to the symbolic structure of the contemporary skyscraper is how corporate economy is elevated through these buildings to a dominant and central position over the life of the city, accurately reflecting the dominance of corporate economy over the political life of the modern city. I would suggest further that these buildings draw from the ancient theme of *axis mundi* the symbolism of sacred and transcendent center, though transformed into materialistic rationalism. They signify a gravity escaping power whose motivating principle is not God but Money: Sears Tower of the Chicago mail-order and now chain-store consumer culture, John Hancock Center of the American sacrament of insurance, Standard Oil Building of the American Oil Empire (for a sensitive discussion of the symbolic nature of skyscrapers see Denney, "The Suppliant Skyscrapers" [1964]).

Museums

The term "museum" derives from an ancient Greek word meaning "a temple of the muses" (those daughters of Mnemosyne, Memory herself), and a museum is described as "an establishment recording and propagating the cultivation, by the people, of the arts and sciences" (Partridge 1958). In many ways museums have become the high temples of modern culture, secular shrines housing the tokens of human culture and technology and natural history. One often sees a hushed reverence among art-museum visitors, for example, as they make their way past icons of the past and present. For this reason many have criticized contemporary museums as mausoleums, empty homages to status conventions that misrepresent their objects by holding them up as sacred, or that cater to large crowds and public whims rather than serving an educative purpose.

Although these criticisms may be correct, museums were still frequently cited by respondents as personally significant symbols of Chicago, offering rich symbolic environments that can be experienced inexpensively within the city and, for many, expressing its vitality.

Whether these things will act as "muses" and inspire aesthetic or educative experiences still depends on what the viewer either brings to the situation or can learn from it. But apart from this fact museums do seem to serve as warehouses of culture, both negatively and positively, in Chicago. The geographical proximity of the Art Institute, the Field Museum of Natural History, the Shedd Aquarium, and the Adler Planetarium in and around Grant Park on the city's lakefront also serves to delineate a visually impressive "neighborhood" of museums. Though others may have expressed it much more eloquently, one Puerto Rican mill worker summed up the importance of museums for many people when he said: "Because they got a lot of nice things there, and it's really like going to another world." When the museum acts as metropolitan symbol, it brings individuals into contact with the broader and more distant spatiotemporal world in a tangible way, and can potentially enrich their conceptions both of self and world.

Lakefront Liminality

Throughout the interviews one common theme was the availability and proximity of "natural" areas, and the lakefront was singled out as a highly valued feature of Chicago because of its beauty, serenity, and numerous beaches. A continuous strip of natural lake and lakefront running through much of the city was seen as contributing to the uniqueness of Chicago. The fact that the lakefront zone has been carefully cultivated was not often mentioned, even though it is obvious that parks have to be "manicured" by the city's Park District or, more significantly, that the city has structured the lakefront area both to appear "natural" and at the same time to be on display. In fact, visitors seldom realize that a vast ghetto exists, in many stretches of the lakefront, only a few blocks away. In this way the natural landscape is cultivated to provide an unnatural facade for the city's social eyesores, even though the lakefront does provide an authentic experience of *urban nature* for all strata of Chicagoans. Not only does it signify nature for those who use it regularly, it also holds the same meaning for many who seldom even see it. Like the Art Institute, Lake Michigan acts as a sign of metropolis whose presence per se and in personal memory far outweighs the actual number of times it is frequented: it signifies a zone where a different set of rules operate, where one can go in reminiscence or in actuality.

Perhaps the lake does not possess the subtle refinement of Seurat's *La Grande Jatte*, which hangs in the Art Institute, and, as Smith (1984) has noted, the lake rarely shows up in Chicago literature; but as one respondent put it, "It's free," and on a fair day in warm weather one can stroll or drive for miles along the lakefront and smell the barbecues as all classes of families and individuals converge for picnics. Lake Michigan was also described as providing a meditative environment where one could "leave the city behind" for the quiet splashing of water on rock. The lakefront serves as a liminal symbol in Victor Turner's sense (1969), as a place where one can temporarilly put aside the normal high-stimulus environment and its rules, and for a time retreat from high-tech culture to a simpler nature. It carries a range of meanings across the life span for those who make the intracity pilgrimage to it: a place of play for children, of games and adventure for adolescents, of picnicing and relaxation for adults, and a source of contemplation for the old. These zones of simplicity and relative control over the environment serve to counteract what Simmel termed "the blasé outlook" imposed by the city:

> There is perhaps no psychic phenomenon which is so uncon-
> ditionally reserved to the city as the blasé outlook. It is at first
> the consequence of those rapidly shifting stimulations of the
> nerves which are thrown together in all their contrasts and from
> which it seems to us the intensification of metropolitan intellec-
> tuality seems to be derived. (Simmel 1971, 329).

In contrast, the lakefront and its parks reduce the overstimulation that work, buildings, crowded streets, and city noise produce, and in effect produce a temporary amnesia in actual experience, a swallowing into the celebratory moment, that yet becomes a memorable sign in the geography of the mind.

Neighborhoods as the Localization of Meaning

For a city to be memorable it is important that it be capable of being personified, and one of the key means to personification seems to be through the localization of meaning to familiar and habituated habitats within the city. Respondents to a checklist of Chicago symbols consistently rated their own neighborhoods, along with the lakefront, more positively than they did any of the other thirty-seven items listed. And this was true of the lower middle-class as well as the upper middle-class. For many of the lower middle-class respondents there was a theme of having "crossed over" the city line into more spacious surroundings at a time when housing was still relatively cheap. One man from a neighborhood in Rogers Park illustrated the importance of locality when he described Chicago, and Rogers Park in particular, as "Home. Why? Of course because I was born here. It's a place I would never pick to live in, but one that I feel comfortable in simply because I know it." He went on to describe the spirit of his neighborhood as embodied in a communal ladder that a former neighbor who had "passed on" left. When asked whether the neighbor had died, he laughed and replied that although it did seem that way, the neighbor had actually moved from Chicago. The ladder symbolized both the former neighbor who was "the real spirit of the neighborhood, he really got things to move," as well the communal spirit of the neighborhood itself, which was most unusual in being able to share a ladder without getting possessive.

A quite different description was given by a young woman from the Near West Side of Chicago, who described her neighborhood as "A dumpy area populated by a lot of dumpy people." Nevertheless, she valued her local bar more than anything else in Chicago, and Chicago was to her the painful memories of her turbulent blues existence. She valued the bar as a place "to drink, gamble, meet people, play pool. I can act crazy and in this place seem normal. I guess you can call it an escape. It's also where I met my husband." When we examine the other valued aspects of her neighborhood, some of the pieces of her life seem to fall together. She mentioned two friends' houses: One where she knew people when she was "down and out" trying to be a singer in a rock band, and which reminds her "of how frustrated I became at life." The source of this frustration was most likely located at the other house, as she said: "Blade's house. I loved him, and lovers are really all I have. Too bad he had to kill himself." One sees in this profile a neighborhood of haunting memories, signs of a self-destructive lifestyle in which even the positive valuation of the bar and its associated activities repeats the same negative pattern.

Another theme that came up for many respondents, especially older ones, was the memory of former neighborhoods. For a number of mostly upper middle-class grandparents who had moved to lakeside condominiums, the memory of former neighborhoods was quite significant. Often they had moved because of fear of increased crime in changing neighborhoods, and despite the greater security afforded by highrises and the lakeside view, there was still a nostalgia for the busy, informal life of the neighborhood that the more cloistered high rise could not match.

Lakefront high-rise buildings, such as those concentrated along the "Gold Coast" on the Near North Side, stand in striking contrast to the lower-class public housing high-rise projects built in Chicago during the 50s and 60s. These buildings, such as the Robert Taylor Housing Project or Cabrini Green Project, are actually high-danger areas, and for this reason offer residents less mobility and chance for social contact than the slums the projects replaced. The failure of low-income high-rise buildings to provide a sense of community for their inhabitants is a literal example of what Alfred North Whitehead called "the fallacy of misplaced concreteness." In these environments, planned solely on the basis of "functional" considerations, little or no attention was paid to such basic functions as how people might interact with each other, or how a community might be built out of the structure itself. Consequently these buildings have exacerbated the already existing ills of ghetto life, and become islands of terror, alienation, and fear; hellish inversions of the status hierarchy of living high above the ground. For the residents, their altitude means entrapment and isolation, not freedom.

The Cemetery

> Whenever the living think about the deaths of others they necessarily express some of their own concern about their own extinction. The cemetery provides them with enduring, visible symbols which help them to contemplate man's fate and their own separate destinies. The cemetery and its gravestones are the hard, enduring signs which anchor each man's projections of his innermost fantasies and private fears about the certainty of his own death—and the uncertainty of his ultimate future—on an external object made safe by tradition and the sanctions of religion (Warner 1959, 280).

Apparently somebody forgot to tell the Chicagoans of my study how the cemetery, as Warner said, "provides them with enduring, visible symbols which help them to contemplate man's fate and their own separate destinies." For cemeteries were hardly ever mentioned as special, and in a simple checklist of thirty-seven Chicago "symbols" (drawn from the results of a prior pilot study), cemeteries were rated most negatively, along with ghettoes, factories, and City Hall. Although one can easily see how ghettoes, factories, and City Hall can represent the decay, blight, and corruption of contemporary Chicago, it is not as obvious at first why cemeteries should be so negatively valued. Certainly the cemetery would have been much more positively valued at the turn of the century as the site of the "family plot," the visible sign of one's roots in Chicago. Yet contemporary average Chicagoans, with the exception perhaps of the old, tend to shy away from the cemetery and the questions it raises.

I asked a class of adults in Chicago to rate cemeteries and found a similar low ranking, and in conversation it became apparent that death is something to be put out of mind in contemporary "feel good" America, not something on which to meditate. One striking exception was a student from Nigeria, who valued cemeteries highly, and when asked why responded, "Because that is where dead people *live*." He went on to describe how he visited his father's grave before he left Nigeria to tell him he was coming to America so that his father's spirit would protect him. And when he returned to Nigeria he planned to go and tell his father personally. On hearing this, the American students, many of whom were themselves black, saw that perhaps there was something significant about cemeteries after all. But it is clear that death and its symbolization in the cemetery is a zone that is heavily repressed in contemporary American culture.

A profound symbolic antidote to the culture of oblivion and death-repression can be found, however, in the cultural life of Chicago portrayed in Saul Bellow's *Humboldt's Gift*. There death, "the only real question" according to Walt Whitman, motivates the deepest meditations of the protagonist of the book, Charlie Citrine. Bellow/Citrine's view of modern life as centered around egocentric individuals and their power and status relations contrasts with his view of death; this view, expressed in one of the book's meditations, requires a shift to the perspective of the periphery and allows a look at the egocentric center. In this way the views on death developed in the book can be seen as a critique of modern culture and what Melville referred to as cultural "Isolatoism."

Perhaps death can be seen as the underbelly of modern culture, something that the bright, ardent view of modern culture cannot see or admit, something that forever foils the American dream of the Fountain of Youth: the denial of the wisdom of old age. When seriously confronted and questioned, death reveals not only cessation of the person and anguish for his or her survivors, but the deeper continuity of human existence preserved as memory. Death is life's final teaching for those who can see and hear and remember and transmit. If social life consists largely in exchange, which is itself a subspecies of transformation, then death represents a final exchange from the carnal to the symbolic, a transformation through remembrance to the legacy of one's acts that lives in others and in this sense is a gift to the living. But of course this implies that death depends on the living, and on a culture of life willing to remember and willing to question the meaning of existence, not content to dream the transient dream of creature comfort and oblivion.

Nighttime Chicago

The symbolic geography of Chicago undergoes a radical shift at night, when it becomes a city of restaurants, nightclubs, and lights; and of cultural events such as concerts, movies, and plays. Museums, as often cited daytime symbols of the city, drop completely out of sight. Similarly, nature tends to become what it was for the ancient city-dweller—a wild area haunted by dangerous barbarians. Only a few of the younger respondents singled out the nighttime lakefront, and even they tended to emphasize the view from the road or a building, not the experience of being on the lake. One exception was a Mexican-American dope dealer, who liked to "get high and swim with friends," and who appreciated the congenial environment of this liminal zone as "good for my business"—selling drugs.

THE EMOTIONAL GEOGRAPHY OF CHICAGO

Most ecological approaches would have us believe that the only sentiments expressed toward the environment are primitive instincts of greed and "territoriality," as if emotions do not form a valid mode of intelligence in their own right. Yet human emotions, quite simply, consist of communicative signs with multiple modes of being—qualitative, energetic, and symbolic—and, like conceptual reasoning, are capable of complex cultivation. One only has to experience a great work of art to realize that sentiment can be one of the most sophisticated forms of human expression, even in our age of abstracted rationalism, which so frequently degrades sentiment into exaggerated forms of sentimentality.

It can also be argued that human sentiment, in the form of customs, traditions, and personal habits, is the vehicle of that vast reservoir of unquestioned assumptions that shape a culture and provide a ground for action. A vital culture furnishes a grammer of sentiments that enables one to act relatively unself-consciously. For this reason "cognitive maps" are not just utilitarian logic systems; they are also moral and aesthetic systems involving sentiment and qualities of feeling.

In an attempt to examine the "emotional geography" of Chicago, respondents were asked what aspects of Chicago made them feel happy, sad, lonely, free, and in touch with other people. Two emotions in particular, "sad" and "free," presented some interesting variations on the themes already described.

In the responses to "sad" expressions of urban blight predominate: buildings and neighborhoods are noted for their decay, and crime and transient people are mentioned as outgrowths of this decay. By contrast, the typical cosmopolitan in Chicago feels freest in urban nature, especially on the inland sea, Lake Michigan. The ghetto was clearly the central aspect of Chicago that makes people feel sad; through its crime and blight, it also represented the greatest threat to the continued vitality of the city. The ghetto, as described in these responses and in the general descriptions of the city, clearly forms one of the most important symbols of Chicago and, indeed, of the contemporary American metropolis. It imposes an all-enveloping symbol of fear upon life in the city, curtailing many nighttime activities, and thwarting the attempts of many ghetto residents toward decent neighborhood life. The feeling of sadness is tinged with nostalgia for a time when Chicago, despite its long history of crime and poverty, allowed a greater freedom of movement and sense of vitality. Hence where memory does become prominent, it is usually to call attention to a less fearful time in the

past now lost. Memory seldom signifies memorability for any of the responses to the emotional geography of Chicago in a sense of living achievement and legacy.

METROPOLIS AND MODERN CULTURE

The partial grammar of metropolitan symbols emerging from this
study suggests some of the main templates or stereotypes that imprint the
memory of Chicago on the minds of its inhabitants. It is not a complete
picture, but only an outline of the most general level of environment as seen
mostly from the personal perspective. For the lived and remembered experience of the city includes not only the increasingly personal levels of community area, neighborhood, and household, and the people, artifacts, and
activities that symbolize these levels but also the broader institutional and
cultural dimensions that shape personal experience. What becomes obvious
from this exploration, however, is that *the environment speaks to us* through
the signs with which we personalize it. In its physical structure a city expresses the culture of its inhabitants as a kind of corporate personality. It tells us
who we are and who we have been, and in this way provides a standard, for
better or worse, for who and what we might become.

One of the primary tasks of the city is to bring out the best in its
citizens, to provide in its educational, civic, occupational, and cultural institutions the means of cultivating and broadening their habits of life. By the
same token a city requires cultivation by its inhabitants if it is to survive and
flourish. The symbols of Chicago reveal a powerfully imageable metropolis,
one potentially *capable* of producing enduring memories and goals. But in
many instances these archetypes of modern culture seem to act more as mere
road signs of the ego rather than living symbols organically related to a way
of life or to a broader, deeply felt community. Perhaps this is due to the level
of analysis: I have chosen to concentrate on signs of the metropolis as a
totality, rather than on the signs of urban living at the levels of community
area and neighborhood. The tradition of community studies in Chicago,
including more recent ones such as Gerald Suttles's study of the "Addams
area" (1968), or Albert Hunter's *Symbolic Communities* (1974), certainly
has revealed the richness of cultural forms in many community areas and
neighborhoods. One might expect the vividness and depth of environmental
signs to increase as they move closer to the individual: the neighborhood
tavern or fair; the houses and people on one's block; the cherished possessions in one's home; the clothing, jewelry, identification cards, or photos on
one's person. All of these things can signify one's identity, but one's identity is
always created out of the surrounding community (including word symbols)
and finds its purpose in the community. Yet in examining the material
indicators of the self in depth, as, for instance, cherished possessions, what
emerges is an overvaluation of the individual self as distinct from its sur-

roundings, from its surrounding community. And yet the broader community of a city, like the individual, is profoundly shaped by the premisses and movement of a culture as a whole.

"There is no collective memory, which does not itself move within a spatial frame," as Maurice Halbwachs said in his work *Collective Memory* (1985, 142; my translation). And memory would soon be irretrievably lost in the flux of time, "if it were not stored daily through the material milieu that surrounds us." It is only with the development of cities that remembrance truly flowers into its broader possibilities for human development. For the city is itself a vast means of externalized memory, a concrete and tangible storehouse of experiences, achievements, of whole lifetimes given to the embodiment of dreams and purposes. Yet so much of modern culture seems to be an attempt to obliterate remembrance in the name of novelty. Where the past, as Wheatley noted (1967, 11), was once normative and required no justification as a model for emulation in building many a traditional city, it came to be regarded as simply a shackle upon the modern vision, something to be completely set aside so that new forms could be created.

It can be argued that the purposes of the eighteenth and nineteenth centuries discussed by Simmel (1971) in "The Metropolis and Mental Life," namely, liberation from constricting historical bonds and social controls, and the development of individual uniqueness, have now been fulfilled in the modern metropolis but with paradoxical and unintended consequences. We see the final product of the mythic quest for the rationalized individual, the original, and the new that so motivates modern culture, in the steel-skeleton skyscrapers of the "international style" of architecture that began to dominate the American cityscape in the 1950s. The shared premiss of the Chicago originators of modern architecture, such as Louis Sullivan, that the skyscraper could express the unique character of the American dream, would seem to have been transformed into a quite different conclusion in the second "school" of Chicago architecture led by Mies van der Rohe. As architecture critic Paul Goldberger has said:

> The notion of the skyscraper as a romantic object, as a building that might have some degree of symbolic quality to it, seemed to disappear. Most of the architects of this time eschewed any overt symbolism for their buildings, although in spite of this their structures still managed to convey a certain kind of message—a message of a rather faceless corporate bureaucracy housed in boxes that looked like other boxes. In this sense then, the skyscrapers of the 1950s were apt. If nothing else, they did give architectural expression to the changing nature of the American corporate structure that caused them to be built. (Goldberger 1981, 109)

It is one of the stranger paradoxes of modern culture that the leaders of this style of building, for example, Le Corbusier or Mies van der Rohe, like many of their contemporaries in philosophy and social thought, sought to scrape away the past, the unquantifiable, the symbolic, in short, everything but pure fact or function, yet it has become obvious that they and their followers achieved one of the most value-laden and time-bound styles of building and thinking yet devised. These buildings may carry personal images of the raw power of Metropolis to the Chicagoans of my study who discussed them, but on a broader level of cultural analysis it can be argued that these buildings signify a culture of jagged individualism, institutionalized idiosyncrasy, and testify to the arrogance and giantism of the rationalist ego rather than to the surrounding city and cosmos. The end result of this modern process of standardized differentiation in all dimensions of cultural life has been the leveling of community *and* individual into the one-dimensional aggregate, as Simmel, Weber, Dewey, and Mumford all foresaw.

In the traditional techniques of memory, one would develop a "syntax" of images based on the structure of a particular building. One's own memory was tied to the memorability of the public sphere, so that theaters and cathedrals were particularly seen as good sources for "mnemonic devices" (Yates 1966). By implication this suggests memorable buildings, that is, buildings whose intrinsic substances lend themselves to memory, and further, to a dimension of public life or culture or urban form that can embody the collective mind of its inhabitants:

> This city which cannot be expunged from the mind is like an
> armature, a honeycomb in whose cells each of us can place the
> things he wants to remember (Calvino 1974, 15).

Consider, by contrast, the characteristic buildings of our own time. Because of the ascetic severity and extreme rationalism of the architectural theories underlying these buildings, they tend to lack publicly visible particulars, visually separable from the rational grid pattern of the whole. They are unsuitable for "hanging memories," and in the decline of modernism are becoming more obvious monuments to the culture of forgetting, the culture of homogeneous mechanical grids that replaced heterogeneous patterns.

If modernity can be characterized as a culture of forgetting, and our own contemporary situation as one of trying to reincorporate memory as a vital component of culture, then how can this be accomplished in a way that avoids degeneration into mere commercialism or historicism? How can memory be reactivated and reincorporated as an *unself-conscious* component of culture? I asked Philip Johnson, critic and architect earlier associated with "the international style" of architecture and now with a neo-ornamental style, these questions at an architectural conference (University of Notre Dame, April 1985). His answer, in the context of public discussion and private conversation, suggested that in a sense historicism is inescapable, that although the absence of apparent ornament may be overly severe, the presence of ornament is simply a question of arbitrary convention and choice. One can see, therefore, why his newer ornamentalism remains a mentalism, in my opinion as virulently rationalist and abstractionist in theory as his earlier "international-style" manifestoes and buildings. We see in this idea of ornament only memory as abstract reference, not as living presence.

Other groping attempts to return memory and community to the built structure itself can be found in the emerging postmodern styles of architecture. One good example in Chicago of a tentative openness to ornament and facade might be artist Richard Haas's *trompe l'oeil* mural covering a Near North Side condominium. The entire east side of the building is painted to give the illusion of the protruding "Chicago Window." The entire south side of the building is painted as a monument for the early Chicago architects: Louis Sullivan, Frank Lloyd Wright, Daniel Burnham, and John Wellborn Root. It even includes one section taken from Adolph Loos's contribution to the Chicago Tribune Building competition of the 1920s. This illusion of architecture was selected for one of the 1981 Distinguished Building Awards in Chicago, and though we see memory attempting to regain a living influence in architecture and city symbolism, the fact that its use in Haas's building is but a clever trick not functionally related to the structure suggests that it may be some time before memory lives again in contemporary architecture, and some time before contemporary architecture and culture catch up to the unconscious relationship of the past to the present in the work of someone like Louis Sullivan. Sullivan's work far surpasses that of most so-called postmodernists in its lack of self-conscious reference and in its organic linking of ornament with the functions of its context. Nelson Algren, it is true, would probably have insisted that Haas's trickery in creating a well-publicized symbol of the Chicago legacy on a high-finance condominium that has nothing architecturally to do with that legacy is a profoundly valid and contemporary symbol of that other Chicago: the city on the make, "Hustlertown."

The final mission of the city, in the words of Lewis Mumford,

> is to further man's conscious participation in the cosmic and historical process. Through its own complex and enduring structure, the city vastly augments man's ability to interpret these processes and take an active, formative part in them, so that every phase of the drama it stages shall have, to the highest degree possible, the illumination of consciousness, the stamp of purpose, the color of love. That magnification of all the dimensions of life, through emotional communion, rational communication, technological mastery, and above all, dramatic representation, has been the supreme office of the city in history. And it remains the chief reason for the city's continued existence. (Mumford 1961:576)

"The color of love" can be found in Chicago, as I have tried to show, but usually as an exception to the color of the stark rational, or impoverished emotional signs that currently predominate, and especially to the color of fear. At the heart of the American city (or rather, in the place of a heart) is the dollar sign, which has appropriated community and cosmos to its own arrogant purposes. The dollar sign does not remember, it simply utilizes the moment; nor does it foresee, it simply calculates for itself. The typical American metropolis today stands as an act of impaired memory and as an external mirror of the culture of forgetting.

What we need to rediscover in the contemporary American city is that relation to the environment in which community itself, as a living relationship and responsibility to those who have gone before, those co-present with us, and those who will inherit the legacy of our time, is the mediating master symbol, and not simply the solitary ego, trapped in a transient present. Even the personal ego is an internalized community to be cultivated in those broader encompassing purposes to which it can give itself.

What the contemporary city needs, and what is the task of a culture that has not yet but which must emerge if we are to reclaim metropolis from oblivion, from the grip of self-destructive rationality and its avatar, necropolis, is a broad cultural transformation, one that recognizes that the personal self is part of a broader set of purposes, and that by critically cultivating these purposes one cultivates the self. For it would take nothing short of a transformation to begin to overcome the spectres of fear, crime, chaos, and the blasé attitude that form "the mind-forg'd manacles" of the contemporary American metropolis. How to renew living memory in urban life and built form is a central task of such a transformation. Perhaps then the modern metropolis could again become what the living city has always, however imperfectly, been: an external organ of social consciousness whose purpose is to nourish, not diminish, human life.

10 Money Is No Object

> For *money*, so long as it is kept in the shape of money, and in the same
> hands, is of no kind of use. In that shape no man can ever make any
> use of it but by parting with it, or at least standing engaged to part with
> it. What value it has, is in the way of *exchange*: value in the way of use,
> it has none.
>
> Jeremy Bentham, Jeremy Bentham's
Economic Writings

REIFICATION, PECUNIARY EMULATION, AND THE CONTEMPORARY POTLATCH

It remains strange, to paraphrase Hugh Dalziel Duncan (1962, 347),
how extraordinarily little is said in sociology and anthropology concerning
the role of money in human relations.[1] Despite the scant attention paid to it,
money is clearly the *axis mundi* of modern life. In many ways money is the
least material of all objects, and at the same time perhaps the most materialistic symbol yet invented. It is abstraction reified. Money is the embodiment of
the exchange process, the "philosophers' stone" that can transform relationships into tangible things, and things into intangible numbers and back
again.

Money mediates. It makes possible the quantification of social life on
a scale of values that all can see. When money assumes the form of a tangible
status symbol it buys us social recognition as possessors of the qualities
symbolized, such as taste or refinement, regardless of whether we truly
possess those qualities or not. We can, for example, be driven to the hospital
to have our life saved in a Ford or Chevrolet ambulance, yet after we are dead
we must have a Cadillac hearse to have an honorable funeral. The Cadillac
signifies our power to purchase the superlative, which becomes the outward

---

1. The translation of Simmel's *The Philosophy of Money* (1978) has perhaps stimulated
growing interest in the social significance of money. Another recent large-scale work is Crump's
The Phenomenon of Money (1981).

sign of the self. And the superlative, in the American death system as well as American culture as a whole, is the money sign. The contemporary American rites of mourning exemplify the money principle itself: from the sensuous activity of a community meal in the home, the rites have progressed to the more abstract form of sending flowers, cards, or money as a token toward the deceased. The secular "parlor," itself an extension of the custom of holding a "viewing" in the home of the deceased, has become more of a funeral "establishment," combining elements of the prestige of money (the funeral home as mansion, the range from low-budget to top-dollar caskets) with religiosity to produce a sacred aura—the last act of consumption, from the grave, as it were.

It is the capacity of money to mediate the exchange process through increasing levels of abstraction, to act as pure symbol, that gives the enormous significance accorded it by modern culture. Yet this great achievement also has been criticized as the root of the dark side of modern culture—the leveling of concrete sensuous qualities and character either to discrete hedonistic sensations or to arbitrary social conventions. It is precisely this reduction to the general, which the culture of money makes possible, that informed the criticisms of Marx, Simmel, and Veblen. Each of these theorists, in his own way, warned us that money owns modern culture; that it lends itself to the ersatz, driving out the real thing; and that we must invest in ways of regaining control over our own creation. For money, as the culture of abstraction, has taken on a life of its own as autonomous system that lends itself to reification, as Marx argued; to a culture of pecuniary emulation, as Veblen contended; and to a "relativity of things" in which inherent quality is eclipsed by what Simmel called "the calculating character of modern times."

After presenting the arguments made by Marx, Simmel, and Veblen concerning the ways money transforms the cultivation of individual character and the sensuous qualities of things into external labels of value, I intend to use contemporary wine and food feasts as metaphors to illustrate their critical perspectives on money. Although other status-rich objects, such as fine art, opera-patron clothing, professionally decorated interiors (Kron 1983), and costly resorts could also (and should also) be explored to illustrate how money buys status not necessarily related to inherent quality, wine and food feasts afford particularly good examples of the appropriation of the sensuous by mechanisms of the abstract. Finally, I will address the implications of the modern culture of nominalism as the true soul of money.

Money as Reification

In Marx's social philosophy self-objectification is the essence of social life and real human being. To be fully human is to realize critically the two-sided objectification process whereby relations with the world, as for example, labor, simultaneously humanize the world while incorporating the

otherness of the world into the person. The object of human activity stands as
something over against the self even as it is the "congealed" form of the self,
which appropriates the qualities of the object. Marx argues that appropriation is not to be regarded as one-sided gratification, not "merely in the sense
of possessing, of having," but as the appropriation of the total essence in its
wholeness, that is, the full realization of the inherent qualities of the thing or
relation:

> On the one hand, therefore, it is only when the objective world
> becomes everywhere for man in society the world of man's essen-
> tial powers [*Wesenkräfte*]—human reality, and for that reason
> the reality of his *own* essential powers—that all *objects* become
> for him the *objectification of himself*, become objects which
> confirm and realize his individuality, become his objects: that is,
> *man himself* becomes the object. The manner in which they be-
> come his depends on the *nature of the objects* and on the nature
> of the *essential power* corresponding *to it*; for it is precisely the
> *determinate nature* of this relationship which shapes the particu-
> lar, *real* mode of affirmation. . . . The specific character of each
> essential power is precisely its *specific essence*, and therefore also
> the specific mode of its objectification, of its *objectively actual
> living being*. . . . Only through the objectively unfolded richness
> of man's essential being is the richness of subjective *human* sensi-
> bility (a musical ear, an eye for beauty of form—in short, *senses*
> capable of human gratification, senses affirming themselves as
> essential powers of man) either cultivated or brought into being.
> (Marx 1964, 140–41).

Marx viewed the activities of life as contributing directly to the
production of self and society, and the inherent qualities of these activities as
becoming part of the object produced and the producer. The most fully
socialized being is thus the most uniquely individual being, because social
individuality, as Marx sees it, is the *objective product* of life activity, not the
precondition for it. We become what we do and what we do ought to have a
specific character that is imparted to us, that confirms us in our individuality,
and that gives us an increased mastery over our development. When the
object of our activity is denied us, when it is absorbed, for example, by
capital, and stands as something over against us rather than as our creation
and means for objectification, then we have alienation (*Entfremdung*) instead of objectification (*Vergegenständlichung*): "Just as man, so long as he is
engrossed in religion, can only objectify his essence by an *alien* and fantastic
being; so under the sway of egoistic need, he can only affirm himself and
produce objects in practice by subordinating his products and his own
activity to the domination of an alien entity, and by attributing to them the
significance of an alien entity, namely money" (Marx 1973, 50). Because

money, as exchange value, can transform the social character of activity, product, and share of individuals in production into relations seemingly autonomous and independent from the individuals involved, it brings about reification, an abstract view of human relations as relations between things (Marx 1973, 157).

The problem in a society ruled by the private interests of money itself is that money, perceived as an alien thing, becomes proxy for the "nature of the object" and the "nature of the essential power corresponding to it." The nature of money is the property of buying everything, thus transforming everything into itself. For this reason money "functions as the almighty being" (Marx 1964, 165), and as "the true *agent of separation* as well as the true *binding agent*—the (universal) *galvano-chemical* power of society" (Marx 1964, 167), conferring on its possessor the inherent qualities of things purchased as social values:

> That which is for me through the medium of money—that for which I can pay (i.e., which money can buy)—that am *I*, the possessor of the money. The extent of the power of money is the extent of my power. Money's properties are my properties and essential powers—the properties and powers of its possessor. Thus, what I *am* and *am capable* of is by no means determined by my individuality. I *am* ugly, but I can buy for myself the most *beautiful* of women. Therefore I am not *ugly*, for the effect of *ugliness*—its deterrent power—is nullified by money. . . . I am bad, dishonest, unscrupulous, stupid; but money is honoured, and hence its possessor. Money is the supreme good, therefore its possessor is good. (Marx 1964, 167)

Marx draws attention to the tendency of money, as an autonomous system of abstract exchange, to undermine the concrete qualities of exchange, qualities of the object and self that arise and are cultivated through *praxis*, intelligible activity. In the place of real activity and objectification, money substitutes nominal value so that the purchased quality is ascribed to the possessor even if it is possessed in name only. Against this culture of reification Marx argues that the nature of human praxis itself calls for the qualities exchanged to be exchanged genuinely, according to the real social needs of the individuals in the relationship, not according to the fictitious realm of the political economists, which consists of primal egoistic individuals with primal property needs. To exchange love there must be love, not just money; to exchange trust there must be a relationship in which trust, not simply money, mediates. To enjoy music, the mere possession of a top-of-the-line expensive stereo unit capable of blowing one's ears off with the latest digitally produced disc is simply not enough; one "must be an artistically cultivated person" as well, because every relation "must be a *specific expression*, corresponding to the object of your will, of your *real individual* life" (Marx 1964, 169).[2] By "artistically cultivated person" Marx does not mean an effete snob, but simply that enjoyment of any art (or any activity) depends on, and is enhanced by, the cultivation in the person of the qualities that form the art's specific medium—in the case of music, the ear. One may *know* the "right" music and musicians to listen to, and derive prestige from this ability to calculate the correct social hierarchy, but only in *hearing* the music for what it is, at one's level of ability, is the music enjoyed. One of the paradoxes of capitalistic individualism as Marx saw it, was that it destroyed the genuine unique individual, whether worker or capitalist, and put in his or her place an "individual" constituted as such not by specifically cultivated qualities but simply by his or her place in the societal money hierarchy.

The Calculating Character of Modern Times

Simmel, although working out of a neo-Kantian framework, in contrast to Marx's Hegelian approach, agreed with Marx that the growth of the money economy brought a corresponding decline in the qualitatively unique individual. As Simmel saw it, money was inseparably bound up with the growth of modern Western urban forms and intellectuality, developments resulting in increased specialization and differentiation, and a dominance of "objective culture" over "subjective culture." To Simmel, money was the social symbol of pure reason, whose critique demanded an analysis somewhat analogous to that undertaken by Kant, an analysis which Simmel originally published in 1900 as *The Philosophy of Money*.

In its ability to reconcile the irreconcilable, to act as the ultimate mediator, money would seem to take on the qualities of the deity, a point made by Marx and echoed by Simmel:

> It may appear as an irony of history that, at the moment when the satisfying and ultimate purposes of life became atrophied, precisely that value that is exclusively a means and nothing else takes the place of such purposes and clothes itself in their form. In reality, money in its psychological form, as the absolute means and thus as the unifying point of innumerable sequences of purposes, possesses a significant relationship to the notion of God. . . . The essence of the notion of God is that all diversities and contradictions in the world may achieve unity in him, that

---

2. "Assume *man* to be *man* and his relationship to the world to be a human one: then you can exchange love only for love, trust for trust, etc. If you want to enjoy art, you must be an artistically cultivated person; if you want to exercise influence over other people, you must be a person with a stimulating and encouraging effect on other people. Every one of your relations to man and to nature must be a *specific expression*, corresponding to the object of your will, of your *real individual* life" (Marx 1964, 169).

he is—according to a beautiful formulation of Nicholas de Cusa—the *coincidentia oppositorum*. Out of this idea, that in him all estrangements and all irreconcilables of existence find their unity and equalization, there arises the peace, the security, the all-embracing wealth of feeling that reverberate with the notion of God which we hold. . . . money actually provides an elevated position above the particular and a confidence in its omnipotence, just as we have confidence in the omnipotence of a highest principle to grant us the particular and the baser at any moment and to be able to transform itself into them. (Simmel 1978, 236, 237).

Unfortunately the divine confidence money can inspire in us may not ultimately derive from money's affinity with divinity but rather from its darker personification as "the root of all evil," as Mephistopheles, bringer of magical means through which all earthly qualities may be gotten for the mere exchange of paper and the cost of a soul. For money is both deity and trickster, of this world and not of this world, the cosmic confidence man in whom we trust but whose impersonal laws seem alternatively to mock and bless us. Money can draw out our deepest wishes and help us to actualize them, or, alternatively, dash them to smithereens.

Money is the paradoxical object that is no object, for its objectifying ability derives precisely from its not being a particular object (Simmel 1978, 436, 441). As a cultural tendency to abstraction, money has created modern individuals in whom *calculative functions* (Simmel 1978, 444) have become the dominant source of personality and basis for social interaction. The calculating character of modern life is the tendency of "transforming the world into an arithmetical problem and of fixing every one of its parts in a mathematical formula" (Simmel 1971, 327). Daily existence, as Simmel noted, has taken on a technical, calculating character, whose profane amulet is the pocket watch.

Simmel's observations at the turn of the century are still further confirmed in the recent general diffusion of the pocket calculator itself, a thing, which, like the home computer, makes the thousand and one details of everyday life more precise, even while it appropriates the average person's practice of arithmetic for itself and leaves in its place the robotic pushing of buttons. Money (and its derived objects) acts "as an intermediate link between man and thing," enabling us to have "an abstract existence, a freedom from direct concern with things and from a direct relationship to nature" (Simmel 1978, 469). Yet this power of abstract rationality produces the impotence of abstract rationality, because though we may seem master of the plethora of objects that money brings us, it is also true that these things absorb our life-energies to their purposes, and perhaps, ultimately to money's purpose (Simmel 1978, 483–84).

In a culture seemingly without a highest principle we are left in a free-floating relativity of *things*, where the transitory value of things, rather than the growing, cultivated *soul*, assumes the appearance of a highest principle:

> In the case of the present age, in which the preponderance of technology obviously signifies a predominance of clear intelligent consciousness, as a cause as well as an effect, I have emphasized that spirituality and contemplation, stunned by the clamorous splendor of the scientific-technological age, have to suffer for it by a faint sense of tension and vague longing. . . . I believe that this secret restlessness, this helpless urgency that lies below the threshold of consciousness, that drives modern man from socialism to Nietzsche, from Böcklin to impressionism, from Hegel to Schopenhauer and back again, not only originates in the bustle and excitement of modern life, but that, conversely, this phenomenon is frequently the expression, symptom and eruption of this innermost condition. The lack of something definite at the centre of the soul impels us to search for momentary satisfaction in ever-new stimulations, sensations and external activities (Simmel 1978, 484).

The externalization of the self, manifest in the search for "momentary satisfaction in ever-new stimulations," represents the dominance of objective culture over subjective culture. In Simmel's view the individual grows through the *creative tension* between objective and subjective culture, and the dominance of one over the other destroys that tension, leaving in its place either a highly differentiated and cosmopolitan facade with no connection to the inherent laws of that individual's unique nature, or a severely limited creature of immediate wants, with no relation to those broader cultural forms and the sustenance they can provide for development. Between unhinged cosmopolitanism and suffocating provincialism there lies the healthy interaction of individuals and objective cultural forms, in which each reciprocally cultivates the other, and in which individuals can develop along the continuum from true provincials to true cosmopolitans. In our time we see in the American food system the extreme dominance of that calculating rationality of money that appropriates nature to the extent of creating square, tasteless tomatoes, whose inherent quality is efficiency, "zombie" bread and cheese that neither live nor die, except through that pecuniary term "shelf-life," and individuals who willingly consume these and countless other "agri-products," thereby illustrating the maxim "You are what you eat."

As further illustration of Simmel's insights on the modern dominance of objective over subjective culture, one can point to the peculiar tendency of twentieth-century art and philosophy to take radically separate "objectivist" or "subjectivist" positions. Cubism in painting, serialism in music, and logical positivism in philosophy were all movements claiming a final triumph of the object over the subject, usually in the name of science. Expressionism in painting, aleatoric music, and existentialism in philosophy were all movements claiming the authenticity of the subject against the dehumanized world of the rational object. Both sides of the modern "split brain" shared (with some notable exceptions) a disregard for past traditions, and yet one could argue that at least in painting and music the tension of their antithetic stance toward the past is what gave them their power. Cubism and expressionism, for example, need to be understood as a reaction to the Western tradition of perspective and representation. When this relation to the past through antithesis gave way in the next generations not only to a lack of concern but also to ignorance of past practices and traditions, one saw a corresponding reduction of framework and vitality in the cultural forms produced, a reduction in inverse proportion to claims for originality. Post–World War II painting and serious music raised originality and freedom from the past to unprecedented levels of importance, and yet, illustrating Simmel's idea that some balance is needed between objective and subjective culture, this was (and perhaps still is) the age of what art critic Harold Rosenberg referred to as "one-idea" artists (See Rochberg 1984a).[3] Another curious link between the opposing sides is the concern with *technique* (Barrett 1978) and the importance of the *idea* being expressed (and this is true of the contemporary subjectivists, such as "minimalists" in art and music), suggesting, in support of Simmel, that our age is stamped with the rationalizing character. We are Descartes' dichotomy, played out in all its unintended consequences.

Simmel saw, in his analysis of money, not only the causes and conditions of modern culture but also, prophetically, the spiritual disturbance that would soon explode in the arts, sciences, and politics of the twentieth century, a seemingly final severing of subject and object, a cultural ideology (perhaps dogma, with its religious connotations, is a better term) of science in everyday life, resulting in a dominant world culture of abstraction, largely devoid of content.

Pecuniary Emulation

Veblen viewed culture as an evolutionary process in which accumulated property increasingly replaces "trophies of predatory exploit as the conventional exponent of prepotence and success" (Veblen 1953, 37), while symbolically retaining predatory significance. Though one might question his use of Henry L. Morgan's stages of cultural development, proceeding from savagery, through barbarism, to civilization, his idea of *conspicuous con-*

---

3. George Rochberg's collection of essays in *The Aesthetics of Survival* (1984a) is a most insightful examination of the consequences of artistic and cultural modernism in the twentieth century.

sumption as a modern expression of an underlying predatory symbol of "invidious comparison" is certainly provocative. Like Freud's *Interpretation of Dreams*, which was published in 1900, Veblen's *The Theory of the Leisure Class* (1899) exposed the underlying fantastic nature of the psyche, in its economic manifestation:

> The possession of goods, whether acquired aggressively by one's own exertion or passively by transmission through inheritance from others, becomes a conventional basis of reputability.
>
> The possession of wealth, which was at the outset valued simply as an evidence of efficiency, becomes, in popular apprehension, itself a meritorious act. Wealth is now itself intrinsically honorable and confers honor on its possessor. By a further refinement, wealth acquired passively by transmission from ancestors or other antecedents presently becomes even more honorific than wealth acquired by the possessor's own effort; but this distinction belongs at a later stage in the evolution of the pecuniary culture. (Veblen [1899] 1953, 37.

According to Veblen the ownership of private property is not based on subsistence needs but on "invidious distinction" and pecuniary emulation. Weath confers honor, and in so doing sets up a distinction by which others realize that if they possessed this wealth, they too would possess honor. Emulation is concerned not so much with the quality and distinctiveness of honor directly, as with the means of acquiring it. In this way the motive of emulation touches all the features of the social structure, especially in a social structure based on the principle of private property (Veblen 1953, 35). Yet the ultimate basis of human nature is not pecuniary emulation, even though Veblen's acrid cynicism might seem to give that impression. It lies instead in what Veblen termed "the instinct of workmanship." In a passage that suggests the influence of one of his teachers at Johns Hopkins University, Charles Peirce, Veblen remarked:

> As a matter of selective necessity, man is an agent. He is, in his own apprehension, a center of unfolding impulsive "teleological" activity. He is an agent seeking in every act the accomplishment of some concrete, objective, impersonal end. By force of his being such an agent he is possessed of a taste for effective work, and a distaste for futile effort. He has a sense of the merit of serviceability or efficiency and of the demerit of futility, waste, or incapacity. This attitude or propensity may be called the instinct of workmanship. (Veblen [1899] 1953, 29–30)

To call a propensity for workmanship an instinct may sound like biological determinism to the contemporary reader, yet Veblen is clearly using the term in the same sense as the pragmatists did, that is, instinct is an ingrained, habituated form of intelligence. The *instinct* of workmanship operates within the context of the act, and contributes to the agency of carrying out the act as an ingrained habit of conduct.

In a pecuniary culture, where the instinct of workmanship becomes transformed into pecuniary emulation, cultivated craftsmanship or practice is not sufficient (or even necessary) as a sign of one's character; instead, an external symbol of wealth will be more convincing, especially if one's "competitors" for social standing are made part of its display. This is apparent in Veblen's discussion of gifts, feasts, and other costly entertainments, which, although probably originating in motives of conviviality and religion, become infused with the money motive of pecuniary emulation, in which the goal becomes the comparison of extrinsic worth rather than the enjoyment of inherent quality:

> Conspicuous consumption of valuable goods is a means of reputability to the gentleman of leisure. As wealth accumulates on his hands, his own unaided effort will not avail to sufficiently put his opulence in evidence by this method. The aid of friends and competitors is therefore brought in by resorting to the giving of valuable presents and expensive feasts and entertainments. Presents and feasts had probably another origin than that of naive ostentation, but they acquired their utility for this purpose very early, and they have retained that character to the present; so that their utility in his respect has now long been the substantial ground on which these usages rest. Costly entertainments, such as the potlatch or the ball, are peculiarly adapted to serve this end. The competitor with whom the entertainer wishes to institute a comparison is, by this method, made to serve as a means to the end. He consumes vicariously for his host at the same time that he is a witness to the consumption of that excess of good things which his host is unable to dispose of singlehanded, and he is also made to witness his host's facility in etiquette (Veblen [1899] 1953, 64, 65).

Later we will see how in a mutual gratification society individuals refine conspicuous consumption to new levels of subtlety by consuming wine and food vicariously for each other, and witnessing each other's "facility in etiquette," all within the social atmosphere of a secret society. Just as praxis is replaced by reification in Marx, and individual character is eclipsed by "the calculating character" in Simmel, the instinct of workmanship is consumed by the modern money culture for Veblen, leaving in its place pecuniary emulation and a world of egocentric display.

We see in these analyses that money is reified abstraction, the paradoxical object that is no object, the means that must be transformed into objects for its power to be realized. Money surrounds itself with a world of objects, which are perceived to be its incarnation and confirmation of quality.

Though the pursuit of money has assumed the status of an ultimate goal in modern life, the mere possession of money itself is not a sufficient sign of prestige and taste: one must possess money's possessions. Money's possessions then act as extensions of the monied self, external labels of character. Money is surely one of the purest *means* yet invented, paradoxically commanding its votaries to see it as purest *goal*. Yet money can and does act as means, and the materialist and nominalist fallacy lies in mistaking the nature of the acquisition of selfhood. In seeing character as *thing purchased*, externally, rather than as *practice cultivated*, the modern consumer-self stands as persona of self-estrangement, as negation of the inherent qualities of life's activities. Selfhood is not a product purchased, it is a gift and a craft and an inheritance. It is the unique nature we are given and are determined to develop through all of life's activities, and whose ultimate purpose is to give itself back to the community. The character of the individual is a social outcome of cultivation, and consumption is essential to its further development. Yet it is a genuine consumption of qualities, a genuine *consummation of a transaction* involving qualitative social enjoyment and suffering, and not merely mechanistic pleasure and pain, that contributes to the real growth of the self.

CONSUMPTION, THE CONSUMMATORY, AND RITUAL WASTE

A feast is made for laughter and wine maketh merry, but money answereth all things

Ecclesiastes, 10:19

Turning to the consumption of quality sought in contemporary wine-tasting feasts, where a high degree of inherent quality of things and palates is juxtaposed with individuals for whom "money is no object" in the upper-class everyday sense, we see the criticisms of money in greater relief.

Consider the following scenario: you are in a group of twenty people gathered from distant places around the world and united solely for the purposes of eating and drinking. The goal of your trek is a stone chateau on Long Island surrounded by a moat, and despite the fact that some of the other pilgrims of the palate have travelled from Paris, Florence, and Fort Worth, you all take the last leg of the journey as a group on three red-and-white helicopters from New York City. Your group has been named *Le Cercle des Vingt*, and includes the wine critic of the *New York Times*, who will memorialize the afternoon in an article named after the old song, "Memories Are Made of This" (Robards 1982a). In seven hours you and your circle will use 1,500 glasses to consume twenty-one kinds of wine valued at thousands of dollars, as well as an eight-course meal prepared by the chef of an exclusive

Philadelphia restaurant who "has abandoned his restaurant with this vow: 'For one day in my life I am going to have fun.'" Abandonment and fun are certainly the order of the day, as the wine critic suggests when he says, "Eight courses are yet to be served, and I take a silent vow to survive by leaving a portion of each on my plate." In this feast of consumption, it is a safe assumption that you have money to burn.

The general law illustrated by these feasts, and by Veblen's biting criticisms, is that the *more* one can publicly consume and waste, especially within the privacy of an elite circle, the more one stands above others as possessing prestige, honor, and distinction. I am not speaking here of "more" only within the confines of the Roman feast complete with vomitorium, or the gaudy modern "balls" still being thrown by Vanderbilts and Rockefellers, but "more" in the sense of that vanishing point of the superlative, that sacrificial stuff on which religions are founded, the consumption of the supreme quality. The term "potlatch" entered into the American vocabulary largely through Veblen's discussions of "conspicuous consumption." Yet the Kwakiutl Indian potlatch was not based on the highly sophisticated money economy characterizing the modern world (though it might be argued that it became increasingly "abstract" as the Kwakiutls became physically and spiritually decimated from contact with whites [Walens 1982]), and when we look at its modern metaphoric equivalent we see directly the invisible hand of money at work.

This feast contains no traditional or inherent reasons for being: the decades-old wines have been purchased, not handed down; the occasion is not a holyday or holiday; the participants are not related as kin, co-workers, neighbors, or nationals, but only by their ability to afford attending and (presumably) by their highly developed "calculating functions" through which they differentiate and judge the esoteric tastes and smells. In other words all external traditional reasons for dining and drinking together are absent—the sole reason for being together is the wine itself, the pure ambrosia. Yet the pursuit of the superlative in its manifestation as wine is itself perhaps one of the supreme conventions of prestige: my knowledge of the best wines reveals me as one of the best; my ability to taste the distinctions of different vintages marks me as a man or woman of taste and distinction— surely one of the right stock; and my ability to purchase and possess the best wines tells those privileged peers who see the cellar or taste the wine that they are seeing or tasting *my* quality, or at least my quality at the level I choose to reveal. Did not Christ himself say that the wine was his body? If the guests are of middling taste I might only want to serve them a slightly better than middling wine—anything better might be lost on them, and besides, they will taste it at their level as the superlative.

In another article aptly titled "A Mutual Gratification Society," Robards describes a similar feast where the twenty-six men comprising "Les

Vingt-Six" challenged the proprietor of a restaurant and his chef "to prepare the best meal that money could buy." This group of gastronomes illustrates the tension between public and private that is involved in the character of money: Money serves to distinguish its possessor, yet to do this it must be "seen" somehow by others. Some sort of public display of a money sign is needed to reveal the potency of money or, to put it another way, money, as a quantitative and relative value, needs to transform itself into quality, or at least into an object signifying quality to others. One of the best ways to do this is through activities and objects themselves unique and so differentiated, such as an exclusive elite or private club, or a collection, that membership or possession alone reveals one, in the light of invidious comparison, as a superior person. Hence the public display of money signs among private peers, such as occurs in art auctions (Baudrillard 1981), is in many ways a more effective status symbol than the public display of money signs to the vulgar public. If you join the Metropolitan Opera Guide, you receive a membership card signifying your prestige as a peer of the elite. Yet the card also puts you in your proper place among the lower echelon of the chosen by telling you on the back: "Not valid for admission to the Eleanor Belmont Room." You may show the front side to your inferiors, but the back side may show you up should you try to overstep your way into the fur-lined Eleanor Belmont Room. Similarly, membership in a wine and food society that considers itself the best in the country is probably more effective than throwing gala events to mark one with the money sign of culture. And when we read Robards's account of this society the self-indulgent joy of elitism is quite apparent. The society's mailing list "has never been made public," and its wine cellar's location is also secret. Robards tells us:

> Induction ceremonies are not held, nor are there ceremonial hats or robes. By most definitions, the society would be considered secret, although little effort is expended to conceal its activities and the members could scarcely be called bashful. It is simply so unobtrusive that few people know about it. . . . The group's existence is well known to certain purveyors of food and drink here and abroad, but to few others, for it makes no effort to be recognized except by other seekers of perfection in the culinary arts. . . . "I modeled it after the Club des Cent," Mr. Berenson, a New York real estate investor in his early 60s, recounted recently, "and there were three prerequisites. No. 1, they had to have a good appreciation of wines and food. No. 2, they had to be able to contribute to a social group. And No. 3, they had to be somebody with whom you and I would like to dine."
>
> The members prefer not to have their names publicly disclosed, for their purpose in belonging is strictly personal enjoyment, not aggrandizement. (Robards 1982b, 90)

Perhaps Robards does not realize that strict personal enjoyment on a limitless budget can itself be a profound expression of aggrandizement, especially when written up for public consumption and emulation by readers of the *New York Times*. Robards describes in perfect seriousness a culture that has seemed to banish pain and unpleasantness from its vocabulary, and to bask in a state of actual or expected pleasures, a world of unashamed, strutting hedonism. We may know the semimystical name of Chateau d'Yquem, perhaps some of us may even be able to afford the initiation fee of one case of fine wine (like the New York Frenchman who on being admitted as the twenty-sixth member had a case of Chateau d'Yquem delivered to the society's secret cellar within the hour by messenger). Yet none of us can enter the sacred circle of Les Vingt-Six (even if we are someone "with whom you or I would like to dine"), and for this reason the society stands unapproachably above us, revealing its twenty-six men (eating their twenty-six breasts of exclusive, not common, pigeon) as true masters of taste by virtue of their membership and their money. There are no free lunches in Les Vingt-Six.

Yet it remains true that wine does possess its own inherent qualities, requiring a differentiating palate that can taste the distinctions. Wine-tasting itself involves a complex process of cultivation developed over years, in which one must develop not only a knowledge of different wines, but a vocabulary of tastes.[4] Yet these kinds of tastes are not what restaurant customers seek. For most people, the various surrounding "labels" are what matter, such as the expensiveness of the wine or meal. Typically, as my informant, Alan Mallory, owner of one of Chicago's superlative restaurants, told me,

> The cheapest bottle of wine on a restaurant list will never sell, the second cheapest will. . . . When status is their object then it attaches to everything, and clearly to restaurants. And wine is one of the vehicles within the restaurant that status achievers will use. They'll also use food. Not nearly as many people order escargot for the taste, I would suspect, as for the opportunity to say the next day, "Oh, we had the escargot at La Fontaine."

---

4. As my wine informant told me: "You need to correlate tasting to a vocabulary. The best tastes are verbal. If you don't have the vocabulary, can you taste it? Maybe you can but maybe you can't isolate it. If you can taste it but can't describe it, then what's the value of having tasted it? It's your experience, yeah, but now what? I think that wine tasting is very much a shared experience. It's an experience the value of which is enhanced by it being a human experience, a social experience. . . . There are two levels of vocabulary—one deals with the actual ingredients of the wine, more technical words correlated to the chemical properties, the other is descriptors, which are more elusive and subjective, and relate to the wines as metaphors, such as pepper, anise, eucalyptus, etc. . . . A lot of this is in the nose. The taste sensations are typically not as complex. Sometimes the taste can be a profound disappointment. You can have five or six tastes in the nose as you agitate the glass, as it breathes. Then the taste in the mouth may be different."

Wine is a particularly good vehicle for the contemporary "Yuppie" upsurge in status symbolism, because wine menus constitute an elaborate pecuniary hierarchy, in which one can show one's ability to pay by ordering at least the second cheapest bottle, and then conspicuously display one's status by having a waiter open and pour the wine in an elaborate and suitably servile fashion. My informant, whose restaurant is located in racially mixed Hyde Park, also commented on class differences in status-seeking among the *nouveaux riches noires:*

> The last ten years that I've been in the restaurant business it has been commonplace, it's a caricature that status seekers will always pay in fifty and one-hundred-dollar bills. And typically that is a black manifestation of status seeking. I think the hundred-dollar-bill user is lower down on the ladder and striving much harder, and is not aware how in some sense there is a gaucheness about handing a waitress a one-hundred bill for a six or twelve-dollar check. It's an absurdity in a sense to carry around money that is unusable.

"Unusable" money is an absurdity in a logical sense perhaps, but cultural life also demands the fantastic, even in a utilitarian culture such as our own, where the fantastic is often reduced to the absurd, where the profane is elevated to the status of the sacred, where sacrificial waste can redeem one's prestige. One can imagine how absurd it would seem to that same man with the hundred-dollar bills to find a group of well-dressed people at a tasting meal nonchalantly spitting wine into the standing champagne buckets customarily placed between each of the participants.[5] Or consider the absurdity of the Chicago area's *Le Français*, rated as one of the five best restaurants in the country. The food is supposed to be so good there that *Chicago Magazine* recommends that one should waste a portion of each course in order to get through the next. Could any Kwakiutl feast match my informant's description of the culinary surrealism one finds there:

5. To investigate wine tasting at first hand I went to an annual wine tasting at Geja's restaurant on the North Side of Chicago with a professional taster. The tasting was an open competition consisting of eight wines (four white and four red) and there was a ten-dollar entry fee. Approximately seventy-five professionals and seventy-five amateurs made their way through the eight tables of decanters, with baskets of bread bits and wine-spitting buckets nearby to cleanse one's mouth. One of the hazards I soon noticed is a tendency toward the last couple of wine buckets for wine poured or spat by others to be carelessly aimed. Contestants were asked to name country of origin (2 points), region or state (2 points), subregion/commune (2 points), winery/chateau/estate (1 point), predominant grape variety (5 points), and vintage (1 point). While the scores were being tabulated, the professional I was with and I went across the street to a bar to join his fellow professional friends, with whom he had been practicing the previous month for this tasting. Though there were some uncertainties, and after checking with the many other professionals who were also waiting at this bar, the general mood was that everyone did fairly

The presentation is when you go in and sit down, the waiters and captains (of whom there are a plethora) go whizzing by in a semi-darkened room carrying flashlights and they bring out monstrous trays three and four feet long and display every product on the menu in a pre-cooked form with gelatin on it so that it all stays in place, with elaborate floral decorations to enhance the presentation. They wheel up monstrous silver carts and flap back these giant domed covers and display these large roasts and fully stuffed birds with the feathers stuck back on them. It's just an incredible display. And rattling off in a very soft tone in French what the items are and what the ingredients are—a *tour de force* of true culinary skill. These things are done with technical perfection. They're not easy. They are complicated, time-consuming, and visually exciting and appetizing I would say (as an afterthought). It's still reputed to be the most expensive restaurant in the three-state area. Also the food is reputed to be the best in the area, one of the five best in the country. The chef is good. His products are tremendously creative—unusual but complementary combinations, with fresh ingredients flown in literally from the corners of the globe. And he also drives four or five $30,000 cars. Clearly ostentatious consumption, but it's clearly a real value in that no where else can you get Madagascar lemurs sautéed in their own fat, or whatever it is that they serve.

... If the display food is not reusable the next night they probably throw it away. It's probably about $500 for showpieces per night and the average table for two spends $300. On this scale of things, what they're throwing away is negligible. Say the dining room seats 80, they serve 200 a night, that's what, $30,000. The waiters there are supposed to make $200 a night.

What a quasi-religious aura one sees in this culinary orgy of the superlative: flashlights, incantations in a foreign tongue, sacrificial displays in full plumage, customers proving their cosmopolitan status by their monied presence. It is nothing less than the ritual transformation of money into bread and wine, the consumption of *haute couture* itself! No matter that culture is merely

---

well. When the scores were revealed, however, it was apparent that this group had not done so well, and out of a possible score of 104, the professional I accompanied scored 19. He was further disheartened when I, not knowing or listing any subregion/communes, winery/chateau/estates, listing California automatically when I guessed USA for country of origin, guessing only one grape variety at all (correctly), guessing that for a ten-dollar entry fee the wines must be fairly recent (three correct), outscored him by one point on the basis of near-total ignorance. He did say that a blind open tasting is much more difficult than a blind tasting of a particular kind of wine.

Though I could taste differences between the eight wines, it was interesting to see how utterly inarticulate I was when it came to verbalizing the tastes. I had no vocabulary of analogy available to describe the qualities and differences.

consumed externally and probably not "digested" at all, it is paid for and seen by others, and can be worn as a verbal trophy in future conversations.

The contemporary money culture of nominalism, with its cultural existence rooted in the world of external labels and names—"packaging"— also has helped create the common assumption that wine in cork-topped bottles is better than that in bottles with metal caps. Yet the purpose of the cork is to allow slow oxidation of the wine, and wines that are meant to be drunk "young" (as they say in the anthropomorphic wine vocabulary) are only given a shorter life by the cork top, not enhanced by it. In this case the cork's chief purpose is to endow the bottle with reputability and distinction, even as it slowly destroys the wine's ability to taste good. And, of course, the restaurant wine cork imparts the qualities of reputability and distinction to the one to whom it is given, just as the ritual smelling and assent to the waiter reveal one to others as someone with taste.

The ritual smelling of the cork seems to be another one of those "alien and fantastic" delusions in which a representative head of the table is selected to pass judgment on the wine (and frequently what qualifies one as a head of the table is simply that one is paying for the meal). One does not want to appear as a cultural dimwit when presented with a cork, so by briefly smelling it and murmuring, "Ah, yes, this is good," one manages not only to save face in front of the waiter or waitress, but to reveal one's cultivated taste to all present. Unless, of course, someone else present thinks that one can tell if the particular bottle is good simply by the tactile *feel* of the cork rather than by its *smell*. Worse still, though, would be to have a professional wine taster present, for he or she will know that a wine cork smells strongly of *cork*, and that the smell and taste of the wine itself is the only sure way to make a judgment: taste is found here in the original sense of the word—in the act of tasting. The professional wine taster will also know, as indeed one told me, that the purpose of the cork ritual is simply to *read* the name inscribed on the cork, to see that it checks against the wine's label.[6] We see in the example of the ritual cork-sniffer the double paradox of an abstract written sign, the name on the cork, being misinterpreted as a sensual sign, the smell of the cork, in order to carry out an action whose purpose is to impress others with abstract ritual appearances of sensual competence. Money, though not

6. Peter Hellman, a wine critic, reports. "The reason a sommelier or waiter hands a newly drawn cork to the patron is not, as is usually thought, so that it can be smelled, but as evidence that a label that says, for example, Chateau Leoville-Barton 1970 says the same on the cork. Corks, after all, are more difficult to substitute than labels."

"A bad cork—what oenologists call 'organoleptic'—does not, in any sense, smell bad necessarily. In my own case, I have certainly tasted wines that appeared to have picked up off-tastes from a bad cork—including, most recently, one of three bottles of an otherwise beautiful Meursault '79 from the reliable house of Ropiteau. But I have never found a cork that itself actually smelled bad" (Hellman 1983, 72).

perhaps an object-in-itself, is an object-for-itself, and has created a world of glittering things and dreams for its single-minded purpose.

MONEY IN THE AGE OF POSSESSION

Money has made possible a whole culture dedicated to consumption, in which things become increasingly cultivated at the expense of souls, in which people become possessed by their possessions, consumed by their consumption, reduced, from what should be a world of unlimited possibilities, to vain dreams, trivial hopes, and ephemeral goals. Behind the culture of money is the culture of nominalism, which asserts that inherent quality is mere sensation, that human social life consists of mere names and conventions, ultimately reducible to things. As Jeremy Bentham, the master materialist who found his version of immortality by writing a proviso in his will that his taxidermied body was to be placed on display as an "auto-icon" sitting upright in a glass case at University College, London, stated in his economic writings:

> If I having a crown in my pocket, and not being athirst hesitate whether I should buy a bottle of claret with it for my own drinking, or lay it out in providing for a family I see about to perish for want of any assistance, so much the worse for me, at the long run: but it is plain that, so long as I continue hesitating, the two pleasures of sensuality in the one case, of sympathy in the other, were exactly worth to me five shillings, to me they were exactly equal.
>
> I beg a truce here of our man of sentiment and feeling while from necessity, I speak and prompt mankind to speak a mercenary language. . . . Money is the instrument for measuring the quantity of pain or pleasure. Those who are not satisfied with the accuracy of the instrument must find out some other that shall be more accurate, or bid adieu to Politics and Morals. (Bentham, *Jeremy Bentham's Economic Writings*, 3: 117)

It could be no plainer who Bentham's true master was—for we hear the voice of money itself, that calculating character which judges all values on a quantitative scale devoid of inherent quality. Money is indeed the pure and accurate instrument of the modern culture of nominalism, in which all the qualities that are essential to human nature, such as sympathy, relation, and community, are diabolically inverted and treated as ephemeral social conventions ultimately reducible to physicalistic sensations, pleasures and pains. In bringing about the public realm of private interests, money has created a world that has largely bid adieu to politics in the traditional sense of a public realm of public interests, a genuine plurality of individuals constituting a community. In the place of politics we have the grotesque abstract cultures of

American exhibitionism and Russian secrecy, each devoid of character, both dominated by the mercenary power of things.

Modern materialism, which places the ultimate laws of existence within the mechanical sphere of things, views money as the instrument of precise, mechanical, and allegedly "natural" law. Money, perhaps the most useless and intangible thing there is, stands paradoxically as the symbol of the utilitarian and materialist age. And its inherent character (if it indeed can be said to possess inherent character) as the measure of all measure in the modern world, has led to the dilemma that money has transformed both the specific qualities of things and the larger purposes of life into mere means to itself. If our age of mechanized petrifaction, of spiritless specialists and heartless hedonists, is to achieve renewal, we need to regain a sense that the instrument serves a larger goal than itself, that of the community, whose purpose is the concrete realization of purpose itself.

11 Reality, Community, and the Critique of Modernism

All my means and methods are sane: my purpose is mad.

Captain Ahab, from *Moby Dick*

What a great number of our contemporaries still mistake for uncon-
ditionally desirable advances in modern civilization looks like an excellent prescription for sending mankind to the loony bin.

Lewis Mumford, *Interpretations
and Forecasts: 1922–72*

MODERNITY AS CULTURAL NOMINALISM

As the twentieth century enters its final years, it becomes increasingly
clear that its chief distinguishing feature, though not, perhaps, its enduring
legacy, is the triumph of abstractionism, so rightly termed by William James
"vicious intellectualism." Not only is the dominance of abstract forms of life
encompassing the whole range of existence characteristic of modernity, but
so is the critique of this problem of overly rationalized existence.

Powerful criticisms of early modernity can be found in the well-
known critiques of capitalism in Marx and Weber. In Marx's case, a distorted
form of production inherently leads to an abstracted culture of personal and
institutional estrangement and domination, while in Weber's perspective the
religious ethos of Protestantism, especially Calvinism, brought about an
increasingly rationalized culture whose continued development combines an
increasingly rationalized expertise with a calculus of sensuality devoid of
heart. Marx optimistically saw capitalism as inevitably giving way to a
socialized society that would place a humanized humanity, and not the
reifications of religion or class interest, at its center. Weber pessimistically
saw not so much the "inevitable" passing away of capitalism as the inevitable
increasing domination of instrumental reason over all spheres of life. The
legacy of humanism (in its broad sense) is a rationalized world and a dehumanized humanity—a Kafkaland where Calvin might awake from uneasy
dreams à la Gregor Samsa of *The Metamorphosis*, to find himself and his
legacy transformed into a gigantic bureaucracy.

230

Neither Marx nor Weber allowed the full possibilities of a semiotic realism that acknowledges the place of the cosmic perspective in human affairs and uses that perspective in the critique of capitalism. The approach developed here attempts to show how a broadened view of reasonableness is needed, one that can accept in part the humanist perspective on reasonableness (that was the very task of modernity over the past few centuries to develop), while rooting that nominalistic perspective within a broadened realist framework that can include sentiment and feeling, the fantastic, and the transformative as constituent features of reasonableness, though not of the modality of abstract cognitive rationality. To move beyond the narrow constrictions of modernity, while incorporating its enduring accomplishments, we must undo our fetishistic attachment to, and domination by, abstract rationality, and return to the community of humankind from which we have severed ourselves, by realizing that we are manifestations of a humanized, yet cosmic, intelligence.

The rise of the specifically modern view in the West has been understood as the result of new technologies, of capitalist modes of production, of the Protestant Ethic, and so forth; and while Marxist, Weberian, and other views contribute to our understanding of modernity and have their own limitations, I wish to develop another approach here.

I would like to concentrate on the culture of modernism as a culture of nominalism. I should make it clear at the outset I do not believe that the late medieval debate between the realists and the nominalists is the cause of the modern worldview, but I do take the rise of philosophical nominalism as one symptom, among others, of the emergence of a new cultural consciousness that can be characterized as *cultural nominalism*. Though this consciousness bore within it numerous positive possibilities for development, it also contained self-contradictory tendencies that, stretched to their furthest implications on the horizon of time, are self-destructive. I take twentieth-century culture as a whole as the self-destructive outcome of the culture of nominalism, and will attempt to frame my discussion through some selected critiques of modernism (centered especially around the exemplary case of turn-of-the-century Vienna) and alternatives to it. Herman Melville and Charles Peirce in particular, present profound insights into the devastating consequences of modern nominalistic culture, and, I believe, in their critiques can be seen the outline of a new mind that has yet fully to take shape. Melville and Peirce each came to react strongly against American rugged individualism and the nominalistic direction of Western culture in general. Each saw the modern quest for absolute freedom and progress as leading ultimately to fragmentation and chaos, an insight which the course of events in the twentieth century has largely served to confirm. I also will turn later to what I take to be other "first filaments" of a new cultural epoch, as found in some contemporary works of social criticism and art. But first, I should clarify what is meant by the terms "nominalism" and "realism"—terms that perhaps mean too many things for too many different people.

The term "reality," like so many other terms in medieval philosophy, has been transformed into the opposite of what it originally meant to scholastic realists. Indeed, as commonly used today, "realism" conforms accurately to the view of nominalism that the real is that which exists completely outside of mind, directly influencing sensation and, through sensation, thought. Yet reality, as conceived by someone like Duns Scotus, was not something *outside* of knowledge and signs; instead, it is by its very nature a "general," that is, a mediating sign (or in Peirce's terminology a "thirdness"). As Peirce described the difference in a letter of 1909 to Lady Welby:

> The realists are those who declare that *some* generals such as are fit each to be predicated of many subjects are Real. The nominalists said in various forms that no general was Real. Now the word "real"—Latin *realis*—was not an old word. It had been invented during the controversy to mean that which is not a *figment*, as of course any word of a particular language is, or, to express the precise meaning of it in terms intelligible today, the Real is such that whatever is true of it is not true because some individual person's thought or some individual group of persons' thought attributes its predicate to its subject, but is true, no matter what any person or group of persons may think *about* it. (Peirce and Welby 1977, 116)

The real, as it emerges in Peirce's discussion and in his modification of scholastic realism, is inseparable from thought in general or mediation. It is more than brute existence, and in a sense is a peculiar kind of social construct; it is not something that is "socially constructed," in Berger and Luckman's sense (1966), because it is not affected by how *we* think of it; rather, it is that which "constructs" us as we imaginatively grow in understanding, and which tempers our opinions in the long run. The effect of nominalism, which displaced scholastic realism in the European centers of learning more from a change of fashions than a resolution of the conflict, was to drive a wedge between thought and things, and to place the real in the realm of the incognizable. Peirce's argument for reality (and modification of scholastic realism) is that reality is not only general and therefore cognizable, but is also the ultimate goal of all cognition.

Key to Peirce's understanding of modern philosophy and modern culture as a whole is the rise of nominalism over scholastic realism:

> In short, there was a tidal wave of nominalism. Descartes was a nominalist. Locke and all his following, Berkeley, Hartley, Hume, and even Reid, were nominalists. Leibniz was an extreme nominalist. . . . Kant was a nominalist; although his philosophy

would have been rendered compacter, more consistent, and stronger if its author had taken up realism, as he certainly would have done if he had read Scotus. Hegel was a nominalist of realistic yearnings. I might continue the list much further. Thus, in one word, all modern philosophy of every sect has been nominalistic. (CP 1.19)

Peirce did not look upon modern philosophy as a march of progress so much as a cancer upon philosophy, a development that admittedly broadened the scope of philosophy but whose foundations were so logically mistaken as to insure misguided conclusions and eventual decay.

The philosophical import of Peirce's realism has been discussed earlier, but here I want to emphasize that the implications of Peirce's realism are quite removed from the contemporary attitude that "the real" or "truth" is simply an ice-cold, bloodless, mechanical, material substratum of existence. The real is inclusive of the imaginative (considered as qualitative possibility) in Peirce's view. He does hold that there is an otherness that tempers our beliefs and opinions over time, but the furthest reaches of Peircean realism involve an extreme animism that would make contemporary objectivists and relativists shudder (as perhaps they will in reading those sections of this book where I have tried, using ideas from Peirce and from George Rochberg, and from my own research on material possessions, to begin to develop a perspective of *critical animism*). In one of the 1898 series of lectures at Harvard he gave in response to William James's request to speak concretely on some "vitally important topics" (and which Peirce titled "Detached Ideas on Vitally Important Topics"), he rounded out a discussion of the principle of continuity with remarks that illustrate the most profound implications of Peircean realism:

> I will not trouble you with any disquisition on the extreme form of realism which I myself entertain that every true universal, every continuum, is a living and conscious being, but I will content myself with saying that the only things valuable, even here in this life, are the continuities. . . . Even in this transitory life, the only value of all the arbitrary arrangements which mark actuality, whether they were introduced once for all "at the end of the sixth day of creation" or whether, as I believe, they spring out on every hand and all the time, as the act of creation goes on, their only value is to be shaped into a continuous delineation under the creative hand, and at any rate their only use for us is to hold us down to learning one lesson at a time, so that we may make the generalization of intellect and the more important generalizations of sentiment which make the value of this world. . . . *Generalization, the spilling out of continuous systems, in thought, in sentiment, in deed, is the true end of life.* (Peirce 1976, 4:345, 346; my emphasis)

A Peircean realism views generalization as the true end of life, not generalization away from concrete existence into increasing levels of abstract rationality, but the generalization of concrete existence in concrete existence. This is generalization in which rationality represents only a portion of reasonableness, and a portion of less value and depth in the affairs of social life than well-tempered sentiment. This view runs directly counter to the hubris of modern rationality by saying that the critical self-consciousness of the rational ego is the least mature of our capacities, while our sentiments and instincts (which to modern rationality were the province of "primitives, women, and children") are in fact our most mature capacities (though admittedly in a problematic way in modern conditions). It recognizes the dangers of reification, of ideas taking on a rational or emotional life of their own to dominate and distort, so that the possibility of critical inquiry is requisite for social life (and always precarious), and yet it allows that all generals from simple action to complex systems of thought are living beings in the semiotic ecology of a greater continuum: real generals, some of which are brought to us through tempered experience or inquiry, others of which are born out of the human heart, but all of which must be humanized. Some of these real generals, such as mathematics or music, are further perceived to be of a higher order of intelligence than the human institutional ways which manifest them are presently capable of knowing. But this is to say that they nourish us while we fulfill them—the cultivation of those objective possibilities inherent in "continuous systems" is a reciprocal process of transaction between our human fallibility and those greater animating forms.

A Peircean realism takes as the basis for cultural life "Concrete Reasonableness," the percolation of generality, of "continuous systems," into the deeper layers of being, into the very fiber of things themselves. It is a cultural perspective in which the growth of intelligence forms a continuum of semiosis from the lowest forms of life to the unlimited community of inquirers; in which evolution is not simply chance reproduction according to mechanical law but also cosmic generalization; in which the acting individual and the broader social structures are conceived as living sign-processes charged with carrying out a purpose greater than can yet be fully understood. Hence it is a view of social life as fundamentally fallible, while yet fundamentally rooted in, and tempered by, an indubitable cosmic evolutionary intelligence.

A culture of nominalism at its most basic level is one in which social life is viewed as based either on conventions themselves ultimately arbitrary or upon untouchable "natural" laws reflecting a mechanical order of things. The latter side of the "split-brain" of nominalism involves a reification of nature. All nature is based on mechanical law that can be partially held in check through social contract or sublimated through social convention. But the law itself remains outside the sphere of human modification. We may, for example, adopt certain economic institutions that serve to mollify socioeconomic inequality, but this does not affect the underlying "natural" human propensity for individual gain, survival, and domination. A number of social critics, across a range from Marx to Melville and Peirce, have shown how this view of supposedly "natural" law actually reproduces the ideology of individualism (in Peirce's words, "the philosophy of greed") and projects it onto nature, denying the place of the social environment by making it epiphenomenal. This view ultimately holds social relation to be a fiction of the social contract, not an essential feature of the underlying reality. In one of its contemporary forms it is called Realpolitik, and whether in its communist or capitalist manifestation it reflects a worldview in which the power of things, not people, ultimately moves the world.

The other side of cultural nominalism is conventionalism, in which all that really matters in social life is based on a world of convention, a world that floats freely above the realm of necessity and biological limitation, an infinitely plastic world, a world largely (and for some, totally) arbitrary at base. Although we live in a world of matter, the place of matter per se is reduced to a minimum; it is its conventional significance only that truly matters. In its theoretical manifestations, this side of nominalism can be seen in various forms of rationalistic "cognitive" theory that see evolution solely in terms of nurture or external environment. Contemporary structuralism and poststructuralism are particularly good examples as well. Here too can be found the reduction of culture to labels and slogans, the brainlessness of American advertising and commercially sterilized television consciousness, in which ideas and emotions are only so many buttons to be pushed. The same holds true of the great propaganda machines of modern totalitarianism, of whatever political persuasion. In place of the living process of interpretation, comes the mere recognition of the label, either through deadening repetition or an attention-grabbing shock. This is a world of "public" relations and advertising, in which all the deepest sentiments and ideas of human life can be "packaged" to sell, a culture in which exchange value so totally dominates cultural life as to obliterate use value, in which transience and the ersatz fulfill one hundred percent of the minimum daily requirements. Nominalism presents us with a system of thought that, although it may seem internally consistent, is based on premises that carried to their full logical conclusion are self-contradictory. Taken in a broader cultural sense, cultural nominalism is rooted in an ultimately dichotomous worldview whose premisses, carried to their full conclusions, are self-destructive. This spectre of Cartesian dualism might be called *mythic relativism*, while its seeming opposite, but actually its other half, might be called *mythic objectivism*.

I am here using Richard Bernstein's (1983) characterization of relativism (which he distinguishes from subjectivism) and objectivism as the central cultural opposition of our time. I only add "mythic" to these terms to signify how both forms of thought seem to me to be avatars of abstraction-ism, of the inherently dichotomous tendencies of the latter stages of the culture of nominalism that sooner or later culminate in a rootless *depersonalized subjectivism* (of individuals or of cultural practices that forever remain incommunicable or incorrectible in their essentials).

The objectivist versus conventionalist/subjectivist legacy of twentieth-century modernity has been the rejection of continuity and tradition, the rejection of growth as a constituent of reality, the unquestioned rejection of any and all boundaries. Both sides of nominalism end with a paradoxical individual, either the solipsistic subject or the lonely referential scientist/philosopher pointing at a "fact." The implications of the culture of nominalism are the increasing diminution of the living continuity of culture and the eclipse of tradition—of a positively or negatively informing past, of an emergent future, of a present that brings cultural legacy to fruition, so as to actualize ideas that themselves can give birth to new possibilities, "ideas of the ceaselessly immortal kind."

Principia Diaboli

So much of the development of twentieth-century arts, philosophy, and social science appears at first as dichotomous—extreme objectivism versus extreme subjectivism—yet with developing perspective we begin to see how these dichotomous developments more closely resemble two sides of a split brain.

Pragmatism may have seemed to provide a link between mind and world early in the century, but pragmatism itself was buried under the combination of caricatures of it (due in great measure perhaps, to the popularity of Jamesian pragmatism, which combined some unresolved nominalistic tendencies toward dichotomism with a looseness of expression) and, more significantly, the turn to positivism in the thirties and the "linguistic turn" that replaced logical positivism in the Anglo-American context. Logical positivism, classic behaviorism, "abstracted empiricism" in sociology, all attempted to displace purpose as a central concern, in favor of the "objective" fact that could be readily pointed to or counted. Other modern movements of thought stressed the importance of the individual or systemic subject as sole center of meaning, as against externally objective determinants (Husserl's phenomenology, Sartre's existentialism, structuralism, and psychoanalysis). These movements, as well as their seeming opposites, shared tendencies toward dehistoricism, in favor of creating a wholly new starting point.

What unites these opposing forms of thought, as well as their counterparts in art and music, is an attempt to create a revolutionary departure that would once and for all cut through the veils of mediation and history, to reveal the truly posthistoric modern condition. If one examines the revolu-

tionary artistic, philosophical, or political movements of the early twentieth
century in Europe, one sees a collective effort to critically self-detach from the
limitations of tradition in order to build anew on solid foundations.

The "Cartesian anxiety" (Bernstein 1983, 16f.), the search for a
fundamental starting point, marked many of the most radical innovations in
the early part of the century. When one looks at the leading figures in such a
key city as Vienna, for example, it is as if they collectively swore as their oath
Descartes' statement in the *Meditations* that "I must once for all seriously
undertake to rid myself of all the opinions which I had formerly accepted, and
commence to build anew from the foundation, if I [want] to establish any firm
and permanent structure in the sciences" (in Bernstein 1983, 16), or, we
might add, in the arts. One sees this purification program in the theories of
architect Adolph Loos, composer Arnold Schoenberg, the *Tractatus Logico-
Philosophicus* of Ludwig Wittgenstein, the phenomenology of Vienna-
trained Edmund Husserl and the metapsychology of Husserl's fellow student
of Brentano, Sigmund Freud.

An inevitable and linear historical progress informed the work of
Loos and Schoenberg. To attain freedom, modern man had to throw off the
dead hand of tradition and separate conceptual reason from mere fantasy and
sentiment. Loos sought to separate decorative items radically from functional
ones, a separation which he believed was an inevitable outgrowth of cultural
evolution: "Cultural evolution is equivalent to the removal of ornament from
articles in everyday use." Loos often stated that a building should either be
functional or decorative, but not both, and perhaps this is why he reacted to
the *Chicago Tribune*'s competition for a monumental *and* functional news-
paper building by submitting a ludicrous giant Greek Column!

In *Wittgenstein's Vienna* Janik and Toulmin describe how the *sound*
of a composition seemed to be a secondary concern to Schoenberg, who was
more interested in the logic of composition:

> Schönberg, unlike Hanslick, considered the question, how a
> composition sounds, as having no importance. . . . So the
> "beautiful" in music is, for Schönberg, a by-product of the com-
> poser's integrity, a function of his search for truth—"The artist
> attains beauty without willing it, for he is only striving after
> truthfulness." (Janik and Toulmin 1973, 110–11)

Schoenberg's unrelenting quest to purify the language of music by subjecting
it to a severe structural logic, had the effect, as with Loos, of placing an
impassable barrier between the received tradition and what was morally or
logically permissible in the modern condition.

One of the direct consequences of both Loos's and Schoenberg's
rejection of tradition is that each created for his art an extremely self-
conscious language, a language based on a strict rational standard. In the

1890s Loos had spent time in Chicago and was familiar with the revolutionary functionalism of Chicago architecture. But where Louis Sullivan called
for form to follow function, in a way in which the decorative could be
organically linked to the context of use, Loos, in the spirit of Karl Kraus, the
Viennese social critic, insisted on a radical separation of fact from value, so
that there could be no organic mediation of function with decoration.
Architecture had to be self-consciously clear of its principles and expression if
it was to free itself from retrograde bourgeois "tatooing."

The fact that Loos's and Schoenberg's works may strike us as compelling and even beautiful is due much more to the artistic character of these
men than to their theoretical formulations. Loos and Schoenberg had the
advantage of creating antitraditional architecture and music, while both men
remained strongly rooted in the traditions they were rejecting. This gave their
work a tension lacking in most of their "heirs" of succeeding generations,
who inherited buildings and music that did not in their substance "remember" their predecessors.

One might say that the old debate between politically "committed"
art and artistic "autonomy" (especially as found in the critical dialogue
between Walter Benjamin and Theodore Adorno), can be seen in this regard
as a dialectic framed wholly within a culture of forgetting. Benjamin, in his
dogmatically Marxist essay written under the influence of Bertolt Brecht,
"The Author as Producer" (Benjamin 1937), claimed that "politically correct" art necessarily includes beauty. Schoenberg believed beauty to be a
function of the composer's striving after truthfulness. Both shared a misguided abstractionist premiss: that a logically correct or politically correct
concept—apparently given in advance—manifested in a logically or politically correct technique, provides the foundation for art. The past, from both
sides, is simply a bourgeois comfort and obstacle to be discarded or overcome, as far as its significance for contemporary work is concerned.

Like Loos, Schoenberg also believed in a kind of linear cultural
evolution for which the past served as a mere springboard, or perhaps a kind
of essential "ladder" for a student composer to "climb" into his craft, but
something which should be discarded as useless and obsolete for a mature
composer working on the edge of the future:

> It is inconceivable that composers should call "serious music"
> what they write in an obsolete style, with a prolixity not con-
> forming to the contents—repeating three to seven times what is
> understandable at once. Why should it not be possible in music
> to say in whole complexes in a condensed form what, in the pre-
> ceding epochs, had at first to be said several times with slight
> variations before it could be elaborated? (Schoenberg 1950, 64)

Schoenberg's emphasis on "condensing" and crystallizing musical ideas has been criticized by composer George Rochberg as leading eventually to a destruction of *redundancy*, which is essential to the "profile of identity" of a piece of music (Rochberg 1984a). Rochberg has used the analogy of mathematician John von Neumann's "parallel and serial operations" to argue that a certain level of redundancy is essential to the way the ear hears and remembers music. In Schoenberg we see a marked decline in redundancy, which later becomes an almost total lack of any redundancy in post–World War II music, whether of the rational "serial" or chance "aleatory" side of the dichotomy. Not only, as Rochberg pointed out, do both sides of the dichotomy sound alike, but the outcome or legacy of this process of decreasing redundancy, which raises the level of self-consciousness to such a degree that the music can no longer be remembered, is something which could only be termed "forgettable music." So-called postmodern minimalists, such as Philip Glass or Steve Reich, have chosen to take a dichotomous stand toward this cultural condition through a self-consciously monotonous music that subverts hearing through redundancy itself. Yet in accepting the same goal of subverting the ear through a technique that denies living pulse and rhythm, not to mention a broad range of emotions, they appear more as the final stage of modernism: one-idea artists.

Freud's case may seem somewhat different from, or even opposed to, those of the other Viennese, since he devoted a great deal of attention to showing how the past is indelibly stamped in us and how symbolic mediation is central to human functioning. But when we turn to the foundation of Freud's model, the "it" or "id" (remembering that Freud used the German vernacular "*das Es*"), we see that it provides the "scientific reality" underlying his model, a reality that the "reality principle" of the "I" must distort and mollify if there is to be any specifically human functioning. Freud punctured the hypocrisy of Viennese life even while showing how it was a necessary fiction.

Peirce's reality "transcends" human consciousness as presently constituted, because we are a partial, fallible, growing life-form, but it is not "transcendent" in the strict philosophical sense: reality is precisely the ultimately knowable object to be realized in and by the unlimited community of inquirers that form the horizon of all inquiry and human development. In philosophical terms real truth is a cognizable aim, as contrasted with Freud's ultimately incognizable "it," whose attainment is not the *alētheia* (truth) of the Greeks, which meant an uncovering and bringing to light and vision, but its diabolical opposite: blindness.

In Freud's view, the id or "it" consists of the mechanically ruled impulses and drives of the physical organism, a seething and uncontrolled chaos outside of history and in itself unmodifiable by human cultivation. Knowledge of Freud's "it," contrary to knowledge of Peirce's "it," means the destruction of all meaning and mediation. When Oedipus in effect answered the questions "What and why is it?" and "Why am I here?," the riddle of the Sphinx, he gained the knowledge that the ultimate goal beneath mediation is incest and murder, and that the attainment of this goal is the destruction of all knowledge, meaning, purpose, and reality. Freud's Oedipal semiotic, with its claim that the id is real, that the ego is a secondary system of representation superimposed on the id, and that therefore the attainment of the reality which lies behind the veil of representation (the very answer to the riddle of the Sphinx) is blindness instead of insight, is fragmentation instead of relation, is murder and lust, or simply hate instead of love—this semiotic reveals itself in the end, despite interesting insights into the fantastic dynamics of the psyche, to be a variation on the myth of Hobbes, subject to the same "fallacy of misplaced concreteness" as Hobbes's is. Freud's use of the Oedipal myth, stripped, as Schorske points out (1980), of all its original political connotations, as the foundation of all human existence itself represents the myth of cultural nominalism, the fallacy that there is a primordial, clear, and distinct dichotomy between a knowing subject and the objective world. Yet there was a kind of historical truth in the idea of a primal horde of sons rising to overthrow the father, not *in illo tempore* as Freud mythologized, but rather in the end of time that was turn-of-the-century Vienna and Europe, when a new constellation rose up across political, cultural, and philosophical life to expunge the past and start from scratch.

Husserl's phenomenology seems to be imbued with the same turn-of-the century spirit to begin anew and thereby in good Cartesian fashion to establish a solid foundation. And though this spirit was generalized throughout Europe, it is perhaps not unrelated that Husserl had studied at the University of Vienna, where he began to turn toward philosophy under the influence of Franz Brentano. In his preface to the 1931 English translation of his *Ideas: General Introduction to Pure Phenomenology* (1913), Husserl claims that his philosophical meditations over the previous decades had a single aim (19, 20): "to discover a *radical beginning* of a philosophy which, to repeat the Kantian phrase, 'will be able to present itself as science.' . . . Lacking as did the traditional schemes of philosophy the enthusiasm of a first beginning, they also lacked what is first and most important: a specifically philosophical groundwork acquired through original self-activity, and therewith that firmness of basis, that genuineness of root, which alone makes real philosophy possible."

The drive to break through the obscuring traditions and mediating abstractions "to the things themselves!" ("zu den Sachen selbst!"), as Husserl said; to create a radical beginning rooted in an original self-activity, ended in Husserl's case with a solipsistic subject privatized from the greater community of inquiriers.

Ludwig Wittgenstein's early picture-theory of representation in the *Tractatus Logico-Philosophicus* embodies an objectivism perhaps diametrically opposed to Husserl's subjectivism, yet one sharing Husserl's extreme ahistorical foundationalism. Both accept the idea so dominant in early twentieth-century philosophy of science that one must begin from a pure beginning, an objective or elementary starting point, rather than from some as yet unquestioned assumptions which then become subject to criticism and modification as inquiry proceeds. Wittgenstein eventually moved toward this latter position, but not before the Vienna Circle has appropriated the *Tractatus* (along with the work especially of Ernst Mach [See Janik and Toulmin 1973]) for its austere program of logical positivism, a movement that itself had great influence upon the course of philosophy, the social sciences, and semiotics.

The ethical and aesthetic spheres were, for early Wittgenstein, outside of what could be rationally expressed in strict propositional form. Where Wittgenstein held these spheres to be the ultimate source of value, "higher" than logical discussion in the sense of being incapable of logical expression and "factual" determination, the Vienna Circle used Wittgenstein's *Tractatus* in order to claim that anything not expressible in rigorous (and narrowly conceived) scientific language was meaningless. By "scientific language" they meant an extreme nominalist standpoint in which verbal or mathematical symbols stand univocally for determinate things or "facts." In attempting to erase all metaphysics the positivists created perhaps the most extreme metaphysics yet devised: an objectivism in which not the community, but the lonely philosopher referentially pointing to a fact, constituted objectivity. To this day linguists and semioticians who profess to be antipositivistic still believe in "syntactics, semantics, and pragmatics," which are rooted in the metaphysical figment of positivism. One cannot underestimate the profound effects this movement had on twentieth-century philosophy and social sciences, and on a more generalized attitude that all spheres of culture should emulate this "scientific" attitude.

As a worldview, the ideology of positivistically based, nominalistically conceived science has shown itself again and again in our time to be destructive to living human culture. In its reduction of the plurality of being to a single technical homogeneity, in its willingness to lend itself to the stunted power-mentality of dictators, generic generals, and the profit industry, in its grand hubris that knows no limits (the question of limits being ethical and therefore nonscientific—in effect, a position above ethics), the ideology of science has shown itself quite willing to destroy a world if only to prove a point: the subservience of the "purist" positivist conception of science to the mercenary power of things. This attitude was immortalized in Tom Lehrer's song about the Nazi/NASA rocket scientist, Werner von Braun: "Once rrrockets are up, who cares vhere zey come down / dat's not my department says Werner von Braun."

Granting that the Vienna Circle ignored what Wittgenstein considered as most important, it remains problematical that what is most important is so utterly outside of language. In the *Tractatus* one confronts a mind incapable of expressing what it considers ultimate, because hemmed in by an extreme nominalistic split between facts and values. In the preface Wittgenstein says, "The whole sense of the book might be summed up in the following words: what can be said at all can be said clearly, and what we cannot talk about we must pass over in silence." When one considers the Greek view of the ethical as the realm of living speech and action, Wittgenstein's banishment of ethics from the social realm of speech to the private realm of silence seems almost a diabolical inversion. Wittgenstein's ineffable realm exists outside of reason, outside of mediation, and can be known only in an inexplicable and incommunicable way. The sad fact of the matter is that, the closer we come to it, the less we can say about it, or inquire into it, or give praise to it. Community has nothing to do with Wittgenstein's reality in the *Tractatus*, for in his objective solipsism reality is a suicidal vanishing point: "Here it can be seen that solipsism, when its implications are followed out strictly, concides with pure realism. The self of solipsism shrinks to a point without extension, and there remains the reality co-ordinated with it" (Wittgenstein 1921, 5.64).

In the early Wittgenstein of the *Tractatus* we see that curious phenomenon of a *depersonalized subjectivism* that underlies so much of twentieth-century culture. He thought he had achieved the "final solution," as he said in his preface, to the problems of philosophy, just as, though it is extremely doubtful he ever read the preface to the *Tractatus*, a certain failed Viennese painter and would-be architect, Adolph Hitler, later thought he could achieve a German radical "foundationalism" through a "final solution" of genocide. Hitler's diabolical terror was, of course, at the polar opposite of the ever ethically haunted Wittgenstein, but the extreme foundationalism of both stems from a larger impulse of the time to achieve a radical closure. Wittgenstein's final solution to philosophy, which he was himself later to recant, had the effect of placing what most mattered utterly beyond the critical communicative community and into a purely privatized realm of the ineffable. Wittgenstein was truly possessed, as few contemporary thinkers are, by the sense of the greater mystery of being, by a longing for that which we in our individual limitations can only partially grasp. Yet Wittgenstein's nominalism (which he did not completely free himself from even in his later turn toward context of use in language) prevented him from bridging the gulf he so painfully felt throughout his life. Could this explain his aphoristic comment made between 1941 and 1944: "Is it some frustrated longing that makes a man mad? (I was thinking of Schumann, but of myself too.)" (Wittgenstein 1980, 44e).

The nominalistic ultimates that motivated all of the Vienna revolutionaries are refracted in a quite different light in Thomas Mann's novel

Doctor Faustus. Though dealing with a fictional composer, Adrian Leverkühn, who is modeled (despite disclaimers by Mann) to some extent after Schoenberg, we might read Leverkühn as a composite figure of the modern temper as a whole.

Leverkühn raises dissonance in his music to the highest level, and, as the name Faustus suggests, makes a pact with the devil in order to achieve twenty-four years of genius time. The devil's depiction of hell reads like a description of modern nominalism, and almost echoes the concluding aphorisms of Wittgenstein's *Tractatus Logico-Philosophicus*:

> Only it is not easy actually to speak thereof—that is, one can really not speak of it at all, because the actual is beyond what can by word be declared; many words may be used and fashioned, but all together they are but tokens, standing for names which do not and cannot make claim to describe what is never to be described and denounced in words. That is the secret delight and security of hell, that it is not to be informed on, that it is protected from speech, that it just is, but cannot be public in the newspaper, be brought by any word to critical knowledge, wherefore precisely the words "subterranean," "cellar," "thick walls," "soundlessness," "forgottenness," "hopelessness," are the poor, weak symbols. One must be satisfied with symbolism, my good man, when one is speaking of hell, for there everything ends—not only the word that describes, but everything altogether. This is indeed the chiefest characteristic and what in most general terms is to be uttered about it: both that which the newcomer thither first experiences, and what at first with his as it were sound senses he cannot grasp, and will not understand, because his reason or what limitation soever of his understanding prevents him, in short because it is quite unbelievable enough to make him turn white as a sheet, although it is opened to him at once on greeting, in the most emphatic and concise words, that *"here everything leaves off."* (Mann [1948] 1971, 244–45)

How would a culture appear that tried to realize to the fullest this particular spiritual realm? It might sound like John Cage's *4'33"* (1952), which consists of a few minutes of silence. Or it might look like the seemingly endless variations on Malevich's all-white canvass, such as Robert Rauschenberg's *Erased Drawing* (1953), in which a drawing by Willem de Kooning was painstakingly erased with forty erasers over the course of a month and the result exhibited as Rauschenberg's own work (see Gablik 1984, 39). More generally it would appear as one of the various forms of minimalism that have dominated art since World War II, forms which deny the active subject rooted in a broader community, and ceaselessly engaged in the task of bringing to humanly perceptible and enduring forms, through craft, the "phantom of life" itself.

Nominalists such as these minimalists want to say that qualities, words, intentions, signs, and social life are simply conventions, and that reality really consists either of the ineffable or of the bare particulars, mechanical motions, the things you can actually point to or touch here and now (as G. E. Moore, in a different context, said about his hands). As we shall soon see in examining Herman Melville's *Moby Dick*, Ahab grasped this, but when he literally grasped "the ungraspable phantom of life," he found that the depersonalized subjectivism that underlies the culture of nominalism is hatred, fragmentation, death, and nothingness; that reality is something more.

Melville's *Moby Dick* gets to the heart of the matter as a prophetic insight into the twentieth century, by revealing the demonic nature of the quest to achieve direct, unmediated, and final knowledge of life itself. Melville wrote to Nathaniel Hawthorne that the book, like Ahab's harpoon, is baptized "in nomine diaboli." And it is in precisely the same sense that our nominalistic age can be characterized not as symbolic, which literally means "to throw together," but rather as "thrown apart" and innately fragmented: "in nomine diaboli."

MELVILLE'S GRASP OF REALITY

The title for *Moby Dick* was suggested to Melville by the story of the legendary white whale, Mocha Dick. According to Viola Sachs:

> Mocha appears to be a condensation of the word mama-cocha used to designate the Peruvian and Chilean cult of the whale; it means mother sea. Thus the name itself might symbolize a return to the primordial waters and womb; yet the word "Dick," that is, devil, points to the presence of evil at the outset of life. (Sachs 1973, 47)

Perhaps, as a synonym for penis, it also suggests the phallic principle in combination with the maternal mother sea: the procreative whiteness of milk and sperm. Another definition of "Dick" from the *1811 Dictionary of the Vulgar Tongue* might also be appropriate:

> *Dick.* That happened in the reign of Queen Dick, i.e., never: said of any absurd old story. I am as queer as Dick's hatband; that is, out of spirits, or don't know what ails me.

It would not be uncharacteristic of Melville, who later found Beauty in a sailor in *Billy Budd*, and Goodness in a swindler in *The Confidence Man*, to seek Truth in an absurd old fish tale in *Moby Dick*. A Freudian could no doubt elucidate further definitions of "Dick" which would also be justified by symbolism throughout the text, but the perspective taken here is that *Moby*

Dick is the story of the quest for the inscrutable white whale who is the essence of reality, "the ungraspable phantom of life."

In the first chapter ("Loomings") the narrator, Ishmael, introduces himself as an alienated and insular soul who takes to the sea as a form of therapy:

> Whenever I find myself growing grim about the mouth; whenever it is a damp, drizzly November in my soul; whenever I find myself involuntarily pausing before coffin warehouses, and bringing up the rear of every funeral I meet; and especially whenever my hypos get such an upper hand of me, that it requires a strong moral principle to prevent me from deliberately stepping into the street, and methodically knocking people's hats off—then, I account it high time to get to sea as soon as I can. This is my substitute for the pistol and ball. With a philosophical flourish Cato throws himself upon his sword; I quietly take to the ship. (Melville [1851] 1964, 23; hereafter cited as *MD*)

Ishmael's journey to the sea can be seen as a rite of passage, a quest involving a return to the primeval womb which can either dissolve and absorb him or cleanse and renew him: In any case it is a journey toward death. Ishmael reveals the key to the novel in the first chapter. He says that chief among his motives

> was the overwhelming idea of the great whale himself. Such a portentous and mysterious monster roused all my curiosity. Then the wild and distant seas where he rolled his island bulk; the undeliverable, nameless perils of the whale; these, with all attending marvels of a thousand Patagonian sights and sounds, helped to sway me to my wish. With other men, perhaps, such things would not have inducements; but as for me, I am tormented with an everlasting itch for things remote. . . .
>   By reason of these things, then, the whaling voyage was welcome; the great flood-gates of the wonder-world swung open, and in the wild conceits that swayed me to my purpose, two and two there floated into my inmost soul, endless processions of the whale, and, mid most of them all, one grand hooded phantom, like a snow hill in the air. (*MD*, 29–30)

Ishmael's vision, which animates his whale quest, is opposed to Ahab's from the start. His soul contemplatively *receives* the vision of whales while Ahab's quest actively pits his will against the white whale who bit off his leg. Swimming "two by two" into Ishmael's inmost soul, like the animals into the ark, is "the whale," and between this procession of whales, representing their grand mediation, is the "snow hill" of the "grand hooded phantom." This white whale is the seemingly transcendental "ungraspable phantom of life," as Ishmael informs us in the first chapter while reflecting on the relation of meditation and water:

> Why did the old Persians hold the sea holy? Why did the Greeks give it a separate deity, and own brother of Jove? Surely all this is not without meaning. And still deeper the meaning of that story of Narcissus, who because he could not grasp the torment-ing, mild image he saw in the fountain, plunged into it and was drowned. But that same image, we ourselves see in all rivers and oceans. it is the image of the *ungraspable phantom of life*; and this is the key to it all. (*MD*, 26; emphasis added)

Later we will see how it is precisely in learning to "grasp" that Ishmael comes to realize the "ungraspable" aspect of the phantom of life. He literally grasps whiteness, the whiteness of social relation, the whiteness that cuts through that narcissism of the modern ego which appropriates the whole world unto itself. To see the "phantom of life" as image of the isolate self, as, for example, Freud was later to do in viewing human relation as only so many cathexes of libido (as if the "phantom of life" is simply an inner hydraulic mechanism) is eventually to go the way of Narcissus. The narcissist can never truly touch the world, only himself or herself. In reaching for the ultimate, the narcissist, the Ahabian, can only attain to a self-image that is simultaneously a death mask. It is the narcissism of modernity that Melville is indicting, a narcissism that would turn the ungraspable phantom of life into an indi-vidualistic self-image, into a *thing* to be possessed. Yet, "He who binds to himself a joy loses it forever" as Blake said; or further, he who would cast aside all human bonds for unbounded freedom would soon find himself the most bound, constricted, and unfree of all.

Anthropologist Victor Turner analyzed the white symbolism of *Moby Dick* in his *Revelation and Divination in Ndembu Ritual*, where he described the transcendent and inconceivable aspects of whiteness: "My principal aim is to point out that whiteness in all three examples represents pure act-of-being. It is everything that cannot be conceptualized, and whenever people attempt to interpret it they are forced to give a long inventory of referents, many of which clearly represent the human standpoint adopted toward the *ipsum esse* (the act-of-being itself)" (Turner 1975, 194).

Although Turner found close parallels in the meanings attributed to whiteness in *Moby Dick* and in the African Ndembu ritual of Chihamba, he believed *Moby Dick* radically differed from the Ndembu ritual because there is no redemption in its tragic ending.

> Melville, identified with Ahab, proud and modern, emhasized the hateful and terrifying aspects of that whiteness which transcends mortality. The Ndembu lay stress rather on the social and com-munal aspects of being, since their social system is basically

structured by kinship ties. . . . But in all of them whiteness represents an attempt to grasp the ungraspable, the embody the invisible. . . . From one point of view *Chihamba* is a long plea for the restoration of the normative order and an act of penance by and on behalf of those who have transgressed moral norms which are believed to have the same validity as natural regularities. Thus *Chihamba*, unlike *Moby Dick*, represents a humble submission to the act-of-being of and behind all phenomena. It emphasizes dependence, whereas *Moby Dick* asserts a suicidal independence. (Turner 1975, 194, 200–201)

Ahab, as modern individualist, is possessed by a cold passion to attain an absolute and immediate knowledge; one that paradoxically requires a suicidal independence and what George Rochberg (1984a) has termed a "rational madness." Consider Ahab's words to Starbuck, a pre-echo of so many twentieth-century manifestos, proclamations, and foundational documents:

> All visible objects, man, are but as pasteboard masks. But in each event—in the living act, the undoubted deed—there, some unknown but still reasoning thing puts forth the moldings of its features from behind the unreasoning mask. If man will strike, strike through the mask!

Ahab is not simply haunted by the spectre of the "Cartesian anxiety" of modernity, the fear of having, as Descartes said, "all of a sudden fallen into very deep water" where "I can neither make certain of setting my feet on the bottom, nor can I swim and so support myself on the surface" (Bernstein 1983, 17). Ahab *is* spectre of the Cartesian anxiety, forever restless until he can touch certainty, until he can tear away the veils of mediation to reveal the divine; fated paradoxically only to touch chaos, to unleash madness, to remain bound, forever restless, to an ungraspable object. In Peirce's terms, Ahab seeks to *know* Firstness, or immediate consciousness in the continual present, a doomed task. His unyielding quest, as Turner and many others have claimed, must fail because of its extreme onesidedness. Yet in examining the text, it becomes obvious that one person is redeemed: Ishmael. Moreover, his redemption results from experiences analogous to those of liminality and communitas described in Turner's work (e.g., *The Ritual Process*).

Three figures touch divinity in *Moby Dick*: Captain Ahab, the lowly black cabin boy Pip, and Ishmael. The highest-ranking and lowest-ranking members of the Pequod, Ahab and Pip, respectively, represent the extremes of consciousness. Pip, after jumping overboard more than once during a whale chase, is left adrift by Stubb (who recognizes that pecuniary interest takes precedence over benevolence) in the vastness of the open sea until the boat crew has completed their task. The engulfing terror of the open sea undoes Pip:

> The sea had jeeringly kept his finite body up, but drowned the infinite of his soul. Not drowned entirely, though. Rather carried down alive to wondrous depths, where strange shapes of the unwarped primal world glided to and fro before his passive eyes; and the miser-merman, Wisdom, revealed his hoarded heaps; and among the joyous, heartless, ever-juvenile eternities, Pip saw the multitudinous, God-omnipresent, coral insects, that out of the firmament of waters heaved the colossal orbs. He saw God's foot upon the treadle of the loom, and spoke it; and therefore his shipmates called him mad. So man's insanity is heaven's sense; and wandering from all mortal reason, man comes at last to that celestial thought, which, to reason, is absurd and frantic; and weal or woe, feels then uncompromised, indifferent as his god. (*MD*, 530)

Pip's experience results in madness, a madness that Ahab intuitively recognizes as profoundly linked to his own obsession. We see in this odd couple a prefigurement of the "split brain" of twentieth-century culture: those extreme primitivisms and rationalisms at opposite poles from each other that yet remain intuitively connected in their eradication of the living human perspective. Between the extremes of unconscious and rational madness represented by Pip and Ahab, is the *via media* that is Ishmael. Ishmael is that other aspect of suicidal modernity, who might yet suffer transformation and rebirth.

The crew of the Pequod represents modern individualist American society; "Islanders" (literally and figuratively) drawn from around the world: "They were nearly all Islanders in the Pequod, *Isolatoes* too, I call such, not acknowledging the common continent of men, but each *Isolato* living on a separate continent of his own" (*MD*, 166).

Ahab, captain of the *Isolatoes*, progressively cuts off his human ties and by these acts becomes increasingly individual and alone. He is truly the modern nominalistic individual who stands at the center of a subjective universe, and, cut off from tradition and left only with will, attempts to attain the ultimate. Ahab is a man who, as Melville once commented about Emerson, lives by the head, but during his torment in the weeks after his leg is bitten off by Moby Dick, Ahab's intellect becomes dominated by his out-of-control heart, and his monomania to attain the white whale takes over. Ahab "piled upon the whale's white hump the sum of all the general rage and hate felt by his whole race from Adam down." Ishmael, by contrast, is the sole individual in the book both to shatter and live through the death grip of the isolating Western worldview by coming to realize the community of humankind.

Ishmael is first initiated into the "continent of men" by Queequeg, the Polynesian harpooner. Queequeg symbolizes all "colored" men and particularly the red and the black men, as seen in his two ritual objects—a tomahawk pipe and his small ebony idol, Yojo. The other two main harpooners are Tashtego, an American Indian, and Daggoo, an African black. These three "aliens" form complementary opposites to the three mates in charge of the whaling rowboats. While hierarchically inferior to the mates, each harpooner is a member of the royalty of his native people. Melville here presents the paradox that the "savages" form a kind of spiritual elite, in counterpart to the material savagery of the whites. Melville's symbology of "alien wisdom" also forms part of his indictment of America as a quest doomed from the start because it is built on the blood and subjugation of the red man and black man (Sachs 1973, 52).

At the inn owned by "Mr. Coffin" (what, dear reader, could this name possibly mean?) where they first meet and share the bed slept in by the Coffins on their honeymoon night (on which Mrs. Coffin, true to her name, later died), Ishmael and Queequeg are symbolically united. They thus meet in a coffin bed, and at the end of the novel Ishmael is finally saved upon Queequeg's coffin, which becomes a lifebuoy.

Ishmael's and Queequeg's "bosom friendship" is sealed in their room where they share "a social smoke. . . from that wild [tomahawk] pipe." This scene of social smoking, sociality from an instrument of death, contrasts with the later chapter, "The Pipe." There Ahab, becoming increasingly estranged, can no longer enjoy smoking and must throw his pipe overboard. At another point he throws his quadrant overboard; with this act he isolates himself from science and guidance from the cosmos above, and demonstrates an increasing reliance on blind will. Melville concretely illustrates the tendency in abstract rationality to throw aside or jettison all that which is not rationality itself. Yet in throwing the quadrant overboard, Ahab jettisons science and the possibility of rationality itself. The blind obsession of rationality to pursue its object singlemindedly through technical means and method, destroys even its own means and its anchor to the starry sky above through its mad narrowing, until all that is left is the blind and empty obsession itself, pure depersonalized solipsism. This is the triumph, as William Barrett, in a different context put it, of the irrational. Rationality becomes its own opposite, devouring itself, making precisely everything it did not want not only possible but actual.

Later in the evening of the "social smoke," Ishmael becomes idolator, humbly making an offering of wood chips and then kissing the nose of the little black idol. This scene contrasts sharply with the false and hypocritical Christian piety of the previous chapter, "The Sermon." The tiny black, touchable idol and the warmth surrounding it stand in stark contrast to the gigantic and incomprehensible white whale. Ishmael reflects:

> As I sat there in that now lonely room . . . I began to be sensible
> of strange feelings. I felt a melting in me. No more my splintered
> heart and maddened hand were turned against the wolfish world.
> This soothing savage had redeemed it. (*MD*, 83)

The name Ishmael literally means "God hears," and in Genesis 16, Abra-
ham's wife's servant, who bore Ishmael, is told: "He shall be a wild ass of a
man, his hand against every man and every man's hand against him, and he
shall dwell over against all his kinsmen." Ishmael has now begun to overcome
the *Isolatoism* inherent in his name. The linking of hands as a sign of
continuity and communion reappears when Ishmael and Queequeg are sign-
ing aboard the Pequod. Against the false piety of the ship's owner, Captain
Bildad, who, though eager to capitalize on Queequeg's expertise as harpooner, questions whether Queequeg is a nominal Christian, stands
Ishmael's wry reply that Queequeg is a deacon at the First Congregational
Church:

> the great and everlasting First Congregation of this whole wor-
> shipping world; we all belong to that; only some of us cherish
> some queer crochets noways touching the grand belief; in *that*
> we all join hands. (*MD*, 128–29)

Bildad's *Isolato* reply is: "Splice, thou mean'st *splice hands.*"
    Ishmael's initiation into "the continent of men," his grasping of the
social basis of reality, culminates in the chapter titled "A Squeeze of the
Hand." With other crew members, Ishmael is squeezing globules of sper-
maceti (a substance from the whale's head used for perfume) back to a liquid
state. In the "bath" and baptism of "inexpressible sperm," Ishmael cleanses
himself of any remnants of hatred, including the diabolic oath he made with
the rest of the crew and with Ahab to kill the white whale: "I forgot all about
our horrible oath; in that inexpressible sperm, I washed my hands and my
heart of it" (*MD*, 532). He experiences an epiphany of the fundamental
continuity of humankind, which transcends social hierarchies and isolato
individuality:

> Squeeze! Squeeze! Squeeze! All the morning long; I squeezed that
> sperm till I myself almost melted into it; I squeezed that sperm
> till a strange sort of insanity came over me; and I found myself
> unwittingly squeezing my co-laborers' hands in it, mistaking their
> hands for the gentle globules. Such an abounding, affectionate,
> friendly, loving feeling did this avocation beget; that at last I was
> continually squeezing their hands, and looking up into their eyes,
> sentimentally; as much to say, -Oh! my dear fellow beings, why
> should we longer cherish any social acerbities, or know the
> slightest ill-humor or envy! Come; let us squeeze hands all
> round; let us all squeeze ourselves into each other; let us squeeze

ourselves universally into the very milk and sperm of kindness. (*MD*, 532)

Ishmael's hands are no longer turned against his fellow men, but rather he has realized "the continent of men" in his experience of squeezing hands. He has "become welded into the universal continuum" (Peirce), in joining hands with his fellow seamen in the "semen" of the "ungraspable phantom of life" itself. In this act, the generative, life-giving aspects of whiteness, as well as the fundamental unity involved in the complementary masculine and feminine principles of love, that is, "the very milk and sperm of kindness," is revealed to Ishmael. Reality is not to be found by a world-negating, individualized turning to ideal mind, but only in and through the community of humankind:

> Would that I could keep squeezing that sperm for ever! For now, since by many prolonged, repeated experiences, I have perceived that in all cases man must eventually lower, or at least shift, his conceit of attainable felicity, not placing it anywhere in the intellect or fancy; but in the wife, the heart, the bed, the table, the saddle, the fireside, the country; now that I have perceived all this, I am ready to squeeze case eternally. In thoughts of the visions of the night, I saw long rows of angels in paradise, each with his hands in a jar of spermaceti. (*MD*, 533)

Melville makes a convincing aesthetic argument for social praxis as essential to the quest for an elusive and fantastic reality. In comparing his view of reality to that of Peirce, we shift perhaps from quest to inquiry, from an aesthetically based argument to a logical one, but community remains an essential ingredient of reality itself.

The story of the Pequod appears to be nothing less than a fantastic documentary of the twentieth century. It is the story of mythic modernism, of the dia-bolic (the tendency toward fragmentation) taken to its extreme, the end of the Western cultural nominalism personified by America. America represents the place where the isolated Western spirit is finally shattered and exposed to world culture. In this sense I am speculating that the twentieth century represents not only the end of the idea of increasingly rationalized progress, and the end of the individualizing Western spirit, but also a large-scale rite of passage, from which a new cultural order must emerge. The pilgrim's progress, the march of the spirit westward, reaches its endpoint in America. It is the land where East and West must finally meet. The spirit can no longer be sought in the new, the original, the ultimate foundation or essence of reality and the associated monomaniacal inquirers; it is rather to be found in our relation to the world through community. Indeed the modern emphasis on novelty for its own sake, on pure originality and individuality, on unlimited rational expansion, seems to reveal ideals which ultimately work against themselves, since differentiation, originality, and individuality can become meaningful only as part of the discourse of the common life. They take on significance only as *means* of vitalizing the social world, not as ends in themselves. We further cultural life through our socially constituted habits of life, those activities through which we encounter the world. These habits embody reality itself for Melville; they are not mere means to otherworldly redemption.

By contrast, we see what happens to Ahab when he attains the ungraspable. As he hurls his final spear at Moby Dick he cries out:

> "from hell's heart I stab at thee; for hate's sake I spit my last breath at thee. Sink all coffins and all hearses to one common pool! and since neither can be mine, let me tow to pieces, while still chasing thee, though still tied to thee, thou damned whale! *Thus*, I give up the spear!" (*MD*, 721)

Ahab's diabolical quest is now at its fragmented but logical endpoint—Hate. At the moment he achieves "absolute knowledge" of Moby Dick, he is an absolute individual, bound to the whale by the line of his spear, submerged in unconsciousness and death, nullified. His "inquiry" has ended, since he has attained final unity with the object. But the object of his quest, the white whale "phantom of life," lives on.

Ishmael, on the other hand, is the sole survivor, who says with Job's messengers, "And I only am escaped alone to tell thee." Ishmael is the paradoxical individual who discovers the generative aspect of whiteness, Love; and realizes that reality is not to be found by an inward turning to the single idea, to rationalized means that betray an irrational and ultimately *isolato* end, but rather, through the greater community of man whose deepest sentiments are those of purposive relation, signifying the underlying continuum of being. Melville is not simply saying that we are "nice guys" underneath it all. *Moby Dick* is a burning indictment of the murderous creatures we are, who would seek to possess and destroy the phantom of life itself; failing, because it is more than our mere conception of it, yet succeeding on the human scale of values if the mad quest for possession means the total self-destruction of the crew of the world-ship. To the extent we wish to possess "the phantom of life" we fall into those forms of hubris, domination, and greed that mark the varieties of human evil. Yet that whiteness that is the phantom of life and that draws us on in our ceaseless quest must forever possess us, even as we endlessly pursue it.

Peirce was not one given to wild, unsupported speculations; his work throughout exhibits his concern with expressing in conclusions only what is warranted by the premises. But what are we to make of the prophetic insight in his 1893 paper "Evolutionary Love"? In discussing the primacy of economics in nineteenth-century science and especially the utilitarian "philosophy of greed" he states:

> The Reign of Terror was very bad; but now the Gradgrind banner has been this century long flaunting in the face of heaven, with an insolence to provoke the very skies to scowl and rumble. Soon a flash and quick peal will shake economists quite out of their complacency, too late. The twentieth century, in its latter half, shall surely see the deluge-tempest burst upon the social order—to clear upon a world as deep in ruin as that greed-philosophy has long plunged it into guilt. No post-thermidorian high jinks then! (CP 6.292)

The image of a deluge-tempest breaking upon a world deeply in ruin and guilt is strikingly similar to the apocalyptic conclusion of *Moby Dick*, where the Pequod is sucked down into the yawning vortex, the all-obliterating whirlpool. Peirce's prophecy, like Melville's, is no mere wishful thinking or mystical intuition; it is a genuine insight into the direction of modern culture which the course of events in the twentieth century thus far has served to confirm. Both men realized that cultural nominalism is not a way of life than can be pursued indefinitely without real and devastating consequences. These consequences are still being played out, but there are some hopeful signs of realization in music, architecture, and art that the quest to obliterate human memory and sentiment under the banner of a scientistic culture, so characteristic of the twentieth century, is self-defeating, and that a renewal must take place by identifying ourselves with a larger tradition (inclusive of those twentieth-century achievements worth preserving) and then cultivating and furthering that tradition and its craft, not simply jettisoning them. In a world without standards, under the domination of a self-destructive rational madness, the very survival of our civilization will depend upon the emergence of a culture rooted in the fullest sense of community. But how can this be brought about?

For a Reanimated Culture

Given the seemingly entrenched, deadly, unhinged rationality of the late twentieth century, it would seem that the new cultural order will not come about through a gradual, imperceptible shift, but through *transformation*, whether brought about through cultural "grace" or inspiration, through the brute necessities of a waning world that has struck at its own vitals, or through a conscious shift in attitude. At present, the mire into which the modern mind has sunk seems so all-pervasive, so encompassing of political right and left, of East and West, of intelligentsia and the common lot, and formed of such a rigid armor of smug self-certainty and habituation, that the most likely way to a new cultural epoch will be brought about through the terrors of mass destruction. The Ahab Imago, mad singular captain possessed by the diabolical quest to grasp and finally possess the ultimate, could, by such a calamity upon the human soul that only an Ishmael Imago could recover, throw the ultimate trickster's dice to silence forever the nervous, hairless biped, or to bring about tragically and paradoxically its renewal and transformation to a new order of being.

Many social interpreters have perceived the destructive tendencies of the twentieth century; Weber in his view of the "iron cage" of instrumentally rational culture, Jung in his more subliminal insight that the twentieth century is under the archetypal sign of the trickster, bringer of chaos and death, but also of the possibility of rebirth, Lewis Mumford in his comprehesive vision of deurbanization and devolution in Western society, manifested on a number of levels ranging from the posthistoric alienated self, to the posthistoric alienated city, to the posthistoric imago that forms the rationalized Western worldview.

Some, perhaps most notably Mumford, have gone further, to try to outline the conditions of a new culture that might offset and replace modernism (in which I include the morass known as "postmodernism"). I will turn now to what seem to me to be "first filaments" of a new mind. Melville and Peirce in their different ways embodied this new attitude, and perhaps this explains in part why they were crushed by their own time, the heyday of the culture of nominalism about to enter its terminal phase. After discussing a few common features of this new attitude I will briefly describe three individuals and one school that suggest fruitful alternatives to the culture of nominalism: Mumford, composer George Rochberg, Doris Lessing (particularly in her "space fiction," *Canopus in Argos: Archives*), and the Vienna School of Fantastic Realism. All share, with Melville and Peirce, a profound sense of the living presence of the past, of the enlarged and subtilized consciousness (in the work as well as the self) that results from living within a broadened sense of community instead of against it, a community whose possibilities may far exceed what we have yet been able to achieve. In this sense all express the superiority of the cosmic self to the personal self. All are realists, not in the degraded materialistic sense the term has taken on in the culture of nominalism, but in the more inclusive sense that recognizes the reality of the imagination. All might be called, with the Viennese painters, *fantastic realists*.

Lewis Mumford

Imagine a social theorist with an understanding of urbanism, modern culture, and rationality surpassing that of Weber and Simmel, with insight into the nature of collective symbolism and the constitution of the self deeper than that of Durkheim, Mead, or Freud, with an ability to generalize that makes Talcott Parsons seem a myopic provincial, and with an attention to the particularities of social life that makes the entire Chicago school of urban ethnography appear to be composed of insensate and unseeing moles. If it seems hard to believe such a sociologist could exist, it is even more unbelievable to accept that such a sociologist has been with us throughout the century, attracting wide and enduring attention except by the field most directly related to his lifework: sociology. What is most remarkable, even if one does not see this person on the same level as those sanctified founders of the sociological canon, is that he could be so long ignored.

Even a brief outline of Lewis Mumford's original contributions to scholarship throughout his long career (his first published article dates from 1911!) would require a book or at the very least a chapter of its own. It suffices to say that even in his early articles and books Mumford cut through the "bright, ardent" view of confident modernity, revealing, for example, the lost history of American literary transcendentalism as well as the shallowness of modern rationalism in architecture, urban planning, literature, and social philosophy.

Mumford's book *The Golden Day* (1926) helped reveal that deeper aspect of the American mind that came to its brief flowering in the early 1850s in the works of Emerson, Hawthorne, Melville, Thoreau, Whitman, and others. Mumford also described the decades that followed as a decline, characterized as "The Pragmatic Acquiescence." His criticism was directed at the enveloping American culture of expediency in general but included philosophical pragmatism specifically. Although Mumford himself appended a biographical note to a 1914 article that "proudly" stated he was a pragmatist, he had moved by the mid-twenties to see Jamesian pragmatism as overly derivative from Emerson, and Deweyan instrumentalism as far too hedged-in by the very technicalism it claimed to be against. In his reply to Dewey's response to *The Golden Day* published in the *New Republic* (1927), Mumford stated his case for a broadened perspective:

> The desiccation and sterilization of the imaginative life has been quite as important an historic fact as the growth of a sense of causality, an insight into what Mr. Dewey calls "means-consequences". . . . Mr. Dewey seems to belive that the "ends" or "ideals" will come into existence of themselves, if only we pay careful heed to the means. I do not share this belief; and in view of what has happened during the last three centuries, it seems to me one of bland complaisance or blind optimism. . . . It is not that we reject Mr. Dewey: that would be ingratitude: but that we seek for a broader field and a less provincial interpretation of Life and Nature than he has given us. (in Kennedy 1950, 56)

One can easily argue with Mumford's characterization of Dewey, citing, for

example, Dewey's discussions of qualitative immediacy, or Dewey's statements in his lead chapter in *Creative Intelligence* that "the pragmatic theory
of intelligence means that the function of mind is to project new and more
complex ends—to free experience from routine and from caprice. . . . action
directed to ends to which the agent has not previously been attached inevitably carries with it a quickened and enlarged spirit. A pragmatic intelligence
is a creative intelligence, not a routine mechanic" (Dewey 1917, 63, 64). But
the deciding fact, it seems to me, is found in setting the enormous body of
Mumford's work next to the massive body of Dewey's work. Much as I
admire Dewey's achievements, it is clear that Mumford's scope, clarity,
vision—his ability to be a "generalist" while yet "labouring well the minute
particulars"—make his not only the more encompassing social theory but,
strangely enough, as my inquiry into the pragmatic attitude draws to a close,
Mumford the more pragmatic of the two—in the broadened Peircean-rooted
sense of pragmatism I have attempted to articulate.

Interestingly, Mumford singled Peirce out as an exception to the
acquiescent attitude of the "Gilded Age": "Peirce was not disrupted by the
compromises and shifts of the Gilded Age: he lived his own life, and made
none. As a philosopher, he thought deeply about logic, science, history, and
the values that ennoble life; and his philosophy was what his own age deeply
needed. . . . Peirce had no part in the pragmatic acquiescence. His voice was a
lonely protest" (in Kennedy 1950, 43–44). In many ways Mumford is far
closer to the Peircean pragmatic attitude than James, Dewey, or Mead (and I
say this in full knowledge of the fact that Peirce viewed the "literary" mind
with as much suspicion as Mumford does the culture of science).

Mumford was to embark in the early 1930s on his "Renewal of Life"
series, a mammoth four-volume and twenty-year undertaking that not only
explores the full scope of Western civilization (and, in the last two volumes,
The Condition of Man [1944] and *The Conduct of Life* [1951], Mumford's
own *Lebensphilosophie*), but even more significantly lays the foundations for
a new cultural order. The first two volumes, *Technics and Civilization* (1934)
and *The Culture of Cities* (1938), establish in an enlarged, historically
informed, and subtilized framework key themes in Mumford's work, the
place of fabrication and urbanism in the development of civilization and
modern life. These same themes are set in even broader context in *The City in
History* (1961) and the two-volume *The Myth of the Machine: Technics and
Human Development* (1967) and *The Pentagon of Power* (1970), which
open fully to the whole horizon of human development.

In both books dealing with the city, Mumford shows the development of modernity to be a gradual *deurbanization* rooted in a cultural
devolution, quite contrary not only to the glib theorists of "modernization"
but also to the more sanguine Simmel and Weber, who saw, respectively, the
emerging individualism and the increasing rationality of the Western city as

progressive, even if problematic. Central to this cultural diminution is the reduction of localized and variegated urban life to single-standard system without limitation, marked, for example, in the consequences of the rise of abstract capitalist economy in the late Middle Ages onward over more localized life-economies. Power replaced polis, and even the concept of "power" became increasingly nominalized, taking on a mechanical sense as physical force and actuality. And as "power" became more forceful, the new power complex displaced purpose as the guiding center of Western life.

Mumford's critique of the dehumanizing system that characterizes modernity, and the organic culture he proposes as its alternative, is perhaps most clearly stated in his *The Pentagon of Power*. In its companion volume, *Technics and Human Development*, Mumford showed the centrality of technics, or fabrication, to the process of human development, even while criticizing the concept of *homo faber*. In Mumford's view the development of civilization is rooted in the myth of the machine—broadly defined as separate from the human element, the myth of an objectivity not involving subjectivity. It is in his view nothing less than the myth of the sun god, that centralized power-source of worship so dear to the ancient pharoahs, and, unexpectedly, so dear to those new sky worshipers, the scientific astronomers such as Copernicus and Kepler, who helped introduce the new mechanical universe: a mechanical world picture at first physically, and later socially, rooted in centralized force and intrinsically devoid of living human purpose.

Central to the mechanical world picture is the erection of and subordination to the *Megamachine*: that combination of both people and things "so organized as to perform standardized motions and repetitive work" (Mumford 1970, 240). As Mumford says, both the advantages and disadvantages of individual machines are increased in the Megamachine: a greater efficiency of quantification coupled with greater rigidity, irresponsiveness to new situations, and "detachment from human purposes other than those embodied in the design of the machine. The chief of these embodied purposes is the exercise of power" (1970, 241). In his critique of Teilhard de Chardin's vision of the ultimate purport of the growth of intelligence, Mumford reveals the inherent self-defeating consequences of the Megamachine, or of what I have characterized as the culture of nominalism:

> Whether presented in the form I have described as the Megamachine, or in the etherialized version upon which Teilhard de Chardin preferred to dwell, as a planetary "film of mind," or abstract intelligence, embracing all human activities, or rather reducing and concentrating those activities for the enhancement of knowledge and power, the final result would be the same: the Big Brain, a universal system of control from which no escape would be possible on this planet—or even *from* this planet.
> . . . Ultimately the purpose of this planetary system . . . would be

to reduce the potentialities of life to those that can be conve-
niently processed and transmuted by its electronic God. In this
the functions that could not be so processed—human histories,
personal and collective artifacts, autonomous activities, transcendent ideals—would be cast aside as worthless: worthless, that is,
to the Megamachine. . . . In short, it is addressed to the enlarging
of the empire of a desiccated and sterilized mind, whose acti-
vated tissues are devoid of vital attributes. . . . One would hardly
guess that love and sex and art and a pullulating dream-world
existed." (Mumford 1970, 319, 318)

Art may, as the expression goes, imitate life, but the Megamachine
clearly tries to *replace* life, overcoming organic creation by mechanical
replicability, variety by homogeneity, and growth by transience or stasis.
This critique is applicable not only to scientific realism but to rationalism as
well: *any* form of thought or expression of mind that holds the rational
(however well defined) as the sole standard of the reasonable. Sooner or later
Ahab *must* cast all human attributes overboard in the name of the Megamachine. Yet ever will the ungraspable phantom of life elude his grasp.

Mumford's critique of modernity stands as deeply and broadly
pessimistic as those of Peirce in philosophy and Melville in literature, and as
characteristically American as theirs in its rooting itself in the broadest
possible historical and biocosmic framework, especially in its allowing for
the possibility of large-scale cultural transformation and renewal. Mumford
proposes an organically based culture as an alternative to the modern pentagon of power, a culture rooted in self-regulating and self-protecting, tempered, organic sources.

Mumford's ideal of the "organic" draws from a rich variety of
sources, including C. Lloyd Morgan's "emergent evolution," Henri Bergson,
Patrick Geddes, Charles Horton Cooley, Alfred North Whitehead, and the
organic architecture of Frank Lloyd Wright. As opposed to the Megamachine, built like a strong chain by a progressive reduction to a single
centralized standard and subject increasingly to the problem of only being as
strong as its weakest link, organic culture is more analogous to the cable, with
many relatively autonomous centers that are yet contextualized within the
whole and give to that whole a strength far more durable than the component
parts. But Mumford's organic culture is, further, an interwoven living cable
or vine, capable of sending tendrils in new directions, of growing through
taking on new purposes not predestined or reducible to a single standard. In
the concept of "organic culture," it becomes clear that the "naturalistic
fallacy" comes not so much from attributing aspects of culture to nature, as
the rabid rationalists of our time are so quick to claim, but in attributing to
nature the qualities of the lifeless machine.

The rationalization of time, so key to the development of the modern Megamachine and mechanical world picture, contrasts sharply with the living time of the organic world picture:

> The past, so far from being left behind, remained vividly present in the individual memory, in the genetic inheritance, in the actual structure of the whole organism; while similarly, an anticipatory, directive, forward thrust became equally visible, engrained in every organic function, carrying those species capable of further development into new situations which demanded new strategies, and opened up new functions and fresh lines of growth. Therewith the central idea of "progressive" or "avant-garde" thought—*the past must be destroyed*—revealed itself as a perverse fantasy, born of ignorance or indifference to the phenomenon of life. "Leaving the past behind" is the equivalent of leaving life behind—and with this, any desirable or durable future. . . .
>
> The conception of time as the flux of organic continuity, experienced as duration, as memory, as recorded history, as potentiality and prospective achievement, stands in frontal opposition to the mechanistic notion of time simply as a function of the motion of bodies in space—along with its spurious imperative of "saving time" by accelerating motion, and of making such acceleration in every possible department the highest triumph of the power complex. (Mumford, 1970, 390–91)

In Mumford's view of time and culture, the organic perspective is no biological reductionism but precisely the means through which humankind and individual are rooted within a vast store of latent and active intelligence far broader than rational mind and, because of this, open to the continued possibility of self-transcendence that mere rationality could never by itself hope to attain. Reality itself is to be found within the web of this historical and biocosmic community: a reality in which evil and regression and death remain as continued presences, but also in which the fantastic and imaginative can meet the methodical within the growing web of organic purpose.

George Rochberg

> Most recently, my search has led to an ongoing reconsideration of what the "past" (musical or otherwise) means. Current biological research corroborates Darwin: we bear the past in us. We do not, cannot, begin all over again in each generation, because the past is indelibly printed on our central nervous systems. Each of us is part of a vast physical-mental-spiritual web of previous lives, existences, modes of thought, behavior, and perception; of actions and feelings reaching much further back than what we

call "history." We are filaments of a universal mind; we dream each others' dreams and those of our ancestors. Time, thus, is not linear, but radial. The idea of the renewal, the rediscovery of music began to haunt me in the early '60s. I came to realize that the music of the "old masters" was a living presence, that its spiritual values had not been displaced or destroyed by the new music. The shock wave of this enlargement of vision was to alter my whole attitude toward what was musically possible today. (Rochberg 1973)

George Rochberg is best known as a leading and controversial contemporary composer, who, beginning in the early 1960s, spearheaded a revolt against modernist compositional means and values by reincorporating tonality within "multigestural" works, thereby generally enlarging the spectrum of possible means. He is less known as an essayist and cultural critic, but it is this aspect of his work and its implications for social theory that I wish to outline briefly here.

Rochberg's early criticism of musical modernism pointed out how post–World War II rationally ordered serial chromatic and aleatory compositions, although seemingly based on opposite principles, paradoxically may sound alike to the ear. Both the totally controlled and the totally uncontrolled sides of the dichotomy have the uninteneded consequence of subverting the way the ear hears—either through the "unplanned indeterminacy" of serialism or the "planned indeteminacy" of "situational" or aleatory music.

In his key essay of 1971, "The Avant Garde and the Aesthetics of Survival" (in Rochberg 1984a), Rochberg discusses John von Neumann's computer analogy between "parallel" and "serial" operations to argue that humans, and specifically the human ear and central nervous system, require clearly perceivable and memorable "input" for meaningful experience. Rochberg's argument is a frontal assault on both the mechanical view of nature and the nominalist assumption that culture is purely arbitrary or conventional. He shows how the ear naturally seeks meaning, and how memory is inseparable from meaningful hearing, i.e., from listening.

In order to meet the ear's need for meaning, a work must have built into itself a perceptible identity, one achieved through specific "structural devices and patterns whose fundamental purpose is *self-perpetuation*" (Rochberg 1984a, 224), as found in almost all Western music from the time of Gregorian chant until approximately 1950. But in the modernist quest to disconnect from the past in the name of originality and novelty, so that a work showing the influence of someone else or some prior mode of expression is by that very fact noncontemporary, one sees a radical reduction in the profile of identity in twentieth-century works, culminating in post–World War II music of rational and chance varieties that lack internally perceivable profiles of identity, that bypass or subvert the listening and remembering ear and body, and that therefore can be literally and metaphorically called "forgettable."

Rochberg's attempt to link music with the body through the ear and central nervous system exposes the avant-garde fallacy of the pastless present even at the micro-level of perception, revealing how simply in order to perceive there must be both a funded organ of perception and a work that can in some way "speak" the language of perceptive feeling—even while paradoxically incorporating (literally) the not-yet-spoken feelings in musical form. The paradox of a contemporary music that can give voice to the speakable as well as the not yet speakable, resonates with the early Wittgenstein's dilemma of the unbridgeable void between the logical language of the "fact" world and the unspeakable silent realm of values. In Rochberg's view this "metaphysical gap" has always existed and, indeed, is at the essence of our human nature: "This gap—or void—has been the primary source and cause of human uncertainty and, equally, the goad to the civilizing process of socialization and culture. Traditionally, before God was declared dead, God or the gods filled it. More recently, it was filled by the answers science gave us which have, for many, turned out to be doubtful or nonanswers. Always it has been filled by art" (Rochberg 1984b, 337). The early Wittgenstein may have consigned the gap to the subjective, and the later, still haunted Wittgenstein may have tried to broaden his perspective through his emphasis on language games and "forms of life," but he did not, in my opinion, come to realize that *Lebensformen* spring from, and attempt to bridge, the gap itself, and that herein is to be found the "grand unified field theory" of human social reality. Though Wittgenstein may have been haunted by the gap, his Viennese logical positivist followers and modernism as a whole were exuberantly certain that it had been nullified. Yet as Rochberg points out in "Can the Arts Survive Modernism?" (1984b), the claim that the metaphysical gap had been rendered nonexistent boomeranged, and what in fact modernism achieved was the dismantling and destruction of those prior bridges thrown across the gap, with the unintended consequence of a much greater abyss than ever before, "now filled with violence and terror and the dread of annihilation."

Rochberg traces the loss of creative tension and energy in twentieth-century modernism, using the mythic metaphor of historic "ages." The "Age of Gold and Age of Silver," between the turn of the century and the opening guns of World War I, characterized the "freshly released energies and unbounded enthusiasms" that marked the explosion of twentieth century-modernism. In the "age of Bronze," between the end of World War I and the beginning of World War II, the intuitive discoveries of the first period gave way to rationalized systematization. In the "Iron Age," between World War II and 1965–70, modernism "moved" to America and became fully institutionalized in the academy as well as the urban landscape. The age that approved everything proved to be the age of nothing: It answered the old question, "Is nothing sacred?" with an earnest "Yes!"

Against the one-sidedness toward forgetting and self-extinction in the name of absolute closure or absolute liberation, Rochberg proposes a new balance, a cultural renewal rooted in our incompleteness, longing, and ability to marvel at and question an open, still mysterious and opaque universe. This cultural renewal would again reconnect certain polarities of human existence that had been sundered into dichotomies in the modern attitude, such as past and present, the fantastic and the logical, culture and nature, and in so doing could reanimate culture with the energy of creative tension that exists in the effort to join these polarities.

The new balance proposed by Rochberg calls not only for a new musical language that signifies in its substance that music is a bodied experience of the transcendent—that there is a deep connection, in other words, between how music is made and how we are made—but more broadly calls for a radical remaking of humankind in general:

> In remaking ourselves it would be well to remember that for countless millennia before the dawn of the age of science man survived without science as we know it. Instead of science he had a profound relation to the cosmos, however fantastic or superstitious that relation may appear from our vantage point. He survived not through rational knowledge or science and technology but through cosmology which peopled his imagination with myth and symbol, poetry and metaphor, image and story and song. . . . The lesson of the avant-garde should be, if we read it correctly, to show us in concrete ways how far removed we now are from any real contact with ourselves or the cosmos, how far we have wandered from home—and that it is time to try to get back, not to some historical past, but to an awareness of the mysterious creatures we are—a secondary, living, organic "language" of the alpha language of the cosmos. (Rochberg 1984a, 231)

The implication of Rochberg's ideas is that we are part of a living cosmic language-game (perhaps one might say song) which bodies forth through the meeting of inner immeasurable imagination and outer rationality in individual works as well as historical epochs. Time itself becomes music through human refraction. Modernism may have explored the fringes and extremes of human emotion and consciousness, of angst and terror, but it did so at the cost of disconnecting itself from the broader range of emotions and the deepest sense of perceptible community and cosmos, a cost whose "days of terror" have yet to be fully paid. Against the "rational madness" of our time, content to ignore all theoretical limits and all possible consequences in its monomaniacal pursuit of truth-power and truth-energy, Rochberg calls for a recontextualized, imaginative reason, one that can place the valid achievements of modernity within broader organs of meaning, one that fully expresses the fantastic reality of life itself.

Fantastic Realism

From the ashes of World War II grew what seems to me perhaps the most vital, and what is in America certainly the most ignored, movement in contemporary painting: the Vienna School of Fantastic Realism. As originally named in 1956 by the late Austrian critic Johann Muschik (see Muschik 1974; an exceptionally lucid discussion of the school is given in Aichele, in press), the school consists of Arik Brauer, Ernst Fuchs, Rudolph Hausner, Wolfgang Hutter, Fritz Janschka, Anton Lehmden, and Kurt Steinwender (now Stenvert). Under the direction of Albert Paris von Gütersloh, a Secessionist and friend of Egon Schiele, this group of young artists cultivated a precise craftsmanship while exploring surrealist ideas and "indigenous" (to Vienna) psychoanalytic concepts.

It is generally accepted that the center of painting moved from Paris to New York after World War II. There, for the first time, American painting achieved an unprecedented hegemony, first through the abstract expressionist school (including painters such as Jackson Pollock, Mark Rothko, Willem de Kooning, Robert Rauschenberg), and through later developments in "pop," "op," "conceptualism," "minimalism," and other styles. Until recently it was an axiomatic assumption in American art criticism that "painterliness," figurative painting, perspective, and the like were relics of the past, whose use signified merely bourgeois, unoriginal, and clearly obsolete styles of painting. The tremendous release from traditional constraints signified by Pollock's "process" or "action" painting brought a liberation that finalized the break with the dead hand of tradition begun earlier in the century. When one did make reference to tradition or figuration, it could only be done in a sly or cynical way, clearly self-conscious, if it was to be authentic (Andy Warhol's *Marilyn Monroe* comes to mind).

Consider then the fantastic realists of Vienna in this context, all of whom based their emerging styles on premises in exact antithesis to those of the New York School: cultivating a precisely controlled craft informed by traditional methods, incorporating collectively the entire range of Western painting within their attempts to come to grips with a shattered world, claiming as a creative source not their own originality but masters ranging from Bosch and Breughel through Vienna's own Klimt, Schiele, Kokoschka, and the "father" and teacher of the school, Albert Paris von Gütersloh, to the seemingly disparate Picasso and Dali. Janschka and Fuchs in particular embody these qualities, as well as others such as love of the erotic, talent for composition, possession of an enormous range of emotions and means of expressing them, and most especially profound *longing* for transcendent beauty and purpose.

Janschka has lived and worked in America for over thirty-five years, and hence is in the peculiar position of not always being counted among the "founders" (as Aichele says, the first published survey of the Vienna school, by Wieland Schmied, *Malerei des phantastischen Realismus/Die Wiener Schule*, [Vienna, 1964], excludes Janschka and Steinwender). His work also clearly cuts against the grain of American postwar styles up to the present. Nevertheless Janschka is perhaps the most subtle of the school. His early *Wohin gehst Du?* (1948), *Where Are You Going?*, stands as a key representative of Janschka's work and the work of the school. In a bombed-out Boschian/Flemish village stands a tableau of Isolato Europeans, most naked, each holding an "icon" of the Western tradition. These "icons" range from literal religious icons to abstract modern art. A strange blue Krishna-like boy walks with a staff in the background. A floating woman is shooting arrows at the man kneeling under a large Picasso painting, suggesting both a firing squad and a shooting-gallery arcade. The Picasso is hung on the outside wall

Fritz Janschka, *Wohin gehst Du?* (1948). By permission of the Museen der Stadt, Vienna.

of a more modern village building, along with works by older masters: an outdoor museum subject to the same floating destructiveness, itself part of the gallery of meaninglessness that confronts the viewer.

Where Are You Going? asks how meaning can be found in the face of such an all-pervasive catastrophic situation. In its subtlety of composition, in which traditional and modern methods and emotions meet in a thoroughly compelling and believable way, it suggests as well an answer: only through a broadened craft and imagination, that can place the contemporary within the timeless, is meaningfulness possible. Indeed Janschka's subsequent work has mapped out what a reanimated spiritual landscape might look like, in its endless variety, once a reconciliation between the fragmented present and an informing tradition is mastered. Perhaps the title of Janschka's painting was addressed to himself and his own need to define his direction as an artist who had been profoundly touched by the war. But the title applies as well to the broadened possibilities for painting that the Vienna School was in the process of developing, and especially to our own time in the spiritual ruins of modern culture.

These ruins are also depicted in Ernst Fuchs's X ray of the contemporary soul, *Psalm 69* (1949–60). In this painting a techno-city reminiscent of Fritz Lang's film *Metropolis*, bellowing lascivious and poisonous smoke and fumes, ruled over by a Roman Caesar-Pope, apparently in the name of God, is set above the suffering, nearly drowned Christ. Psalm 69 reads: "Save me, O God! For the waters have come up to my neck. I sink in deep mire, where there is no foothold; I have come into deep waters, and the flood sweeps over me. I am weary with my crying; my throat is parched. My eyes grow dim with waiting for my God. . . ." The opening lines of this psalm resonate with the imagery of the "Cartesian anxiety" of having "all of a sudden fallen into very deep water," with those drownings of *Moby Dick*, and, through the refraction of Fuch's painting, with Peirce's remarkable 1893 allusion to the "deluge-tempest" that would break upon and clear the social order in the latter half of the twentieth century. Here is the spiritual image of Mumford's Megamachine, utterly dominant, and in its arrogant hubris ready to crush human organic transcendence. The Death Spectre rises up from the water, true master of this rational anarchy.

Dire though this condition be, the suffering Christ remains as a sign of possible transcendence in Fuchs's vision. Indeed the beads of sweat on his face and the blue surrounding shroud were the first manifestations of what were to become cherubs in later paintings, signs of reconciliation of Fuchs's personal spiritual struggles, and, as with Janschka, signs that the transcendent remains as an inherent possibility of the deepest levels of human existence. As Fuchs himself has said,

the tendency of art in our time to shun the pictorial element, the

Ernst Fuchs, *Psalm 69* (1949–60). Courtesy of the artist.

image, is a form of affliction, a plague. This is why we should all learn to contemplate images again, for it is in images that the language of the spirits, the messages from Heaven, manifest themselves, as they did in the tongues of the prophets. . . .

For it is art that opens us up to the Thou, the other, the Unknown. In the obscurity of one's own creative process one knows even without the aid of reason how significant the work is. It is as in dreams, where images create themselves and utter the ineffable to which no analysis can do justice.

Images alone enable us to grasp the overabundance of the incomprehensible. By their means that which cannot be articulated can be revealed. Language is itself a work of art; who can ever encompass it in all its possibilities? . . . How does one find those keys without resort to language, to logic? I call it contemplation. Whoever is capable of dreaming with his eyes on an image can come close to its meaning. (Fuchs 1979, 181, 189)

Fuchs's words, like his images, are diametrically opposed to the depersonalized subjectivism of the early Wittgenstein and other turn-of-the-century figures who sought to fully encompass language and, in some cases, to deny that the "ineffable" may somehow be partially grasped and revealed. In the Vienna School of Fantastic Realism we see yet another transformation by Viennese culture, which by the turn of the century had retreated from the public sphere of the Ringstrasse to an increasingly depersonalized subjectivity. While retaining the interest in self-exploration characteristic of Schiele and Kokoschka, the fantastic realists have set their explorations within a public sphere of traditions, craft, and the attempt to find a way out of the spiritual emptiness of our megatechnic time. As Aichele has said,

> even in their self-portraits the Fantastic Realists revealed intimate meanings in the context of a public message. For a public stunned by the realization that established tradition was all too vulnerable to the ravages of atomic and conventional warfare, the painters of the Vienna School attempted to restore a sense of continuity between past and present. In doing so, they revived an idea expressed earlier in the 20th century by Alberto Savinio, composer and theorist of the Metaphysical School. "Memory," Savinio wrote, "is our culture." (Aichele, in press)

Klimt, Kokoschka, and Schiele were eclipsed by the admittedly powerful developments in turn-of-the-century Paris (so that in the 1950s one could buy erotic drawings by Schiele in Vienna for one dollar!), only to have been "rediscovered" more recently. Perhaps in the sorting out that is now going on, in the gropings toward figuration, "painterliness," neo-expressionism, and the like, the central position in art, since World War II, of the fantastic realists will begin to be recognized, as the faulty premises of the various New York cults of abstractionism become more evident. The "new realism," for example, that has become fashionable in the past few years is all surface and glitter, mere dull gropings, in effect, toward what the fantastic realists carved out years ago and are still creating anew.

Lessing's "Space Fiction"

Doris Lessing's recent *Canopus in Argos: Archives* series seems to me to constitute a radical break with the modern ego-centered novel, yet one that has not been recognized as such by critics. She has devised a new cosmic perspective as source of the narrative in what she calls her "space fiction," one that restores the "I am" to its bounded position within the broadest imaginable perspective. Remarking on the first of the series, *Shikasta*, she says:

> as I wrote I was invaded with ideas for other books, other sto-
> ries, and the exhilaration that comes from being set free into a
> larger scope, with more capacious possibilities and themes. It was
> clear I had made—or found—a new world for myself, a realm
> where the petty fates of planets, let alone individuals, are only
> aspects of cosmic evolution expressed in the rivalries and interac-
> tions of great galactic Empires. . . . I feel as though I have been
> set free both to be as experimental as I like, and as traditional:
> the next volume in this series, *The Marriages between Zones
> Three, Four, and Five*, has turned out to be fable, or myth. Also,
> oddly enough, to be more realistic. (Lessing 1979, xi)

What Melville foresaw in *Moby Dick* as the single-minded journey of the modern ego, resulting ultimately not only in Ahab's death but in the destruction of the world-ship itself, a destruction from which Ishmael alone was saved because redeemed through Queequeg into the world community, is told again in Lessing's series, but now from the far side of the "Century of Destruction." Queequeg and his fellow primitive aliens are now space aliens: the galactic empires of Canopus, Sirius, and Puttoria/Shammat. Canopus, a civilization so mature as truly to represent God relative to us (though itself seeming to exist within a web of higher orders), does not prevent evil or contingency from occurring, because it must itself obey *the Necessity*, a higher governing principle organically embodied in the Canopean mind.

Lessing constantly portrays figures in transition and transmutation, from a base lower realm to a wider, mysterious, and yet increasingly intelligible higher realm, a new order. The Queen in *The Marriages between Zones Three, Four, and Five* and Ambien II in *The Sirian Experiments* both exhibit this position of transition, toward a transcendence that is made possible only through a coming to terms with, and reintegration of, the higher and lower, sacred and mundane, future and past. In her cosmic evolutionary view, the passage to a new order that appears at present incomprehensible (but only because it is more comprehensive) is key, yet contingency, evil, regression, and decay are not external to the process but inescapable elements of its living reality. In *The Sentimental Agents* the terrible experiences of *Shikasta* ("the broken one")—read modern self-destroying earth—inform the future actions of the Canopeans (read deity relative to us at present, or the unlimited community in its unending inquiry and cultivation, or that new kind of creature Peirce alludes to for whom rational mind is instinct), enabling them to better cope with their striving toward *the Necessity* in their present, by tempering them with experiences that become part of their very substance.

Lessing presents beings for whom reason is apparently mature instinct, beings who have passed to a new balance in their carrying out of purpose but who are still struggling to serve even higher purposes, i.e., they remain eminently fallible. Her work is a diagram of critical common-sensism, not only of the Canopeans, but of that projection of our present highest possibilities in the modern mode, the "Sirians."

The root metaphor of the Canopean mind is the concept of *the Necessity*, an attitude developed in the Canopean past, perhaps as the result of some crisis. Lessing's concept of the Necessity is anything but necessitarian; not a linear, mechanical, utilitarian universe, but a universe of growing purpose, subject at times to the limits and regressions of evil, as well as unforseeable contingency, yet nevertheless growing in and toward truth. In this sense it is a quite different concept than the realm of necessity discussed by Hannah Arendt, who viewed the private sphere of the household as that concerned with necessity, as opposed to the public sphere as the realm of freedom. Arendt saw the rise of the laboring mentality and of necessity as manifestations of the emergent "social" realm of modern life, a social realm ultimately destructive of public and private spheres alike.

The modern age has indeed raised necessity—survival of the fittest, the "natural" laws of the market, Realpolitik—to the status of ultimate end, but it is a fictitious necessity, the dream of modern nominalistic individualism. Lessing's use of "the Necessity" restores the paradoxical marriage needed between the two levels of necessity and freedom that are utterly divorced in Arendt's neo-Kantian political theory. Lessing's Canopean Necessity is a kind of necessity of freedom: There is a guiding purpose that tempers us, and in diverging from it we are lost in falsity; yet we must each choose in some way to be absorbed in and guided by this purpose. Her concept of the Necessity resonates with Peirce's "critical common-sensism."

The Necessity is our need to push ourselves to the limits of our feelings, perceptions, and thoughts, so that we may make possible the next transformation. Contemporary theories of evolution have finally been coming to realize the profound significance of evolution by revolution—by sudden, dramatic transformation—though they have yet to work through the obvious implication that we humans, as the fruit of this evolutionary process, are creatures of transformation. This seems to me precisely what Lessing maps out in adopting a perspective recognizing cosmic contingency and purpose. She suggests a view that we are creatures of transformation in a universe of transformations beyond what we can presently see; that we must press and inquire to bring about the conditions through which the transformation of our being and the realization of the larger purpose can occur; that the Necessity floats in the possibility of creative transformation.

We now see that the Einsteinian universe displaced what seemed the airtight truth of the Newtonian universe, just as the Newtonian universe displaced the Ptolemaic and other seemingly complete of final views of the universe. We now realize that the Einsteinian universe is itself only the best approximation we can come up with at present, that there may be what seem to us an endless series of better approximations to the order of the universe (grand unified theories notwithstanding), and that we stand as minute and ever so ignorant creatures relative to those scientific visions of the future.

Yet when we come to reflect on the ultimate, as is particularly clear in religious formulations of the nature of God but also is true in the other dimensions of human thought, including social theory, we act as if we stand in full knowledge, so that our meager conception frequently poses as a fixed and final image of the ultimate. This is mere idolatry. Our conception of the ultimate is framed within the limitations of our being, and we are but filaments of perhaps limitless series of higher orders of intelligence, each of which may be so comprehensive as to be "deity" to that subordinate to it. In this sense we can read Lessing as suggesting that our task is to give embodiment to the larger orders of purposeful being through what means we are capable of, to further reality through those fantastic transformative powers that are the inmost possibilities of our being. All this is involved in the story of the Necessity unfolded in the five novels of this series.

From the point of view of those intensely devoted to the rationalist position, who have never admitted to themselves that side of human consciousness relating to the never-ending stream of nonverbal images and pictures (iconic signs), or thought through the endgame abstractions forming the consequences of a pure verbal rationalism which denies the uses of the imagination, Lewis Mumford and these contemporary artists of fiction, music, and painting I am describing as "filaments of a new mind," may appear as simply soft romantics in a hard world. But if it be romanticism of any kind, it is a romanticism that seeks to restore the full dimensions of human feeling, emotion, and imagination that are indeed operative forces in social life— whether admitted or not. This is to be a realist in the broader, thoroughly social, Peircean sense I have proposed throughout this book. If the usual meaning of "romantic" these days is one of total unrealism (a meaning which turns out to be, under closer inspection, a deprecation of the truer social sense of reality), Mumford gave the lie to this view when he pointed out, almost forty years ago: "As so often has happened during the last quarter century, the self-styled practical men turned out to be the weak irresponsible dreamers, afraid to face unpleasant facts, while those of us who were called dreamers have, perhaps, some little right to be accepted—at least belatedly—as practical men. By now history has caught up with our most dire prophecies. This is at once the justification of our thinking and the proof of its tragic failure to influence our contemporaries" (Mumford 1947, 8).

Although written almost forty years ago, these words have only grown truer. And even to "our contemporaries" today the incorporation of the past in the work of Mumford, Lessing, Rochberg, or the fantastic realists shows them to regressive rather than progressive. But this kind of criticism reveals how ensconced in mythic modernity the critic happens to be. This is particularly true of so-called "postmodernist" critics, who retain the unrealistic modernist fantasy that a new work or even a new culture must be wholly different from anything that has gone before if it is to be authentic.

And then there is that other kind of critic, who believes that social science is concerned solely with describing the "facts out there," that the depiction of statistical regularity is the sole task of a social science, and that meaning and purpose are irrelevant. This type of critic manifests in political theory an advocacy of "Realpolitik" as the fundamental reality of human sociopolitical life—the power of things moves people, not the reverse. This type of critic, who denies the reality of meaningful purpose, simply appears over and over again as the plaything of meaningless purpose, of a purpose that clothes itself with the aura of scientific legitimation, but whose real purpose is to turn the whole world into itself, into Mumford's "Megamachine": a system in which *living scientific inquiry* itself would be impossible, not because its means and methods are soberly sane and rational, but because its purpose is mad, is rational madness.

In reading Rochberg's 1970 "Humanism versus Science" (in 1984a), one feels the direct impress of Mumford's *The Pentagon of Power*, although through the artistic perspective on science and technics. There Rochberg describes an imaginary science-fiction story that remarkably resembles, in its outlook and feeling-tone, the *Canopus in Argos: Archives* series that Lessing was to write in the next decade. In his story's picturing of a remembrance of the "days of terror" of our time (or as also can be heard in his *Symphony No. 3*), one also feels a visual resonance with those questioning recollections of terror in the fantastic realists—of Janschka's *Wohin gehst Du?* or his sardonically named series "Interiors for Fallout Shelters" (for example, *Nuclear Trinity*, 1963), or of Ernst Fuchs's *Psalm 69* or his *Die Hochzeit des Einhorns* (Marriage of the Unicorn).

These works are not the "works of terror" themselves: those de-humanized productions of social theory, painting, music, architecture, or fiction in which signs of human warmth and generosity, of impassioned purposiveness and imagination, have been excluded in favor of emotional and/or rationalist extremes. The works that I have suggested are filaments of a new mind yet to take complete shape are instead signs of the days of terror that in their very substance point beyond the culture of nominalism to a new cultural configuration that *recenters* the human personality within a *reconstructed* perception of cosmos.

This culture, as seen in its first filaments, will be rooted precisely in those qualities now so despised by terminal modernism: living imagination, living memory, a profound respect for the limitations, as well as possibilities, in organic life itself, a community of personalities animated by the very task of creating a new organic culture that can give voice and form and body to the deepest human longings for relation. This new cultural epoch, should the human spirit survive the "days of terror," "century of destruction," and age of abstractionism, will be realistic in that imaginative and fantastic, and ultimately animistic, sense that semiotic realism involves: the fullest sense of community; that organized and localized body of humanized, cosmic intelligence whose horizon is the unlimited community of creative interpretation incarnate.

Epilogue: Social Theory
in the Pragmatic Attitude

If it is true that social theory is in a restructuring phase, as Bernstein (1976, 1983), Geertz (1983), and others have suggested, and indeed, if modern culture as a whole is in a restructuring phase in which the guiding premises of modernism have exhausted themselves as living sources for belief, the question remains: *Wohin gehst Du?* To judge from some works in contemporary sociological theory that have received widespread critical attention, such as Jürgen Habermas's *Theory of Communicative Action*, or Anthony Giddens's work on structuration, social theory has returned to the questions of meaning that animated much of classical sociological theory, while updating its theoretical vocabulary in ways that attempt to encompass large-scale and small-scale orders of meaning, of historical development and change, and of postindustrial and postmodern conditions.

The now canonical "founding fathers" of modern social theory, such as Marx, Weber, and Durkheim, were alarmed by the destructiveness inherent in modern culture, and particularly by the ways in which it erodes the life-world. These concerns were largely eclipsed in mid-century abstractionist sociology in America and somewhat earlier by Nazism in Germany. A renewal of interest in meaning and the place of critique has been underway, but too frequently without the deeply felt anxieties and vital concerns of the earlier theorists. The new attempts to develop a broadly based theory of meaning seem largely dominated by the technical abstractionism they purport to explain (as is particularly clear in semiotics, but also in the other interpretative theories).

The domination of rationalized technique over all spheres of life in modern culture as a whole has been a central theme in much critical social theory of the twentieth century, as seen in Dewey, Scheler, Mumford, the Frankfurt School, Arendt, and others. And yet, it seems ironically true that what distinguishes recent attempts to restructure social theories of meaning from those attempts earlier in the century, is precisely a kind of domination by theoretical technique in the contemporary works, one that has taken the place of the profoundly disturbing sense of immanent or already existing loss of meaning, of the collapse of Western civilization itself, that one reads in a Weber or, later, in a Mumford or an Adorno.

The recent proliferation of interpretative orientations in German, French, and Anglo-American schools of thought does, however, suggest that we are in the midst of a transformation of social theory, one in which commonly accepted premises are now being questioned, in which new premises are beginning to suggest themselves. In the best work a real dialogue of theories is occurring, one which attempts to overcome the limitations of a single-minded view by reconciling what is best from a variety of sources.

One approach that should be particularly important for contributing to an emerging social theory is critical theory. It seems to me, on the one hand, that a comprehensive social theory must in some way take up the question of the relation of its conclusions to the society it is interpreting, and that social theory is for this and other reasons inescapably critical. It also seems crucial for social theory to show how critical interpretation is essential for any free society. On the other hand, one of the problems of modern societies is the loss of commonly accepted assumptions that can serve as a reservoir or motivation for action. It is not critical interpretation that has taken the place of unquestioned beliefs in modern culture, but the rationalizing mind that substitutes technical expertise for both "intuitive" relations to the world *and* reasoned critique.

Are the emerging critical theories of action broad enough to include the unreflective, generative act that always precedes self-conscious reflection as an essential element in a free communicative society? Is there an overemphasis on the critical in critical theory that makes it yet another manifestation of modern rationalization rather than an antidote to it? In its critical emphasis does it ignore the *common-sensical*, those unquestioned beliefs whose vitality as a living resource for action, the species achievement of past praxis reaching back beyond historical humankind, may be as necessary to a living culture as reasoned critique? To go beyond the constrictions of the modern rationalization of society, a truly comprehensive theory of social life should involve a reconstructed view of nature, feeling, and sentiment in communicative life. In this sense, though we certainly need to renew reflective or critical life, it may be as or more important in this crucial time when the vitality of modern culture seems to be at an ebb, to renew our generative, spontaneous, and unself-conscious life in practice as well as in our theories of conduct and communication, instead of merely consigning this dimension to the "irrational."

Another way of saying this is that at present there is virtually a repression of nature in social theory. Giddens and Habermas, for example, represent supposedly critical positions, but in my opinion they acritically accept the received mechanical view of nature. Why must criticism stop at the concept of nature? This mind-set, which refuses to investigate the assumption, shared by sociobiologists and their conceptualist antagonists, that nature is a mechanical system, is not only insufficiently critical but reveals the deep-seated prejudices of the culture of nominalism in its theoretical manifestation.

When the ground for spontaneous action, for the generation of new living cultural forms, for a direct relationship to a larger cultural milieu is eroded away from a rationalized criticism that sees no other standards or modes of being except its own, then critical theory, broadly considered, becomes part of the pathology of modern culture rather than an antidote. The goal of rationality should not be an imperialistic gobbling up of everything for itself, into itself, but the germination of fruitful modes of conduct, the natality of spontaneous and felt cultural forms that may not yet *know* why they are, but, as the conclusion of the prior form of reason is the premiss on which their heritage is based, they have a firm grounding on which to grow into self-consciousness. Again, meaning is at basis a living sign-process of cultivation, subject to real laws of growth, and not simply a system of abstract rational code or arbitrary conventions.

The return of interest in meaning takes up many of the same problems and theories as did "classical" modern social theory, but they have a way of becoming theoretical armament, illustrating a clever technical virtuosity rather than ways and means of coming to terms with the most urgent issues of our time. Meaningfulness itself becomes a secondary concern, when it is addressed at all, as if a social theory of meaning can limit itself to a technical discussion of "the code" or "the situation," or "the social system," without addressing the questions, Why am I (or we) here? Where am I (or you, or it) going? In its concern with meaning and interpretation, contemporary social theory has attempted to break out of the abstracted empiricism that so dominated mid-century American sociology, but whether it has succeeded in breaking out of the arid and sterile technocracy of what Mills called "grand theory" is quite another question. Perhaps it is no surprise that the spectre of Talcot Parsons, who was C. Wright Mills's "ideal type" of grand theorist and whose ponderous work seemed to many to be eclipsed by the turn to interpretation, has reemerged in the recent work of Habermas, Jeffrey Alexander, and Richard Münch, while Mumford, a contemporary of Parsons, remains unheard.

If the restructuring of social theory is to be successful, it must do more than simply return grand, abstracted theory to the shelf of sociological commodities; it must bring back the possibility of a broad theoretical framework that does full justice to living human purpose and suffering, in style and in substance. One of the key marks of the domination by technique is a system that promises all the answers, because such a system usually ignores the essential place of the *questions* in the structure of the system itself.

Such a system usually represses the place of uncertainty in practice and the begetting of new problems and possibilities that are essential to all conduct from the most personal to the broadest institutional levels. More importantly, systems that promise all the answers ignore the inescapable mystery and wonder at the heart of all life, including human social life, and that will forever outrun rational understanding even while animating it. The imagination is today regarded as merely "imaginary" by both sides of the modern split-culture of nominalism; at best it is regarded as merely a creator of conventional fictions, but certainly not as an essential feature of reality itself.

Yet the pragmatic attitude, as outlined in various ways throughout this book, is one rooted in the reality of the imagination. Peirce's Firstness, iconic signs, abduction, and indeed, pragmaticism itself, all in different ways inhabit a world that acknowledges the reality of qualitative possibility, as does Dewey's qualitative immediacy and problematic situation, and the "I" of Peirce and James and Mead. In attempting to carve out this mode of being so neglected or repressed by modern thought, it becomes apparent that pragmatism is quite the opposite of a mere philosophy of expediency or even of a "homo faber."

In his late work Peirce considered individuality a social fact of qualitative, indexical, and purposive import. Because of his devotion to logic, however, he did not in my opinion fully realize to what extent qualitative individuality is an essential ingredient in the life not only of the localized community and culture but also of the broader community of inquirers, helping the community to "body forth" in new and fruitful ways. Dewey and Mead devoted much closer attention to qualitative social individuality but shied away from the broader implications of the biocosmic perspective developed by Peirce. Although, as I have tried to show, there is a great deal of value in Dewey and Mead's situationalism when broadly understood (as is too infrequently the case), one of the costs of their situationalism was an optimism that undervalued the self-destructive trends of modernity. Social theorists and others interested in pursuing the pragmatic attitude in its most articulate form should turn to the person who has perhaps achieved in social theory and cultural critique what Peirce achieved in his philosophy: Lewis Mumford.

The concept of the unlimited community of inquirers, which provides the ultimate foundation for our knowledge of reality through the possibility of continued inquiry and imaginative and self-correcting interpretation stretching into the horizon of the indefinite future, suggests to the contemporary mind the image of increasingly rationalized and etherealized beings, bloodless and logical, earnest and aloof, utterly desensualized. Yet if my understanding of Peirce is correct, the unlimited community, over time, increasingly develops into creatures of sentiment, whose deepest sentiments and instincts become increasingly infused with "concrete reasonableness."

Critical inquiry itself, in this view, does not increasingly absorb the life-world into itself, but gives itself to a life-world that represents a more encompassing, tempered, and animating *body* of intelligence. If my interpretation of the unlimited community of inquirers becoming increasingly creatures of senti- ment in the long run is correct, this suggests to me a radically different view of the direction of human development than that given in modern social theory. From this perspective, the chief end of humankind, in Peirce's words, is: "To actualize ideas of the immortal, ceaselessly prolific kind. To that end it is needful to get beliefs that the believer will take satisfaction in acting upon, not mere rules set down on paper, with lethal provisos attached to them" (CP 2.763).

A social theory that limits itself to "mere rules"—whether those of a code or even those of a "theory of communicative action"—and in so doing does not include the central fact of a living human purpose that will never be encapsulated or harpooned by the standards of abstract rationality, is not likely to meet the needs of the emerging cultural mind. Similarly a theory that denies "ideas of the immortal, ceaselessly prolific kind," whose being it is our task to imagine and actualize, and which in turn endow us with far greater possibilities for animated development than mere abstract rationality could ever do, ignores, in my opinion, the most pressing need of our time—to break out of the hubris of abstraction, to reconnect our critical capacities of rationality with our admittedly repressed or dormant, but in the end far more mature, capacities for "critical" sentiment and perception. More than ever, in our modern hubris, have we closed ourselves up through our "mind forg'd manacles." More than ever must "the doors of perception" be cleansed through a critical animism that acknowledges the true social continuity of being, the relative immaturity and great tendency to err of our rational ego, the tempered maturity of the human capacity to marvel and to imagine—a critical animism that can transform those imaginings into humanized, cosmi- cally rooted practices.

Bibliography

Aichele, P. In press. "Self-Confrontation in the Early Works of the Vienna School." In Mary Matthews Gedo, ed., *Psychoanalytic Perspectives on Art*, vol. 3, Hillsdale, New Jersey.

Althusser, L. 1979. *For Marx*. Translated by Ben Brewster. London: Verso Editions.

Apel, K. O. 1980. *Towards a Transformation of Philosophy*. London: Routledge and Kegan Paul.

———. 1981. *Charles S. Peirce: From Pragmatism to Pragmaticism*. Amherst: University of Massachusetts Press.

Arato, A., and Gebhardt, E., eds. 1982. *The Essential Frankfurt School Reader*. New York: Continuum.

Arendt, H. 1946. "The Ivory Tower of Common Sense." *The Nation* 19: 447–49.

———. 1958. *The Human Condition*. Chicago: University of Chicago Press.

Aristotle. 1941. *Politics*. R. P. McKeon, ed., *The Basic Works of Aristotle*. New York: Random House.

Arlow, J. 1980. "Object Concept and Object Choice." *Psychoanalytic Quarterly* 49: 109–33

Bandura, A. 1969. *Principles of Behavioral Modification*. New York: Holt, Rinehart and Winston.

Barrett, W. 1958. *Irrational Man: A Study in Existential Philosophy*. New York: Doubleday, Anchor Books.

———. 1978. *The Illusion of Technique: A Search for Meaning in a Technological Civilization*. Garden City, New York: Doubleday, Anchor.

Barthes, R. 1977. *Elements of Semiology*. Translated by Annette Lavers and Colin Smith. New York: Hill and Wang.

———. 1980. *Writing Degree Zero*. Translated by Annette Lavers and Colin Smith. Preface by Susan Sontag. New York: Hill and Wang.

———. 1985. *The Responsibility of Forms*. Translated by Richard Howard. New York: Hill and Wang.

Basch, M. 1976. "Theory Formation in Chapter VII: A Critique." *Journal of the American Psychiatric Association* 24: 61–100.

———. 1980. *Doing Psychotherapy*. New York: Basic Books.

Batiuk, M. E. 1982. "Misreading Mead: Then and Now." *Contemporary Sociology* 11 (March): 138–40.

Baudrillard, J. 1981. *For a Critique of the Political Economy of the Sign*. Translated with an introduction by Charles Levin. St. Louis: Telos Press.

Becker, H. S. 1982. *Art Worlds*. Berkeley: University of California Press.

Bellow, S. 1975. *Humboldt's Gift*. Viking Press.

Benjamin, W. [1937] 1982. "The Author as Producer." In *The Essential Frankfurt School Reader*. Edited by Andrew Arato and Eike Gebhardt. New York: Continuum.

Bentham, J. [1823] 1948. *The Principles of Morals and Legislation*. New York: Harper and Row.

———. 1954. *Jeremy Bentham's Economic Writings*. W. Stark, ed. London: George Allen and Unwin.

Berger, P., and Luckman, T. 1966. *The Social Construction of Reality*. New York: Doubleday.

Berger, P. L.; Berger, B.; and Kellner, H. 1973. *The Homeless Mind*. New York: Random House.

Bernstein, R. 1964. "Peirce's Theory of Perception." In E. C. Moore and R. S. Robin, eds., *Studies in the Philosophy of Charles Sanders Peirce* (second series). Amherst: University of Massachusetts Press, 165–89.

———. 1967. *John Dewey*. New York: Washington Square Press.

———. 1971. *Praxis and Action*. Philadelphia: University of Pennsylvania Press.

———. 1976. *The Restructuring of Social and Political Theory*. New York: Harcourt, Brace, Jovanovich.

———. 1977. "Why Hegel Now?" *The Review of Metaphysics* 31, no. 1: 29–60.

———. 1983. *Beyond Objectivism and Relativism: Science, Hermeneutics, and Praxis*. Philadelphia: University of Pennsylvania Press.

Blake, W. 1788. From Annotations to Swedenborg's "Wisdom of Angels Concerning Divine Love and Divine Wisdom." In *The Portable Blake*. New York: Viking Press (1946).

Blumer, H. 1967. "Society as Symbolic Interaction." In Jerome G. Manis and Bernard N. Meltzer, eds., *Symbolic Interaction*, p. 141. Boston: Allyn and Bacon.

———. 1969. *Symbolic Interactionism: Perspective and Method*. Englewood Cliffs, N.J.: Prentice-Hall.

———. 1973. "Comment on 'Symbolic Interaction as a Pragmatic Perspective: The Bias of Emergent Theory'." *American Sociological Review* 38: 797–98.

———. 1977. "Comment on Lewis' 'The Classic American Pragmatists As Forerunners to Symbolic Interactionism'." *The Sociological Quarterly* 18 (Spring): 285–89.

———. 1980. "Mead and Blumer: The Convergent Methodological Perspectives of Social Behaviorism and Symbolic Interactionism." *American Sociological Review* 45 (June): 409–19.

———. 1983. "Going Astray With a Logical Scheme." *Symbolic Interaction* 6, no. 1: 127–37.

Bobrick, B. 1981. *Labyrinths of Iron: A History of the World's Subways*. New York: Newsweek Books.

Borges, J. L. 1967. "Borges and I." In *A Personal Anthology*, translated by Anthony Kerrigan, pp. 200–201. New York: Grove Press.

Bourdieu, P. 1968. "Structuralism and Theory of Social Knowledge." *Social Research* 35 (Winter): 681–706.

————. 1973. "The Berber House," In Mary Douglas, ed., *Rules and Meanings*, Middlesex, Eng.: Penguin Books.

————. 1977. *Outline of a Theory of Practice*. Translated by Richard Nice. Cambridge: Cambridge University Press.

————. 1984. *Distinction: A Social Critique of the Judgement of Taste*. Translated by Richard Nice. Cambridge, Mass.: Harvard University Press.

Breicha, O., ed. 1981. *Der Art Club in Österreich, Zeugen und Zeugnisse eines Aufbruchs*. Vienna: Jugend und Volk.

Buchler, J., ed. [1940] 1955. *Philosophical Writings of Peirce*. New York: Dover Publications.

Bürger, P. 1984. *Theory of the Avant-Garde*. Translated from the German by Michael Shaw. Minneapolis: University of Minnesota Press.

Burke, K. 1966. *Language as Symbolic Action*. Berkeley: University of California Press.

Calvino, I. 1974. *Invisible Cities*. New York: Harcourt, Brace, and Jovanovich.

Campbell, J. 1982. "Review of American Sociology and Pragmatism: Mead, Chicago Sociology, and Symbolic Interaction." *Transactions of the Charles S. Peirce Society* 18 (Winter): 105–8.

————. 1983. "Mead and Pragmatism." *Symbolic Interaction* 6, no. 1: 155–64.

Caplow, T. 1982. "Christmas Gifts and Kin Networks." *American Sociological Review* 47: 383–92.

————. 1984. "Rule Enforcement without Visible Means: Christmas Gift Giving in Middletown." *American Journal of Sociology* 89 (6): 1306–23.

Carnap, R. 1967. *The Logical Structure of the World and Pseudoproblems in Philosophy*. Translated by Rolf A. George. Berkeley and Los Angeles: University of California Press.

Chapin, F. S. 1935. *Contemporary American Institutions*. New York: Harper and Row.

Cherry, C. 1957. *On Human Communication*. Cambridge: MIT Press.

Choron, J. 1968. "Death and Immortality." In *Dictionary of the History of Ideas*, vol. 1. New York: Charles Scribner's Sons.

Coleridge, S. T. 1960. *Shakespearean Criticism*. T. M. Raysor, ed. London and New York: Dent.

Cooley, C. H. [1902] 1964. *Human Nature and the Social Order*. New York: Schocken.

————. [1909] 1962. *Social Organization*. New York: Charles Scribner's Sons.

Coser, L. A. 1976. "Sociological Theory from the Chicago Dominance to 1965." *Annual Review of Sociology* 2: 145–60.

Crump, Thomas, 1981. *The Phenomenon of Money*. London: Routledge and Kegan Paul.

Csikszentmihalyi, M., and Rochberg-Halton, E. 1981. *The Meaning of Things: Domestic Symbols and the Self*. New York: Cambridge University Press.

————. 1978. "People and Things: Reflections on Materialism." *The University of Chicago Magazine* (Spring): 6–15.

Dallmayr, F. 1984. *Polis and Praxis*. Cambridge: MIT Press.

Davis, J. 1955. "Living Rooms as Symbols of Social Status: A Study in Social Judgement." Ph.D. dissertation, Harvard University.

Denny, R. 1964. *The Astonished Muse*. New York: Grosset and Dunlap.

Denzin, N. K. 1984. "On Interpreting an Interpretation." *American Journal of Sociology* 89: 1426–33.

Derrida, J. 1978. *Writing and Difference*. Translated with an Introduction by Alan Bass. Chicago: University of Chicago Press.

Dewey, J. 1896. "The Reflex Arc Concept in Psychology." *Psychological Review* 3 (July): 357–70.

———. 1916. *Essays in Experimental Logic*. Chicago: University of Chicago Press.

———. 1917. "The Need For a Recovery of Philosophy." In J. Dewey et al., eds., *Creative Intelligence: Essays in the Pragmatic Attitude* pp. 3–69. New York: Henry Holt.

———. 1925. *Experience and Nature*. Chicago: Open Court.

———. [1927] 1954. *The Public and Its Problems*. Chicago: Swallow Press.

———. [1934] 1958. *Art as Experience*. New York: Capricorn Books, G. P. Putnam's Sons.

———. 1938. *Logic: The Theory of Inquiry*. New York: Holt, Rinehart and Winston.

———. 1939. *Theory of Valuation*. Chicago: University of Chicago Press.

———. 1946a. *Problems of Men*. New York: Philosophical Library.

———. 1946b. "Peirce's Theory of Linguistic Signs, Thought, and Meaning." *The Journal of Philosophy* 43, no. 4: 85–86.

———. 1960. "Qualitative Thought." In R. J. Bernstein, ed., *Dewey on Experience, Nature, and Freedom*, pp. 176–98. Indianapolis: Bobbs-Merrill.

Dewey J., and Bentley, A. F. 1949. *Knowing and the Known*. Westport, Conn.: Greenwood Press.

Downs, R. M., and Stea, D., eds. 1973. "Cognitive Maps and Spatial Behavior: Process and Products." In *Image and Environment*. Chicago: Aldine.

Duncan, H. D. 1962. *Communication and Social Order*. London: Oxford University Press.

———. 1968. *Symbols in Society*. New York: Oxford University Press.

———. 1969. *Symbols and Social Theory*. New York: Oxford University Press.

Duncan, J. S., ed. 1982. *Housing and Identity: Cross-cultural Perspectives*. New York: Holmes and Meier.

Durkheim, E. [1915] 1965. *The Elementary Forms of the Religious Life*. Translated by Joseph Ward Swain. New York: The Free Press.

———. 1982. *The Rules of Sociological Method and Selected Texts on Sociology and Its Method*. Edited with an Introduction by Steven Lukes. Translated by W. D. Halls. New York: The Free Press.

———. 1983. *Pragmatism and Sociology*. Translated by J. C. Whitehouse. Edited with an Introduction by John B. Allcock, Preface by Armand Cuvillier. Cambridge: Cambridge University Press.

Eco, U. 1976. *A Theory of Semiotics*. Bloomington: Indiana University Press.

———. 1979. *The Role of the Reader: Explorations in the Semiotics of Texts*. Bloomington: Indiana University Press.

———. 1984. *Semiotics and the Philosophy of Language*. Bloomington: Indiana University Press.

Eisenstadt, S. N. 1982. "Symbolic Structures and Social Dynamics." In I. Rossi, ed., *Structural Sociology*, pp. 149–79. New York: Columbia University Press.

Eldredge, N., and Gould, S. J. 1972. "Punctuated Equilibria: An Alternative to Phyletic Gradualism." In T. J. M. Schopf, ed., *Models in Paleobiology*, pp. 82–115. San Francisco: Freeman, Cooper.

Eldredge, N., and Tattersall, I. 1982. *The Myths of Human Evolution*. New York: Columbia University Press.

Fairbairn, W. R. 1954. *An Object Relations Theory of Personality*. New York: Basic Books.

Fisch, M. H. 1978. "Peirce's General Theory of Signs." In T. A. Sebeok, ed., *Sight, Sound and Sense*. Bloomington: Indiana University Press.

Freud, S. [1900] 1962. *The Interpretation of Dreams*. New York: Avon.

———. [1901] 1953. *The Psychopathology of Everyday Life*. London: Hogarth.

———. [1905] 1962. *Three Essays on the Theory of Sexuality*. New York: Avon.

Fuchs, E. 1979. *Ernst Fuchs*. New York: Harry Abrams.

Gablik, S. 1984. *Has Modernism Failed?* New York: Thames and Hudson.

Geertz, Clifford. 1973. *The Interpretation of Cultures*. New York: Basic Books.

———. 1980. "Blurred Genes: The Refiguration of Social Thought." *American Scholar* 49 (Spring): 165–79.

———. 1983a. *Local Knowledge*. New York: Basic Books.

———. 1983b. "Interview: Notions of Primitive Thought." In Jonathan Miller, *States of Mind*. New York: Pantheon Books.

Gehlen, A. 1980. *Man in the Age of Technology*. New York: Columbia University Press.

Giddens, A. 1978. *Emile Durkheim*. New York: Viking.

———. 1979. *Central Problems in Social Theory*. London: Macmillan.

———. 1982. *Profiles and Critiques in Social Theory*. London: Macmillan.

———. 1984. *The Constitution of Society: Outline of the Theory of Structuration*. Berkeley: University of California Press.

Gimenez, M. 1982. "The Oppression of Women: A Structuralist Marxist View." In I. Rossi, ed., *Structural Sociology*, pp. 292–324. New York: Columbia University Press.

Glaser, B., and Strauss, A. 1965. *Awareness of Dying*. Chicago: Aldine.

Godelier, M. 1970. "System, Structure and Contradiction in *Das Capital*." In Michael Lane, ed., *Introduction to Structuralism*, pp. 340–58. New York: Basic Books.

———. 1982. "The Problem of the 'Reproduction' of Socioeconomic Systems: A New Epistemological Context." In I. Rossi, ed., *Structural Sociology*, pp. 259–91. New York: Columbia University Press.

Goffman, E. M. 1949. "Some Characteristics of Response to Depicted Experiences." Master's thesis, University of Chicago.

Goldberger, P. 1981. *The Skyscraper*. New York: Alfred A. Knopf.

Gonos, G. 1977. "'Situation' versus 'Frame': The 'Interactionist' and the 'Structuralist' Analyses of Everyday Life." *American Sociological Review* 42 (December): 854–67.

Gould, S. J. 1979. *Ever Since Darwin*. New York: W. W. Norton.

———. 1983. *Hens' Teeth and Horses' Toes*. New York: W. W. Norton.

Habermas, J. 1973. *Theory and Practice*. Boston: Beacon Press.

———. 1981. *Theorie des kommunikativen Handelns*. Band 2, *Zur Kritik der funktionalistischen Vernunft*. Frankfurt: Suhrkamp.

————. 1983. "Modernity—An Incomplete Project." In Hal Foster, ed., *The Anti-Aesthetic: Essays on Postmodern Culture*. Port Townsend, Wash.: Bay Press.

————. 1984. *The Theory of Communicative Action*, vol. 1. Translated by Thomas McCarthy, with original German. Boston: Beacon Press.

————. 1985. *Der philosophische Diskurs der Moderne*. Frankfurt: Suhrkamp.

Halbwachs, M. 1985. *Das kollektive Gedächtnis*. Übersetzt von Holde Lhoest-Offermann. Frankfurt: Fischer.

Hazlitt, W. C. 1907. *English Proverbs and Proverbial Phrases*. London: Reeves and Turner.

Hellman, Peter. 1983. "The Romance of Opening Wine." *Food and Wines* 6(1): 72.

Hinkle, R. C. 1960. "Durkheim in American Sociology." In Kurt H. Wolff, ed., *Emile Durkheim*, pp. 267–95. Columbus: Ohio State University Press.

Hobbes, T. [1651] 1978. *Leviathan*. Introduction by C. B. MacPherson. New York: Penguin Books.

Huber, J. 1973a. "Symbolic Interaction as a Pragmatic Perspective: The Bias of Emergent Theory." *American Sociological Review* 38: 272–84.

————. 1973b. "Reply to Blumer: But Who Will Scrutinize the Scrutinizers?" American Sociological Review 38: 798–800.

Hull, C. 1952. *A Behavior System* New Haven: Yale University Press.

Hunter, A. 1974. *Symbolic Communities*. Chicago: University of Chicago Press.

Husserl, E. 1973. *Cartesian Meditations: An Introduction to Phenomenology*. Translated by Dorian Cairns. The Hague: Martinus Nijhoff.

Jacobsen, T. 1963. "Ancient Mesopotamian Religion: The Central Concerns." In *Cuneiform Studies and the History of Civilization*. Proceedings of the American Philosophical Society 107/6.

James, H., ed. 1926. The Letters of William James. 2 vols. Boston: Little Brown.

James, W. [1890] 1950. *The Principles of Psychology*. 2 vol. New York: Dover.

————. [1909] 1977. *A Pluralistic Universe*. Cambridge, Mass.: Harvard University Press.

Janik, A., and Toulmin, S. 1973. *Wittgenstein's Vienna*. New York: Simon and Schuster.

Joas, H. 1985a. *G. H. Mead: A Contemporary Re-examination of His Thought*. Translated by Raymond Meyer. Cambridge: MIT Press.

————. ed. 1985b. *Das Problem der Intersubjektivität: Neuere Beiträge zum Werk George Herbert Meads*. Frankfurt: Suhrkamp.

Johnson, G. D. 1983. "Mead as Positivist: A Review of American Sociology and Pragmatism." *Theory and Society* 12: 273–77.

Johnson, G. D., and Shifflet, P. A. 1981. "George Herbert Who? A Critique of the Objectivist Reading of Mead." *Symbolic Interaction* 4 (Fall): 143–155.

Jonte-Pace, D. In press. "Rorschack's Movement Response, Object-Relations, and Religion: Toward a Projection Theory of Religion." *American Imago*.

Junker, B. 1954. "Room Compositions and Lifestyles: A Sociological Study in Living Rooms and Other Rooms in Contemporary Dwellings." Ph.D. dissertation, University of Chicago.

Kaplan, S. 1976. "Adaptation, Structure and Knowledge." In G. T. Moore and R. G. Golledge, eds., *Environmental Knowing*. Stroudsburg, Pa.: Dowden, Hutchinson and Ross.

Kennedy, G., ed. 1950. *Pragmatism and American Culture*. Boston: D. C. Heath.

Kernberg, O. F. 1976. *Object-Relations Theory and Clinical Psychoanalysis*. New York: J. Aronson.

———. 1980. *Internal World and External Reality: Object Relations Applied*. New York: J. Aronson.

Ketner, K. L. 1981. "Peirce's Ethics of Terminology." *Transactions of the Charles S. Peirce Society* 17, 4:327–47.

Kohut, H. 1971. *The Analysis of the Self*. New York: International Universities.

———. 1977. *The Restoration of the Self*. New York: International Universities.

Korosec-Serfaty, P. 1982. *The Main Square*. Hassleholm, Sweden: ARIS.

———. 1984. "The Home, from Attic to Cellar," *Journal of Environmental Psychology*, 4.

———. 1985. "Experience and the Use of the Dwelling." In I. Altman and C. Werner, eds., *Human Behavior and Environment*, vol. 8, *Home Environments*. New York: Plenum Press.

Kron, J. 1983. *Home Psych: The Social Psychology of Home and Decoration*. New York: Clarkson N. Potter.

Kuipers, B. 1982. "The 'Map in the Head' Metaphor." *Environment and Behavior* 14: 202–20.

Kuklick, H. 1984. "The Ecology of Sociology." *American Journal of Sociology*. 89: 1433–43.

Laumann, E. O., and House, J. S. 1970. "Living Room Styles and Social Attributes: The Patterning of Material Artifacts in a Modern Urban Community." *Sociology and Social Research* 54: 321–42.

Lehrer, A. 1983. *Wine and Conversation*. Bloomington: Indiana University Press.

Lessing, D. 1979. *Shikasta*. New York: Alfred A. Knopf.

Levine, D. 1981. "Rationality and Freedom: Weber and Beyond." *Sociological Inquiry* 51: 5–25.

Lévi-Strauss, C. 1966. *The Savage Mind*. Chicago: University of Chicago Press.

———. 1967. *Structural Anthropology*. Translated by Claire Jacobson and Brooke Groundfest Schoepf. Garden City, N.Y.: Anchor Books.

Lewis, J. D. 1976. "The Classic American Pragmatists as Forerunners to Symbolic Interactionism." *The Sociological Quarterly* 17: 347–59.

———. 1977. "Reply to Blumer." *The Sociological Quarterly* 18: 291–92.

———. 1979. "A Social Behaviorist Interpretation of the Meadian 'I'." *American Journal of Sociology* 85: 261–87.

Lewis, J. D., and Smith, R. L. 1980. *American Sociology and Pragmatism: Mead, Chicago Sociology, and Symbolic Interaction*. Chicago: University of Chicago Press.

Locke, John. 1959. *An Essay Concerning Human Understanding*, vol. 1. New York: Dover.

Lynch, K. 1960. *The Image of the City*. Cambridge, Mass.: MIT Press.

MacAloon, J., ed. 1984. *Rite, Drama, Festival, Spectacle*. Philadelphia: Institute for the Study of Human Issues.

MacCannell, D., and MacCannell, J. F. 1982. *The Time of the Sign*. Bloomington: Indiana University Press.

Mahler, M. S. 1979. *The Selected Papers of Margaret S. Mahler, M.D.* New York: J. Aronson.

Maines, D. 1977. "Social Organization and Social Structure in Symbolic Interactionist Thought." *Annual Review of Sociology* 3: 235–59.

Mann, T. [1948] 1971. *Doctor Faustus*. Translated by H. T. Lowe-Porter. New York: Vintage Books.

Manning, P. K. 1978. "Structuralism-Survey Review." *Contemporary Sociology* 7(2): 139–43.

Marx, K. 1964. *The Economic and Philosophic Manuscripts of 1844*. Translated by Martin Milligan. Edited by Dirk J. Struik. New York: International Publishers.

———. 1973. *Grundrisse*. Translated by Martin Nicholaus. New York: Vintage Books.

———. 1978. *The Marx-Engels Reader*. 2d ed. Robert C. Tucker, ed. New York: W. W. Norton.

Mauss, M. [1925] 1967. *The Gift: Forms and Functions of Exchange in Archaic Societies*. New York: W. W. Norton.

McPhail, C., and Rexroat, C. 1979. "Mead vs Blumer: The Divergent Methodological Perspectives of Social Behaviorism and Symbolic Interactionism." *American Sociological Review* 44 (June): 449–67.

———. 1980. "Ex cathedra Blumer or ex libris Mead?" *American Sociological Review* 45 (June): 420–30.

Mead, G. H. 1917. "Scientific Method and Individual Thinker." In J. Dewey et al., eds., *Creative Intelligence: Essays in the Pragmatic Attitude*, pp. 176–227. New York: Henry Holt.

———. 1932. *The Philosophy of the Present*. Edited by Arthur E. Murphy, with prefatory remarks by John Dewey. LaSalle, Illinois: Open Court.

———. [1934] 1974. *Mind, Self and Society*. Edited by Charles Morris. Chicago: University of Chicago Press.

———. [1938] 1942. *The Philosophy of the Act*. Edited by Charles Morris. Chicago: University of Chicago Press.

———. 1964. *Selected Writings*. Edited by A. J. Reck. Indianapolis: Bobbs-Merrill.

Meltzer, B. N.; Petras, J. W.; and Reynolds, L. T. 1977. *Symbolic Interactionism: Genesis, Varieties, and Criticism*. London: Routledge and Kegan Paul.

Melville, H. [1851] 1964. *Moby Dick*. Indianapolis: Bobbs-Merrill.

Merleau-Ponty, M. 1962. *Phenomenology of Perception*. Translated by Collin Smith. New York: Humanities Press.

Milgram, S. 1970. "The Experience of Living in Cities." *Science* 67 (March 13): 1461–68.

Miller, D. L. 1982. "Review of J. D. Lewis and R. L. Smith, *American Sociology and Pragmatism*." *Journal of the History of Sociology* 4: 108–14.

Mills, C. W. [1959] 1977. *The Sociological Imagination*. New York: Oxford University Press.

Mills, P. J. 1982. "Misinterpreting Mead." *Sociology* 16 (February): 116–31.

Morris, C. 1927. Unpublished letter to E. A. Burtt. Morris Archives at the Peirce Edition Project. Indiana University–Purdue University at Indianapolis.

———. 1938a. "Scientific Empiricism." In *Encyclopedia and Unified Science*. Chicago: University of Chicago Press.

———. 1938b. *Foundations of the Theory of Signs*. Chicago: University of Chicago Press.

———. 1938c. "Peirce, Mead, and Pragmatism." *Philosophical Review* 47: 109–27.
———. 1946a. "Reply to Dewey's Article." *The Journal of Philosophy* 43, no. 7: 196.
———. [1946b] 1955. *Signs, Language, and Behavior.* New York: George Braziller.
———. 1964. *Signification and Significance.* Cambridge, Mass.: MIT Press.
———. 1970. *The Pragmatic Movement in American Philosophy.* New York: George Braziller.
———. 1971. *Writings on the General Theory of Signs.* The Hague: Mouton.
Mukerji, C. 1983. *From Graven Images: Patterns of Modern Materialism.* New York: Columbia University Press.
Mumford, L. 1926. *The Golden Day.* New York: W. W. Norton.
———. 1934. *Technics and Civilization.* New York: Harcourt, Brace and World.
———. 1938. *The Culture of Cities.* New York: Harcourt, Brace and World.
———. [1944] 1973. *The Condition of Man.* New York: Harcourt, Brace, Jovanovich.
———. 1947. *City Development.* London: Secker and Warburg.
———. [1951] 1970. *The Conduct of Life.* New York: Harcourt, Brace, Jovanovich.
———. [1956] 1972. *The Transformations of Man.* New York: Harper Torchbooks.
———. 1960. "Concluding Address." In C. Kraeling and R. McC. Adams, eds. *The City Invincible.* Chicago: University of Chicago Press.
———. 1961. *The City in History.* New York: Harcourt, Brace and World.
———. 1967. *The Myth of the Machine: Technics and Human Development.* New York: Harcourt, Brace, Jovanovich.
———. 1970. *The Myth of the Machine: The Pentagon of Power.* New York: Harcourt, Brace, Jovanovich.
———. 1979. *Interpretations and Forecasts: 1922–1972.* New York: Harcourt, Brace, Jovanovich.
Muschik, J. 1974. *Die Wiener Schule des Phantastischen Realismus.* Vienna: Jugend und Volk.
Ogden, C. K., and Richards, I. A. 1923. *The Meaning of Meaning.* New York: Harcourt, Brace and World.
Orleans, P. 1973, "Differential Cognition of Urban Residents: Effects of Social Scale on Mapping." In R. M. Downs and D. Stea, eds., *Image and Environment.* Chicago: Aldine.
Parsons, M. J. 1980. "James Mark Baldwin and the Aesthetic Development of the Individual." *The Journal of Aesthetic Education* 14: 31–50.
Parsons, T. 1960. "Durkheim's Contribution to the Theory of Integration of Social Systems." In Kurt H. Wolff, ed., *Emile Durkheim*, pp. 118–53. Columbus, Ohio: Ohio State University Press.
Partridge, Eric. 1977. *A Short Etymological Dictionary of Modern English.* Macmillan.
Peirce, C. S. 1931–58. *The Collected Papers of Charles Sanders Peirce.* Vols. 1–6 ed. C. Hartshorne and P. Weiss, vols. 7–8 ed. A. Burks. Cambridge, Mass.: Harvard University Press.
———. 1958. *Charles S. Peirce: Selected Writings.* P. P. Weiner, ed. New York: Dover.
———. 1976. *The New Elements of Mathematics.* Vol. 4. Carolyn Eisele, ed. Atlantic Highlands, N.J.: Humanities Press.

Peirce, C. S., and Welby, V. L. 1977. *Semiotic and Significs: The Correspondence between Charles S. Peirce and Victoria Lady Welby.* Edited by Charles S. Hardwick. Bloomington: Indiana University Press.

Perinbanayagam, R. S. 1974. "The Definition of the Situation: An Analysis of the Ethnomethodological and Dramaturgical View." *Sociological Quarterly* 15 (Autumn): 521–41.

———. 1985. *Signifying Acts: Structure and Meaning in Everyday Life.* Carbondale: Southern Illinois University Press.

Piaget, J. [1929] 1975. *The Child's Conception of the World.* Totowa, N.J.: Littlefield, Adams.

Popper, K. [1934] 1968. *The Logic of Scientific Discovery.* New York: Harper Torchbooks.

Rathje, W. L. 1974. "The Garbage Project." *Archaeology* 27.

Ricoeur, P. 1976. *Interpretation Theory: Discourse and the Surplus of Meaning.* Fort Worth, Texas: Texas Christian University Press.

———. 1978. *The Philosophy of Paul Ricoeur.* C. Reagan and D. Stewart, eds. Boston: Beacon.

Robards, T. 1982a. "Memories Are Made of This." *New York Times Magazine,* January 10.

———. 1982b. "A Mutual Gratification Society." *New York Times Magazine,* May 2.

Rochberg, G. 1973. Liner notes to *String Quartet No. 3* New York: Nonesuch Records.

———. 1984a. *The Aesthetics of Survival: A Composer's View of Twentieth-Century Music.* Ann Arbor: University of Michigan Press.

———. 1984b. "Can the Arts Survive Modernism? (A Discussion of the Characteristics, History, and Legacy of Modernism)." *Critical Inquiry* 11, no. 2 (December): 317–40.

Rochberg-Halton, E. 1977. "Object Relations Among the Crabdancers." *Canadian Drama* 3, no. 2 (Fall): 115–21.

———. 1979a. "The Meaning of Personal Art Objects." In J. Zuzanek, ed., *Social Research and Cultural Policy.* Ontario: Otium Publications.

———. 1979b. "Cultural Signs and Urban Adaptation: The Meaning of Cherished Household Possessions." Ph.D. dissertation, University of Chicago.

———. 1982. "The Real Relation between Pragmatism and Chicago Sociology." *Contemporary Sociology* 11 (March): 140–42.

———. 1983a. "The Real Nature of Pragmatism and Chicago Sociology." *Symbolic Interaction* 6, no. 1: 139–53.

———. 1983b. "Contemporary Domestic Symbols and the Archaeology of the Self." Lecture at the Field Museum of Natural History, Chicago, May 10.

———. 1985a. "Life in the Treehouse: Pet Therapy as Family Metaphor and Self-Dialogue." In Marvin B. Sussman, ed., *Pets and the Family.* New York: The Haworth Press.

———. 1985b. "City Semiosis." Special session on "Landscape Images" of the Annual Meeting of the Association of American Geographers, Detroit, April 23.

———. Forthcoming. "The Triadic Theory of Meaning: Why Peirce's Semiotic Is as

Simple as 1, 2, 3." In Jeffrey Crane and Barry Johnston, eds., *The Laughing Picarro: Essays in Sociological Interpretation.*

Rorty, R. 1979. *Philosophy and the Mirror of Nature.* Princeton: Princeton University Press.

Rosensohn, W. L. 1974. *The Phenomenology of Charles S. Peirce.* Amsterdam: B. R. Gruner.

Rosenthal, S. B. 1983. "The Pragmatic World of Charles Peirce." *Transactions of the Charles S. Peirce Society* 19, no. 1: 13–22.

Rossi, Ino, ed. 1982. *Structural Sociology.* New York: Columbia University Press.

———. 1983. *From the Sociology of Symbols to the Sociology of Signs.* New York: Columbia University Press.

Rowles, G. D. 1978. *Prisoners of Space: Exploring the Geographical Experience of Older People.* Boulder, Colo.: Westview Press.

Sachs, V. 1973. *The Myth of America: Essays in the Structures of Literary Imagination.* The Hague: Mouton.

Sahlins, M. 1976a. *Culture and Practical Reason.* Chicago: University of Chicago Press.

———. 1976b. *The Use and Abuse of Biology: An Anthropological Critique of Sociobiology.* Ann Arbor: University of Michigan Press.

Saussure, F. de 1966. *Course in General Linguistics.* Translated by Wade Baskin. New York: McGraw-Hill.

Scheler, M. [1927–28] 1976. "Die Stellung des Menschen im Kosmos." In Manfred S. Frings, ed. *Gesammelte Werke*, Bd. 9, *Späte Schriften.* Bern and Munich.

———. [1954] 1958. *Philosophical Problems.* Translated by Oscar A. Haac. Boston: Beacon Hill.

———. [1960] 1980. *Problems of a Sociology of Knowledge.* Translated by Manfred S. Frings. Edited with an Introduction by Kenneth W. Stikkers. London: Routledge and Kegan Paul.

Schlereth, T. J., ed. 1982. *Material Culture Studies in America.* Nashville: The American Association for State and Local History.

Schmied, Wieland. 1964. *Malerei des phantastischen Realismus/Die Weiner Schule.* Vienna.

Schneider, L., ed. 1967. *The Scottish Moralists.* Chicago: University of Chicago Press.

Schoenberg, A. 1950. *Style and Idea.* New York: Philosophical Library.

Schorske, C. 1980. *Fin-de-Siècle Vienna.* New York: Alfred A. Knopf.

Schudson, M. 1981. "All That Glitters Is Not Sold." *In These Times* (December).

———. 1984. *Advertising, the Uneasy Persuasion.* New York: Basic Books.

Schutz, A. 1962. *Collected Papers*, vol. 1, *The Problem of Social Reality.* M. Natanson, ed. The Hague: Martinus Nijhoff.

———. 1970a. *On Phenomenology and Social Relations.* Edited and introduced by Helmut R. Wagner. Chicago: University of Chicago Press.

———. 1970b. "The Homecomer," in H. R. Wagner, ed., *Alfred Schutz on Phenomenology and Social Relations.* Chicago: University of Chicago Press.

Schwartz, B. 1976. "Images of Suburbia: Some Revisionist Commentary and Conclusions." In *The Changing Face of the Suburbs*, edited by B. Schwartz. Chicago: University of Chicago Press.

————. 1981. *Vertical Classification: A Study in Structuralism and the Sociology of Knowledge*. Chicago: University of Chicago Press.

Scully, V. 1977. *Empathy, Sign, and the Vernacular*. The Robert B. Mayer Memorial Lecture Series on Art and Architecture in America Since World War II. Chicago, April 13.

Sebeok, T. A., ed. 1977. *Sight, Sound and Sense*. Bloomington: Indiana University Press.

Simmel, G. 1971. *On Individuality and Social Forms*. D. Levine (ed.), Chicago: University of Chicago Press.

————. 1978. *The Philosophy of Money*. Translated by Tom Bottomore and David Frisby. London: Routledge and Kegan Paul.

Singer, M. 1968. "Culture." *International Encyclopedia of the Social Sciences*. New York: Macmillan.

————. 1972. *When a Great Tradition Modernizes: An Anthropological Approach to Indian Civilization*. New York: Praeger.

————. 1977. "For a Semiotic Anthropology." In Thomas A. Sebeok, ed., *Sight, Sound, and Sense*. Bloomington: Indiana University Press.

————. 1980. "Signs of the Self: An Exploration in Semiotic Anthropology." *American Anthropologist* 82: 485–507.

————. 1984. *Man's Glassy Essence*. Bloomington: Indiana University Press.

Skinner, B. F. [1953] 1965. *Science and Human Behavior*. New York: The Free Press.

Smith, C. S. 1984. *Chicago and the American Literary Imagination*. Chicago: University of Chicago Press.

Smith, M. B. 1978. "Perspectives on Selfhood." *American Psychologist* 33 (December): 1053–1063.

Stea, D., and Blaut, J. M. 1973. "Notes Toward a Developmental Theory of Spatial Learning." In R. M. Downs and D. Stea, eds., *Image and Environment*. Chicago: Aldine.

Stebbins, R. A. 1967. "A Theory of the Definition of the Situation." *Canadian Review of Sociology and Anthropology* 4 (August): 148–64.

Stokols, D. 1978. "Environmental Psychology." *Annual Review of Psychology* 29: 253–95.

————. 1983. "Environmental Psychology: A Coming of Age." In A. Kraut, ed., *G. Stanley Hall Lectures*, vol. 2. Washington, D.C.: American Psychological Association.

Stone, G. P., and Farberman, H. A. 1970. "On the Edge of Rapprochement: Was Durkheim Moving Toward the Perspective of Symbolic Interaction?" In Stone and Farberman, eds., *Social Psychology through Symbolic Interaction*, pp. 100–112. Waltham, Mass.: Ginn-Blaisdell.

Strauss, A. 1961. *Images of the American City*. New York: The Free Press.

————. 1968. *The American City: A Sourcebook of Urban Imagery*. London: Penguin.

Strauss, A.; Schatzman, L.; Erlich, D.; Bucher, R.; and Sabshin, M. 1963. "The Hospital and its Negotiated Order." In E. Freidson, ed., *The Hospital in Modern Society*, pp. 147–69. New York: The Free Press.

Stryker, S. 1980. *Symbolic Interactionism: A Social Structural Version*. Menlo Park, Calif.: Benjamin/Cummings.

Sturrock, J., ed. 1979. *Structuralism and Since: From Lévi-Strauss to Derrida*. Oxford: Oxford University Press.

Suttles, G. 1968. *The Social Order of the Slum*. Chicago: University of Chicago Press.

Swift, J. [1726] 1960. *Gulliver's Travels*. New York: Signet Classic.

Thomas, W. I. 1909. *Source Book For Social Origins*. Boston: Richard C. Badger.

————. 1966. *W. I. Thomas on Social Organization and Social Personality*. Morris Janowitz, ed. Chicago: University of Chicago Press.

Thomas, W. I., and Thomas D. S. [1928] 1970. "Situations Defined as Real Are Real in Their Consequences." In G. Stone and H. Farberman, eds., *Social Psychology through Symbolic Interaction* pp. 154–55. Waltham, Mass.: Ginn-Blaisdell.

Tolman, E. C. [1948] 1973. "Cognitive Maps in Rats and Men." In R. M. Downs and D. Stea, eds., *Image and Environment*. Chicago: Aldine.

————. 1961. "A Summary Discussion of Purposive Behavior." In T. Parsons et al., eds., *Theories of Society*. New York: The Free Press.

Turner, V. 1967. *The Forest of Symbols*. Ithica, N.Y.: Cornell University Press.

————. 1969. *The Ritual Process*. Chicago: Aldine.

————. 1975. *Revelation and Divination in Ndembu Ritual*. Ithica, N.Y.: Cornell University Press.

————. 1982. *From Ritual to Theater: The Human Seriousness of Play*. New York: Performing Arts Journal Publications.

————. 1984. "Liminality and the Performative Genres." In J. J. MacAloon ed., *Rite, Drama, Festival, Spectacle*. Philadelphia: Institute for the Study of Human Issues.

Veblen, Thorstein. [1899] 1953. *The Theory of the Leisure Class*. Introduction by C. Wright Mills. New York: Mentor Books.

Walens, S. 1982. "The Weight of My Name Is a Mountain of Blankets: Potlatch Ceremonies." In Victor Turner, ed., *Celebration: Studies in Festivity and Ritual*, pp. 178–89. Washington, D.C.: Smithsonian Institution.

Warner, W. L. 1959. *The Living and the Dead: A Study of the Symbolic Life of Americans*. New Haven: Yale University Press.

Weber, M. 1981. "Some Categories of Interpretative Sociology." Translated by Edith E. Graber. *The Sociological Quarterly* 22 (Spring): 151–80.

Weigert, A., and Hastings, R. 1976. "Identity Loss, Family and Social Change." *American Journal of Sociology* 82: 1171–85.

Wheatley, P. 1967. *City as Symbol*. London: H. K. Lewis.

Williams, R. 1958. *Culture and Society: 1780–1950*. London: Chatto and Windus.

————. 1981. *The Sociology of Culture*. New York: Schocken Books.

Winnicott, D. W. [1951] 1958. "Transitional Objects and Transitional Phenomena." In *D. W. Winnicott Collectd Papers*. New York: Basic Books.

Wittgenstein, L. [1921] 1974, *Tractatus Logico–Philosophicus*. Translated by D. F. Pears and B. F. McGuiness. London: Routledge and Kegan Paul.

————. 1980. *Culture and Value*. Translated by Peter Winch. Chicago: University of Chicago Press.

Wolff, J. 1981. *The Social Production of Art*. New York: St. Martin's Press.

Yates, F. 1966. *The Art of Memory*. Chicago: University of Chicago Press.

Index